Catherine of Siena

Spiritual Development in Her Life and Teaching

Thomas McDermott, OP

Paulist Press
New York/Mahwah, NJ

Scripture quotations are from the New Revised Standard Version Bible, copyright © 1989 National Council of the Churches of Christ in the United States of America. Used by permission. All rights reserved.

Cover design by Cynthia Dunne
Cover art: "St. Catherine of Siena Receives the Stigmata" by A. Franchi (1898), chapel of the motherhouse of the Sisters of the Poor of St. Catherine of Siena, via dei Rossi, Siena. Used with permission.

Book design by Lynn Else

Copyright © 2008 by the Dominican Province of St. Albert the Great

All rights reserved. No part of this book may be reproduced or transmitted in any form or by any means, electronic or mechanical, including photocopying, recording, or by any information storage and retrieval system without permission in writing from the Publisher.

Library of Congress Cataloging-in-Publication Data

McDermott, Thomas, 1952–
    Catherine of Siena : spiritual development in her life and teaching / Thomas McDermott.
       p. cm.
    Includes bibliographical references and index.
    ISBN-13: 978-0-8091-4547-8 (alk. paper)
    1. Catherine, of Siena, Saint, 1347–1380. 2. Spirituality—History—Middle Ages, 600–1500. 3. Spiritual formation—History of doctrines. I. Title.
    BX4700.C4M33 2008
    282.092—dc22

                                                                2008006015

Published by Paulist Press
997 Macarthur Boulevard
Mahwah, New Jersey 07430

www.paulistpress.com

Printed and bound in the
United States of America

To

Mary O'Driscoll, OP
Giacinto D'Urso, OP+
Giuliana Cavallini+
Suzanne Noffke, OP
Kenelm Foster, OP+

*for their contributions to
catherinian studies in our time*

L'amore si transforma nella cosa amata.

Santa Caterina da Siena, il *Dialogo* LX

CONTENTS

Acknowledgments vii
Abbreviations ix
Foreword xiii
Introduction 1
Biographical Notes 7

1. SPIRITUAL DEVELOPMENT IN THE LIFE OF CATHERINE OF SIENA 11

Introduction 11
Sources and Their Historical Value 12
Childhood Experiences 18
In the Cell (c. 1363–67) 26
Siena and Its Environs (c. 1367–75) 34
Beyond Siena (1375–80) 58
Conclusion 73

2. CATHERINE OF SIENA'S PRINCIPAL TEACHINGS AND SPIRITUAL DEVELOPMENT 78

Introduction 78
"The Truth of God the Father" 80
God Becomes "Little" So That We Can See the Truth 82
The Blood That Reveals the Truth and Re-creates Us 84
The Christ-Bridge as "The Way of Truth" 89
"I Will Draw All Things to Myself": Progress on
    the Bridge as Spiritual Development 101
The Truth of the Human Person 104
"The Way of Self-Knowledge" 117

Contents

"On Two Feet You Must Walk My Way":
  Love of God and Love of Neighbor 131
Conclusion 134

3. *"I TRE STATI DELL'ANIMA"*: STAGES OF SPIRITUAL DEVELOPMENT 137

Introduction 137
The First *Scalone* 161
The Second *Scalone* 169
The Third *Scalone* 183
Catherine's Life in Relation to Her Teaching 206
Conclusion 219

CONCLUSION 225

Catherine's Teaching 225
Catherine's Life 231

APPENDIX: Outline of the *Dialogue* of Catherine of Siena ... 234

NOTES 235

WORKS CITED 323

INDEX 339

Acknowledgments

In the *Dialogue* the eternal Father tells Catherine of Siena that, in his providence, he did not give to any one person the knowledge of doing everything necessary for life so that everyone would have to turn to others for their help. I began this work during a period of more than two years (2003–5) in which I lived at Convento Santa Maria sopra Minerva in Rome, where the research and writing were done close to the tomb of "the virgin of Fontebranda" in the adjoining basilica. With gratitude I acknowledge some of the many people who assisted me:

The Dominican friars at the Minerva and San Clemente in Rome, San Domenico in Siena, the Dominican House of Studies in Washington, DC, and St. Dominic Priory in St. Louis; John Cunningham, OP, Elisabetta Valgiusti, Wolfram Hoyer, OP, the faculty, staff, and students at Kenrick-Glennon Seminary in St. Louis, Matthew Powell, OP, Christian Steiner, OP, Paul-Marie Chango, OP, Moreno Fiori, OP, Alfonso V. Morales Huerta, Reginald Onyekwere, Gloria Falcão Dodd, the staff at Centro di Studi di S. Caterina da Siena in Rome, the late Professor Giuliana Cavallini, Don Emanuele Musso, Nancy Denman, Elizabeth Frenzel, Lesa McDermott and Douglas Hodgins, Madre M. Imelda Fortuna, OP, Suzanne Noffke, OP, Father Anthony Oelrich, Joseph Phan Tan Thanh, OP, Connie Henrion, Paul Murray, OP, Father Ejike Anyanike, Keith D. Miles, Kevin J. H. N. Stephens, OP, and the Canonichesse della Santa Croce at the Minerva.

I especially want to thank the Dominican Province of St. Albert the Great (USA) for its generous sponsorship of this project. In

Catherine of Siena

particular, I thank Edward Ruane, OP, former provincial, Michael Mascari, OP, provincial, and Donald Goergen, OP, regent of studies.

Above all, I express my gratitude to Mary O'Driscoll, OP, who first introduced me to Catherine and whose advice was invaluable.

"Per li quali tutti ti rendo grazie. Amen." (*Orazione* III)

ABBREVIATIONS

AAS	*Acta Apostolicae Sedis*
CCC	*Catechism of the Catholic Church*, 2nd ed., 1997
CCSL	*Corpus Christianorum. Series Latina.* Turnhout. 1953ss
D	The *Dialogue* of Catherine of Siena. When followed by Roman numerals it indicates the chapter number in *Il Dialogo*, ed. G. Cavallini, 1995; followed by the page number in Arabic numerals, for example: *D* LXIII, 159. When followed by Arabic numerals it indicates the chapter number in the *Dialogue*, trans. S. Noffke, 1980; followed by the page number in Arabic numerals, for example: *D* 121, 231.
L	The letters of Catherine of Siena. Followed by "T" indicating the numbering system of the letters of N. Tommasèo, then the edition of the letters consulted and, if applicable, the relevant volume in Roman numerals. The editions consulted are: *Le lettere di S. Caterina da Siena*, 6 vols, ed. P. Misciattelli, 1939; *The Letters of Catherine of Siena*, 4 vols., trans. S. Noffke, 2000, 2001, 2007, 2008; *I, Catherine: Selected Writings of Catherine of Siena*, trans. K. Foster and M. J. Ronayne, 1980; *Saint Catherine of Siena as Seen in Her Letters*, trans. V. Scudder, 1927.

Catherine of Siena

Legenda major Raymond of Capua. *The Life of Catherine of Siena*, trans. C. Kearns, 1980. Followed by § and the chapter and page numbers in Arabic numerals.

Legenda minor Fra' Tommaso da Siena detto "Il Caffarini." *S. Caterina da Siena. Legenda minor*, trans. B. Ancilli, 1998. Followed by upper case Roman numerals indicating the part of the work (I, II, III), lowercase Roman numerals indicating the chapter number, and Arabic numerals indicating the page number, for example: *Legenda minor* II, ii, 63.

P The prayers of Catherine of Siena. Followed by the number of the prayer in Arabic numerals as found in *The Prayers of Catherine of Siena*, 2nd ed., trans. S. Noffke, 2001, followed by Roman numerals in parentheses indicating the number of the same prayer as found in *Le orazioni di S. Caterina da Siena*, ed. G. Cavallini, 1978, followed by the page number in Arabic numerals in the Noffke edition.

PG *Patrologiae cursus completus. Series Graeca.* Paris, 1857ss

PL *Patrologiae cursus completus. Series Latina.* Paris, 1844ss

Processo (Taur.) *Santa Caterina da Siena nei ricordi dei discepoli*, ed. I. Taurisano, 1957. (Italian translation of the depositions of Cortona, Maconi, and Dominici in *Il Processo Castellano*, ed. M. H. Laurent, 1942). Followed by the page number in Arabic numerals.

SCG St. Thomas Aquinas. *Summa Contra Gentiles.* 5 vols., trans. V. J. Bourke, 1956 and 1975.

Sent. S. Thomae Aquinatis. *Scriptum super Sententiis*, 4 vols. Paris, 1947.

Abbreviations

ST
St. Thomas Aquinas. *Summa Theologica*, 3 vols., trans. Fathers of the English Dominican Province, 1947.

Supplementum (Tin.)
Vita di Santa Caterina da Siena, ed. G. Tinagli, 1938. (Italian translation of Pars I and II, tract. I–VI, of Caffarini's *Libellus de Supplemento*). Followed by I or II indicating Pars (Libro) I and II, followed by Roman numerals in lowercase indicating the chapter, and by Arabic numerals indicating the section and page number, for example: *Supplementum* (Tin.), II, ii, 8, 81.

Foreword

The grace of God that elicits an inner faith leading to Christ, even though it is supernatural, becomes manifest in incarnational ways. God leads us through the mediation of various gifts. Some people are inspired toward a deeper spiritual life by the force of theological arguments. Others are touched by the example of saints living among us. Still others are moved by vivid images that are used to distill the salvific truth locked in Catholic doctrine. Each of us is enriched by the living Word of God and by the sacraments administered in the church.

Catherine Benincasa of Siena was a woman who enjoyed great intimacy with Christ. Enriched by extraordinary graces not enjoyed by most of us (and which always require a profound, sometimes dark faith in their reception), she had an attractive, powerful personality. Her vivid encounter with God flowed out into her relationships, her dynamic activity, and her convincing words. It was obvious to those who knew her that she was a woman of God, so much so that soon she had a circle of disciples that included laity, priests, and religious. People wanted to hear her, to receive her advice, to listen to her words. Even though she had no formal education—she was probably illiterate—she had the capacity to assimilate what she heard being taught by preachers and to present it in a forceful way. Her teaching was not that of a professional theologian or a preacher who shares his prepared lectures and notes. Catherine would sit next to a person, attentive to his or her intellectual capacities and spiritual needs, and she would impart a direct teaching that flowed from her personal knowledge of Christ and his mysteries. What she heard from theologians was corroborated by her personal experience, and then, with a deep concern for the good of the other, she presented it to the listener in vivid language. The gifts of the Holy Spirit alight in her soul would inspire her to speak about the Christian life, the renewal of the church, or God's loving concern for us. She was intent on igniting in the souls of all who met her a passionate desire for God, and on inspiring the soul—the "eye of the intellect"—to focus on the mystery of the living God.

Catherine's involvement in several of the major concerns of fourteenth-century Europe—including peace among the Italian cities, the Crusade, the return of the pope from Avignon to Rome, and church renewal—is well known. In some cases she was successful; in some not. But underlying all of them was her ardent desire that a close relationship with Christ be lived out in practice, a relationship that is ultimately manifested not through such extraordinary experiences as locutions, vision, stigmata, and levitations, but through the simple but real living of the theological virtues of faith, hope, and charity.

The colorful images that Catherine used in rapid succession to explain the mysteries of faith without great concern for their inner coherence can be baffling. Readers of her letters or the *Dialogue* have often been perplexed by the confusion and inconsistencies of her imagery. This perplexity is rooted in the mistaken expectation that in the writings of St. Catherine of Siena, doctor of the church and co-patron of Europe, a theological system can be found. Unlike St. Thomas Aquinas, Catherine was not a systematic theologian; nor was she an author of a practical, step-by-step guide to sanctity. Theologians dealing with spiritual theology have tried to articulate the principles of the encounter with God and to describe the necessary stages in growth. These attempts are always limited, because growth in sanctity is not a technique that can be learned by training. Nor is it true that having attained a certain stage, one can only proceed forward, never falling back. Each person's encounter with Christ is unique, bound up as it is with the personal history of the individual and the personal touch of Christ. It is no surprise, therefore, that Catherine's description of the stages of spiritual

Foreword

growth, vividly depicted through the image of "steps leading across the bridge that is Christ," appears chaotic and confusing. An attentive and faith-disposed reading of her writings, however, discloses in them not only her personal journey of faith and her passionate attempt to explain through colorful images the challenges of spiritual authenticity, but also the profound Catholic doctrine that underlies her teaching.

Thomas McDermott does not attempt to deny or minimize the difficulties in interpreting Catherine's works, and therein lies the value of his book. While he focuses on the salient points of Catherine's spiritual journey and her teaching, he is aware that it is primarily Catherine's word itself that can inspire and bring about a greater fidelity to Christ. Father McDermott's insightful guide through the writings of the great Dominican saint may help us to remember that, as we read what she has written, it is not a theological manual that we are to expect, but Catherine herself, who with strong images and colorful comparisons is, as it were, grabbing us by the elbow and pointing beyond herself, toward Christ our Savior.

Father Wojciech Giertych, OP
Theologian of the Papal Household
Palazzo Apostolico
Vatican City

Introduction

A member of the Pontifical Academy of Theology recently wrote: "Catherine [of Siena] was, together with Teresa of Avila, the first woman declared a Doctor of the Church in 1970, *yet the ecclesial reception of her doctorate is still not fully complete, especially in the world of academic theology.*"[1] While biographies and articles on the life of Catherine continue to appear, very little attention has in fact been given to her spiritual teaching or doctrine. When we consider that Catherine was declared a doctor of the church nearly forty years ago, and that critical editions and translations of her writings are more readily available today than ever before, it is surprising that relatively few scholarly articles or books—particularly in English—have been written in recent times on her teaching.

In this study we will examine in a systematic way the subject of spiritual development and its stages in the teaching of Catherine of Siena. We will also consider how her own life and spiritual development correspond with her teaching. Our sources for her teaching will be Catherine's own words as found in the *Dialogue*, her letters and prayers, and the writings of various contemporary commentators. Regarding her life, we will consult the various primary biographical sources in addition to the autobiographical portions of her own "writings"[2] as well as the works of commentators. This study is a straightforward presentation of what Catherine actually says on the subject of spiritual development and its stages with some analysis and commentary, including appropriate references to her possible sources. It is not, however, an application of her teaching nor is it a psychological or existential commentary on it.

One of the reasons why I have chosen the subject of spiritual development is because of its central place in Catherine's doctrine.

Catherine of Siena

Spiritual development is not the only theme found in Catherine's writings but it is undoubtedly the most important. Everything for her, including the much-needed reform of the church, hinged on the interior reform of the individual. However, the expression "spiritual development" does not appear in her writings; instead, Catherine uses such expressions as "going the way of truth,"[3] "rising"[4] on the bridge of Christ crucified, or "the three states and grades of the soul."[5] The theme is treated in various parts of the *Dialogue* but most especially in "The Bridge" (*Dialogue* 26–87), where spiritual development is presented as three stairs *(scaloni)* on the bridge of the body of Christ crucified and in "Tears" (*Dialogue* 88–97) as different types of life-giving tears.

Another reason the subject of spiritual development and its stages was chosen is that it is that part of the *Dialogue* which, I think, would be of most interest to people today. R. Byrne points out that as a result of the influences of existential and process philosophies as well as modern psychological insights into the developmental phases of human maturity, many Christians today see in the journey theme an apt metaphor for spiritual experience.[6] In presenting Catherine's teaching, which many people find somewhat difficult to understand, I hope others will be able to grasp more easily the richness of her message and make some practical applications of it.

After studying Catherine of Siena, I would describe her, in a qualified way, as a "doctrinal mystical theologian." Of course she is not a theologian in the sense of someone who explores the truths of faith in an intellectual way; rather, she is a mystic who experienced contact with God and who then communicated this experience, affective and experimental, to others—often through images.[7] She presents religious truth, as E. Ancilli says, not so much as the result of reasoning as of an intimately lived experience.[8] Her knowledge of God was primarily a result of a personal, loving relationship with God that was informed by the truths of the faith as she encountered them in scripture, homilies, conversations, and books. Her temperament and intellect were exceptional. Her teaching covers

Introduction

the major points of faith: the Trinity, creation, sin, the incarnation, redemption, the church, sacraments, and eternal life.

In reading Catherine's works for the first time, one can have the impression, as I did, that she has no system or precise terms and is confused or even contradictory. This impression is due, in part, to the fact that Catherine does not use definitions or formulas but rather images to convey some truth. It is often necessary to consult not only the *Dialogue* but also the letters and prayers to understand what a particular catherinian concept or term such as "self-knowledge," "truth," or "gathering together the soul's three powers" means. This apparent lack of clarity is also due to other factors: Catherine's writings were actually dictated to others and, in the case of the *Dialogue*, during mystical experiences that occurred over a period of approximately one year. The more one perseveres in studying Catherine, however, the more one realizes that Paul VI was indeed correct when he referred to the "definite coherence of her teachings" and how "the various sections of Catherine's teaching form a closely-knit, compact whole."[9] Also, the more one studies Catherine the more one is surprised to discover deeper and subtler layers of meaning in her teaching.

Catherine was a teacher from the moment of her first known religious experience as a child. Raymond of Capua relates how, after her vision of the royal Christ at the age of six, she "drew to herself a number of little girls like herself to gather round her, and they used to listen with delight to her pious exhortations."[10] In each of her numerous extant letters, the earliest of which was written some twenty years after this vision, she is always teaching (or preaching)—no matter to whom the letter is addressed. Almost all of her letters are treatises on the truths of faith that she had experienced personally as expressions of God's love. In the last three years of her life her theological thought underwent a great synthesis that resulted in the dictation of the *Dialogue*, which Catherine called simply *il libro*, or the book. Our study of Catherine's teaching on spiritual development will primarily focus on the *Dialogue*, which Cavallini says is "the work of Catherine's full spiritual maturity"[11] and which M. O'Driscoll describes as "a compendium of her theological thought."[12] However, as I have already said, in order to arrive at a clearer understanding of what Catherine is saying I have also consulted widely the rest of her works, especially the letters.

The English translation of texts of Catherine's writings are generally taken from current published editions of translations as indicated in the footnotes. However, in several cases I have translated the text myself or, when using a published translation, substituted another word in brackets that I regard as more correct. All other translations, unless otherwise indicated, are my own.

The *Dialogue* is an account of a dialogue between Catherine and God "the eternal Father."[13] By far the greater part of the book is the eternal Father's replies to Catherine's questions. Because the entire work is Catherine's, humanly speaking, I sometimes quote the words of the eternal Father as Catherine's (for example, "Catherine says").

The fact that Catherine has a distinctive teaching or doctrine is confirmed by the fact that she was declared a doctor of the church. A mystic such as Catherine apprehends the truth of God in a different way from a theologian, although both speak of the same truth. Every doctor of the church must have an "eminent doctrine." J. Galot explains the significance of this term in the Church today:

> The doctor is one who has set forth revealed doctrine manifesting deep *understanding* of this doctrine and giving it an *expression* worthy of admiration, so that a special charism of light granted by the Holy Spirit can be recognized in him. What distinguishes the charism of the doctor, in fact, is the excellence of the doctrine, the way in which he understands and expounds revelation. This charism implies an effort of doctrinal penetration, reflection and elucidation, with regard to the mysteries of the faith.
>
> This requires a certain *personal originality*, so that it is possible so to speak of a real contribution to doctrinal development.[14]

Introduction

Catherine's deep understanding, indeed penetration, of doctrine is evident throughout her teaching, and her imagery is the full fruit of this understanding as well as an expression of her personal originality. She herself has something to say in the *Dialogue* about what being a doctor of the church means: The doctors have been enlightened by a supernatural light and have become lights for others dispelling the darkness of error and showing the way of truth.[15] Along with the martyrs and confessors, they catch "souls with their sounds."[16]

In chapter 1 we examine the primary biographical sources to illustrate how Catherine's faith, as reflected in her actions, mystical experiences, and her own words, developed in the course of her life. This is important for several reasons. First, spiritual development, as we have said, is a major theme in Catherine's teaching and yet the biographical sources barely suggest that she herself underwent much if any development in terms of her own faith. It is often assumed, however, that Catherine's teaching flowed, at least in part, from her own experience. Second, in Catherine's well-known teaching on the bridge of Christ crucified and its three *scaloni* or stairs (representing three spiritual stages) she is insistent on the necessity of everyone moving along them and therefore developing spiritually.[17] She herself developed and that development must be rescued from neglect. In chapter 2 we will consider the most important catherinian concepts and themes as they relate to spiritual development: the truth of God the Father, the blood, the Christ-bridge, the human person, sin, the soul's three powers, the way of self-knowledge, and the place of the neighbor. In chapter 3 we will examine comprehensively Catherine's teaching on the stages of spiritual development as found principally in the *Dialogue*. We will also consider to what extent Catherine's life and spiritual development, as described in chapter 1, correspond to her teaching. In the Conclusion we consider the fundamental message of both her teaching and life.

We should approach Catherine's teachings as affording us a privileged glimpse into the theological world view and faith of one of the most remarkable women of the fourteenth century.

Biographical Notes[1]

1347	On March 25, the feast of the Annunciation, Catherine is born at Siena with her twin sister Giovanna, the twenty-third and twenty-fourth children of the cloth dyer Jacopo di Benincasa and his wife Lapa di Puccio Piagenti.
1353	Catherine experiences her first vision, "the vision of the royal Christ," while walking down the via del Costone near her home.
1354	Catherine makes a vow of virginity.
1362	Her favorite sister, Buonaventura, dies. Shortly thereafter, Catherine cuts off her hair to forestall her parents' plans to marry her off. Fra' Tommaso della Fonte, OP, a cousin who grew up in her home, becomes her confessor.
1363 (c.)	Catherine declares publicly that she has no intention of ever marrying. She begins fasting. She is clothed in the habit of the *Mantellate* or Dominican Sisters of Penance and begins living in seclusion in a "cell" or small room in the family house for three years.
1367 (c.)	She experiences the mystical espousals with Christ and then receives the mission of working in the world in his name for the salvation of her neighbor. She gradually leaves her cell and performs corporal works of mercy. She is granted a vision of the soul's beauty. A "family" of spiritual disciples begins to gather around her.
1368	A year of great political turbulence and upheavals. On August 22, Catherine's father dies. Around this

	time Fra' Bartolomeo Dominici, OP, joins her circle of disciples and eventually becomes her second confessor.
1370	The summer was one of great mystical experiences for Catherine: the mystical exchange of hearts with the Lord, mystical death, and other wonderful gifts.
1372	Catherine writes her first political letters for the sake of peace in Italy. Her fasting is now almost total.
1373	With the support of the pope, Catherine promotes the idea of a Crusade.
1374	She goes to Florence at the time of the general chapter of the Dominicans. Fra' Raymond of Capua is assigned as her confessor, and becomes her friend and biographer. Catherine reenters Siena where the plague has again struck; she nurses the plague stricken and cures Raymond and Matteo di Centi. The plague ends and she goes to Montepulciano for the first time.
1375	Journey to Pisa, where on April 1 she receives the invisible stigmata in the chapel of Santa Cristina. Returning to Siena, she converts and assists Niccolò di Toldo, a prisoner condemned to death. Florence revolts against the pope and war begins.
1376	On March 31, Florence is put under papal interdict. Catherine, at the request of the Florentines, goes to Avignon to intercede for them and to encourage the pope to return to Rome. Gregory XI leaves Avignon on September 13. Catherine passes through Tolone, frees Varazze of the plague, and encourages Gregory at Genova. She returns to Siena in December.
1377	On January 17, Gregory XI enters Rome. Catherine writes to him and pleads on behalf of Siena, which has now joined with Florence in the antipapal rebellion. In the summer she sets forth on an extended mission of peace and reconciliation among the noble families

Biographical Notes

	in the Val d'Orcia, after having begun work to transform the castle at Belcaro, close to Siena, into a monastery for cloistered nuns. In late summer she sends Raymond of Capua to Rome with certain proposals for the reform of the church. After an intense mystical experience, Catherine begins dictating the *Dialogue* sometime around October. On December 13, she is sent by the pope to Florence to sue for peace.
1378	On March 27, Gregory XI dies and Urban VI is elected on April 8. On June 18 Catherine is nearly killed by a mob in Florence during the revolt of the Ciompi and she retires for a little while outside the city. Peace between Florence and the pope is reached on July 28. She again goes to Siena and finishes dictating the *Dialogue*. On September 20, the antipope Clement VII is elected at Fondi, resulting in schism. Catherine is called to Rome by Urban VI, leaves Siena with the *"bella brigata,"* her band of approximately forty disciples, and arrives at the Eternal City on November 28. She is immediately received by the pope and speaks before the cardinals. In December at the port of Ostia she says farewell for the last time to Raymond of Capua, who has been sent by the pope on a mission to France pertaining to the schism.
1379	During the year Catherine sends letters and messengers from Rome to every part of the Christian world in support of the cause of the true pope. She calms the Romans who revolt against the pope and blesses Tommaso d'Alviano, who defeats the antipapal troops at Marino resulting in the recovery of Castel San Angelo in Rome. Most of her prayers were recorded during this time.
1380	Amid terrible physical and moral trials, Catherine's physical condition worsens day by day. With difficulty she walks every day to St. Peter's Basilica where she

spends the day praying for the church. On January 29–30, she has her final great mystical experience in which she offers her life for the church. She dies in Rome during the morning of April 29. She is buried at the church of Santa Maria sopra Minerva in Rome; her head is later transferred to the church of San Domenico in Siena.

1461	On June 29, Catherine is canonized by Sienese Pope Pius II (Piccolomini).
1866	On April 13, Pope Pius IX declares her a co-patron of Rome.
1939	On June 18, Pope Pius XII proclaims Catherine, with St. Francis of Assisi, patron of Italy.
1970	On October 4, Paul VI includes Catherine in the catalogue of doctors of the universal church together with St. Teresa of Avila. They are the first women saints to be declared doctors.
1999	On October 1, John Paul II proclaims St. Bridget of Sweden, St. Catherine of Siena, and St. Teresa Benedicta of the Cross [Edith Stein] co-patronesses of Europe.

1
SPIRITUAL DEVELOPMENT IN THE LIFE OF CATHERINE OF SIENA

Introduction

The biographical sources (apart from the autobiographical parts of her own writings) give the impression, at first glance, that Catherine of Siena did *not* experience much if any development in terms of her own faith. For example, there is no indication that she ever had any mortal sins to renounce: She had her first vision of Christ at the age of six when, according to her confessor Raymond of Capua, she was "transformed into him";[1] in her family home she was said to have been mystically whisked up the stairs;[2] around the same age she is said to have levitated, a mystical phenomenon that she would later consider to be a sign of the soul's perfect union with God;[3] around the age of seven she made a vow of virginity.[4] In short, it would seem that Catherine's starting point on her own spiritual "journey" (if it can even be described as such) was very near to its end (that is, union with God). Common sense, however, tells us that her love of God and neighbor could not possibly have remained static throughout her lifetime.

After we examine the reliability of the sources, we will look at what they indicate about Catherine's spiritual development during the various periods of her life: her childhood, the years in the cell (c. 1363–67), her activity in Siena and its environs (c. 1367–75), and then beyond Siena until her death in Rome (1375–80).

Catherine of Siena

Sources and Their Historical Value

Sources

The most important primary biographical sources of Catherine of Siena are the *Legenda major*, the *Supplementum* (or *Libellus de Supplemento*), the *Processo Castellano*, the *Legenda minor*, and her writings: *epistolario*, the *Dialogue*, and prayers.[5]

The *Legenda major* is the most important single biographical source.[6] Raymond of Capua, Catherine's confessor, friend, and disciple from 1374 until her death in 1380, who later became the master of the Dominican order, wrote the work between 1385 and 1395.[7] He drew upon his own experience and intimate knowledge of her, the witness of others (including her mother), and the notes of Tommaso della Fonte, her relative and first confessor.[8] These notes, which have not survived, were probably "a series of little notes, one might almost say 'jottings,' written from day to day."[9]

The *Supplementum* is a compilation of stories about Catherine by Tommaso di Antonio di Siena (also known as "Caffarini") that were not included in the *Legenda major*. Caffarini, a Dominican, was also a disciple and occasional confessor of hers.[10] His sources were his own experience and, as with the *Legenda major*, the testimony of others as well as the notes of Tommaso della Fonte. From 1411 to 1414 he compiled testimonies of many of Catherine's former disciples for the *Processo Castellano* for her canonization.[11] After this he produced the *Legenda minor*, an abbreviated popular version of Raymond's *Legenda* to which he added some personal recollections.[12]

Lastly, the autobiographical parts of Catherine's own writings, particularly the letters, are a rich source of information on her life.

A Legenda *with a Difference*

The genre of the *Legenda major*, the most important of the primary sources and the one to which we will refer most often, is the hagiographical form of the medieval *legenda*. C. Kearns observes[13]

Spiritual Development in the Life of Catherine of Siena

In Raymond's time and for centuries previously the word *legenda* was a technical term for the biography of a saint. In Latin *legenda* in one of its senses means "to be read", and the title was apt for lives intended *to be read (aloud)* for purposes of edification. At that date the term contained no implication that the contents of the *legenda* were of doubtful authenticity or veracity, as do the words *legend* and *legendary* in modern usage.[14]

Every *legenda*, then, had the purpose of edifying the Christian faithful so as to build them up spiritually.[15] Miracles were a standard part: "[T]here was nothing incredible in the frequent occurrence of miraculous happenings in the lives of holy persons. It was their absence that would have appeared incredible."[16] S. Noffke notes:

> All the primary sources of our knowledge of Catherine of Siena are clothed in the myth of fourteenth-century Italy.... Myth in its noblest sense is simply the result of any attempt to wrap into story the truth that is beyond the mere factual. There is little truth beyond the nakedly scientific that is not wrapped in this kind of myth.[17]

Raymond had another purpose in writing his *Legenda* besides edification: to depict Catherine as someone chosen by God for a particular mission of reform and conversion in the church. Raymond, who, as master of the Dominicans, would later instigate a reform movement in the order, also wanted to portray Catherine as a supporter of the order's reform—which, in fact, she was.[18]

In the context of medieval hagiography, the *Legenda major* is unusual. For example, Raymond, who was a canon lawyer, cites his sources at the end of every chapter. At the end of Chapter II of Part One, for example, he says:

> As for what has been narrated in this chapter, my informant was for the most part Catherine's mother Lapa. Some of the facts, especially in this last part, I was told by Catherine her-

self and by that Lisa whom I have just mentioned. Besides, apart from this last incident, I have the testimony of quite a number of witnesses, both her earliest confessor [Tommaso della Fonte] (who was brought up from childhood in her parents' house), and several worthy women, neighbors or relatives of Catherine's parents.[19]

Raymond's *legenda* with its scientific criteria of checks and citations is unique in medieval hagiography.[20] Furthermore, what Raymond himself admits about his own methodology is almost disarming in its frankness. For example, in the Second Prologue he refers to "allowing for the human fallibility of my search for the truth":

> I solemnly declare to all who read this book, calling as my witness the Truth himself who can neither deceive nor be deceived, that I have recorded in it nothing feigned, nothing fabricated, and, allowing for the human fallibility of my search for the truth, nothing that is false in any way in the substance of the facts narrated.[21]

Later, in Part Two, after a rather long quotation of a divine message to Catherine, Raymond says:

> Now, however, I want to make it clear that with regard to many matters about which she spoke to me time and time again, I cannot actually remember all the exact words she used.... [W]herever the course of my narrative calls for a report of what Catherine said, I give it in the words which seem to me most likely to be the ones she used, judging by what I can recollect of them, and by the subject-matter itself. But I must frankly add…that often, as I am writing, many and many a thing comes back to mind which up to that had escaped my recollection. This is Catherine's doing. I often feel she is present with me as I write, and in a way dictating to me the very things I am to record. The reader should keep this reservation constantly in mind, as a stan-

dard by which to measure what I write. It applies only to the *words* which I report, not to the *facts*. For as regards the facts, I never write down any but what I know with perfect certitude, on the authority of witnesses or written documents, or by my own personal observation. And indeed I remember equally well a great number of the actual words which I report, especially the words in which doctrine is formulated.[22]

Raymond comes across as a very credible biographer. The *Legenda major* is a "*legenda* with a difference."[23]

Nonetheless, the historical value of the sources, including the *Legenda major*, came under serious attack beginning in 1921 with the publication of Robert Fawtier's *Sainte Catherine de Sienne: essai de critique des sources*, vol. 1, *Sources hagiographiques*. Using a positivistic historical method, Fawtier denied the historical value of almost all the events described in the primary biographical sources saying that the hagiographers fabricated their accounts in order to promote Catherine's canonization and the glorification of the Dominican order. The *Legenda major*, Fawtier claimed, was a conscious work of deformation. In 1930 the second Fawtier volume, *Les oeuvres de Sainte Catherine*, appeared in which he evaluated her own works as biographical sources. However, he claimed that these too had been interfered with to varying degrees for the same purposes and therefore were not altogether reliable sources. In 1948 Fawtier and L. Canet produced a biography of Catherine based on their findings: *La double experience de Catherine Benincasa (Sainte Catherine de Sienne)*.[24]

Fawtier's conclusions, however, did not go unchallenged by his peers, namely, I. Taurisano, E. Jordan, P. Mandonnet, and G. Pardi.[25] One of the flaws in Fawtier's methodology, A. Curtayne says, was "an arbitrary use of the Letters, amounting in some cases to *misuse*."[26] Today, some eighty-seven years after the appearance of Fawtier's first work, few scholars would completely dismiss the historical value of the biographical sources. There was, however, a positive outcome from the "Fawtier controversy," as A. Levasti notes:

> Fawtier's destructive theses were exaggerated, but they had the good effect of awakening students of Saint Catherine to the situation, and of opening to them doors that led to new ways of approach....There was a revival of interest in Catherinian studies, and a strictly scientific methodology began to be applied to them.[27]

The new era of catherinian studies saw the appearance of solid academic works by Dupré Theseider, Taurisano, F. Valli, and M. H. Laurent, among others.

In his own rebuttal of Fawtier's attack on the historical value of the biographical sources, the eminent Dominican Père Mandonnet of Fribourg University writes:

> The life of St. Catherine of Siena, or to speak more precisely, the authority of the historical documentation of her life, remains after these new researches that which it was before....Even more, the weak and arbitrary critique, in my opinion, that the historical documentation has just undergone only serves to better bring out again their value and solidity. I do not believe that there exists in the XIV century, in all the hagiography, a personality whose life presents itself in its whole and its detail with similar guarantees of historicity.[28]

With this conclusion in mind, we can assume that the biographical sources, particularly the *Legenda major* and Catherine's own works, have historical value—although the exact extent, of course, cannot be determined.

Role of Hagiography

Because some of these sources are in the genre of hagiography, events in Catherine's life that may have been found "unedifying" or too "ordinary" (for example, faults, sins, temptations) were undoubtedly either played down or not recorded at all. There may be other reasons, too, why more of Catherine's human side was not included in the records: Perhaps out of a desire to speak more of God's goodness in her life she may not have told Raymond about all of her previous struggles. Also, what she did share with Raymond he may have downplayed as we see in the *Legenda major* itself when Catherine, after telling him something she had done that she regarded as a sin but that he thought was only a small transgression, complained: "[W]hat a spiritual father I have now, finding excuses for my very sins!"[29] Catherine, as can be seen in her letters and prayers, frequently refers to herself as a sinner.

In view of the incomplete picture that hagiography affords of saints, the task of discerning evidence of Catherine's spiritual development in the biographical sources is not without difficulty. Mentions of the reality of sin in her life and of the ordinary struggles of faith and human weakness are few and far between, and what development can be discerned pertains mostly to growth in, quite literally, perfection. However, a careful reading of the sources reveals some hints of Catherine's more ordinary side. Some examples of these are when, after her vow of virginity, she listened to her sister Buonaventura and as a result gave more attention to her personal appearance, and when she followed her mother Lapa to the sulphur baths. Also worthy of note are her unwillingness to come out of the cell to help her neighbor, the time she hid on the roof of her house to avoid helping a small child thought to be possessed, judging priests, possible jealousy in love, sexual thoughts, and her delay in leaving Siena to carry out the Lord's commands.[30] In fact, her inner struggles can be glimpsed in those periods that the hagiographers call "diabolical assaults." Additionally, her very practical knowledge of life in all its facets suggests that Catherine had more life experience than the biographical accounts indicate.

Since our sources are of historical value, and since the subject of spiritual development figures so prominently in her teaching, our investigation into Catherine's spiritual development can be justified if we keep in mind these limitations.

Catherine of Siena

Childhood Experiences

"The Great Vision of the Royal Christ"[31]

Around the age of six, Catherine had her first vision, which Caffarini says "was so efficacious that it transformed her entire life."[32] Because of its importance in her life, it is worth quoting Raymond's account at length:

> It was when she was about the age of six. She went one day with her little brother Stefano—not much older than herself—to the house of her sister Buonaventura the wife of Niccolo whom I have mentioned already. We may suppose they went to bring some parcel or message from their mother Lapa, for mothers are fond of visiting their married daughters, or of sending affectionate inquiries after their welfare. The children did as they had been told, and set out on the journey home. As they began to come down a certain slope called in Italian Valle Piatta, Catherine raised her eyes and glanced across the valley. There in the sky above the roof of the church of the Friars Preachers, she saw the vision of a splendid audience-hall, furnished like a royal court. Within it was the Saviour of the world, our Lord Jesus Christ, seated on a lordly throne, clothed in pontifical vestments, and wearing on his head a tiara, the regal mitre of the pope. With him were the Princes of the Apostles, Peter and Paul, and blessed John the Evangelist. Entranced and rooted to the spot, she fixed her eyes on the sight. Wide-eyed she looked upon her Saviour, lovingly contemplating him with the eyes both of body and of soul. And he who was so wonderfully showing himself to her on purpose to draw to him her love, fixed her with his majestic glance, and smiling on her with surpassing affection stretched out his hand over her and made the Sign of the Cross, graciously imparting to her, in the way that prelates do, his own everlasting blessing.

Spiritual Development in the Life of Catherine of Siena

So powerful was the grace this blessing brought her that she was transported out of herself, and transformed into him upon whom her loving gaze was fixed. She lost all consciousness not only of the journey she was making but of her very self. Timid child as she was, she stood rooted in the public roadway, eyes raised aloft and head unmoving, whilst the crowded traffic of men and beasts passed by. She would undoubtedly have continued to gaze on motionless as long as the vision lasted had not another person intervened to bring her back to herself. For while our Lord was carrying out the actions just described, Stefano, her little brother who was with her, had kept on for a time on his way downhill alone after she had stopped, thinking she was coming just behind. After a little, he noticed that she was not with him any longer, and was not following behind. He turned around and saw her a good way back, standing still and staring at the sky. He called out to her two or three times to attract her attention. But as she neither replied to him nor took any notice, he turned and went back to her, calling out as he went. As it was all no use he took hold of her and pulled her, saying: "What are you doing there? Why don't you come?" Like a person awaking from a heavy sleep she lowered her eyes for an instant and said: "Oh, if you but saw what I am looking at, you would never try to take me away from a sight so delightful." As she said this, she raised her eyes to the sky again. But the vision had dissolved and vanished, for such was the will of him who had shown himself in it. Its disappearance was to her like a stab of pain unbearable, and with tears she chid herself for having glanced away.

From that moment onwards the little one began to grow up spiritually in a remarkable way: in virtue, in conduct, and in sound sense. Her way of life became no longer that of a baby nor even a young girl, but rather that of one advanced alike in years and in the estimation of those about her. The flame of love of God had been enkindled in her heart....[33]

In this passage, Raymond says that the Lord wanted "to draw her on to be zealous for the better gifts" and that Catherine grew spiritually after the vision. He also says that she was "transformed into him." The primary effect of the vision, however, is perhaps found in the words: *"The flame of love of God had been enkindled in her heart."*

An image of the royal Christ, instead of the child Jesus or Holy Family, is not one we would expect a small child to have.[34] The vision was attractive and it may have instilled in her a lasting sense of the beauty of God such that, years later, she would wonder why, on seeing his goodness, we do not abandon all attachments and run after him, following his "fragrance"?[35] Often, and in various ways, Catherine uses the word *beauty*:[36] "Everything was made by me, and without me nothing can exist. Therefore, if it is beauty that you want, I am beauty";[37] "O eternal Father! O fiery abyss of charity! O eternal beauty!";[38] "Beauty above all beauty!";[39] the human person is created to share in God's supreme eternal beauty;[40] the beauty of the human soul.[41]

Catherine may have intuited in the vision her future mission at the service of the church.[42] She learned from its painful disappearance that we should never remove our glance, even momentarily, from God.[43] The vision left her "thirsty" in the sense of wanting to be in communion with the Lord.[44] Raymond describes its immediate effect on Catherine:

> [S]he learned and took to heart the virtues and the way of life of the ancient Egyptian Fathers of the desert, and the life-stories of some of the saints, especially Saint Dominic. So powerful became the ardent longing of her soul to imitate these holy men that she could give her mind to nothing else. Accordingly, a number of unusual features began to show themselves in her conduct to the astonishment of those who observed them. She would seek out hidden places, and there,

Spiritual Development in the Life of Catherine of Siena

in secret, lash her tender body with a little scourge. She no longer played the games of children, but took on the practice of prayer and meditation. Unlike other children she grew daily more silent and reserved. She was unlike other children in this too, that as she grew bigger she took less to eat instead of more. By her example she drew to herself a number of little girls like herself to gather round her, and they used to listen with delight to her pious exhortations, and to imitate what she did, in their own little way. They had a certain secret meeting-place in her house, and there they would scourge themselves in company with her, and repeat a number of times, following a plan which she laid down for them, the *Our Father* and the *Hail Mary*. All this foreshadowed, as the sequel will show, what was to come in after years.[45]

[T]he great vision of the Royal Christ...stirred Catherine so deeply and so powerfully that from that time onwards every spark of love for the things of this world was quenched in her heart. In its place was kindled a holy and all-absorbing love for our Lord Jesus Christ, the only Son of God and of the glorious Virgin Mother. All else, from then on, she counted but as garbage, that she might possess her Saviour. Taught by none other than the Holy Spirit, she came to understand that she should serve her Creator with an unblemished purity, holy both in body and in soul. With all her heart she longed to make virginal purity her possession.[46]

"The great vision of the royal Christ" signals the beginning of Catherine's spiritual development.

Subsequent Experiences

Despite her young age, the vision of the royal Christ apparently enkindled in Catherine a desire to make a radical response. In imitation of the desert Fathers, who withdrew into the desert, one day she left the walls of the city and found a cave where she could pray. Raymond says that as soon as she began praying she rose up to the top of the cave and remained there for several hours. After she returned to the ground "[s]he was enlightened by our Lord to understand that, whilst she was indeed to afflict her flesh for his sake, yet the time to do so had not yet arrived, nor was it in this way that he had planned for her to leave her father's house."[47] In this experience the Lord speaks to Catherine for the first time and discloses that he does in fact have a plan for her that would in the future entail penances and leaving her father's house.

The next significant event in her spiritual journey, as indicated by the biographical sources, is her vow of virginity around the age of seven.[48] Catherine had been praying continually to Mary asking her to obtain from her Son "clear and firm guidance in the ways of the Spirit, so as to do what would be most pleasing in his eyes, and most fruitful for the saving of souls."[49] Catherine makes her vow to Mary, saying:

> [G]ive me as my Spouse the One I long for from my inmost heart, your own all-holy and only Son, our Lord Jesus Christ; and I promise him and promise you that to no other spouse will I ever give myself, but in my own humble measure I too will keep my virginity for ever spotless for him.[50]

This act of self-surrender or dedication to the Lord was the first step toward Catherine's mystical espousals with Christ some fourteen years later.

We are told that she grew daily in holiness and, despite her age, was on fire for the salvation of souls. She had a particular interest in saints, such as St. Dominic, who worked for the salvation of souls. She used to kiss the footsteps of the Dominican friars from the nearby church of San Domenico as they walked by her house. In time she herself wanted to be a Dominican so that she could help save souls. When she had the impression that it would not be possible, she decided to follow the example of St. Euphrosyne of Alexandria, a woman who had disguised herself as a man in order to join a monastery.[51]

Spiritual Development in the Life of Catherine of Siena

The next event of significance in Catherine's spiritual development, as far as the records indicate, happened five years later and, while not a mystical experience, had a great impact on her. Raymond says that at the age of twelve her family began to keep her at home in preparation for marriage, as was the custom. Lapa was particularly anxious that Catherine should take more care about her appearance although she showed absolutely no interest. Catherine's beloved older sister Buonaventura was brought in to convince her to change. As a result, Catherine agreed but, Raymond says, privately resolved to keep her vow of virginity. After this "the fervour of her prayer cooled off and the continuity of her state of reflection was broken."[52] When Buonaventura died shortly thereafter, Catherine was brought back to her original resolve and deeply regretted that she had loved her sister more than God. According to Raymond, she still confessed this "sin" years later and would weep over it. She is said to have never again loved anyone more than God. She now "began to seek again the endearments of her eternal Spouse with warmer affection and keener eagerness than before."[53] Catherine intensified her prayer and mortification, shunning human contact and telling people of her promise to espouse only Christ.[54]

Her family, however, did not relent in their efforts to find a husband for her. They now enlisted the help of a Dominican friar to convince her to marry. After listening to Catherine, the friar took her side and convinced her to take the radical step of cutting off her hair to show her seriousness and end the family's harassment. The family was enraged and the opposition increased: "A family edict went forth that Catherine was no longer to have any place to withdraw to by herself, household tasks were to be heaped upon her, and neither time nor place allowed her in which she could be with her Spouse in prayer."[55] A period of persecution by the family now began in which abuse was daily heaped on her. With her room and solitude taken away, we are told that she

> made for herself a secret cell within her own heart, and made up her mind never to go forth from it no matter what

the business on which she was engaged in. The result was that she who formerly had been sometimes inside and sometimes outside the walls of that material cell which she then possessed, now remained uninterruptedly within the walls of that inner cell of the heart which no one could take from her.[56]

This "secret cell within her own heart" led to Catherine's subsequent teaching on "the interior cell":

It was at this time, according to the same biographer [Raymond], that she discovers the secret of the *interior cell* which thereafter she always loved to recommend to all souls thirsty for perfection, especially to religious. It is a "mental cell" made with the help of Jesus the divine guest in the voluntary exercise of removing every occupation of the mind which is far from the thought of God. Such a cell could not be taken from her so long as she could recollect herself to her liking even while performing the daily chores. "The other dwelling place is spiritual," she wrote later to her faithful companion Alessa dei Saracini, "and you should carry it with you constantly. This is the cell of true self-knowledge of the goodness of God in you. There are two cells in one…" [letter T49].[57]

This "interior cell" would one day make it possible for Catherine to move out of the seclusion of her house and Siena itself without losing her spiritual composure. During this period she also learned to endure suffering: "She endured not only with patience but with joy all the suffering that came upon her. The speed of her advance increased from day to day, and the joy that filled her soul brimmed over."[58]

God's plan for Catherine was about to be partly disclosed in a way that would please her. St. Dominic appeared to her in a dream and told her to take courage and not to lose heart, that one day she would wear the habit of the Dominican *Mantellate*.[59] "At these words," says Raymond, "a thrill of happiness went through her and she wept for very joy."[60] Raymond says that the dream always remained impressed on her memory.[61] Fra' Bartolomeo Dominici,[62] one of her closest disciples, relates the dream to Catherine's zeal for the salvation of souls. God says to her:

> [St. Dominic] longed with all his strength to lead, by example and word, many souls to my love. And since he could not function all the time and everywhere, as was his desire for the well-being of souls, I inspired him to found the Order of Preachers so that, with the help of his children, his work would be extended and realized more easily.... If therefore you want to be mine and his genuine daughter, you also must exert yourself with great zeal for my honor and the salvation of souls.[63]

Caffarini also mentions the dream but with an additional detail: After St. Dominic showed the habit to Catherine, the devil appeared and offered her a wedding dress.[64]

The dream apparently emboldened Catherine because that same day she called a family meeting where she disclosed that she had earlier made a vow of virginity and would never have any other spouse than Jesus Christ: "This is a matter in which I have not the slightest intention of yielding to your will. I must obey God rather than man."[65] After this her father, who had witnessed a mysterious sign in the form of a white dove on Catherine's head while she was once praying, granted her the freedom to do what she wanted and warned the family not to interfere. Raymond says that at this meeting she went from being a silent and reserved girl to a self-possessed adult.[66] She had demonstrated her absolute determination.[67]

Catherine was now poised to take the next radical step in her response to the Lord: entering into almost complete seclusion in a tiny "cell" in the family house, an event that occurred shortly after she received the Dominican habit.

Catherine of Siena

In the Cell (c. 1363–67)

Penance and Prayer

After her father's assent, Catherine, who was then about sixteen or seventeen years of age, requested "to have a tiny room entirely to herself, and when this was given her she began to live in it as in the desert, herself alone with God alone, and to mortify her body to her heart's content."[68] Her withdrawal into a cell again reflects the influence the stories of the desert Fathers had on her. She may have been particularly familiar with the story of St. Anthony, the most famous of the Egyptian Fathers, who withdrew to a cave in the desert where he fought the devil. At that time there was a small church dedicated to St. Anthony close to her house.[69]

Catherine's entry into the cell marked the beginning of a period of great austerities and penances. Lapa, who disregarded her husband's injunction, still hoped to wean her daughter away from such an unusual way of life and so decided to bring her to the fashionable sulphur baths not far from Siena.[70] We may wonder why Catherine, after delivering such an uncompromising speech to her family, agreed to such a trip. Caffarini provides the explanation: "Catherine, more shrewd than the mother, prudently thought to please her by not disturbing her and to take advantage of those delightful baths for the purpose of afflicting her body much more than if she had stayed in the cell."[71] Once at the baths Catherine went to the place where the hot water entered the pool and, exposing her flesh to water, did indeed inflict more pain on herself than had she stayed in her cell.

Sometime after the incident at the baths, if Raymond's account is chronological, Catherine was clothed in the habit of the Dominican Mantellate in a ceremony at San Domenico that her mother attended.[72] The event was significant in her life: It was probably public (or quasi-public), was officially linked to the Dominican order, and was commonly regarded as irreversible (there is no indication after this of Lapa trying again to dissuade her). K. Foster comments on its implications:

Spiritual Development in the Life of Catherine of Siena

It is worth insisting on the immense importance for Catherine of being able to carry on her work under the wing of the Order; in the medieval church the Order of St. Dominic was relatively more important than it has ever been since. In those days the Dominicans as a body were the highest theological authority in the church, at once an intellectual élite and a touchstone of orthodoxy. Catherine could no more have done what she did had she been merely a laywoman than she could have done it had she been an enclosed nun. And her Dominican connection was a special advantage.[73]

The usual choice in those days for a young woman with a religious vocation would have been the cloister. We have no indication, however, that Catherine ever considered becoming a nun. D'Urso says that "for such a woman, the cloister would have been almost a diminution, like half a vocation. Instead, the Dominican ideal which is both monastic and apostolic seemed made for her, particularly in the form of the Third Order which left open the way to action for a woman."[74]

Caffarini records a vision Catherine had soon after receiving the Dominican habit that would later have a significant impact on her teaching on spiritual development. In this vision she saw a magnificent tree full of rich fruit but surrounded at its base by thorns. Not far from the tree was a mound of what appeared from afar to be a pile of wheat but that was actually nothing more than inedible chaff. Three types of persons approached the tree for its fruit. Some came and looked at the tree but when they saw the thorns they lost interest and went toward the "wheat." Others went through the thorns at the base of the tree but then became discouraged when they saw how high the fruit was; they too turned around and headed for the chaff. Lastly, only a few people made it through the thorns and up the tree to the fruit. J. Jorgensen comments:[75]

> In this vision Catherine's fundamental view of life which was to grow fuller and deeper with the coming years, was already given. Man is placed, so she feels, between two

powers, *both of which appeal to his love*. One of these two powers is truth, life, peace, happiness and everlasting life; the other is delusion, the world, the ever enchanting and ever disappointing mirage of Satan.[76]

The importance of the vision can be seen in the fact that Catherine refers to it in the *Dialogue*.[77] As we will see in the next chapter, she apparently used the fruit tree and the three types of persons who approach it as an image (perhaps her original image) for stages of spiritual development prior to her use of the image of the bridge.

Catherine's concern at this time was to have complete dominion over her nature, including carnal stimulations contrary to her vow of virginity, as well as natural stimulations of hunger, thirst, rest, and sleep.[78] As Raymond says, "The honey she ranged for was the opportunity and means of denying still more everything of self that was in her, and of becoming ever more closely united with her Spouse."[79] She would flagellate herself three times daily for one-and-a-half hours each time: for her own sins, the sins of the living, and for the sins of the dead.[80] Later in life, the blood of Christ as the indisputable proof of divine love would become one of her principal teachings. In her corporal penances she saw herself as giving "blood for blood," love for love. Around this time Dominici saw Catherine for the first time in her cell and, despite her extreme lifestyle, observed that "she was a young girl looking very cheerful."[81]

Divine Visitations

Besides penance and prayer, her years in the cell were also characterized by divine visitations that became more frequent and familiar.

> He [our Lord] could not continue any longer to leave this chosen lamb without a shepherd's guidance, or to leave so apt and diligent a pupil without an expert master. The Teacher he chose for her was neither man nor angel but his own self. I had it from herself that as soon as she began this

Spiritual Development in the Life of Catherine of Siena

life of seclusion in her cell, our Lord Jesus Christ began in his goodness to appear to her, and to give her full instruction on every aspect of her spiritual life.[82]

Raymond says that the visits became so frequent that "it would be hard to find two people who spent their time so constantly in each other's company as these two did."[83] At a certain point Christ seemed to be continually present to her, even when she was in the company of others.

During this period, despite her isolation from other people, Catherine's wisdom increased. Occasionally she would receive visitors such as Tommaso della Fonte and Dominici.[84] She would leave the cell only for daily Mass or confession. It is likely that there was preaching every day at Mass at San Domenico, although the record is not entirely clear.[85] The reaction of many people to Catherine's wisdom, as noted by Raymond and Dominici, was like that of the people of Nazareth: "Where did this man get this wisdom?" (Matt 13:54).[86] Dominici says, "Some rivals...believed that she was taught by us friars, while instead the opposite was true."[87] Catherine's ability to "read" (which might be described better as guessing since Raymond said she could hardly spell or recognize the letters in words) is an insight into her mental powers that were wholly intuitive: "[S]he knew without being able to give a reason for her knowledge."[88]

Many of her most important teachings were acquired during this period. By far the most important was the "fundamental maxim": "Do you know, daughter, who you are and who I am? If you know these two things you will have beatitude within your grasp. You are she who is not, and I AM HE WHO IS."[89] As we will see in the next chapter, this would become a major part of Catherine's famous teaching on self-knowledge. Other principles revealed to her at this time were: the difference between a true and false vision;[90] the maxim: "Daughter, think of me; if you do, instantly I will think of you";[91] the right order of love: God first and others second; the importance of loving others in God;[92] the rooting out of self-love and the planting of holy self-hatred of one's lower nature.[93]

Catherine of Siena

Crisis

Catherine would now face a severe crisis similar to Anthony's assaults by the devil and that would shatter the tranquility of her life in the cell. From the experience she would learn more truths pertaining to spiritual growth. The crisis had various aspects: sexual temptations, seemingly friendly voices suggesting that she stop her penances and suffering and take a husband and have children like the holy women in the Bible, and the cessation of the divine visitations.[94] Raymond describes this part of the crisis as one of diabolical assaults. Modern psychology would argue that the thoughts and temptations that Catherine experienced were simply her own—a reflection of her ordinary struggles, conflicts, and doubts. Can we not imagine the voice of Catherine herself in the following words of her "attackers"?

> "[W]hat is the point of all this affliction? What will all these excruciating sufferings bring you in the long run? Do you imagine you can keep them up for ever? Impossible! unless you want to kill yourself and end up as a suicide. Be wise in time. Drop this nonsense before it leads to a complete breakdown. It is not yet too late to enjoy the delights which life can offer. The resilience of youth is on your side; your body can win back its freshness and vigour. Live the life that other women do. Take a husband. Be a mother of children. Bow to the law of human nature to increase and multiply. None of this can hinder the fulfillment of your desire of pleasing God. Have not saintly women been wives and mothers? Think of Sarah and Rebecca."[95]

Some might contend that the purposes of hagiography perhaps required that the cause of the crisis be attributed to another source.

Catherine, although distressed, continued praying and mortifying herself. During her last assault by the "demons," Catherine declared:

Spiritual Development in the Life of Catherine of Siena

"I have made choice of suffering as the well-spring of my strength. It is no hardship for me, but rather a delight, to endure for my Saviour's name all you have been inflicting on me, and more besides, for as long as it shall please his Majesty." At these words the demon horde turned tail and fled pell-mell, and a great light from heaven flooded the little room. And there, at the heart of the brightness, was our Lord Jesus Christ himself, nailed upon the cross and covered with his blood, in that very form in which, by his own blood, he entered into the Holy Place. From that cross he spoke to her these words: "My daughter Catherine, look at what I have suffered for your sake. Do not take it hard, then, when you too must suffer something for my sake."[96]

Then the Lord changed into his more familiar appearance and moved closer to her. Catherine asked him where he had been and he said, "Hidden in your heart, I was guarding it from your enemies on every side; but on the outward side I was allowing you to be distressed in as far as this would help to save your soul."[97]

The crisis taught Catherine a lesson that would stay with her for the rest of her life and that would become part of her spiritual teaching: the importance of accepting suffering in joy and that one's love of God is not proven by the enjoyment of spiritual pleasures but rather by perseverance. She also came to believe more firmly in God's abiding presence, especially during difficult times. Because of her perseverance, the Lord, who now addresses Catherine as "my daughter," promised to show himself more frequently and familiarly in the future.[98] Being addressed as "daughter" thrilled Catherine. Later, in her spiritual teaching, being a "son" or "daughter" of God would be her image for the highest stage of spiritual development.

The divine visitations did indeed become more frequent and familiar. Caffarini says that the two would speak like "the father with the daughter or like the most diligent teacher with his best disciple."[99] Raymond says that sometimes Christ would come with his mother or St. Dominic, St. Mary Magdalene, St. John the Evangelist, or the apostle Paul, "[b]ut for most of the time he came alone and held long conversations with her like one intimate friend with another. Further, as she reluctantly admitted to me more than once herself, our Lord would even recite the Psalms with her as they walked to and fro in her room, like two religious or two clerics reciting their office together."[100] During this time her vocal prayer decreased and her ecstasies grew to such a point that she could barely finish the Our Father without going into one.[101] Caffarini reports that at such times she would often repeat the words, "O Love, o Love!"[102]

Mystical Espousals

Catherine's seclusion in the cell reaches its climax c. 1367 with "the mystical espousals" when she was about twenty-one.[103] As the divine visitations increased, so did Catherine's desire

> to attain to the perfection of the virtue of faith, such a faith as would confirm her immutably in self-surrender to her Spouse and render her still more dear in his eyes. After the example of the disciples in the Gospel she began to beg our Lord to increase her faith and to grant her that virtue in such fullness that never for the future would any hostile power be able to unsettle or uproot it. He answered her in one short sentence: "I will espouse you to me in faith."[104]

The mystical espousals occurred on Shrove Tuesday when Mary took Catherine's right hand and held it toward her Son and asked him to espouse Catherine to himself in faith.

> The only-begotten Son of God most graciously consented. He drew out a gold ring set with four pearls and surmounted by a splendid diamond. With his all-holy right hand he placed it on the ring-finger of Catherine's right hand, saying as he did so: "Behold, I espouse you in faith to

me, your Creator and your Saviour. That faith will be ever kept untarnished until the day when you will celebrate with me the everlasting wedding-feast in heaven. So now, daughter, do manfully. From now on you must never falter about accepting any task my providence may lay upon your shoulders. Remember, you have been confirmed in faith, and will prevail over all your enemies."[105]

From then on Catherine had a permanent awareness of her confirmation in grace or predestination to heavenly glory.[106]

Her mystical espousals symbolize a perfection of Catherine's faith in which her self-surrender to God becomes irreversible. Like all of Raymond's descriptions of her most significant mystical experiences, the mystical espousals effect Catherine's "usefulness" to others: Now she will be able to withstand "manfully" any obstacle that comes her way and to accept any task that the Lord gives her. There is no explicit mention of union, as one might expect; rather, the mystical espousals are described as a preparation for greater service to God and neighbor. As D'Urso says, "[T]he divine Spouse had not given her the ring of mystical union so that she could enjoy by herself the celestial joys; because she was united to Him, she would also then have to go out of the little paradise of her retreat to pour out on others the richness of her graces."[107] Caffarini sees the mystical espousals as a preparation for her later involvement in public life for the salvation of souls:

> As the first Catherine [of Alexandria], queen and martyr, having obtained victory over unfaithfulness, was espoused to Jesus Christ, so this second Catherine, after the victory of many battles, as a sign of her firmness of faith and of her four purities (the pearls of the ring) of mind, heart, word and works, was confirmed in grace.
>
> Having in fact to present herself in public in an unusual way for a woman, like the other great holy preachers that were helped and confirmed by divine virtue for the salvation of souls, this virgin [Catherine of Siena] was confirmed

in a solemn way before the saints in heaven so that she could safely go forth with such trust to accomplish those great undertakings....[108]

Caffarini records another event after the mystical espousals worth mentioning:

> While she was in her room praying and intensely desiring Jesus' friendship, it was as if she was repeating: "Kiss me with a kiss of your mouth," and the Lord appeared to her and gave her a kiss with which she was exceedingly delighted.[109]

As we will see in chapter 3, the kiss of peace at the mouth of Christ marks the soul's arrival on the third *scalone* or stair of the bridge.

After the mystical espousals, Raymond refers to Catherine as "a spouse of the Lord...called on by him to bear children to him in the spirit."[110] Later in her teaching, Catherine would repeatedly speak of "conceiving" and "bearing" the virtues in the lives of one's neighbors. Indeed Catherine was soon to "give birth" to the virtues in her relationships with others.

Siena and Its Environs (c. 1367–75)

Out of the Cell: "Works of Mercy Towards Her Neighbour"[111]

After the mystical espousals Catherine began "to mingle with other people, but unobtrusively and with disciplined restraint"[112] in Siena and its environs. Sometimes during a divine visitation the Lord would abruptly say to her, "Leave me now. It is dinner-time and your family are sitting down to table; go and join them; and afterwards you can come back to me."[113] She would then burst into tears, saying that he was driving her away from him, that she did not want to be separated from him for even a moment, that mealtimes meant nothing to her, that she had turned her back on human companionship in order to find him, and that she had no desire to go back or do anything that might lead to her being separated from him. The Lord's reply is significant:

> "Dearest daughter, let it be so for this reason, for so it is right for you to fulfill *all* justice; for my grace in you must now begin to bear fruit not only in yourself but in other souls as well. *I have no intention whatever of parting you from myself, but rather of making sure to bind you to me all the closer, by the bond of your love for your neighbour.* Remember that I have laid down two commandments of love: love of me and love of neighbour. 'On these two commandments,' as I myself bore witness, 'depend the Law and the Prophets.' It is the *justice* of these two commandments that I want you now to fulfil. On two feet you must walk my way; on two wings you must fly to heaven. Cast back your mind and remember how from childhood days your heart has been filled with zeal for the salvation of souls, a zeal which I planted there, and watered, and made to grow. Remember how you used to plan to put on man's attire and enter the Order of Preachers in foreign parts to labour for the good of souls. Remember how, from that time forward, you burned with eagerness to put on the habit which you now wear, so as to satisfy your loving devotion to my faithful servant Dominic, who founded his Order above all to labour zealously for souls. Why then are you surprised, why are you sad, because I am now drawing you on to the work which you have longed for from your infancy?"[114]

The neighbor was not to be a means of separation from God for Catherine but rather the means of a closer and more intimate bond with him.[115] Years later Catherine would tell Raymond of Capua that the command to leave the cell so distressed her that "her heart was at times…pierced with anguish that it seemed to be cut in two or to be breaking asunder."[116] Perhaps an allusion to her fear at this time can be found in the *Dialogue* where she makes an analogy to the disciples fearfully huddling together in the Upper Room but who later, after the descent of the Spirit, leave it to preach.[117] Catherine's obedience in leaving the cell "was a victory over her personal tastes which would have to be repeated more than once in the life of this lover of solitude who, notwithstanding appearances, felt as if in exile among the anxieties of the world."[118] It was "the central point of all catherinian experience."[119]

In the above text the Lord commands Catherine to leave the cell so as "to bear fruit not only in [herself] but in other souls as well." She begins by first going to the family table and helping once again with household tasks; then her work gradually extends to the poor. "After the espousals to the Lord," writes Raymond, "she realized more than ever that the more she practiced works of mercy towards her neighbour, the more she would be pleasing to him."[120] Comparing her to St. Nicholas or St. Martin of Tours, he says that she would get up early in the morning so as not to be seen and deposit gifts of wine, corn, and oil on the doorsteps of the poor. From charity to the poor she extended her work to nursing the sick, beginning with an old woman named Tecca who had leprosy and who was about to be put outside the city walls, as was the rule. Catherine took care of her, seeing in Tecca her divine Spouse. Catherine was now putting the virtues into practice in her relationships with her neighbors. Raymond lists those virtues as charity, humility, patience, faith, and hope.[121]

The second elderly person Catherine helped, according to the *Legenda major*, was the Mantellata Palmerina.[122] She posed a different challenge for Catherine: "Some smoldering spark of envy and pride, which she cherished in her heart, flamed into a burning hatred against Catherine. She could not bear the sight of her: she could not even hear her name spoken without undergoing a paroxysm of hatred."[123] The Lord, however, showed Catherine the beauty of Palmerina's soul, albeit blemished by sin. On seeing it Catherine could not bear to think that it might be lost forever and so she intensified her prayers for the woman. Eventually Palmerina was brought around, went to confession, and received the sacraments before dying. The Lord then granted Catherine a vision of Palmerina's soul after the old woman's death:

> As he showed it to her our Lord said: "Look, dear daughter, at this soul. When it was already lost, I won it back through you. Is it not a thing of splendor? Would not anyone endure the greatest trials in order to win so exquisite a creature? I myself am Beauty Supreme from which all other beauty is derived. Yet so enchanting is the beauty of the souls of men that I gladly came down upon this earth and shed my Blood in order to redeem them. How much more should you yourselves take on you toil and labour for the sake of one another, so that so splendid a creature may not be lost? That is why I have given you a vision of this soul: to rouse you still more to spend yourself for the salvation of souls...."[124]

This vision of the soul's beauty prompted Catherine to ask for a particular mystical gift: the ability to see the state of the soul of anyone she would meet. The Lord granted her request, saying:

> I now endow you with a power of spiritual insight by which you will be able to see the beauty or the ugliness of all the souls that come into your presence. From now on, the senses of your soul will perceive the qualities of spirits as distinctly as the senses of your body perceive the qualities of bodies.[125]

This is the first indication we have of Catherine having an extraordinary gift. It would impel her to spend herself for the salvation of souls. Catherine once said to Raymond:

> "Father!...if you were to see the beauty of the human soul, I am convinced that you would willingly suffer death a hundred times, were it possible, in order to bring a single soul to salvation. Nothing in this world of sense around us can possibly compare in loveliness with a human soul."[126]

Catherine of Siena

The vision of the soul's beauty was an important part of Catherine's preparation for her future work beyond the walls of Siena.

Catherine's spiritual growth during this period is manifested not only in her works of charity but also in an increase in devotion to the Eucharist and in the experience of ecstasy. Her fasting from food became almost total at this point while her desire for daily reception of the Eucharist grew.[127] She would say to Raymond, "Father, I'm hungry; for God's sake give my soul its Food."[128] Her exuberance for communion often caused a disturbance in church: She would cry so much during Mass that her confessor told her not to sit near the altar.[129] Every time she received communion she would go into ecstasy, lying stiffly on the ground for at least three hours and sometimes speaking out loud.[130] She sometimes desired communion so much that her teeth rattled audibly.[131] When the priest would give her the chalice with unconsecrated wine to cleanse her mouth, she would fix her teeth so firmly on its rim that she left permanent marks on it.[132] Not surprisingly, various restrictions were placed on her: The prior would sometimes deny her permission to receive communion.[133] At times she was forbidden to receive communion from any priest at will.[134] Some priests ordered her to leave the church immediately after receiving the sacrament so that her ecstasies would not disturb others and so that the building could be closed on time.[135] Some unsympathetic friars were even known to have thrown her outside the church or to have kicked her while she was in a state of ecstasy.[136]

Her ecstasies began to occur wherever she was.[137] "She found her mind drawn so overpoweringly and, as it were, so connaturally, towards union with [the Lord] at every moment," writes Raymond, "that no outward action or pre-occupation of her bodily powers came between her soul and his spiritual endearments."[138] Stefano Maconi, a member of Catherine's "family" of followers and one of her closest disciples, recounts in his deposition for the *Processo Castellano*:

> If sometimes she was constrained to listen to things of the world, or things which were of no use to one's well-being,

she was immediately rapt in ecstasy, the body staying without movement as if it had been in prayer. In this way she was rapt every day, as we ourselves have seen, I don't say a hundred or thousand times, but much more; her members remained so cold and insensible that they would rather break than bend.[139]

There are so many accounts in the biographical sources of her being in ecstasy that, after reading them, one would think that she spent most of her life in that state. Her way of praying when not in ecstasy was also exceptional: She would frequently be in a pool of perspiration; she would laugh and cry simultaneously; her colloquies with the Lord would be interspersed with periods of silence as she listened to his reply.[140]

Catherine's ministry to sick and elderly women reached a climax with her care of another Mantellata, Andrea, when she dramatically demonstrated her fulfillment of the Lord's command "to walk on two feet" (to love God and neighbor in the same way). Andrea had breast cancer and the decay was so bad that no one could stand to be around her.

> When Catherine heard this she realized that this invalid, abandoned by practically everyone else, was being assigned specially to herself by God. At once she went to the house, approached the sufferer with a friendly smile, and cheerfully offered herself as her nurse, to attend her as long as her sickness would last.[141]

Despite the repugnant smell, Catherine took great care of the woman. One day, as she was changing her bandage, an even more revolting smell came forth and she was on the verge of vomiting. Then

> she bent over the sick woman and pressed her mouth and nose upon the festering sore, and in that posture she remained a long time, until she felt that the power of the Spirit had subdued the nausea of the flesh, and that she had stamped out the rebellion of the flesh against the spirit.[142]

Catherine of Siena

Andrea, however, eventually turned against Catherine and falsely accused her of unchastity. The accusation was repeated to such an extent that the Mantellate summoned Catherine to a meeting and berated her. Despite the accusations, she continued nursing Andrea. Once while praying in her cell

> the Saviour of the world appeared to her. In his right hand he held a crown of gold, studded with pearls and precious stones; and in his left a crown of thorns. And he said: "Dear Daughter, I want you to know that it is marked out for you to wear both of these crowns in turn. Make your choice, then. Either choose to wear the crown of thorns in this life here below, and then I will keep the jewelled crown for you in the life which is to come. Or else choose this jewelled crown in your present life, and the crown of thorns will await you after death." To this she replied: "The doing of my own will, Lord, I have irrevocably renounced this long time past; I have made my choice to follow your will, and your will alone. I have no longer, then, any possibility of making a choice of my own. But since it is your express will that I should give an answer now, this is it: My choice is, in this life, invariably to follow the pattern of your own most blessed passion, and always, for your sake, to take suffering to myself as the refreshment of my soul."
>
> With these words she resolutely seized the crown of thorns with both hands....[143]

This vision seems to continue the line of the earlier vision of the crucified Christ after the crisis in the cell. There would be more mystical experiences involving the cross or the passion of Christ, with the climax coming in 1375 with the stigmata.

The story of Andrea continues. One day when Catherine was removing a bandage, the odor was so overpowering that she was again revolted and her stomach turned. Dominici says that she then heard a voice saying, "What great pride you have there; you are not ashamed to detest Christ in your neighbor."[144] Catherine quickly came back to herself. Raymond of Capua records what happened next:

> Fresh from her recent conquests in the power of the Holy Spirit, and strong in the heroic virtues [the Lord] had brought her, she could not bear that her body should again rebel against her spirit. Turning on it with a holy indignation she cried: "As the Lord lives, who is the beloved Spouse of my soul, you will be made to swallow down the thing for which you show such deep disgust." So saying, she gathered into a bowl the water with which the ulcer had been washed and the corrupt matter which had come away with it, and going to one side she swallowed it.[145]

Catherine, who had previously "put her mouth" to Andrea's wound, now drinks at her "opened side." The Lord would soon invite her to do the same with him in one of her deepest mystical experiences. Her love of neighbor now mirrored her love of God.

Christ's Opened Side

The following night, after the above incident with Andrea, the Lord appeared with his five wounds while Catherine was praying and said:

> "[Y]esterday the intensity of your ardent love for me overcame even the instinctive reflexes of your body itself: you forced yourself to swallow without a qualm a drink from which nature recoiled in disgust. In response to this I now say, that as you then went far beyond what mere human nature could ever have achieved, so I today shall give you a drink that transcends in perfection any that human nature can provide or has ever heard of." With that, he tenderly placed his right hand on her neck, and drew her towards the wound in his side. "Drink, daughter, from my side," he said, "and by that draught your soul shall become enraptured

with such delight that your very body, which for my sake you have denied, shall be inundated with its overflowing goodness." Drawn close in this way to the outlet of the Fountain of Life, she fastened her lips upon that sacred wound, and still more eagerly the mouth of her soul, and there she slaked her mystic thirst for long and long.[146]

From that day on, says Raymond, "her soul was so inundated with grace that she lived, practically without interruption, in a state of actual contemplation of the things of God. Her mind cleaved so utterly to her Creator and ours that the lower sense-faculties of her soul remained for the most part inactive."[147] Drinking at the opened side was Catherine's most profound mystical experience so far.

Entrance into the opened side "has a precise meaning in the catherinian imagination: a complete communion of friendship and affection with the Lord."[148] The second recorded instance of it in the *Legenda major* was on July 17, 1370, at the church of San Domenico when Catherine went into ecstasy after receiving communion. She later told Raymond about the experience:

> "I must describe for you, Father," she said, "the way our Lord dealt with my soul that day. He did just what a mother does with the baby in her arms which she loves so tenderly. She offers him her breast, but at the same time she holds him a little away from her, and he begins to cry. As soon as he does, she chuckles at him and hugs him to herself and kisses him, and then she lets him have the breast to his heart's content, and her own delight is one with his. So did our Lord deal with me that day. He showed me his sacred side, but from a distance; and I shed many tears by reason of the longing thus provoked in me to slake my thirst there. And then he seemed to smile at my tears, and to leave me to them for a little while; but in the end he ran to me and clasped my soul in his arms, and set my mouth to the wound in his most sacred side. Driven by a mighty yearning, my soul pressed on until it found its way inside his

breast, there to plunge itself in such knowledge and fruition of the Godhead that, could you realise it, you would wonder that my heart does not burst for very ardour, and that this body is able still to contain a soul transfigured into a living flame of love."[149]

A new image now appears: the breast of Christ. Catherine enters the opened side and "journeys" to the breast where she is plunged into "knowledge and fruition of the Godhead." During another experience, the Lord again drew her into his side "and there revealed to her nothing less than the mystery of the Trinity."[150] It was after Catherine mystically drank at the opened side of Christ that her body parts would become rigid during ecstasy, her eyes tightly closed, and her ears impervious to sounds.[151]

Caffarini says that the Lord showed her his opened side again and again, once even when she was traveling on a road outside Siena.[152] Sometimes the Lord merely showed her his opened side. At other times he would open it for her to enter. One such experience is particularly important in terms of Catherine's later teaching on spiritual stages.

> It happened around the feast of the Holy Cross that, when the virgin was meditating on the love of Christ and the effect of his passion, she felt herself completely plunged in Christ's blood.
>
> Then the Lord appeared to her carrying a cross of gold and said to her: "Take this, daughter, and come with me." And she went with him. After that she saw another large cross on which Christ ascended and said to her: "Put your mouth to the wound on my side." And she put it there and tasted the divine sweetness of the Lord.
>
> Then she found herself lifted up on high, and it seemed to her that Jesus offered her his lips and she did likewise to give a kiss. Such was the impression that she had that for several days it seemed to her that she could feel the face of

Jesus resting on top of hers and at that time she received a great many graces from the Lord.

During these divine experiences it seemed to her that Jesus said: "My daughter, go on these three ways *[tres status]* that I will show you and then you will always be dear to me. The first thing is that I want you to fix your eyes well on the feet on the cross; that is, I want you to keep far away from yourself every earthly affection so that you will enjoy my sweetness." As a second thing, he drew her to the opening of the wound on his side, opened it, and the virgin entered and received there such sweetness, love, clarity and knowledge, so much light from God that she could not find the words to describe the richness of the gifts that had been communicated to her. As a third thing, he embraced and kissed her, giving her peace.[153]

Catherine would gradually find the experience of drinking at the opened side and breast inexpressible; she would taste "a sweetness that she did not know how to describe."[154] The opened side would be a venue for other mystical events: One time the Lord drew from it a bloodred dress and gave it to her as a pledge of future glory;[155] at another time he dipped a piece of bread into his side and gave it to her, saying, "Daughter, take it and eat it";[156] at another time a vine of grapes flowed from Christ's breast and side.[157]

The experience of drinking at Christ's opened side results in Catherine being in a profound state of communion with the Lord, who now expects more from her: "[S]he had not yet gathered in for him that harvest of the souls of her neighbours which her life here below was destined to bear."[158] Raymond describes a vision that occurred sometime after Catherine had first drunk at the opened side:

On a certain day, then, [the Lord] appeared to her as she was at prayer in her little cell, and told her of the coming of this new marvel into her life. "I am now making known to you beforehand, my daughter," he said to her, "the unwonted conditions under which the rest of your mortal life is to be lived out. The gifts I am now about to shower on you are so rare, that they will cause amazement and incredulity in the minds of ignorant and fleshly-minded men. Even your friends will come to doubt you, and suspect that you are the victim of delusions. But the root cause of all this will be the great love I bear you. For I intend to flood your soul with such an abundance of divine grace that its effects will brim over upon your very body, which will begin to take on an abnormal way of life, totally different from that of the common run of men. Besides this, your heart will now be so filled with burning zeal for the salvation of souls that you will lay aside the conventional restraints imposed upon women, and break entirely with the habits of reserve in this regard which you have trained yourself in up to this. Indeed, you are now to plunge boldly into public activity of every kind with but one thought in mind, the salvation of souls, whether they be men or women."[159]

Catherine would, therefore, enter upon a new chapter in life where she would "break entirely" with her reserved habits and "plunge boldly into public activity" for the salvation of souls. At another time the Lord would be more explicit and say that her assignment would take her outside Siena.

Conversion of Sinners and Peacemaking

Before venturing outside Siena, Catherine's work within the city and its environs would expand beyond works of charity to the poor and sick to the conversion of sinners and "settling affairs" among individuals and families. There are many accounts of how she interceded with God for someone's conversion and later obtained it. In the case of one hardened sinner, the Lord told her not to bother because he deserved eternal death; Catherine argued with God, reminding him that he had appointed her especially for the salvation of souls and that "the only consolation left to [her] in this world is to see [her] neighbors' souls converted to you; this alone is what enables [her] to endure [her] exile from your presence."[160] Now that her fasting from ordinary food was virtually total, she spoke of "eating souls" in regard to her efforts for the conversion of sinners. Dominici summarizes her work with people at this time:

> Who in fact could say enough about all the people and the types of people she brought back to a better life through her holy exhortations! How many noble matrons she induced to wear the religious habit! How many noble young women were moved by her words and the example of her life of virginity and the voluntary observance of extraordinary austerity! How many young men were converted and entered different orders! How many religious she led to a better life! How many prostitutes she brought back to a chaste life! How many murderers and men who had gone astray through grave and old enmities did she reconcile with lasting peace, and owing to her holy admonitions, were reunited in sincere and good friendship!
>
> It would take too long and in any case would seem incredible to tell how she, with her admirable speech, sweetly comforted the pious, frightened and confounded the arrogant and insolent; and not only the ignorant and the common people, but also princes, barons, soldiers, great prelates, illustrious doctors of the two laws, medical doctors and expert professors in sacred theology; with a few words she would ignite the more pious sentiments of the good people who spoke with her, and miraculously and beneficially she confounded the crafty and bad ones.[161]

Although Catherine was the recipient of exceptional mystical experiences, and her own way of life was anything but ordinary, in her relations with others she apparently came across as fully alive, friendly, and capable of bringing out the best in others. We are told that people were often converted just through conversation with her[162] and that she had an "outgoing affability in her charity,

Spiritual Development in the Life of Catherine of Siena

and a charming graciousness in her dealings with others" so that people enjoyed being around her.[163] Caffarini says that a woman once told her confessor that every time she met Catherine she "would cry out of happiness and feel inclined to pray."[164] "She had a special charm and as many people approached her, be they men or women, of every rank and of every profession, she made them all better and brought them back to God."[165] Her effect on people can also be seen in his account of Catherine meeting a poor woman at the door of the church who was at the point of desperation:

> The virgin, impassioned with love towards God and neighbor, forgot herself and began to console the poor woman and succeeded so much that the woman started to laugh with joy and then said to one of the companions of the virgin: "This virgin comforted me so much that I feel quite at peace with my whole self."[166]

Dominici relates his own first encounter with her and its effect on him:

> I attest that since the first time I entered into her small cell, although she was a young girl looking very cheerful, I never felt, although being myself a young boy too, any stimulus of the senses, but rather, the more I talked with her and came closer to her the more any disordered emotion calmed down, which was the opposite of what I experienced every day in conversation with other women.[167]

He also says that she was usually happy and joyful.[168]

At this point the biographical accounts begin to mention miracles: Catherine healed a Mantellata who had fallen through the roof of her house; she healed Raymond and Dominici of the plague;[169] she exorcised the little girl Lorenza of evil spirits.[170] She also had the gift of prophecy:

Catherine of Siena

For Catherine possessed the charism of prophecy in so perfect a measure, and it was so continuously present in her that, as far as we could see, nothing was hid from her that concerned herself or those about her, or those who sought her help for the salvation of souls. Those of us who lived with her could not in her absence do anything of any moment, whether good or bad, but she was aware of it. This we knew by experience repeated again and again: it was constantly happening. What was more wonderful still was the fact that our inmost thoughts were known to her....[171]

Although she was unlettered, Catherine's wisdom and theological knowledge were impressive and manifested her own spiritual development. Dominici says that learned people, both religious and laity, tried to stump her with questions or uncover some heresy in her teaching:

God then diffused on her lips so much grace that as time passed, when because of the will of God, she began to talk openly with everyone, as it says in the *Legenda [major]*, I saw the greatest number of learned and clever men, religious and learned laity, run to her from diverse places and at different times not so much for devotion but rather to denigrate and confound her, but after one talk with her they were edified by her teaching and preached the virtues.

I will not say much so as not to prolong too much [accounts of] the miraculous conversions of religious of various Orders who in every possible way and with every effort looked for a way in her private talks or in her public preaching to the people to defame her, and who after having spoken with her not only changed in their opinions and habits but, won by the Truth, were constrained to praise her spontaneously and miraculously in their preaching, and they did not even want to stop praising her virtues which they themselves had experienced despite the fact that everyday they had to withstand serious harassment from their confreres.[172]

Spiritual Development in the Life of Catherine of Siena

Mystical Exchange of Hearts and Other Experiences

Another mystical event was about to occur during this period when Catherine was performing works of charity in and around Siena. Raymond of Capua says that sometime after Catherine's first experience at the opened side she had prayed, "Create a clean heart in me, O God, and renew a right spirit within me."[173] The Lord then appeared to her and seemed to open her left side and remove her heart. A few days later she was in the Mantellate chapel in San Domenico praying. As she was about to return home, she was surrounded by a heavenly light in which the Lord came to her with a heart in his hands. "Our Lord approached her, opened her left side once more, and placed within it the heart which he was carrying. 'See, dearest daughter,' he said, 'a few days ago I took your heart from you; now, in the same way, I give you my own heart. For the future, it is by it that you must live.'"[174] This event, the miraculous exchange of hearts, occurred in the summer of 1370 and as a result Catherine could no longer say, "Lord, I commend to your care this heart of mine."[175]

This was "the great summer of 1370, which [Catherine] spent entirely in putting on the will of God, clothing herself as a new being, assuming Christ."[176] The miraculous exchange of hearts represents a closer union of wills between Catherine and Christ, an intensification of the union that had begun at the mystical espousals. It also had another effect:

> Another thing that followed on this miraculous exchange of hearts was a consciousness that grew up in her that she was no longer the same person she had been. "Do you not notice, Father," she would say to her confessor, Father Thomas, "that I am no longer the same person, but have become totally transformed?"…"Such joy and jubilation possess my soul," she said, "that I am filled with wonder that it can still remain within my body. So intense is the fire that burns in me that mere material flame seems a cold,

dead thing by comparison, fit to freeze rather than to warm a person. While this fire is burning in me it seems to renew and rejuvenate my inner self, bringing a sense of moral purity and humble dependence which makes me feel I am a child of four or five years once more. It brings, as well, a boundless love for my neighbour, so that I would readily undergo death itself with joy and gladness for any neighbour's sake."[177]

Here we see how yet another of Catherine's mystical experiences is directed toward her neighbor. Catherine's will is now "identical" to Christ's,[178] and her love of others is also Christlike: She is now prepared to die for her neighbor. The exchange of hearts was another step in the Lord's preparation of Catherine for her work for the salvation of souls on a wider scale than she had previously known. It also prepared her for the next major mystical experience: the mystical death.[179]

At this time, Catherine's mystical experiences associated with the Eucharist increased: She saw an infant or youth in the consecrated host; the priest at Mass appeared to merge with a living fire when he consumed the host; she perceived a wonderful perfume after receiving communion; and whenever she was in the presence of the Blessed Sacrament her heart would beat so loudly ("a strong, resonant thudding") that it caused a disturbance.[180] We are told that while in a state of ecstasy she would often teach, "sometimes speaking of these sublime things in broken whispers, so that some of what she said could be taken down in writing."[181]

The sources continue to describe the increasing difficulty she now had in explaining her mystical experiences to others. This was especially true with an extraordinary three-day vision that began on the feast of the Conversion of St. Paul and in which she experienced, according to Raymond, a "flood of graces and revelations and visions."[182] After one such vision (perhaps the same one), Catherine reported to her confessor that "she had seen God and that she had felt such a pleasure that she did not know how to express it but through these words: *'the supreme Good.'*"[183] At another time, when an ecstasy was finished, she exclaimed, "Oh Father, today I cannot speak with anyone, because all that I see appears to me as wrapped in a deep darkness."[184]

Raymond records her levitating in front of others on August 18, 1370:

> Then, when she had received the Sacrament, she felt her soul enter into God, and God into her soul, in the same way as a fish in the sea is in the water, and the water is in the fish. All drawn in and gripped by God, she could barely totter home to her tiny cell. Once there, she sank down and lay motionless on that bed of boards which I described already. Then, after a long time, her body found itself raised aloft into the air, and remained suspended, without any material support. This took place in the presence of three witnesses, who testify to the fact and whose names I give below. At length her body sank back on the bed; and then she began to speak in a whisper such words of life, so full of deep meaning and sweeter than honey and the honeycomb, that the bystanders hearing them were moved to tears. After that we prayed for many people, some of them by name, and her confessor in particular.[185]

Under obedience, she later told Raymond more of what had happened: She had had a vision while she was praying for the eternal salvation of himself and others. When the Lord promised her their salvation, she asked him for a token or pledge. He then told her to stretch out her hand:

> "I did so. He took a nail, rested the point of it on the centre of the palm of my hand, and pressed it into my hand with such force that it seemed to pierce right through it, and I felt agony as if an iron nail had been driven through it with a hammer. So now, Father, by the grace of my Lord Jesus Christ, I bear this stigma in my right hand; and

though others cannot see it, its reality is testified to myself by the evidence of my senses and by the pain it gives me, which never ceases."[186]

Catherine's Sins

Not surprisingly, the hagiographical sources do not mention that Catherine ever committed any serious sins. However, in the *Dialogue* Catherine herself admits to a certain "sin" *(una infermità occulta)* in her past: judging others, especially priests.[187] Also, in her letters and prayers she often refers to herself as a sinner:

> I have sinned against the Lord. Have mercy on me! Never have I come to know myself in you. But it is your light that allows us to see whatever good there is to know.[188]

> Then was the soul's [desire] stirred up. She considered her own and others' imperfection.[189]

> No, because of my sins my life is a burden and pain to everyone, near and far. May God in his mercy free me from so many sins![190]

Several of her teachings that pertain to imperfections have an autobiographical sound to them. For example:

> Do you know how you can tell when your spiritual love is not perfect? If you are distressed when it seems that those you love are not returning your love or not loving you as much as you think you love them. Or if you are distressed when it seems to you that you are being deprived of their company or comfort, so that they love someone else more than you.[191]

Raymond records two minor "transgressions," the memory of which always caused pain to Catherine. The significance of these events can perhaps be seen by the fact that they are mentioned in more than one of the biographical accounts. The first occurs after Catherine emerged from the above-mentioned three-day vision that began on the feast of the Conversion of St. Paul. Her confessor at the time, Tommaso della Fonte, and another friar stopped at her house to ask if she would like to accompany them to visit a well-known hermit outside Siena. Raymond makes sure to state that Catherine was still groggy, having been "caught up to the third heaven" like Paul, and was "sunk in her supernatural lethargy, intoxicated, as it were, by the Spirit of God." When Tommaso asked her if she wanted to join them in visiting the hermit, Catherine said that she did. "But no sooner had the words passed her lips," says Raymond, "than like a flash, she was struck with remorse of conscience for the lie. So acute was her sorrow that it stung her back to complete consciousness. And then, for another three days and nights, corresponding to those she spent in ecstasy, she wept continually for that 'sin.'"[192]

The second "sin" during this time happened in San Domenico on the vigil of the feast of St. Dominic in the presence of Dominici. Catherine had a vision of St. Dominic during which she was describing the saint's physical features to him. Just then one of her own brothers was passing by and Catherine briefly removed her glance from St. Dominic to look at him. "But at once she was overcome, both soul and body, by a storm of weeping, and was unable to continue what she had been saying."[193] Afterward she told Dominici that both the Virgin Mary and Paul appeared to her and scolded her for removing her glance.

Neither incident appears to us as serious but they may indicate Catherine's extreme sensitivity to any imperfection at this point in her life.

Catherine's "Community"

Catherine was not an aloof mystic who preferred isolation from others.[194] In her teaching she would consistently lay emphasis on love of neighbor; in her life, her own love for neighbor can be seen especially in her relations with the *"caterinati,"* her group of followers, as reflected in her letters to them and in their depositions at the canonization process years later. We have already seen how the dimension of "the other" surfaced very early in Catherine's life when, at the age of six, she gathered around herself a group of other little girls whom she instructed.[195] Dupré Theseider says:

> Catherine was temperamentally not a hermitess and perhaps would not have adapted even to the cloistered life. The needs and vicissitudes of the neighbor and the possibility of helping him in some Christian way attracted her. It is not without significance that around her there formed spontaneously a so-called "family": a voluntary gathering of a few tens of people, profoundly religious and of a certain culture and doctrine, all animated by a same ideal of life, according to the Spirit; a group not really organized to a clerical mode, but clearly united in a manner moved by Catherine, the *"mamma,"* who was in her time very much connected to them, as is seen in her numerous letters.[196]

Raymond, in fact, says that those who lived with her "had come…to enjoy the satisfaction of living in her company, a blessing which filled with extraordinary delight all those who were privileged to share it."[197] It was a mixed group of men and women, young and old, priests and laity, Mantellate, drawn from various ranks of society but especially, it would seem, from the nobility. The community was mobile to a certain extent and would follow Catherine on her travels outside Siena.[198] Catherine was called *"mamma"* and acted as a kind of superior who would occasionally give commands "in virtue of holy obedience."[199] The community was at times a source of suffering for her; one member violently abused and insulted her and then, like Judas Iscariot, stole money from the common purse.[200] The atmosphere in the community was apparently relaxed as seen in some of Catherine's letters dictated to secretaries who would sometimes sign off using humorous nicknames such as "Giovanna *pazza* [crazy]" and *"stolta* [stupid] Cecca."

The fact that Catherine had disciples at all, that they were of "a certain culture," and her relations with them were warm and cordial, suggests that her personality was attractive to others.

Mystical Death

The momentous summer of 1370 comes to a climax with Catherine's mystical death a few weeks after the miraculous exchange of hearts and brings to a close this period of her spiritual development. As with her other major mystical experiences, the *Legenda major* says it was in answer to prayer. Catherine, who wanted to die so as to be with the Lord, prayed that, if she were to remain in this life, Christ would allow her to be one with him in his sufferings. The Lord granted the request and from that day onward she began to feel his sufferings and declined in health.

> Accordingly, there surged up within her so overmastering a force of love that her heart could no longer keep it pent up, and was rent asunder by its impetuosity. So does it happen when a vessel holds a liquid which is full of power and hidden potency. Its pressure grows too strong for what contains it; its imprisoned energy shatters the restraining walls of the vessel and its power forces its way out.
>
> Need I say more? Need I delay to work out the comparison? The force of Catherine's pent-up love had mounted, till at last her heart was rent in two from top even to the bottom; the blood-vessels on which life depends had ruptured. As a result, not for any natural cause, or for any other reason than the sheer intensity of her love for God, she breathed her last.[201]

The mystical death lasted four hours and was so real that neighbors crowded into the house to console Lapa and the family. Raymond of Capua, who was not present, later asked Catherine to tell him what had happened during the experience. "So immense was the fire of my love for God, and of my longing to be one with him,"

Catherine said, "that even had my heart been made of stone or iron itself, it would have been torn apart and shattered all the same." She went on to say that her soul separated from her body "and I saw the secret things of God, things which it is not given to any pilgrim here below to utter, for no memory can recall them when they are past, nor can human words alone come anywhere near expressing them."[202] Then she told him:

> [M]y soul saw and grasped all that there is in that next world which is normally invisible to us here below. I saw the glory of the saints and the punishment of sinners. But, as I said already, my memory no longer can recall all that I saw, nor would words suffice to express it. However, I will tell you what I can. Take it as certain, then, that my soul saw the divine Essence.[203]

More than any previous one, this experience was indescribable for Catherine.

During the mystical death the Lord spoke again about the new and strange next chapter of her life:

> "Do you see what great glory those souls who offend me are robbed of, and what penalties they are punished with? Go back to earth, then, and show them their peril, show them the harm they are doing to themselves." The thought of going back revolted my soul, but he went on to add: "You must go back; the salvation of many souls demands it. It demands, too, a radical change in the way of life that has been yours up to this. Your cell will no longer be your dwelling-place. For the salvation of souls you will even have to leave your own city. But I will be with you always. I will lead you forth, and will lead you back again, and you will carry with you the honour of my name. You will give proofs of the Spirit that is in you, before small and great, before layfolk and clergy and religious, for I will give you a mouth and a wisdom that none shall be able to resist. I

will bring you before Pontiffs and the Rulers of churches and of the Christian people, in order that I may do as is my way, and use what is weak to put to shame the pride of the strong." Whilst with these and suchlike words, (continued Catherine), he kept speaking in a purely spiritual or intellectual vision to my soul, suddenly, in some mysterious way, I know not how, my soul found itself back in the body once more.[204]

Probably after her mystical death Catherine began writing her first letters; Gardner says she began in 1372, but Noffke says 1370 or even before.[205] The earliest extant letters, which Noffke says were written before the plague of the summer of 1374, were addressed mostly to religious and her own brothers. Catherine's letter writing took on a more universal scope after her journey to Pisa in 1375.

If the Lord had foretold to Catherine in 1370 that she would leave her cell and Siena for the salvation of souls, why did it take another five years before she embarked on her first major journey outside Siena? We can only surmise as to the reason. It is possible that the development (both spiritual and human) of Catherine the worker of charity, settler of affairs, and converter of sinners in Siena to Catherine the peacemaker and preacher to popes and cardinals on an international stage simply required more years of preparation. Also, it is possible that her age posed a practical problem: When she finally left Siena for Pisa in 1375 she was twenty-seven or twenty-eight, whereas had she left in 1370 she would only have been twenty-three. It might have been impossible for Catherine to have received a hearing outside Siena had she been so young. Catherine had to rise above the restricted conception at the time of a woman's duty in public life, especially a "woman of the people" as she was.[206] Furthermore, when she was twenty-three the Dominican order had not yet appointed an official spiritual director for her as it would do in 1374 in the person of Raymond of Capua. Perhaps the support and accompaniment of Raymond, a respected theology master of a noble family, encouraged her to begin this new and radically different phase of her life. It is deserving of note that her first major trip out of Siena was to Pisa, also in Tuscany, and that it happened about a year after Raymond's appointment and that he went with her.[207]

Catherine had made several trips beyond Siena before going to Pisa but all were in the environs of Siena itself. In the spring or early summer of 1374 she went to Florence where the general chapter of the Dominican order was taking place. It is possible that she was summoned to the chapter, so this cannot be taken as the beginning of her travels beyond Siena.[208] After Florence, Catherine and her followers went several times to Montepulciano and Val d'Orcia, both of which are in Tuscany.[209]

The time had now come for a dramatic change in Catherine's living out of her zeal for the salvation of souls and fulfillment of the Lord's commands. She would leave behind her reserved ways, rise above the medieval concept of an ordinary woman's role, leave Siena, and become a player on a much larger stage. Perhaps her words in a letter to Dominici and Caffarini recall the voice of the Lord to her around this time: "[D]o not be satisfied with little things, because God wants great things!"[210]

Beyond Siena (1375–80)

Leaving Siena: The Stigmata

As we have said, the first trip beyond the environs of her hometown was to Pisa, some 125 kilometers northwest of Siena, in 1375. Raymond's account of it contains some important details:

> [I]t happened that a considerable number of the inhabitants of Pisa were very eager to see Catherine. They had heard people sounding the praises of her virtue, and they wanted to hear her doctrine, which was said to be "marvellous," and which was so in reality. These included men and women, religious and layfolk: and most eager amongst them were

certain nuns of the city. However, since for the majority of those who wanted to see her, it was not possible and would not be proper to come to her in Siena, she received numerous requests from them, both by letter and by messenger, begging her to be so kind as to travel to Pisa. In order to prevail on her to come, they promised her in their letters that a great harvest of souls awaited her there, and so the glory of the Lord would be greatly served by her visit. Catherine was never one for much travelling about, but she felt the force of these requests, so numerous and coming so thick and fast, one upon another. Some of her close disciples felt she should go, others were strongly opposed. In her decision she turned as usual to prayer, humbly asking the Lord to direct her. Several days passed, and then, (as she later confided to me), he appeared to her in vision and told her to accept the invitation without delay. Truly obedient as she was, she humbly bowed to this command. She informed me of it and, with my permission, made the journey to Pisa.[211]

It is deserving of note that Raymond says that the idea of going to Pisa was not Catherine's but was the result of an invitation from different groups of people there, especially some cloistered nuns; that her interest in going pertained to the possibility of saving many souls; that Catherine did not usually travel about; that the proposed trip to Pisa was controversial among some of her followers; and that the Lord told her to go without delay.

Raymond may have exaggerated Catherine's hesitancy so as to stifle her critics who later said: "Why is that one gadding about so much? She's a woman. Why doesn't she stay in her cell, if it's God she wants to serve?"[212] However, as we have said, the trip to Pisa represented the beginning of a radical departure from the role of women in public affairs of the time, as well as in Catherine's own lifestyle up to that point, that such a decision had to be well considered.

Catherine's future bold participation in the public forum was probably inspired, to a certain extent, by her namesake Catherine of Alexandria and, more especially, by Mary Magdalene, both of whom are portrayed as fearless preachers in popular medieval legends and who are also patronesses of the Dominican order.[213] In the widely disseminated *Legenda aurea*, a collection of hagiographical stories of the saints written by the Dominican Jacopo de Voragine (d. 1298), Catherine of Alexandria is shown as preaching at various times before a pagan emperor and his subjects and converting many to the faith before her eventual martyrdom.[214]

In the *Legenda major* Raymond of Capua says that Catherine had a special devotion to Mary Magdalene, who would appear to her frequently,[215] that Christ's mother gave the Magdalene to Catherine to be her "mother and teacher,"[216] that at another time Christ himself also gave her to Catherine to be her mother and that "afterwards [Catherine] referred to her as her mother."[217] There can be little doubt that the hagiographical stories and the New Testament accounts of the Magdalene influenced Catherine, as seen in two of her letters. In letter T61 she refers to the Magdalene as an "apostle" whose love of Christ was manifested in her love for "his creatures when after his holy resurrection she *preached* in the city of Marseilles,"[218] a reference to the hagiographical story of the Magdalene's capture after the resurrection when she was set adrift in the sea in a rudderless boat that miraculously landed in Marseilles, where she immediately began preaching boldly before pagans and even the governor.[219] Besides being an "apostle" and fearless "preacher" before pagans, the Magdalene is commended by Catherine in letter T165 for another admirable characteristic: not caring what others might say or how things might look.

> She was no more self-conscious than a drunken woman, whether alone or with others. Otherwise she would never have been among those soldiers of Pilate, nor would she have gone and stayed alone at the tomb. Love kept her from thinking, "What will it look like? Will people speak ill of me because I am rich and beautiful?" Her thoughts

weren't here, but only on how she might find and follow her Master.[220]

Without wanting to detract from Catherine's uniqueness and strength of character, she undoubtedly saw in Mary Magdalene a female precedent and role model for her future work as an *apostola* and preacher.[221] However, unlike the Magdalene, there would be nothing mythical about Catherine's activities.

The fact that the trip was controversial among her own followers indicates that she was about to do something unprecedented. She had made other trips outside Siena, as we have already said, but the trip to Pisa was different. When she eventually leaves her hometown the weightiness of the moment is not lost on Dominici who compares her to Abraham, "who not only left his paternal house, but also his hometown and his own country, and then wandered to different cities and places."[222] Catherine was to spend almost the entire year of 1375, off and on, in Pisa.[223]

It was in Pisa, on April 1, 1375, that Catherine received the invisible stigmata. Raymond was present and describes what happened.

> It happened in the city of Pisa, and I was present at it myself and witnessed it all. She had arrived in that city accompanied by a large group of followers including myself, and had gone to stay in the house of a gentleman of the city near the church or chapel of Saint Christina, Virgin. In that church one Sunday morning, at her own earnest request, I had celebrated Mass and had—to use the popular expression—"communicated" her. Afterwards, as was her habit, she remained for a considerable time in a state of abstraction from her bodily senses....The rest of us were waiting till she would return to her senses, in the hope that she would then have some words of spiritual comfort for ourselves, as often happened. Suddenly, before our eyes, her emaciated body, which had been prostrate on the ground, rose up to a kneeling position; she stretched out her arms and hands to

their full length; her face grew radiant. For a long time she knelt like that, bolt upright, her eyes closed. Then, whilst we looked on, of a sudden she pitched forward on the ground as if she had received a mortal wound. A few minutes later she returned to her senses.

In a little while she sent for me, and spoke to me privately apart from the others. "Father," she said, "I must tell you that, by his mercy, I now bear the stigmata of the Lord Jesus in my body....I saw our Lord, fastened on the cross, coming down upon me in a blaze of light. With that, as my spirit leaped to meet its Creator, this poor body was pulled upright. Then I saw, springing from the marks of his most sacred wounds, five blood-red rays coming down upon me, directed towards my hands and feet and heart. Realising the meaning of this mystery, I promptly cried out: 'Ah, Lord, my God, I implore you not to let the marks show outwardly on my body.' Whilst these words were still upon my lips, before the rays had reached me, their blood-red colour changed to radiant brightness, and it was in the form of clearest light that they fell upon the five parts of my body—hands, feet, and heart."[224]

The stigmata was the culmination of a series of mystical experiences that had begun approximately seven years earlier. First, she had the experience of light after the crisis in the cell in which the Lord appeared on the cross, covered in blood, and said, "My daughter Catherine, look at what I have suffered for your sake. Do not take it hard, then, when you too must suffer something for my sake."[225] Second, in the summer of 1370, after Catherine had drunk "at the opened side" of the old woman Andrea, the Lord appeared and offered her two crowns, one of thorns and one of gold, and told her to choose one; Catherine chose the crown of thorns, saying that she wanted "to follow the pattern of your own blessed passion, and always, for your sake, to take suffering to myself as the refreshment of my soul."[226] Third, the Lord then showed her his five wounds and drew her to his wounded side from which she drank. Fourth, on August 18, 1370, when she prayed for the salvation of Raymond and others, the Lord promised that they would be saved and gave Catherine a token of it in the form of an invisible stigma in her right palm.[227] Fifth, shortly after this, Catherine prayed that she would experience all of Christ's sufferings on earth, which resulted in her mystical death at the end of the summer of 1370.[228] Dominici tells us that after the mystical death she had a better understanding of the passion. He also records that Catherine, after having asked the Lord to allow her to experience the same pains he felt on the cross, felt thereafter the pain of three nails in her head, chest, and side.[229]

The mystical espousals, mystical death, and the stigmata are the three most important mystical events in Catherine's adult life.[230] The stigmata marked the last and greatest chapter of her life.[231] But what did it mean? Dominici says that the presence of continual pain after the stigmata assured her of the Lord's presence, which made her stronger and more joyful in her work for the honor of God and the salvation of souls.[232] R. Garrigou-Lagrange says that all true stigmatization results in a greater love of the cross and a greater desire to conform oneself to Christ:

> The meaning of the stigmata comes from this: that the physical pains caused by the visible and invisible wounds are connected to a spiritual participation in the moral sufferings of the Savior and to a profound compassion for his crucifixion.
>
> The highest end that God sometimes proposes to grant to a saint in this extraordinary grace is to revive in the soul the memory of the Passion of the Savior and the love of the Cross.
>
> This highest end is evident in the effects of the true stigmatization. There is a greater knowledge of vanity or of the emptiness of the things of the world, of all that which will pass; an insatiable desire for the eternal goods; a greater love for Jesus crucified and for the pain, which, if it is accepted with love, makes us similar to Him. The ser-

vants of God who receive such a grace understand the sense of the words of the Canticle of Canticles: "My beloved is for me as a bunch of myrrh"; *they enter into the depth of the Passion of Jesus, of his abasement, of his immolation for the salvation of sinners.*[233]

For Catherine, the stigmata primarily represented a participation in the passion and death of Jesus Christ, that is, in his *mission* for the salvation of souls. The stigmata is "a sign of the profound symphony with the mission of Christ who has come to make peace between heaven and earth."[234]

The "Investiture Vision" of April 1, 1376

The relation of the stigmata to mission is supported by the fact that on its first anniversary Catherine had another important vision in which her sense of mission was confirmed and specified. She described the event to Raymond in letter T219 shortly after it happened:

> Love, love, love one another! Be glad, be jubilant! Summertime is coming! For on the night of April first [1376] God disclosed his secrets more than usual. He showed his marvels in such a way that my soul seemed to be outside my body and was so overwhelmed with joy that I can't really describe it in words. He told and explained bit by bit the mystery of the persecution holy church is now enduring, and of the renewal and exaltation to come. He said that what is happening now is being permitted to restore her to her original condition....
>
> *The fire of holy desire was growing within me as I gazed. And I saw the people, Christians and unbelievers, entering the side of Christ crucified. In desire and impelled by love I walked through their midst and entered with them into Christ gentle Jesus. And with me were my father Saint Dominic, the beloved John, and all my children. Then he placed the cross on my shoulder and put the*

olive branch in my hand, as if he wanted me (and so he told me) to carry it to the Christians and unbelievers alike. And he said to me: "Tell them, 'I am bringing you news of great joy!'"

Then my soul was fuller than ever. It was immersed in the divine Being, along with the truly joyful, in union with love's affection....

Then I was marvelously happy. I was so confident about the future that it seemed I was already possessing and enjoying it. Then I said, like Simeon, "Now you can dismiss your servant, Lord...." And there were such mysteries as words can never describe, nor heart imagine, nor eye see. Now what words could ever describe the wonderful things of God? None from this poor wretch! So I'd rather keep silent and give myself completely *to seeking God's honor, the salvation of souls, and the renewal and exaltation of holy church.* And by the grace and power of the Holy Spirit I intend to persevere until I die.[235]

In this highly important vision Catherine received from the Lord a mandate to bring the cross and the olive branch, symbols of the faith and peace, to Christians *and* non-Christians. From now on she dedicated herself completely to God's honor, the salvation of souls, *and* "the renewal and exaltation of holy church."

It is curious that Raymond never refers to this vision in the *Legenda*. The modern biographer Drane does not seem to mention it either. Jorgensen, on the other hand, describes it as "decisive."[236] The vision seemed to have greatly motivated Catherine to work for the reform of the church without being discouraged. D'Urso comments that letter T219 is one of the most important of Catherine's letters and "it reveals the perception of a vocation so vast that it cannot be called other than ecumenical [=universal]."[237]

> The giving to her of the cross on the shoulder, as the Lord carried it, and the olive branch of peace in the hand, to bring them "to one people and to another," that is to say, to believers and non believers, is certainly the symbol of

conferment of mission.... Here we have the full consciousness, on the part of our Saint, of her universal vocation. The vision is a charismatic confirmation of this ecumenical mandate, clear and precise in her conscience.[238]

The vision's message is a radical extension of the Lord's previous two messages during the summer of 1370 when he had told her that she would leave Siena for the salvation of souls. The fact that the cross and olive branch are to be brought to believers and nonbelievers suggests that Catherine's mission might well have taken her outside Europe had she lived longer.[239] As D'Urso says:

> Now the apostolic commission and the peacemaking, the cross and the olive branch, have as their borders the world, since the Christian people and the unbelievers are destined for it. And before she assumes this commission, Catherine must enter into the side of Christ, where all people are brought together, believers and unbelievers. In fact, all of humanity, without distinction, is called to know the love of Christ, who was immolated on the cross of love for everyone. Catherine must take her mandate there, because she must go to the center of love, from which radiates all the ways that lead to individual souls....[240]

The year 1376, in which the "investiture vision" took place, was, says D'Urso, "a year marked not only by great historical events but by the attainment of extremely important interior levels" and it was "the season of great syntheses" for Catherine, then twenty-nine years old:

> By word and with the letters, she launched in many directions bold messages of faith shot through with a notable charge of conviction. Everyone admired the efficacy of her expression, not only on the level of exhortation but also on that of doctrine. There was nothing of the banal in those writings; rather, to those to whom they were addressed

there was a complex of substantial and orthodox thought that even surprised the learned.[241]

Avignon

The above-mentioned "investiture vision" of April 1, 1376, resulted in almost immediate action on Catherine's part. Within days of writing letter T219 to Raymond of Capua, news reached Siena that Florence had been placed under papal interdict. Catherine left Siena in May and first went to Florence where she offered to be a mediator between the city and Pope Gregory XI. The offer was accepted.[242] Shortly after that she moved on to France and arrived in Avignon on June 18, 1376.[243] She had various reasons for going there, but Raymond says the principal one was "to urge him [Gregory XI] to give orders for the launching of the Crusade."[244] Catherine had already corresponded with the pope: Four of her extant letters to Gregory were written prior to her arrival in Avignon; an additional six letters were written while she was there.[245] The pope, on his part, had some prior knowledge of her. In 1374 he had commissioned Raymond to advise her when it was learned that she and her followers were promoting the Crusade. Also in the same year he had sent a bishop, Alfonso da Vadaterra, the confessor of St. Birgitta in Rome, to ask Catherine to pray for him and the church.[246]

Nonetheless, Catherine was not met with open arms by Gregory and his advisors. Dominici, who was with her, reports that "almost all the Roman Curia reacted against her" but later, after having listened to her, they were "miraculously transformed in their feelings and actions, so that those who were at first her persecutors then became her friends and benefactors."[247] Stefano Maconi, one of her closest disciples, was also present in Avignon and says that many times Catherine preached so well before the pope and cardinals that "they were all astonished, and in amazement said: 'No man has ever spoken in such a way, and without doubt it is not a woman who speaks but the Holy Spirit, as can be seen clearly.'"[248] Raymond relates how Catherine broke with custom in Avignon, stood up before the pope, and "assumed an astonishing majesty of bearing, and poured out these words like a torrent":

> "The honour of Almighty God compels me to speak bluntly. The truth is, that even before I left my native city I was more conscious of the evil odour of the sins committed in the Roman Curia than were the persons themselves who were committing them; yes, and who continue to commit them daily." The Pontiff was silent. For my own part I was completely stunned. I was careful, however, to imprint on my memory that striking picture of her as, radiating authority, she spoke to the pope in such terms face to face.[249]

It is generally thought that Catherine played a role in Gregory's decision to return to Rome on September 13, 1376.

Catherine's spiritual development also manifested itself in a growing sense of authority that was remarkable. For example, at different times Raymond quotes her as having said to him, "What kind of way is that to speak?" or "How can you deny to my face a fact?" He also records that she rebuked him for having convinced the pope to cancel a plan to send her to Naples and how she would dispatch Raymond on some assignment. She promised Raymond that after her death she would give him a stroke of the discipline whenever he made a mistake. Raymond attributes Urban VI's entering St. Peter's barefooted to Catherine.[250] Catherine "was absolutely sure of herself. It never occurred to her that she might be wrong."[251] No doubt her self-confidence was related to the strength of her authoritative encounters with Christ, her conformity to him, and his daily visitations. Foster says: "She was a woman, she was young, she was not of noble birth, she had never been to school; she was not even a nun; the wonder is not that her position, depending as it did entirely on her personality, aroused opposition, but that it aroused so little."[252]

> All her writings are marked by the tone and authority which experience alone can give. No saint has more evi-

dently exemplified the words of St. Paul, "the spiritual man judges all things and is himself judged by no man." Her judgment—fortunately—was the authentically spiritual sort that includes self-judgment, humility. And humility she learned at the source, from the humble *dulce Agnello*. But having learned this lesson, her judgment was henceforth free, and she used it with a candour, a courage and also (despite appearances to the contrary) on the whole with a certain sweetness and charm which make Savanarola, for example, seem by comparison heavy-handed, tactless and harsh. Admittedly, Savanarola had his own peculiar difficulties and was not a woman.[253]

Her sense of authority, however, did not make Catherine cold or emotionally distant from others. For example, when Urban sent her dear friend Raymond of Capua on a diplomatic mission to France, he says that Catherine "took hard the prospect of my absence" and on the day of his departure accompanied him to the ship and wept.[254]

The Vision That Preceded the Dialogue *and Near Martyrdom in Florence*

The next significant spiritual event in Catherine's life, as far as our sources indicate, is the vision she had that preceded writing the *Dialogue*. Catherine describes it in letter T272 to Raymond, dated to October 10, 1377, or shortly thereafter.[255] Sometime after the feast of St. Francis (October 4), she went to Mass and made four petitions that would later serve as the framework for the *Dialogue*: for the reform of the church, for the salvation of the entire world, for Raymond's salvation in particular, and for an understanding of God's providence in relation to the salvation of an unnamed person. In a vision, the Lord replied to each petition. Letter T272 reflects the final stages of a synthesis in Catherine's theological thought. It is in this letter that the most famous catherinian image of the bridge first appears as well some other teachings found in the *Dialogue*, which she probably began dictating soon afterward and may have finished before November 1378.[256] Raymond alludes to the vision:

> [A]bout two years before her death, God poured so abundant a light of truth into her mind that she felt compelled, in her turn, to pass it on to others in written form. She requested her secretaries, therefore, as already described, whenever they observed that she was rapt in ecstasy, to be alert to take down whatever they should hear her say. It was in this way that, in a brief space of time, a certain *Book* was compiled, containing a *Dialogue* between a Soul and the Lord. The Soul presented four petitions to the Lord; he replied to them, and furthermore instructed the Soul concerning a variety of truths of momentous significance.[257]

Catherine's entry into the passion and death of Christ for the salvation of souls was almost literally realized when she was nearly martyred on June 18, 1378, in Florence where she had gone to make peace during the revolt of the Ciompi.[258] At a certain point the crowds turned and went in search of her. On finding her, like Jesus in the Garden of Gethsemane, she offered her life:

> I am Catherine; Do with me whatever our Lord may permit….I am all right here. Where else should I go? I am ready to suffer for Christ and his church. It is what I have been wanting this long time, and asking for with all my heart. Why should I now take flight, when I have found what I wanted? I offer myself as a living victim to my eternal Bridegroom.[259]

After this the mob broke up and went away. Catherine "showed nothing but regret, weeping and saying: 'Oh! what a disappointment. I thought that this day the Lord Almighty would bring my glory to consummation!'"[260]

Spiritual Development in the Life of Catherine of Siena

Final Mystical Experience

Pope Urban VI, soon after the election of the anti-pope Clement VII, invited various holy people to come to Rome to pray for him and advise him.[261] On November 28, 1378, Catherine arrives in the Eternal City where, in a little more than a year, she would have her final great mystical experience.[262] In her last letter (T373) to Raymond, written about two months before her death, she refers to it:

> Father! Father and sweetest son! Stupendous mysteries has God accomplished since the Feast of the Circumcision [January 1], such that the tongue alone cannot tell of them. But passing over all that period, let us come to Sexagesima Sunday [January 29], for it was then those mysteries occurred that you will hear of in the brief account I am giving you [cf. letter T371], quite unlike anything I have ever experienced. So intense was the pain in my heart that my tunic was torn through my clutching at as much of it as I could while I writhed in the chapel like one convulsed. Had anyone tried to hold me, he would surely have robbed me of life.[263]

She then goes on to describe how the devils terrorized her, throwing her to the floor, whereupon her soul seemed to separate from the body. Her followers thought she may have died.

> Then the humble Lamb became present to my soul saying: "Fear not, for I will accomplish your own desires and those of my other servants. I want you to see that I am a skilled Master Potter, reworking and remodeling vessels as he pleases. I know how to rework and remodel these vessels of mine, and that is why I am now taking the vessel of your body and refashioning it in the garden of holy church in quite a new way."[264]

For the next two days she experienced diabolic assaults ("the most terrible I have ever endured"). "I simply do not know," Catherine writes to Raymond, "what the divine Goodness will choose to do with me but, judging how my body feels, it seems to me that I must seal all this period with a fresh martyrdom in my soul's beloved, that is, in holy church."[265]

The second part of the letter (T371) is a description of the religious experience of Sexagesima Sunday to which she had earlier referred. It is one of her greatest letters in which she describes her ultimate great mystical experience before her death. In it we can see the final synthesis of her mysticism, a mysticism that is deeply doctrinal and yet directed outward toward the church. God showed her how many people approach "this Bride [the church] for her outer shell, that is, for her temporal substance, while she is quite empty of any who seek her marrow." The Lord was grieved because he found no one to minister to his church; all had abandoned her.

> And as her [Catherine's] sorrow and the fire of her desire increased, she cried out before God, saying: "What can I do, O inestimable Fire?" And his Graciousness replied: "Offer your life once more, and never let yourself rest. This was the task I set you, and now set you again, you and all who follow you."...[266]

Then the Lord showed her a practical plan for the reform of the church: She was to tell the pope to make peace and to grant it to anyone willing to receive it; she was to tell the cardinals to come together and adopt an ordered way of life. If the cardinals did this, he would give them light and they would see what needed to be done and then would make it known to the pope, who, he assured her, would cooperate.[267]

Catherine's description of the vision continues:

> God placed me before him—though I am always present to him since he contains in himself all things—but [now] in a new way, as if memory, understanding and will had nothing whatever to do with my body. And his Truth became so luminously clear that in that abyss the mysteries of holy church

were renewed, as were all the graces past and present I have received throughout my life, including the day on which my soul was espoused to him. But all of this was driven into oblivion for me by the growing intensity of the fire, and I paid heed only to what could be done, which was to offer myself in sacrifice to God for the sake of holy church and in order to remove the ignorance and negligence of those whom God has put into my hands. Then the devils began yelling destruction at me, trying with their terrors to hinder and diminish the ardour of my free and burning desire. But while they were striking at the shell of the body, my desire burned ever hotter and I cried out: "O eternal God, receive the sacrifice of my life into this mystical body of holy church. I have nothing to give except what you have given me, so take my heart and squeeze it out over the face of the Bride." Then, turning [to me] the eye of his Lovingkindness, God eternal plucked out my heart and squeezed it out into holy church. And such was the force with which he had drawn it to himself that had he not immediately (not wishing the vessel of my body to be broken) girded it with his might, my life would have ended there and then.[268]

Here we see Catherine make her supreme act of self-sacrifice for the church. She died exactly three months after this vision on April 29, 1380.

Conclusion

In this chapter we have traced the development of Catherine's faith as reflected in her own words, actions, and mystical experiences, during various periods of her life: her childhood experiences beginning at the age of six, followed by her three years of seclusion in a "cell" in her family house beginning around the age of sixteen, the following seven years of activity in and around Siena, and finally the last five years of her life in which she launched out beyond Siena. Let us summarize each of these periods.

The vision of the royal Christ was an "awakening" in which Catherine was attracted to the beauty of God and wanted to be with him, as reflected in her making a vow of virginity a year later. Her subsequent childhood experiences, many of them learned in her relations with her family, taught her the importance of pleasing God over human beings, the value of suffering and the ability to endure it with joy, and the ability to be recollected in the midst of the world. Her interest in others emerges early in her life as seen by her gathering around herself a group of little girls as well as in her interest in saints who worked for the salvation of souls.

Her three years in the cell was a time of withdrawal, purification, enlightenment, crisis, and mystical espousals. Her withdrawal and penitential practices, aimed at the complete eradication of self-will, were influenced by the example of the desert Fathers. Her enlightenment was the result of visitations by Christ in the role of a father, teacher, or friend, who communicated to her various principles of the spiritual life but most especially the fundamental maxim, "You are she who is not, and I AM HE WHO IS," which would become the cornerstone of her life and teaching. It was also a time of crisis in her relationship with God characterized by his withdrawal of spiritual consolations and a subsequent feeling of abandonment. As a result of this crisis she learned that genuine love of God is independent of consolations, the importance of perseverance in one's spiritual journey, and the necessary role played by suffering in the life of the disciple. The mystical espousals, the climax of her time in the cell, symbolized the union of Catherine's will with God's will, the strengthening of her faith in preparation for her future work, and the expectation that she would now "bear children to him in the spirit"[269] (that is, bring others to life spiritually).

Catherine's emergence from the cell and her work in and around Siena during the next seven years was a time characterized by the performance of corporal works of mercy, another crisis, arrival at perfect love of neighbor, drinking at Christ's opened side, the settling of feuds, the conversion of sinners, the mystical exchange of hearts, and the mystical death. The emergence from the cell represented her victory over self-love after years of purification. Her performance of corporal works of mercy for the poor and sick represented a sharing with others of the graces and virtues she had received as well as her effort to love others in the same way she loved God. Just as there had been a crisis in her love of God when she was in the cell, so now there was a crisis in her love of neighbor when those for whom she was caring withdrew their love and persecuted her. From this crisis she learned some equivalent lessons: that genuine love of neighbor is independent of any self-interest, the importance of persevering in our love of neighbor, and the inevitable role of suffering in the practice of genuine love of others. Catherine's "drinking" at Andrea's wound represented her arrival at a level of love of neighbor that now mirrored her love of God. As a reward, Christ invited her to drink at *his* wounded side where she had a further mystical experience of union that left her feeling more concerned about the salvation of souls. The mystical exchange of hearts was a further perfection of the union of her will with Christ's, which gave her a "boundless love of neighbor"[270] for whom she was now prepared to die. The climax of these seven years was her experience of mystical death that was a preparation for her entry into Christ's mission for the salvation of sinners through his suffering and death. During the mystical death she glimpsed the punishment of sinners and was told to return to life so as to work for the salvation of souls. Her mystical experiences were now increasingly indescribable.

Around the age of twenty-eight she launches out far beyond Siena. The last five years of her life are characterized by her entry into the mission of Jesus Christ, a synthesis of her theological thought, and an increasing concern for God's honor, the salvation of souls, and the reform of the church, which ultimately leads to her final self-offering and death in 1380. The stigmata marked her definitive entrance into the passion and death of Christ *for* the salvation of sinners. The investiture vision on the first anniversary of the stigmata represented the bestowal of mission, one that was universal and directed toward peace, conversion, and the reform of the church. During this period of her life, "[h]er love of Jesus expands, grows insatiable, infinite, is transformed into love of His Mystical Body, of the all-comprehensive, all-embracing Holy Catholic church."[271] The vision of October 1377, described in letter T272, which preceded the writing of the *Dialogue*, signaled a synthesis in Catherine's theological thought. In her final great mystical experience she offers her life in sacrifice for the renewal of the church and then dies three months later.

Her spiritual wisdom grew from an initial insight, "the fundamental maxim," to dictating, some seventeen years later, an entire compendium of spiritual thought in the form of the *Dialogue*. In terms of a growth in her relationship with others, we see how she went from anonymously dropping off food at the doorsteps of the poor in Siena to peacemaking, concern for the salvation of souls and the reform of the church. In her relationship with God she went from experiencing a vision of Christ at the age of six to entry into Christ's universal mission to all people and final self-offering of her life for the reform of the church.

We note that the mystical experiences generally represent "union" and "mission." The mystical espousals, drinking at the opened side, and the exchange of hearts represent union with Christ; the mystical death, stigmata, and investiture vision represent entry into his mission. (Her final great mystical experience is a consummation of her entry into Christ's mission.) However, all Catherine's experiences of union are directed toward mission. This is clearly reflected in Raymond's description of nearly all the mystical experiences that he consistently relates to Catherine's eventual mission for the salvation of souls.

The biographical sources, which are generally reliable, therefore reflect the fact that Catherine grew spiritually. Her faith, from which sprang love of neighbor, union with God, and mission, was not static but deepened and matured over the years. This can be seen dramatically in the fact that within eight short years an uneducated sixteen-year-old girl "of the people" goes from being a shy recluse in her parents' house in Siena to standing boldly before the pope in Avignon and telling him that she can smell the stench of sin in the papal court. In particular, her spiritual growth can be seen in terms of growth in wisdom and relationship with God and others.

In chapter 3, after having looked at Catherine's teaching on the stages of spiritual development, we will examine whether her life bears any correspondence with her teaching. In the next chapter, however, we will consider her principal teachings as they pertain to spiritual development.

2
CATHERINE OF SIENA'S PRINCIPAL TEACHINGS AND SPIRITUAL DEVELOPMENT

Introduction

The people of Pisa, according to Raymond of Capua, invited Catherine of Siena to visit them because "they wanted to hear her doctrine, which was said to be *'marvelous,'* and which was so in reality."[1] In this chapter we will examine her doctrine or teachings as they relate to spiritual development. These teachings pertain to creation, incarnation, redemption, the human person, sin, prayer, and the social dimension of our faith.

Our starting point will be Catherine's teaching on truth because it is the foundation of her entire spiritual thought. Next we will look at her teaching on Christ and his blood, which reveals the truth and makes its fulfillment possible by means of a bridge to God. We will then examine what she says about the human person in all of his or her facets as they relate to spiritual development. Catherine's teaching on self-knowledge, a prelude to prayer, and its role in the spiritual life will also be considered. Lastly, we will look at the important place Catherine gives to the neighbor.

At the outset we must admit that Catherine's doctrine is not always easy to grasp. It is often necessary to consult more than one text in the catherinian corpus to understand what a particular term or teaching means. Owing in part to the fact that her theological language is in the form of images instead of definitions, many who have attempted to study her teachings find them oblique and give up.² As quaint as her images may be, they can be frustrating for the reader who tries to connect one with another in a logical way so as to arrive at a semblance of systematic theological thought. She frequently has several images for the same thing: The soul is a house, a city, a vineyard, God's spouse; conscience is a worm, watchdog, judgment seat, attorney, prod. Needless to say, one image does not always connect with another: The soul is a little boat, but Jesus Christ is a bridge and also a staircase; the church is "the mystic body of Christ," but it is also a small shop on the bridge of Christ crucified; the bridge leads to a peaceful sea while spanning a river.³

An additional difficulty arises when we consider the *Dialogue:* repetitions, inconsistency in terminology, and interruptions. The reader who craves order and clarity will often feel frustrated. Yet Pope Paul VI was undoubtedly correct when he referred to the "definite coherence" of Catherine's teachings, which are in fact not contradictory.⁴

Another challenge to understanding Catherine's teaching arises from her diverse themes. Some commentators have tried to identify which is the most important so as to have a "key" to "open" and better understand the whole of her teaching. The Trinity, Christ, truth, blood, knowledge, love, mercy, or the will have each been seen by one or more commentators as her central theme. However, such attempts are unsuccessful owing to the fact that her teaching is so diffuse, as W. Hinnebusch notes:

> There is no agreement among scholars concerning the chief characteristics of Catherine's teaching. Her approach is so personal and her writings so affective and rich in themes that its leading thought defies capture. With almost kaleidoscope rapidity Catherine varies her metaphors and images and, even in the more orderly *Dialogue*, links in intimate union themes which professional theologians would look at one by one. Her doctrine, nevertheless, reflects an inner consistency and unity. It is a single gem but, turned

at different angles to the light, its facets emit varying colors, shades, and tints. Some writers maintain that Catherine's dominant topic is the Precious Blood; others love, living faith, or divine Providence. Many localize her central idea in the knowledge of God and self. That so many attempts have been made, indicates the futility of the attempt.[5]

Even to identify a catherinian "spiritual itinerary" or spiritual plan of life based on her teaching is difficult.[6]

Despite these problems, it is possible to present Catherine's principal teachings as they relate to spiritual development in a clear and systematic fashion as we have done in this chapter. In the conclusion we will show how all the various teachings come together in the spiritual development of the human person.

"The Truth of God the Father"

Catherine places great emphasis on *truth* and on the necessity of our seeing, knowing, and understanding it. She frequently refers to God the Father as "eternal Truth" or "sweet First Truth" and he in turn will refer to the Son as "my Truth."[7] There is one supreme truth that Catherine calls "the truth of God the Father."[8] She refers to it in numerous places in her writings:

> Since [my children] had no share in the good for which I had created them, they did not give me the return of glory they owed me, and so my truth was not fulfilled *(non s'adempiva la mia verità)*. What is this truth? That I had created them in my image and likeness so that they might have eternal life, sharing in my being and enjoying my supreme eternal tenderness and goodness.[9]

This "supreme eternal truth of God" is that God, out of love, created us in his own image and likeness so that he could be in a personal, loving relationship with us in which he would share his life and joy.[10] Catherine says that God loved us even *before* creating us: "With unimaginable love you looked upon your creatures, within your very self, and you fell in love with us."[11] God loved us so much that he drew us out of himself and, like a mad lover, was "compelled" to create us.[12]

Catherine's entire doctrine relates in one way or another to the truth of God the Father, which she often refers to simply as "truth." The truth, she says, is both *"antica e nuova."*[13] It is old in the sense that God's love for us has never changed and new insofar as it has been revealed to us in history by the shedding of Christ's blood. However, the truth has been largely obscured by humanity's selfish self-love, which "blinds" us from seeing it. Because it pertains to humanity's origin, purpose, and destiny, there is an urgent need for the truth of God the Father to be known so that it might be *fulfilled*.

Humanity's destiny to be in an eternal relationship of love with God was forestalled by Adam's sin with the result that we could no longer know the truth about ourselves or God, nor could we be in a love relationship with him. Catherine views the effects of original sin from various perspectives. She compares the human person (or the heart or soul) to a clay vessel that is meant to be filled with Truth, divine love, eternal life, or grace, as we go on our earthly pilgrimage toward God. Unfortunately, the "clay of humankind was spoiled by the sin of the first man, Adam, and so all of you, as vessels made from that clay, were spoiled and unfit to hold eternal life."[14] Using another image, she says that original sin destroyed the road leading to everlasting life: "I want you to realize, my children, that by Adam's sinful disobedience the road was so broken up that no one could reach everlasting life."[15] She also compares original sin to a deadly wound healed by Christ.[16]

All these images reflect the fact that, because of original sin, the truth of God the Father could not be fulfilled: "[B]ecause of their sin they never reached this goal and never fulfilled my truth, for sin closed heaven and the door of my mercy."[17] Original sin distorted the image of God in the human person so that the possibility of our uniting with him was now impossible:

> The fall of Adam broke this image...: man now forgot his creator; no longer discerned the divine goodness; no longer returned love for God's love. Ideally, human life should chime in unison with the "processions" in the Trinity—proceed, that is, from being or power into intelligence and love, both these acts bearing upon God. Now the harmony was broken. But the decisive act in the sin had been the will's free choice of the finite instead of the self's infinite Origin. This choice, the original prototypal sin, broke man off from God. And because that sin was consummated in the will, the faculty of love, it disrupted in a special way man's relation to God the Holy Spirit; he fell into a state of war against the Trinity, and in particular against the Third Person.[18]

By choosing the finite, humanity offended God and thereafter was incapable of rectifying the situation.[19]

God Becomes "Little" So That We Can See the Truth

The incarnation, according to Catherine, was the first step in God's disclosure of truth after Adam's sin. God is compared to a lover who goes in search of his beloved: "She the soul runs away from you and you go looking after her. She strays and you draw closer to her. You clothed yourself in our humanity, and nearer than that you could not have come."[20] The full revelation of truth, however, would come later with the shedding of the God-man's blood.

Catherine has other images to illustrate God's action in the incarnation: Having made us in his own image and likeness, he then took *our* image and became one of us;[21] he became one with us;[22] he gave us a very personal gift as one friend to another;[23] he engrafted the live tree of his divinity onto the dead tree of our fallen humanity so as to restore us to life.[24] She also describes the incarnation as God's veiling, hiding, kneading, or wrapping his divinity in our humanity:

> For you cannot see me as I am. This is why I covered the divine nature with the veil of your humanity, so that you would be able to see me. I who am invisible made myself, as it were, visible by giving you the Word, my Son, *veiled in your humanity*.[25]

> I united my nature with you, *hiding* it in your humanity.[26]

> [H]is divinity is *kneaded (impastata)* into the clay of your humanity like one bread.[27]

> Therefore, so that I might see and know you in myself and thus have perfect knowledge of you, you made yourself one with us by descending from your Godhead's great exaltedness to the very lowliness of our humanity's clay. So that I, then, with my littleness, would be able to see your greatness, you made yourself a little one, *wrapping up (rinchiudendo)* the greatness of your Godhead in the littleness *(piccolezza)* of our humanity. Thus you were revealed to us in the Word, your only begotten Son.[28]

God took our humanity, therefore, so that we might be able to see him and know the truth of God the Father. Catherine's teaching echoes the Gospel of John: "I am the way, and the *truth*, and the life"; "For this I was born, and for this I came into the world, to testify to the *truth*."[29]

Catherine is forever amazed at the love and humility of the Creator who would condescend to being one of his own creatures. This kind of love demands a genuine return of love from us such that all selfish self-love and pride are removed: "Who, oh who would be so stupid, so bestial, as not to return love for love, and completely get rid of perverse selfish love, the source and root of our every evil?"[30] If our response to the truth of God the Father is indeed that of love, then we will gradually be united with him in love:

We are your image and now by making yourself one with us you have become our image, veiling your eternal divinity in the wretched cloud and dung heap of Adam. And why? For love! You, God, became human and we have been made divine![31]

In another place Catherine says that the incarnation restores humanity to life and grace: "Think of it! I gifted you with my image and likeness. And when you lost the life of grace through sin, to restore it to you I united my nature with you, hiding it in your humanity."[32] It is through grace that we will be united to God.[33]

Another reason for the incarnation was to make amends for Adam's sin: "[O]ur heart should burst right out of our body at the realization of the status and dignity to which infinite Goodness has appointed us—first by creating us in his own image, and then by joining his divine nature with our humanity to ransom us and create us anew."[34]

In summary, there are three reasons for the incarnation in Catherine's spiritual thought: the satisfaction of justice through obedience, the showing of divine love, and giving us a share in God's divinity.[35]

The incarnation was God's first step in revealing the truth of God the Father; the shedding of the God-man's blood would be, as we have said, its full manifestation.

The Blood That Reveals the Truth and Re-creates Us

For Catherine, the shedding of Christ's blood on the cross was the most radical and undeniable proof of God's love for us:[36] "It removes every doubt about the reality of this divine love."[37] In her writings she repeatedly refers to the blood and sees almost everything in its light and encourages others to do likewise.[38] The blood of Christ is undoubtedly one of her most important themes.[39] Some may not be comfortable with Catherine's frequent references to blood but, like many of her images and teachings, it is clearly rooted in scripture:

> "Drink from it, all of you; for this is my blood of the covenant, which is poured out for many for the forgiveness of sins." (Matt 26:27–28)

> In him we have redemption through his blood. (Eph 1:7)

> For if the blood of goats and bulls, with the sprinkling of the ashes of a heifer, sanctifies those who have been defiled so that their flesh is purified, how much more will the blood of Christ...purify our conscience from dead works to worship the living God! (Heb 9:13–14)

Christ's blood for Catherine was "the symbol of symbols." As Foster says:

> God really did bleed, and all that Catherine does is to dwell on this fact as the supreme image of divine love and the chief motive of ours. It haunted her day and night. An unconscious poet, she thought with symbols, and, the blood became the symbol of symbols in which to express her experience and understanding of Christianity. And I suppose her readers will always divide into those who find her indelicacy in this matter rather repulsive and those who find it (as I do) magnificent.[40]

Let us now look more closely at Catherine's teaching on the blood of Christ, the main tenets of which can be seen in the following text from letter T304:

> In ourselves we find the blood that manifested the love that God has for us; in which blood we receive our redemption: having lost the being of grace, we were recreated in grace.

Catherine of Siena

We are that vessel that received the blood, because it was shed only for us.[41]

Three effects of Christ's blood are given: it "manifested the love that God has for us," in it "we receive our redemption," and are "recreated in grace."

1. *The blood "manifested the love that God has for us."* The shedding of Christ's blood reveals the various facets of the truth of God the Father. First, as Catherine repeatedly says, the blood reveals God's immeasurable love: "The blood manifests to you the love God has for you."[42] Secondly, the blood reveals that God, out of love, created us in his own image and likeness: "Since in the blood of Christ crucified we know the light of the supreme eternal truth of God, which is that he created us in [his] image and likeness, not out of any debt but through love and grace."[43] Thirdly, the blood reveals that he created us out of a desire to share his being, joy, and beauty with us in an eternal union of love: "[The] blood manifests to us the truth of God the Father. His truth was this: that he created us for the glory and praise of his name, and so that we might participate in his eternal beauty."[44]

2. *In the blood "we receive our redemption."* The blood of the God-man also *satisfies* for Adam's sin and thereby reconciles humanity with God. Catherine describes the problem and its solution by means of the blood:

   > For my divine justice demanded suffering in atonement for sin. But I cannot suffer. And you, being only human, cannot make adequate atonement. Even if you did atone for some particular thing, you still could make atonement only for yourself and not for others. But for this sin you could not make full atonement either for yourself or for others since it was committed against me, and I am infinite Goodness.
   >   Yet I really wanted to restore you, incapable as you were of making atonement for yourself. And because

> you were so utterly handicapped, I sent the Word, my Son; I clothed him with the same nature as yours—the spoiled clay of Adam—so that he could suffer in that same nature which had sinned, and by suffering in his body even to the extent of the shameful death of the cross he would placate my anger....
>
> In the union of these two natures I received and accepted the sacrifice of my only-begotten Son's blood....[45]

Christ's blood restores us to a right relationship with God and makes it possible for us to grow in grace.

Catherine also has another image of the redemption that she was perhaps fonder of. This image stresses the work of the redemption more from the perspective of *merit* (that is, the superabundance of Christ's reward that is passed on to his "relatives and friends"). This is the image of Christ as a wet nurse *(baglia)* and it is Catherine's more important image of the redemption:[46]

> So the pus was drained out of Adam's sin, leaving only its scar, that is, the inclination to sin and every sort of physical weakness—like the scar that remains after a wound has healed. Now Adam's sin oozed with deadly pus, but you were too weakened to drain it yourself. But when the great doctor came (my only-begotten Son) he tended that wound, drinking himself the bitter medicine you could not swallow. And he did as the wet nurse who herself drinks the medicine the baby needs, because she is big and strong and the baby is too weak to stand the bitterness. My son was your wet nurse, and he joined the bigness and strength of his divinity with your nature to drink the bitter medicine of his painful death on the cross so that he might heal and give life to you who were babies weakened by sin.[47]

The wet nurse takes the place of the child and suffers on its behalf by taking the bitter medicine that restores it to life (grace) again.[48]

Although Catherine regards creation and redemption as the greatest manifestations of God's love, the redemption is the greater of the two because it entailed the shedding of God's blood.[49] Catherine sees the redemption as reconciling humanity with God in a way that addresses what she regards as the three greatest evils confronting humanity:

> The same love that moved God to create man in order that a creature might share in the uncreated divine life, moved him to recreate man when, by misusing his inborn freedom, he had in effect refused that destiny. It was one and the same love, only now even more ecstatically displayed; for not content with giving being to a creature bearing his image, God now, in the person of the Son, so identified himself with this creature as to share its very nature, human nature. This is the Incarnation—a love union of God with humanity that aimed at *reconciliation*. And this reconciliation, considered from God's side, has three aspects corresponding to the three main evils involved in human sinfulness: disobedience, ignorance (especially of God's love), and the love of self in preference to God....
>
> The remedying of these evils by the incarnate Word is seen by Catherine almost exclusively in terms of the Crucifixion.[50]

3. *"We were recreated in grace."* The blood also represents grace. In baptism "the soul is kneaded with my blood"[51]—"[i]n ourselves we find the blood"—and then the soul grows in grace so as to arrive at full communion with God in eternal life. "And in my unspeakable love for you I willed to create you anew in grace. So I washed you and made you a new creation in the blood that my only-begotten Son poured out with such burning love."[52]

Having considered the effects of the blood, it is apt to note that Catherine frequently enjoins people to bathe, immerse, wash, nourish, satiate, fortify, drown, forget, warm, inebriate, or clothe, themselves "in the blood."[53] Catherine's use of the expression "in the blood" is equivalent to the Pauline expression "in Christ."[54] "In the blood," says Foster, means entry into the field of a new force:

> And as love, for her, is always *active*, the blood of Christ expresses and symbolizes a positive active force; and to enter the blood is to enter the field of this force and so, *ipso facto*, to begin to be purified from the self-love which is its direct contrary. The force of Christ, so to say, is a God-love, so to enter it willingly is to renounce self-love.[55]

The blood manifests the truth—not only the truth of God the Father, but also the truth of Christ's teachings and his way of life. We now see that we cannot go to the Father except through the Son. "[H]is teaching…is the rule and way for the perfect and the imperfect alike."[56] Catherine speaks, therefore, of the *"catedra [sic] of the Cross"*[57] and refers to Christ himself as "the glorious book."[58]

Because of Christ's blood, therefore, humanity is restored to a right relationship with God so that growth in grace (or spiritual development) leading to union with God is possible. The "vessel" that each person carries through life can now be filled with grace.[59] Progress, as we shall see, involves an increase in knowledge and love of Truth. We must always "lift the eye of the intellect" to Christ crucified and to his blood in order to know the truth about God and ourselves.[60] As we become more fully who we are meant to be, truth is at last fulfilled in us.

The Christ-Bridge as "The Way of Truth"

The bridge (*ponte*) of Christ crucified is first mentioned in letter T272 to Raymond of Capua in which Catherine recounts a recent mystical experience that later led her to write the *Dialogue* (*"il libro"*). The experience is dated to approximately October 10, 1377.[61] In the letter, Catherine says that she made four petitions to

God, one of which was for Raymond himself. In response to this particular petition, the eternal Father says:

> [H]e [Raymond] shall [then] be my dearest son, and will repose on the breast of my only-begotten Son, whom I made a bridge so that everyone may come to taste and receive the fruit of your labors. Know, dearest children, that the road was broken through the sin and disobedience of Adam in such a way that no one could attain to his end *(termine)*; so my truth was not being fulfilled *(non s'adempiva la mia verità)*, that I had created him in my image and likeness, so that he may have eternal life, and participate in and taste me, I who am the supreme and eternal Good.[62]

We find almost the same thing when the bridge is mentioned for the first time in the *Dialogue*:

> Then he [Raymond of Capua] shall be my very dear son and shall rest, he and the others, on the breast of my only-begotten Son, of whom I made a bridge so that all can attain their end *(fine)*, and receive the fruit of your labor that you have sustained because of love for me. So carry on manfully *(virilmente)*![63]

> I told you that I have made a bridge of the Word, my only-begotten Son, and such is the truth. I want you to realize, my children, that by Adam's sinful disobedience the road was so broken up that no one could reach everlasting life. Since they had no share in the good for which I created them, they did not give me the return of glory they owed me, and so my truth was not fulfilled.[64]

We note that the Word became a bridge so that humanity could attain its goal: to be in an eternal love union with God and to become like him so that truth might be fulfilled. As we will see, this goal cannot be attained instantaneously but involves a process of spiritual development. As Cavallini says:

> In love, therefore, that configures [man] with the first Love, man finds the full perfection of his own being and the end of all his aspirations. But he can never attain to such a height only by his own power, so much less so after sin had carved out an abyss between heaven and earth and put discord among the powers of the soul. To restore the harmony of the human person and to return to man the possibility of reaching his end, the Word of God made of himself a bridge between heaven and earth assuming human nature; he made himself the only way that leads to salvation.[65]

Catherine, staying close to scripture again, relates the image of the bridge with Christ's words, "I am *the way*, and the truth, and the life."[66] The Christ-bridge is the only way to reach our end or goal; it is "the way of truth," the way in which the truth of God the Father will be fulfilled. Everyone is obliged to pass along this bridge and is able to do so: "This is the way you must all keep to no matter what your situation, for there is no situation that rules out either your ability or your obligation to do so. You can and you must, and every person gifted with reason has this obligation."[67]

Development of the Image of the Christ-Bridge

We may wonder why the bridge, Catherine's most important image for spiritual development, appears so late in her extant writings. One reason may be that she already had two other images for spiritual development: the tree and the staircase,[68] examination of which will illuminate our consideration of the bridge.

The tree and the three types of people who approach it for fruit is an image that originated in one of Catherine's early visions as mentioned in chapter 1.[69] It was apparently her original image for spiritual development and contains several elements that she later retains in her teaching on the stages of spiritual growth: the implication that spiritual progress toward the "fruit" does not proceed on an even plane, the necessity of enduring suffering so as to arrive at our end or goal, the necessity of seeing the truth of things, and that we can approach the tree for its fruit in different ways. The essential meaning of the image would seem to be this: With clear knowledge of the truth and a desire strong enough to endure suffering, we can attain the end for which we were created and thus enjoy the "fruit." In Caffarini's account of the vision there is no indication that the tree represents the crucified Christ, but when the same vision is recounted in the *Dialogue* some thirteen years later it clearly does.[70]

Another image for spiritual growth begins to appear in some letters (letters T34, T74, T75, T120) possibly written after February 1376.[71] It is that of the staircase *(scala)* on the body of the crucified Christ with three stairs *(scaloni)* going to his feet, opened side, and mouth. According to Dupré Theseider, the earliest of these is letter T75 addressed to "the nuns of San Gaggio near Florence and to the nuns of Monte San Savino," which he dates to March 1376.[72]

> To make it possible for us to climb to this perfection, Christ actually made for us a staircase *(scala)* of his body.
>
> If you look at his feet, you see that they are nailed fast to the cross to form the first *[scalone]*. This is because we have first to rid ourselves of all selfish will. For just as the feet carry the body, desire carries the soul. Reflect that we can never have any virtue at all if we don't climb this first *[scalone]*. Once you have climbed it, you arrive at deep and genuine humility.
>
> Climb the next *[scalone]* without delay and you come to the open side of God's Son. There you find the fiery abyss of divine charity. At this second *[scalone]*, his open side, you find a storehouse filled with fragrant spices. There you find the God-Man. There your soul is so sated and drunk that you lose all self-consciousness, just like a drunkard intoxicated with wine; you see nothing but his blood, shed with such blazing love.

Then, aflame with desire, you get up and climb to the next *[scalone]*, his mouth. There you find rest in quiet calm; there you taste the peace of obedience. A person who is really completely drunk, good and full, falls asleep, and in that sleep feels neither pleasure nor pain. So too the spouse of Christ, sated with love, falls asleep in the peace of her Bridegroom....This, then is where she finds herself conformed with Christ crucified, united with him.[73]

This image of the staircase on the body of Christ allows Catherine to speak now of *stages* of spiritual development for the first time. As we will see in the next chapter, the three *scaloni* on the body of Christ represent different degrees of love of God and neighbor.

We come now to the image of the bridge itself, which, as we have said, first appears in letter T272 written c. October 10, 1377, and which is fully developed in the *Dialogue*, which was probably written between October 1377 and November 1378.[74] In this work Catherine transposes her earlier image of the staircase of Christ's body onto the image of the bridge and relates this new composite image to the three spiritual stages *(i tre stati dell'anima)*:

Before I show you what I want to show you, and what you asked to see, I want to describe the bridge for you. I have told you that it stretches from heaven to earth by reason of my having joined myself with your humanity, which I formed from the earth's clay.

This bridge, my only-begotten Son, has three *[scale]*. Two of them he built on the wood of the most holy cross, and the third even as he tasted the great bitterness of the gall and vinegar they gave him to drink. You will recognize in these three *[scaloni]* three spiritual stages *(tre stati dell'anima)*.

The first *[scalone]* is the feet, which symbolizes the affections. For just as the feet carry the body, the affections carry the soul. My Son's nailed feet are a *[scalone]* by which you can climb to his side, where you will see revealed his inmost heart. For when the soul has climbed up on the feet of affection and looked with her mind's eye into my Son's opened heart, she begins to feel the love of her own heart in his consummate and unspeakable love. (I say consummate because it is not for his own good that he loves you; you cannot do him any good, since he is one with me.) Then the soul, seeing how tremendously she is loved, is herself filled to overflowing with love. So, having climbed the second *[scalone]*, she reaches the third. This is the mouth, where she finds peace from the terrible war she had to wage because of her sins.[75]

In letter T272 Catherine says that the image of the bridge came to her in a vision before Mass when she made her four petitions to God.[76] In the letter, however, there is no mention of three *scaloni* going to the various parts of Christ's body, although she does speak of three stages. The vision may have occurred during Catherine's sojourn at Val d'Orcia in the autumn of 1377.[77]

Where might Catherine have found the image of the bridge, humanly speaking? Noffke says that she might have conceived it after seeing the great *Ponte vecchio* spanning the Arno in Florence when she first visited there three years earlier.[78] Jorgensen, on the other hand, says that Catherine may have developed it from hearing the legend of one of Siena's patron saints, San Galgano, who, it was said, was led by the Archangel Michael to a long bridge that led to a beautiful meadow.[79] D'Urso, on the other hand, believes that Catherine may have taken the image from a story found in the *Dialogi* of Gregory the Great, which Domenico Cavalca, OP (d. 1342), condensed and included in his vernacular *Vite dei santi padri*.[80] As we shall see, it is almost certain that Catherine had contact with Cavalca's works, especially *Lo specchio della croce*, which contains many sayings also found in her own writings.[81]

No matter what her sources may have been, Catherine opts for the bridge as her primary image to illustrate the human person's spiritual development toward union with God. The advantages of the new image over the former one of the tree are somewhat obvious: A bridge is made for people so that they can make progress safely toward their destination. Catherine's bridge is a covered bridge with a variety of components (walls, a roof, a shop, stairs, gate) that provided her with further possibilities for other images.[82]

Description of the Bridge

This should be our first consideration regarding the bridge: It is Jesus Christ *himself*, "the way, and the truth, and the life." Catherine says that it "stretches from heaven to earth" indicating that the bridge is the result of God's initiative and not ours.[83] As we have seen, the bridge has three *scaloni*, stone walls, and a roof. The three *scaloni* or stairs represent the three spiritual stages;[84] the stones are Christ's virtues that direct pilgrim travelers to their final end and the mortar that holds them together is Christ's divinity mixed with the blood of his humanity.[85] The roof is God's mercy, which protects pilgrim travelers from the "rain of divine justice" so that they pass along the bridge without fear.[86] On the bridge there is a *bottiga* that represents the church. According to G. Gigli, it is a word of Spanish origin meaning an apothecary or a place where curative treatments are kept.[87] Cavallini calls it simply "a small building standing on the bridge: in it the body and blood of Christ are kept and distributed to passers-by so that they may not faint on the way."[88]

One feature of the original tree image reappears in the image of the bridge: the thorns *(spine)*. Just as the tree has thorns at its base, so the bridge has thorns around its entrance, requiring that those who want to cross the bridge must first pass through them. The thorns represent the inevitability of suffering in one's spiritual journey. Those who pass through them must remove their sensual will and put on the "shoes" of God's will with which they will no longer suffer in spirit.[89] At the end of the bridge there is a gate *(porta)* through which the pilgrim travelers pass to reach their final end:[90]

> At the end of the bridge is the gate (which is, in fact, one with the bridge), which is the only way you can enter. This is why he said, "I am the Way and Truth and Life; whoever walks with me walks not in darkness but in light." And in

another place my Truth said that no one could come to me except through him, and such is the truth.[91]

Passing through the gate, pilgrim travelers "enter into [God], the sea of peace."[92]

Lastly, Catherine says that after Christ's ascension the Christ-bridge no longer exists on earth as before; what exists now is the bridge of Christ's *teaching and virtues*, which was "firmed up" by the coming of the Holy Spirit:

> When he had been raised on high and returned to me, his Father, I sent the teacher, that is the Holy Spirit, who came with my power and my Son's wisdom and his own clemency. He is one thing with me, the Father, and with my Son. He strengthened *(fortificò)* the way of doctrine that my Truth left behind in the world. And although the presence [of the Son] had left, what did not leave was the doctrine and the virtues, true stones placed over this doctrine, the way of which he made for you this sweet and glorious bridge.[93]

> ...So first I made for you the bridge of my Son, as was said, [when he was] actually talking with people; the actual bridge was raised up, [but] the bridge and the way of doctrine remains *(e levato il ponte attuale rimase il ponte e la via della dottrina)*.[94]

In several places in the *Dialogue* Catherine refers to "the bridge of the *teaching (dottrina)* of Christ crucified."[95] However, Christ's teaching is one with the actual Christ-bridge: "Now I have fully described for you and shown you the [actual] *(attuale)* bridge and the teaching that is one with it."[96]

The "Stones of Virtue" on the Bridge[97]

Catherine hardly mentions the Commandments but she speaks often of the virtues, beginning in the opening sentence of the *Dialogue*: "A soul rises up, restless with tremendous desire for God's honor and the salvation of souls. She has for some time exercised herself in *virtue*."[98] Her emphasis on virtue (or virtues) is not unique. The Fathers emphasized them as "the best response to the primordial question of happiness posed by the human heart."[99] The virtues are the fruit of prayer and self-knowledge.[100]

The first virtue to come from self-knowledge is humility when we know the truth about ourselves. The second one is charity when we see how much God loves us; it is the most important virtue and the "mother" of all others:[101] "Every perfection and every virtue proceeds from charity. Charity is nourished by humility. And humility comes from knowledge and holy hatred of oneself, that is, of one's selfish sensuality."[102] Catherine compares charity to a tree from which the other virtues grow.[103]

Another important virtue for Catherine is patience, which indicates whether or not one actually possesses the other two virtues:

> O dearest daughter, this patience is a queen who stands guard upon the rock of courage. She is an invincible victor. She does not stand alone, but with perseverance as her companion. She is the very heart of charity, and it is she who reveals whether the mantle of this charity is a wedding garment or not. She lets it be known if it is torn by imperfection, for she senses at once its opposite, which is impatience.
>
> All of the virtues can at times simulate perfection when they are really imperfect, but they cannot deceive patience. For if this gentle patience, the very heart of charity, is present in the soul, she shows that all the virtues are alive and perfect.[104]

Catherine does not, however, speak much about the three theological virtues as a group.[105] However, in letter T69, one of her earlier extant letters, she mentions them:

> These three virtues flow from one another, because there is no love without faith, nor faith without hope. They are

three pillars that uphold the fortress of our soul so firmly that no wind of temptation, no hurtful word, no creaturely flattery, no earthly love—even of spouse or children—can strike it down. No, in every one of these cases it will be supported by these three dependable pillars.[106]

Catherine seems to regard all the virtues as "theological" in the sense that they relate us, directly or indirectly, to God; all virtues are connected to charity.[107]

Another virtue that Catherine extols is discretion *(discrezione)*.[108] Cassian, whose *Conferences* were immensely influential in Catherine's time, regarded discretion as the most important virtue for the monk and speaks of it at length.[109] Discretion meant more or less the same thing for Catherine as it did for Cassian. It is "the virtue which preserves from all excess the zeal for perfection and maintains it in a proper balance."[110] In letter T213, Catherine's fullest teaching on the virtue, discretion is the prudence that regulates our charity to neighbor and, especially, our corporal penances.[111]

The virtues are represented by the stone walls of the bridge. Before the bridge of Christ crucified, the virtues were human virtues that pertained only to peaceful living in society. After Christ's passion, however, the virtues were infused with grace (his blood) and now direct us toward our ultimate end.[112] Through Christ's blood the human virtues become "theological" or God-oriented virtues because all are found and have their origin in God's Son and thus direct us to him and eternal life:

> The bridge has walls of stone so that travelers will not be hindered when it rains. Do you know what these stones are? They are the stones of solid virtue. These stones were not, however, built into the walls before my Son's passion. So no one could get to the final destination even though they walked along the pathway of virtue. For heaven had not yet been unlocked with the key of my Son's blood, and the rain of justice kept anyone from crossing over.

But after these stones were hewn on the body of the Word, my gentle Son, (I have told you that he is the bridge), he built them into walls, tempering the mortar with his own blood. That is, his blood was mixed into the mortar of his divinity with the strong heat of burning love.

By my power the stones of virtue were built into walls on no less a foundation than himself, for all virtue draws life from him, nor is there any virtue that has not been tested in him. So no one can have any life-giving virtue but from him, that is, by following his example and teaching. He perfected the virtues and planted them as living stones built into the walls with his blood. So now all the faithful can walk without hindrance....[113]

It was he who crushed that precious body to extract from it enough blood to give us life and bind the stones together. Now *every* virtue, when laid on Christ and soaked in his blood, avails and gives us life.[114]

As our love of God grows so do the virtues increase in us. To live in Christ is to possess the virtues, as Catherine explains using another image: "So the soul rests on the breast of Christ crucified who *is* my love, and so drinks in the milk of virtue. In this virtue she gets the life of grace...."[115] Just as milk is necessary for the nursing infant, so the virtues are necessary in the life of the pilgrim traveler in his or her passage on the Christ-bridge.

The Stormy River

Besides the bridge as the "way of truth" there is the tempestuous river underneath it that "is not the way of truth."[116] The river first appears in letter T272:

"This sin [of Adam's] sprouted thorns and brambles in the form of many difficulties, along with a river continually dashing with its waves. And that is why I have given you my

Son as a bridge, so that you won't drown while crossing the river...."

"But beware of taking the way down below, because it is not the way of truth. Do you know who they are who cross the river below the bridge? They are the wicked sinners for whom I am asking you to pray to me, and for whom I am asking your sweat and tears because they are lying in the darkness of deadly sin. They are making their way through the river, and unless they take up my yoke and put it on, they will come to eternal damnation."[117]

Its first appearance in the *Dialogue* is in chapter 21:

With sin came at once the flood of a stormy river *(un fiume tempesto)* that beat against them constantly with its waves, bringing weariness and troubles from themselves as well as from the devil and the world. You were all drowning, because not one of you, for all your righteousness, could reach eternal life.[118]

The river that flows to eternal damnation, then, is the abode of sinners. It is not tranquil, in contrast to the "peaceful sea," but stormy and brings weariness and troubles to those in it.

The river is the reverse image of the bridge: Sinners are traveling, too, just as the pilgrim travelers on the bridge are. The devil draws people to himself just as Christ does:

The others, in contrast, hold to falsehood, which gives them the water of death. The demon calls them to this, and they, blind and mad, do not realize it, because they have lost the light of faith. It is as if the devil said to them, "Let all who are thirsty for the water of death come to me, and I will give it to them."[119]

Catherine describes those in the river as dead to grace, blind to God's truth, remembering nothing of God's mercy, having wills that are dead to God's will but who still have their free will. When the "worm of conscience" nibbles, however, it can hardly be felt because it has been blinded by their sins.[120] The river is the way of falsehood and it too has a gate at the end:

> Thus will those miserably come to their end who travel by the way beneath the bridge, through the river. They never turn back to admit their sins or to ask for my mercy, so they came to the gate of falsehood because they follow the teaching of the devil, who is the father of lies. And this devil is their gateway through which they come to eternal damnation.[121]

"I Will Draw All Things to Myself": Progress on the Bridge as Spiritual Development

To pass along the Christ-bridge is to have *personally* accepted the gift of communion with God so that the truth of God the Father might be fulfilled.[122] Catherine never speaks of "the bridge of Christ" but most often of "the bridge of Christ *crucified*" to underscore that it is by the passion, death, and resurrection of Christ that God makes possible the gift of communion with himself.[123] Our acceptance of this gift and growth in it is the application of the merits of Christ's redemption in our lives.

For Catherine, the possibility of spiritual development and passage on the bridge of Christ crucified is found in Christ's words, "And I, when I am lifted up from the earth, will draw all people to myself."[124] Her well-known dictum, "The human heart is always drawn by love," is Catherine's interpretation of this text.[125] Although we are by nature disposed toward God, we must still exercise our free will in going to him. This is expressed clearly in another dictum of hers that paraphrases Augustine: "For I created you without your help, but I will not save you without your help."[126]

That is, if we are to be saved we must genuinely will it as expressed in Catherine's insistence on our being "thirsty":

> If you would make progress, then you must be thirsty *(avere sete)*, because only those who are thirsty are called: "Let anyone who is thirsty come to me and drink." Those who are not thirsty will never persevere in their journey. Either weariness or pleasure will make them stop. They cannot be bothered with carrying the vessel that would make it possible for them to draw the water. And though they cannot travel alone, they do not care for the company. So at the first sight of any prick of persecution (which they consider their enemy) they turn back.[127]

The people on the bridge are the "pilgrim travelers" *(i viadanti peregrini)*[128] who travel in different ways: imperfectly, more perfectly, and most perfectly.[129]

We said earlier that Catherine compares the pilgrim traveler (or the heart or soul) to a vessel.[130] As we progress on the Christ-bridge our vessel is emptied of selfish self-love and is then gradually filled with grace, which directs us toward union with Christ the "living water"[131] where we find ourselves in God, the "sea of peace":

> So walk on carrying your heart like a vessel emptied of every desire and every disordered earthly love. But no sooner is your vessel emptied than it is filled. For nothing can remain empty. If it is not full of something material, it will fill up with air. Just so, the heart is a vessel that cannot remain empty. As soon as you have emptied it of all those transitory things you love inordinately, it is filled with air—that is, with gentle heavenly divine love that brings you to the water of grace. And once you have arrived there you pass through the gate, Christ crucified, to enjoy that living water—for now you find yourself in me, the sea of peace.[132]

Catherine of Siena's Principal Teachings and Spiritual Development

The human person's entry into the "peaceful sea" occurs when the "created Trinity" (the soul's divine image and likeness) so perfectly reflects the uncreated Trinity that they unite.[133] God is not indifferent to our progress on the Christ-bridge; the same love with which he created us and then sent the Word to die for us is now at work helping us to reach our goal: "So I can and want to and will help whoever wants my help,"[134] says the eternal Father.

The process of emptying one's vessel of selfish self-love and filling it with grace makes for progress and involves *knowledge* and *love*—an important key idea in Catherine's teaching.[135] She knew that the human soul consists of intellect and will and that the soul's progress to God must involve both: "[I]t is impossible to live without seeing and loving *(senza amare e senza vedere non si può vivere),*" she writes to the Contessa Salimbeni.[136]

Another of Catherine's key ideas that appears numerous times in her works is "love follows knowledge." It first appears at the very beginning of the *Dialogue*:

> A soul rises up, restless with tremendous desire for God's honor and the salvation of souls. She has for the first time exercised herself in virtue and has become accustomed to dwelling in the cell of self-knowledge in order to better know God's goodness towards her, since upon knowledge follows love *(al cognoscimento seguita l'amore).*[137]

Because God is love,[138] spiritual development entails a growth in love: "If then God is charity, it goes without saying that possession of charity is the necessary condition of any knowledge of God...the man who has nothing in himself of what God is in essence is incapable of knowing God."[139] Catherine also says that "love transforms one into what one loves" *(l'amore si transforma nella cosa amata).*[140] "Slavish fear" *(timore servile)*, on the other hand, is not enough to bring one to God.[141]

Catherine of Siena

The Truth of the Human Person

For Catherine, progress on the bridge or spiritual development involves the whole person. Her theological anthropology can be glimpsed in the first chapter of the *Dialogue* when "the gentle loving Word" says to her:

> "Open your mind's eye and look within me, and you will see the dignity and beauty of my reasoning creature *(la mia creatura che à in sé ragione)*. But beyond the beauty I have given the soul by creating her in my image and likeness, look at those who are clothed in the wedding garment of charity, adorned with many true virtues: They are united with me through love. So I say, if you would ask me who they are, I would answer," said the gentle loving Word, "that they are another me, for they have lost and drowned their own will and have clothed themselves and united themselves and conformed themselves with mine."[142]

In this rich passage, Catherine lays out the characteristics of the human person: He or she is God's "reasoning creature," who has "dignity and beauty," who is present in God ("within me"), is made in his "image and likeness," and who is meant to be united with him and become "another himself" "through love" after having eradicated the selfish will and "conformed themselves with mine." Concerning Catherine's perception of divine and human beauty

> [o]ne may say that Catherine is enamored by the beauty of man, of his soul made in the image and likeness of God, and who for that reason participates in the same beauty of God, in the natural order.... Catherine's anthropology is therefore a description of the beauty, above all spiritual, of man, as a reflection of the same beauty of God.[143]

God's presence in the human person is the central fact in Catherine's anthropology. It is reflected in her well-known adage,

"[T]he soul is in God and God in the soul, just as the fish is in the sea and the sea in the fish."[144] As we will see when we consider her teaching on self-knowledge, knowledge of *God in us* is an essential part of our progress along the Christ-bridge.[145] Another saying that reflects the human person's affinity to the divine is "I am the fire and you are the sparks."[146] We see something similar also in prayer 14 (VII): "O God eternal, Oh boundless Love! Your creatures have been wholly kneaded into you and you into us—through creation, through the will's strength, through the fire with which you created us, and through the natural light you gave us."[147]

The human person's beauty will be brought to perfection, Catherine says, when he or she wears "the wedding garment of charity, adorned with my true virtues"[148] and is then united with God. Our vocation is to divinization when God, as he says to Catherine, shall make us "another myself" *(un altro me)*.[149] However, Catherine is not unaware of "the tendency within man to give a negative response to God's love, to rebel against his creator."[150] More will be said about our proneness to selfish self-love later. For Catherine, however, the essential fact of the human person is not this but rather God's presence in us, that we are loved by him, and therefore have dignity and beauty.[151]

The Soul

The human person's dignity and beauty lie chiefly in the soul where spiritual development takes place, leading the soul to ultimate resemblance with God.[152] Catherine's teaching on the beauty of the soul undoubtedly had its beginning in the mystical experience described in chapter 1 in which the Lord gave her the gift of seeing the soul's natural beauty.[153] Because God is supreme Beauty, and because the soul is made in his image and likeness, the soul mirrors divine beauty. God created the soul out of love and for love with the result that "[t]he soul cannot live without love. She always wants to love something because love is the stuff she is made of, and through love I created her."[154]

The soul's creation in the divine image and likeness is not a finished state but a dynamic reality that is meant to grow.[155] Through the gift of grace the soul becomes the dwelling place of God: "'Heaven' I call [the soul], because I made it heaven wherever I lived by grace, concealing myself in it, and making mansions through the affection *(affetto)* of love."[156] Catherine also speaks of the birth of Christ in the soul by grace: "You see this gentle loving Word born in a stable while Mary was on a journey, to show you pilgrims how you should be constantly born anew in the stable of self-knowledge, where by grace you will find me born in your soul."[157] She has several images for the soul such as a house,[158] a vineyard (with free will as its worker),[159] and a city (with three gates for each of the soul's three powers[160] and the watchdog of conscience at the gate of the intellect).[161] She also says that God is the spouse of the soul.[162]

The soul's divine image is a reflection of the Trinity. In *Dialogue* 13 Catherine introduces an important theme in her spiritual thought: the soul's three powers *(tre potenze)*:

> You said, "Let us make humankind in our own image and likeness." And this you did, eternal Trinity, willing that we should share all that you are, high eternal Trinity! You, eternal Father, gave us *memory (memoria)* to hold your gifts and share your power. You gave us *understanding (intelletto)* so that, seeing your goodness, we might share the wisdom of your only-begotten Son. And you gave us *free will (voluntà)* to love what your understanding sees and knows of your truth, and so share the [clemency] *(clemenzia)* of your Holy Spirit.[163]

As we see here, the soul's three powers are associated with the three divine Persons of the Trinity and their appropriations: Memory is associated with the power of the Father, understanding with the wisdom of the Son, and will with the clemency of the Holy Spirit. All three powers of the soul work together just as the three Persons of the Trinity work in concert. Catherine's teaching on the soul's three powers is perhaps the clearest evidence in her doctrine of Augustinian influence.[164] In the Augustinian triad of memory, understanding, and will, Catherine found a useful image to reflect the soul's creation in the image and likeness of the three Persons of the Trinity.[165]

For Catherine, the soul's three powers not only reflect the soul's divine origin in the Trinity but are also the means by which the soul will be united to God:

> You made us in your image and likeness so that, by the three powers which we possess in one soul, we reflect your trinity and unity. They not only create a resemblance but a unity. Thus by memory we resemble and are united *(si assimigliasse e unissesi)* to the Father, to whom Power is attributed; by the intellect we resemble and are united to the Son, to whom Wisdom is attributed; and by the will we resemble and are united to the Holy Spirit to whom Clemency is attributed and who is the love of the Father and the Son.[166]

In order for the soul to be united with God, its three powers must be "gathered together":

> You must be thirsty, then, and you must gather together *(congregarvi insieme)*, as he said, two or three or more....
>
> He says, then, "If two or three or more are gathered in my name, I shall be in their midst."...
>
> These two cannot be gathered together in my name without three—that is, without the gathering of the three powers of the soul: memory, understanding, and will. The memory holds on to my blessings and my goodness to the soul. Understanding contemplates the unspeakable love I have shown you through the mediation of my only-begotten Son, whom I have set before your mind's eye for you to contemplate in him the fire of my charity. The will, finally, is joined with them to know and desire me, your final goal.
>
> When these three powers of the soul are gathered together, I am in their midst by grace.[167]

Catherine of Siena

Catherine interprets Christ's words, "where two or three are gathered in my name, I am there among them,"[168] as referring to the necessity of the soul "gathering together" its three powers "in my name" so that Christ will be present in the soul through grace.

The clause "in my name" is crucial because the soul's powers can be united in another name which is *not* of God:

> [F]or your soul's three powers are united in the name of the devil, whereas they ought to be united in my name.[169]

> I have already told you that the world's pleasures are all venomous thorns. Understanding is deluded at the sight of them, and the will in loving them (for it loves what it should not love), and the memory in holding on to them. Understanding is acting like a thief who robs someone else, and so the memory holds on to the constant thought of things that are apart from me, and in this way the soul is deprived of grace.[170]

To be "gathered together in my name" means that the soul knows (="remembers" and "understands") and loves God in a successive progression leading to the soul's eventual union with Truth. It also means to do whatever is in agreement with the truth of God the Father so that one is truly disposed to love him more perfectly:

> Those who are motivated by slavish fear climb and gather their powers together only imperfectly. When they see the penalty that must follow upon their sin, they climb up and gather together their powers: memory to recall their vices, understanding to see the punishment they expect for their sin, and finally the will to hate it.
>
> Since this is the first [rising] *(salita)* upward and the first gathering together, they must act on it.[171]

While the soul's "gathering together" in fear of punishment is a necessary first step, it is not sufficient to bring one to God. Only love of the good can do that:

> "When two or three are gathered together in [my] name, I am in their midst." This is really so. It seems our Savior meant to say, "Let the soul's three powers be gathered together, so that memory is filled with [my] blood and with God's blessings, the eye of understanding sees and focuses on God's inexpressible love for humankind, and the will loves." It follows that when these three powers are gathered together, all our actions and works are gathered together in God's name, because everything is done for him. Then our soul rejoices because we see that God is in our midst through grace and through the sweet effects of love.[172]

When the soul's three powers are truly gathered together "in my name," the soul is united in itself and in harmony with God. Like a three-stringed instrument, it emits a beautiful sound.[173] As we will see in the next chapter, at the highest stage of spiritual development the soul's memory is *filled* with blessings, understanding *sees* the truth, and the will is *united* to God.[174]

We have seen that when the soul's powers are "gathered together in my name," Christ is present by grace.[175] The presence of grace is the beginning of spiritual development leading to union with God:

> I said that having been raised up, he would draw everything to himself. This is true in two ways. First, the human heart is always drawn by love, as I said, and with all its powers: memory, understanding, and will. If these three powers are harmoniously united in my name, everything else you do, in fact or in intention, will be drawn to union with me in peace through the movement of love.[176]

By the gift of grace the truth of God the Father is fulfilled and the soul unites with God and shares in his being:[177] "[W]ith the infusion of habitual grace man is raised to a level completely transcending the abilities and exigencies of his nature. He acquires a *supernatural* likeness to God and is therefore the supernatural image of God."[178]

Catherine of Siena

Sensuality and Reason

Catherine regards the body and soul as a unity.[179] When she speaks of the soul she quite often means the whole person, as we see in the opening sentence of the *Dialogue:* "A soul rises up, restless with tremendous desire for God's honor and the salvation of souls. She has for some time exercised herself in virtue and has become accustomed to dwelling in the cell of self-knowledge...."[180] Nonetheless, in *Dialogue* chapter 98 she echoes St. Paul in saying that the body contains a "perverse law" that causes its members to rebel against the Creator.[181] Catherine calls the perverse law "sensuality" *(sensualità)*, which is a source of many other sins. Other sources of sin are selfish self-love *(amore proprio)* and self-will *(la propria voluntà)*.[182] To a certain extent, sensuality, selfish self-love, and self-will are vestiges of original sin.

However, there is also personal or actual sin that the human person freely chooses. Personal sin, according to Catherine, is the result of defective knowledge and disordered desire. The eye of the intellect can be darkened or altogether blinded by disordered desire when one is so absorbed in self or in the things of this world that the truth cannot be seen and responded to in love:

> And just as the dead do not see, so they, with the pupil of their eye covered over as I told you, do not see. They do not know that of themselves they are nothing. They do not recognize the sins they have committed. Nor do they know my goodness to them, that I am the source of their very being and of every grace beyond that.[183]

The habit of persistently loving oneself or created things wrongly results in a further darkening of the intellect.[184] Sin mars the soul's natural beauty and impedes its union with God. Catherine regards selfish self-love as the worst sin, as Foster notes:

> Self-love for her is the root of all evil, and the whole world stinks with its horrible fruit. She attacks it again and again.

> Her extremely acute sense of its presence and power in the soul is why she so insists on the need for self-knowledge. To know oneself is to know sin; and there is no way to God except through hatred and love: hatred of self and love of Christ.[185]

Catherine describes "the effects of sin in terms of all that was most unpleasant in medieval life, stench, sickness, filth, cruelty, wounds, blindness, rottenness."[186]

Let us briefly consider some more of Catherine's descriptions of sin and its effects. Because God is the soul's spouse, to selfishly love oneself instead of God is adultery.[187] Those who only love themselves have "spurned the blood and trampled it underfoot with their disordered passions."[188] Sin is also an injustice against God and neighbor. Catherine says that God loves us gratuitously, but that we *owe* him love as a debt; therefore, not to love him is not to pay our debt, which is an injustice.[189] It is a matter of justice that we love our neighbor because God has commanded it. Sins against our neighbor, including sins of omission, are also an injustice. When we are not the kind of person God intends us to be, we, in effect, withhold some good due our neighbor and are therefore guilty of injustice.[190]

Sin is also "loving what God hates and hating what God loves."[191] Because sin has no being, to love it is absurd and an egregious affront to God, who is supreme Being and Love.[192] Catherine also says that sin is a rebellion against God and *ourselves:* "My creatures found rebellion in themselves, for as soon as they rebelled against me, they became rebels against themselves."[193] Speaking again from a Thomistic perspective, "what makes an action morally wrong is the harm it does to the perpetrator."[194] Sin, therefore, is primarily a diminishment of oneself. Catherine's understanding of this can be seen in her treatment of the effects of sin on one's neighbors in which she says that the sinner himself or herself is the "chief neighbor," the one who is most affected by the sin:

> I would have you know that every virtue of yours and every vice is put into action by means of your neighbors. If you

hate me, you harm your neighbors and yourself as well (for you are your chief neighbor), and the harm is both general and particular.[195]

Catherine describes several other effects of sin. Sin leaves one dissatisfied because it has no being *(non è cavelle)*;[196] only God, who is infinite and greater than ourselves, can ultimately satisfy our desire.[197] Sin causes weariness.[198] Sin is like a tyrant who takes away our freedom and leaves us fearful.[199] In short, sin is disintegrative to the unity of the soul and leaves us out of harmony with the ground of our being.

The natural opponents of sensuality, selfish self-love, and self-will, are reason, assisted by conscience and holy self-hatred *(odio santo di sé)*:

And if difficulties make her selfish sensuality want to rise up against reason, her conscience must use [holy] hatred to pronounce judgment and not let any impulse pass uncorrected. Indeed, the soul who lives in [holy hatred] finds self-correction and self-reproach in everything—not only in those [movements] which are against reason but often even in those which come from me.[200]

The struggle between sensuality and reason is extreme: "You need to cut-off and not just loosen. Because he who does not cut-off remains bound."[201] She advises that no one "let pass even one thought outside of God that may not be correct without great reproach."[202]

Catherine frequently refers to the human person as "the creature who has reason" *(la creatura che à ragione)*, reflecting the importance she places on reason, which allows us to know the truth. Sensuality or selfish self-love is a mortal enemy because it darkens or extinguishes the light of reason so that one cannot see the truth and thus safely go his or her way along the Christ-bridge. Reason, however, gives everyone enough light to know *some* truth: "Every person is enlightened in knowledge of the truth, if he so wants, providing he does not remove the light of reason by disordered self-love."[203]

The "Light of Faith"—Free Will

In baptism we receive more light, "the light of faith," which allows us to see the truth of God the Father and thereby know ourselves and our final end. With this light (or "lamp") we can now make our way on the bridge: "So you must follow the way courageously, not in the fog but with the light of faith that I gave you as your most important adornment in holy baptism."[204] Catherine describes the other effects of baptism using various images. Baptism repairs the wound of original sin and the crack in the leaking vessel.[205] In baptism we are given a knife to be used by our free will with which to fight against sensuality *and* to plant the virtues.[206]

Catherine strongly emphasizes the human person's free will, as we see in letter T69:

> When God created man, he said to him: "Be it done according to your will", that is, "I make you free, subject only to myself". O infinitely precious Fire of Love! You show forth the nobility of your creature, creating all things to serve him and him to serve you. And yet we, miserable creatures, go and love the world and all its luxury and splendour, so that our soul loses its sovereignty and is degraded to the service of sin, with the devil as its master.[207]

Consider Foster's observation about Catherine's emphasis on free will:

> An immediate consequence of the divine image in the soul is its *non*-subjection to anything but God. "You alone", declares Catherine to God, "are greater than we"; and what she has in mind above all is the freedom of the human will, the power of "the creature endowed with reason" to decide "freely and for itself"—a power such that "no evil or any

other creature whatsoever can constrain the soul to a mortal sin against its will". This phrase—an echo perhaps of Romans 8:35—recurs frequently, with slight variations, in the letters, and always in connection, implicitly at least, with the idea of creation.[208]

No one can take away our free will, but we can give it away, in which case it may be used as a weapon against *us*.[209]

We should exercise our free will in such a way that our will, one of the soul's three powers, gradually conforms and unites with the divine will.

"A Soul Rises Up, Restless with Tremendous Desire"[210]

In these opening words of the *Dialogue* Catherine speaks of *desiderio*, a word that occurs hundreds of times in her writings.[211] The desire for God was a theme in monastic writings such as the *Conferences* of John Cassian and the *Rule* of Benedict and reached a high point of development in the writings of Gregory the Great and especially Augustine.[212] The theme was inspired, to a certain extent, by scripture, particularly the Psalms.[213] Catherine adapts the theme of desire for her own purposes.

For Catherine, desire is the holy longing in the human person for the fulfillment of the truth of God the Father, or, to put it in another way, the human person's infinite longing, always sensed but not always identified, for the Infinite, for "union with the divine essence." Desire is an expression of the will (or heart). As a modern Thomist says, "God has left us, at the deepest level of everything, a desire to return to him."[214] Catherine speaks at some length about desire in letter T29:

> The reason we cannot have this sort of peace in this life is that our desire is not completely satisfied until we reach this union with the divine Being *(essenzia)*. As long as we are pilgrim travelers in this life we have only desire and hunger:

> desire to follow the right path, and hunger to reach our final destination *(termine)*. This desire makes us run along the way, the road cemented by Christ crucified. For if we had no longing for God as our destination, we would have no concern for wanting to know the way. I want you, then, to have an ever greater true holy desire to follow this way, the road that will bring you to your destination.[215]

Because this infinite desire in us can never be completely satisfied in this life, we experience a certain restlessness and even torment.[216] Finite persons and things, as good as they may be, can never ultimately satisfy this desire; only the infinite Good can do so.[217] Evil, Catherine says, is the result of *disordered* desire born of selfish self-love and holding things apart from God.[218]

Desire, like God's image and likeness in the soul, is a divine "mark" or vestige in us and therefore is not an effect of grace.[219] Our desire is actually a reflection of God's own desire for our salvation so that in eternity he can share his divine life with us. This divine desire was manifested on the cross:

> Take your lesson from gentle First Truth, who in his restlessly yearning hunger and thirst for our salvation cried out from the wood of the most holy cross, "I thirst!" It is as if he were saying: "I am more longingly thirsty for your salvation than I can show you through this finite suffering." Yes, he is tortured with physical thirst, but that suffering is finite. It is the pain of holy desire, shown us in his thirst for the human race, that is infinite.[220]

God's desire to save us and to be in an eternal relationship of love with us is so great that Catherine says he is "constrained" to be merciful: "I am constrained *(costretto)* to this [leading souls back to grace] by the same immeasurable love with which I created them, as well as by prayers and desires and sufferings of my servants";[221] "I am not scornful of desire. No, I am the one who answers holy [desires] *(santi desideri)*."[222] The church, the Eucharist, and the Lord's faithful servants, such as Catherine herself, are ongoing signs in history of God's eternal desire to be in relationship with us.[223]

Our desire responds to the attraction of God's love and desire for us:

> Then eternal Truth seized her desire and drew it more strongly to himself. Just as in the Old Testament when sacrifice was offered to God a fire came and drew to himself the sacrifice that was acceptable to him, so gentle Truth did to that soul. He sent the fiery [clemency] of the Holy Spirit and seized the sacrifice of desire she had made of herself to him....[224]

Commenting on this text, the Italian Dominican I. Colosio says:

> The desire for God is by definition always a *projection* of the soul towards the good which is loved and desired, but even more so and better, it is...an *attraction* perceived always more consciously and which is exercised by the Object loved. As the soul progresses it begins to experience that Object which is loved and desired—that is, God—as infinite good, gradually "robbing" it and drawing it, so to speak, towards itself and freeing it from the dross of self-love, from egotism.[225]

Desire increases in proportion to one's knowledge.[226]

Catherine teaches that desire is a necessary part of every prayer or good work; without it, such things would be finite and heartless:

> So your desire is an infinite thing. Were it not, could I be served by any finite thing, no virtue would have value or life. For I who am infinite God want you to serve me with what is infinite, and you have nothing except your soul's love and desire.[227]

Continuous desire to be with God constitutes for Catherine the Pauline injunction to "pray constantly": "This is why I told you that holy desire, that is, having a good and holy will, is continual prayer."[228]

Desire, being an expression of the will or heart, is also an expression of the soul's love. Accordingly, in letter T26 Catherine describes the union of the human person with God as a union of desire: "But you may ask, 'What is this food of angels?' My answer is that it is the desire of God which draws to itself the desire that is in the depths of the soul, in such a way that together they make one thing."[229] Because desire is infinite it continues on in heaven. Just as the risen Christ continues to desire the salvation of those on earth, so also the blessed continue to experience infinite desire:

> But once the soul is separated from the body and has reached me, her final goal, she does not on that account give up her desire so as to no longer desire me and the charity of her neighbors.... She never ceases her constant offering of her desires....[230]

Because God is infinite, our desire for him is endless. The blessed carry with them to heaven their desire for the honor of God and the salvation of souls. Heaven will be an experience of "interior surprises" in which there will be "an inextinguishable thirst to enjoy God; this thirst is a continuation of desire....From one satisfied desire there will spring another and then another according to a vital chain."[231]

"The Way of Self-Knowledge"

The Cell of Self-Knowledge: "You Are She Who Is Not, and I AM HE WHO IS."

We now come to one of Catherine's most well-known but frequently misunderstood teachings: the cell of self-knowledge (*cella del cognoscimento di sé*).[232] As we have seen, the convergent progression ("gathering together") of the soul's three powers of memory, understanding, and will, "in my name," gradually leads the soul to union with God. Self-knowledge, as taught by Catherine, is essential to the soul's progress. The teaching pertains chiefly to the intellect (the soul's powers of "memory" or "understanding"); however, self-knowledge is inseparable from the will because "love follows knowledge."[233] For Catherine, self-knowledge is the foundation of prayer[234] as well as an expression of the Christian's basic attitude or stance in life. The reader may be surprised at how seldom Catherine explicitly mentions prayer in the *Dialogue*. The reason is that self-knowledge, to a certain extent, *is* prayer.[235]

Knowledge of self and knowledge of God did not originate with Catherine but was a popular theme in medieval spirituality largely derived from St. Augustine.[236] As B. Hackett notes,

> Possibly the best introduction to, if not the very basis of, Augustine's spirituality is his *nouerim me, nouerim te* (May I know myself. May I know you!). To know the soul and to know God was, he said, the whole endeavour. The soul and God are the twin poles around which his reflections of the spiritual life revolve....It has been noted that Augustine's quest for self-knowledge is directed towards *amor* as distinct from *appetitus* for other kinds of knowledge. In simple terms, to know oneself is humility—the antidote to the wrong kind of love, *amor sui*, meaning perverse self-love. But self-knowledge also leads to knowledge of God, since the soul is made in the image of God, and knowledge of God inevitably generates love of God and, when perfected, union with him, in other words, direct vision and enjoyment of God himself, the supreme good. But there can be no advance towards the perfection of charity, unless perverse self-love is eradicated.[237]

Many of the medieval writings on the subject were anonymous and associated not only with Augustine but also with Anselm, Bernard,

Hugh of St. Victor, and others.[238] The theme, to a certain extent, was inspired by scripture:

> Desire without knowledge is not good, and one who moves too hurriedly misses the way. (Prov 19:2)
>
> Before judgment comes, examine yourself; and at the time of scrutiny you will find forgiveness. (Sir 18:20)

The ancient Greeks, of course, also had great appreciation for self-knowledge as seen in the famous inscription "Know thyself" on the shrine at Delphi.[239] To what extent these antecedents may have influenced Catherine's own teaching is unclear, but it is evident that she elaborates the basic elements of the tradition in a form that is personal and that has a practical function in the spiritual life.[240]

Catherine's understanding of herself and of God developed in the course of her lifetime, as did her teaching on self-knowledge. However, in its initial stage her teaching on self-knowledge was directly related to a mystical experience that occurred at the beginning of her three years of solitude in the "cell" of her family house. Raymond of Capua records it in the *Legenda major*:

> The life of the Spirit is received and lived out in practice through the word of the Lord. Accordingly I take as my starting-point that pithy word of doctrine which was spoken to her at the outset by her Teacher, the Creator of the universe. She often recounted for her confessors, including my unworthy self, what took place when our Lord Jesus Christ first began to appear to her. He appeared to her one day while she was at prayer, and said: "Do you know, daughter, who you are and who I am? If you know these two things you have beatitude in your grasp. *You are she who is not, and I AM HE WHO IS.* Let your soul become penetrated with this truth, and the Enemy can never lead you astray"....[241]

This is the "fundamental maxim"[242] that would become the foundation stone of both Catherine's spiritual life and teaching. Its importance is underscored by Raymond:

> Take note, Reader, that this is the solid foundation which our Lord laid down in the beginning for Catherine's life of union with him. This is his betrothal pledge to her. Assuredly it is a foundation fit to carry a building of the loftiest spiritual perfection, holding it erect and unshaken, come what may of wind or tempest.[243]

"You are she who is not, and I AM HE WHO IS." The second part of the fundamental maxim is an adaptation of God's words to Moses in the burning bush:

> But Moses said to God, "If I come to the Israelites and say to them, 'The God of your ancestors has sent me to you,' and they ask me, 'What is his name?' what shall I say to them?" God said to Moses, "I AM WHO I AM."[244]

The first part of the maxim, "You are she who is not," is its antithesis. What could this maxim possibly have meant to a teenage Tuscan girl of the *trecento*? One scholar says it meant that "at the root of our being there is nothing of ours, but only a gift of God."[245] Another says that its meaning is consistent with 1 Corinthians 4:7, "What do you have that you did not receive?"[246] Years later, the words of the fundamental maxim would appear in the *Dialogue* with Catherine's own commentary:

> [F]or I am who I am, whereas you have no being at all of yourselves. What being you have is my doing; I am the Creator of everything that has any share in being.[247]

> [F]or I am she who is not. And if I should claim to be anything of myself, I should be lying through my teeth.... For you alone are who are, and whatever being I have and every

other gift of mine I have from you, and you have given it all to me for love, not because it was my due.[248]

I want her to be humble, to see that of herself she is nothing and to recognize that her existence and every gift beyond that comes from me, that I am her life.[249]

The fundamental maxim was much more than a philosophical understanding for Catherine whose "whole life was a witness to this basic attitude…that man owes his existence to God, and this existence is the gift of a loving Father."[250]

"And in This Cell Is Found Another Cell, the Cell of the Knowledge of God's Goodness in Us."[251]

Catherine's understanding of self-knowledge initially may have been only that we participate in God's being and that apart from him we are nothing. In the course of her lifetime, however, her understanding of its truth deepened to the extent that in the *Dialogue*, written years later, the eternal Father tells Catherine that self-knowledge alone is *not* enough: "So, as I told you in the beginning, knowledge of the truth comes through self-knowledge; not pure self-knowledge, but seasoned *(condito)* and united with the knowledge of me in you *(cognoscimento di me in te)*."[252] "Knowledge of me in you" or "knowledge of God's goodness in you" *(cognoscimento della bontà di Dio in te)*[253] becomes a second and deeper dimension of Catherine's doctrine of self-knowledge after that of the fundamental maxim.

Self-knowledge's two dimensions appear for the first time in one of Catherine's earliest extant letters written some three years before the *Dialogue*. In letter T41 to Tommaso della Fonte, the cell of self-knowledge is compared to a well *(pozzo)* in which one passes through the dry earth of self-knowledge to the living water of knowledge of God:

> If we were to ask that gentlest most loving young man and most merciful father, this is how he would answer us:

> "Dearest children, if you wish to discover and experience the effects of my will, dwell within the cell of your soul." This cell is a well in which there is earth as well as water. In the earth we recognize our own poverty: we see that we are not. For we *are* not. We see that our being is from God. Oh ineffable blazing charity! I see next that as we discover the earth we get to the living water, the very core of the knowledge of God's true and gentle will which desires nothing else but that we be made holy. So let us enter into the depths of this well. For if we dwell there, we will necessarily come to know both ourselves and God's goodness. In recognizing that we are nothing we humble ourselves.[254]

Later, in two letters written toward the end of 1377, Catherine uses yet another image to express the two dimensions of self-knowledge: "the cell within a cell *(nella quale cella trova un'altra cella)*"[255] or "the cell of two rooms *(due celle in una)*:"[256]

> This is the cell of true self-knowledge, and there you will find knowledge of God's goodness [in you] *(in te)*. This cell is really two rooms in one, and while you are in the one you must at the same time be in the other; otherwise your soul would end up either in confusion or presumption. For if you stayed in self-knowledge, spiritual confusion would be the result. And if you stayed only in knowledge of God, you would end up in presumption. So the one has to be seasoned by the other, and the two made to be one. When this is accomplished you will arrive at perfection. Here is why. From knowledge of yourself you will gain hatred for your selfish sensuality, and because of that hatred you will be a judge. You will mount the bench of your conscience and demand an account of yourself, letting no sin pass without doing it justice. From this knowledge issues the spring of humility....
>
> In the knowledge of God you will discover the fire of divine charity, where you will find your pleasure on the

cross with the spotless Lamb, searching out God's honor and the salvation of souls in continual and humble prayer.[257]

The first cell, therefore, is the dimension of the dry earth in the previous image of the well. It is here that we know our poverty and nothingness *apart* from God that results in knowledge and hatred of one's puny rebellion against him by our "selfish sensual will." It is here, especially, that we perceive our vices and "uproot" them. It is in the second cell, the "cell within the cell," that we discover the "living water" and the second part of the truth of God the Father, that is his "true and gentle will which desires nothing else but that we be made holy."[258] Here we discover "the fire of divine charity," God's radical love for us. It is here also that we see the virtues in God, and because God is present in us we also discover the virtues, at least in a germinal state, in ourselves.[259] Catherine urges us to "plant" the virtues, the first of which to begin "growing" are humility, charity, and patience.

The existence of a second dimension of self-knowledge conveys the truth that knowledge of self invariably includes knowledge of God and his goodness in oneself, "[j]ust as the fish is in the sea and the sea in the fish."[260] The two dimensions are absolutely inseparable. Because the doctrine of self-knowledge in both its dimensions pertains to *all* truth, Catherine can confidently say that it is the fundamental principle of spiritual development: "Herein lies all our perfection. There are many other things, but this is the principal one."[261]

Catherine, however, does not retain the images of the well or the cell within a cell in the *Dialogue*, although the substance of the teaching appears in another form. In the work she speaks only of "knowledge of yourself, and of me in yourself"[262] or "the goodness of God in oneself"[263] and of the necessity of keeping both kinds of knowledge together:

> I mean that I do not want [the soul] to, nor should she, think about her sins either in general or specifically without calling to mind the blood and greatness of my mercy. Otherwise she will only be confounded. For if self-knowledge and the

thought of sin are not seasoned *(condito)* with remembrance of the blood and hope for mercy, the result is bound to be confusion.[264]

Catherine now leaves behind the images of the well and two cells and introduces her final image of self-knowledge, which is more comprehensive and better able to express the various dimensions of truth found in it.

The Image of "The Peaceful Sea"

Catherine's teaching on self-knowledge comes to maturity in her image of the *mare pacifico*, which appears in both the letters and the *Dialogue*. In letter T226 to Raymond of Capua, she writes:

> For when a soul sees not self for self's sake, but self for God and God for God, inasmuch as he is supreme eternal Goodness, all-worthy of our love—contemplating in him the effect of his fiery and consummate love—it finds in him the image of his creature, and in itself, that image, it finds him. That is, the love a man sees that God has for him, he, in turn extends to all creatures, and so at once feels compelled to love his neighbour as himself, for he sees how supremely he himself is loved by God, when he beholds himself *(sagguardando sè)* in the wellspring *(fonte)* of the sea of the divine Essence. He is then moved to love self in God and God in self, like a man who, on looking into the water, sees his image there and seeing himself, loves and delights in himself. If he is wise, he will be moved to love the water *(fonte)* rather than himself, for had he not first seen himself, he could not have loved or been delighted by himself; nor removed the smudge on his face revealed to him in the well.
>
> Think of it like this, my dearest sons: we see neither our dignity nor the defects that mar the beauty of the soul unless we go and look at ourselves in the still sea *(mare pacifico)* of the divine Essence wherein we are portrayed;

for from it we came when God's Wisdom created us to his image and likeness.²⁶⁵

In this passage we see Catherine's teaching on self-knowledge and its two dimensions in its final form. Four moments can be identified: when one "sees how supremely he himself is loved by God," "beholds himself in the wellspring of the sea of the divine Essence," is "moved to love the water," and sees "the defects that mar the beauty of the soul." Let us look more closely at each.

1. *"He sees how supremely he himself is loved by God."* As we know, Catherine repeatedly stresses the importance of "opening the eye of the intellect" (*l'occhio dell'intelletto*), the pupil of which is faith, to see the truth about God and his love for us.²⁶⁶ The blood of the Crucified, as we have said, reveals this truth most clearly:

   > Your mind's eye, illuminated by faith, ought to be fixed on my only-begotten Son, Christ crucified....²⁶⁷

   > O dearest daughter whom I so love, you who are my bride, rise above yourself and open your mind's eye. Look at me, infinite Goodness, and see my unspeakable love for you and my other servants.²⁶⁸

   In other words, one begins by "contemplating in [God] the effect of his fiery and consummate love." God wants us to take this first step; indeed, he invites us to gaze into him.²⁶⁹

2. *"He beholds himself in the wellspring of the sea of the divine Essence."* Catherine saw the sea for the first time in 1375 when she went to Pisa and was so taken by its beauty that thereafter she would often refer to God as a peaceful sea.²⁷⁰ If the *mare pacifico* is beautiful, then the human person's image reflected in it is also beautiful: "He is then moved to love self in God and God in self, like a man who, on looking into the water, sees his image there and seeing himself,

loves and delights in himself." In this regard, in the very last chapter of the *Dialogue* we read:

> This water is a mirror in which you, eternal Trinity, grant me knowledge; for when I look into this mirror, holding it in the hand of love, it shows me myself, as your creation, in you, and you in me through the union you have brought about of the Godhead in your humanity.[271]

Now we see that we are made in God's image and likeness, that God dwells in us and we dwell in him, and that we reflect his beauty and goodness; we also realize that we have no being apart from him any more than a reflection on water can exist apart from the water itself. This moment, therefore, includes one's realization of the truth of the fundamental maxim, "You are she who is not, and I AM HE WHO IS," as well as the first part of the truth of God the Father: We are made in God's image and likeness. Catherine uses another image, "the gentle mirror" (*lo specchio dolce*), to express the latter point:

> As the soul comes to know herself she also knows God better, for she sees how good he has been to her. In the gentle mirror of God she sees her own dignity: that through no merit of hers but by his creation she is the image of God.[272]

3. "*Moved to love the water*," we are, by implication, gradually transformed into it.[273] Because love always tends toward union with the beloved, the human person's desire for union with God now emerges. To love the water is to be gradually united with it, the prospect of which Catherine sets before us in the opening chapter of the *Dialogue* when she speaks of the soul's "continual humble prayer, grounded in the knowledge of herself and of God" by which "the soul is united with God."[274] Furthermore, as the soul progresses toward union with God it perceives another facet of the truth of God the Father: *his* desire to be united with us,

"sharing in [his] being and enjoying [his] supreme eternal tenderness and goodness."[275] Union with God, however, will require a response on our part.

4. *"Defects that mar the beauty of the soul"* are also perceived. In the beauty of the peaceful sea one sees not only one's likeness to God but also one's dissimilarity: "the smudge *(difetto)* on his face."[276]

> And in the mirror of God's goodness she sees as well her own unworthiness, the work of her own sin. For just as you can better see the blemish in your own face when you look at yourself in a mirror, so the soul who in true self-knowledge rises up with desire to look at herself in the gentle mirror of God with the eye of understanding sees all the more clearly her own defects because of the purity she sees in him.[277]

We see how selfish self-love or the "selfish sensual will" has disfigured our personal reflection of the divine beauty and grasp the urgent necessity of its removal.[278] As a twentieth-century Dominican says, "We become more acutely aware of our inadequacy before the mystery as we are brought closer to it."[279] In the light of God's infinite beauty, we see how sin has prevented the fulfillment of the truth in us. Sin is literally "no-thing" and to love it is to be transformed into it. "And where does the soul learn the gravity of its sin? [Again,] in self-knowledge."[280] Foster notes:

> Her insistence on the need for self-knowledge is not only, or even primarily, a way of saying that we must recognize ourselves to be sinners, and so acquire humility. Of course it is that; but Catherine always looks *through* the sin to the goodness that it thwarts and distorts—that is, to the soul's radical "likeness" to the Creator whose image it bears.[281]

This new knowledge of how selfish self-love has disfigured the soul's divine likeness and prevented it from fully sharing in God's being and happiness causes "holy hatred" to rise up in oneself: "[W]e love God and hate ourselves—not the self that is [God's] creation, but the self we see rebelling against our Creator."[282] Knowledge of our poverty must also be joined with knowledge of God's mercy if despair is to be avoided: "[S]elf-knowledge must be seasoned with knowledge of me, or it would end in confusion."[283]

Let us now briefly summarize Catherine's fully developed teaching on self-knowledge as found in the image of the peaceful sea. In contemplating God's love and beauty, we see his image and likeness in ourselves; we discover God's presence in ourselves and our presence in him "as the fish is in the sea, and the sea is in the fish." In God we see the virtues and then discover them within ourselves and realize that they are meant to grow. We also see that we have no existence or being apart from God; everything we have is his gift to us. As we contemplate God's love for us, we return love for love. We crave union with God, the ground of our being and supreme Beauty, and come to see that he too desires to be in a personal love union with us in which he will share more fully his being and joy. The more clearly we see God the more we realize how our choice for selfish self-love has disfigured our reflection of divine beauty and prevents the fulfillment of truth in us and thus the urgent necessity of "uprooting vice" and "planting virtue." As selfish self-love falls away, we grow toward union with God.

Knowledge of self and of God (or simply "self-knowledge," as Catherine often refers to it) is a theme that appears in the earliest of Catherine's extant letters and then reappears hundreds of times in all her works. She never tires of insisting on the necessity of one's returning or living in the "cell of self-knowledge." The exercise of self-knowledge is meant to be ongoing owing to our frailty, proneness to self-love, *and* God's infinite nature. Self-knowledge is a "holy abyss" because knowledge of God is wonderfully endless.[284] Catherine also speaks of the "*grace* of knowledge of ourselves and God."[285] Through self-knowledge Christ is born in our souls through grace and we ourselves are born again.[286] It is, therefore, through our capacity of knowing and loving that we receive the divine indwelling.[287] This experience of spiritual rebirth is meant to continue and increase just as grace is meant to grow. The blessed in heaven enjoy a perfect communion of knowledge and love of God. In one of her prayers, Catherine extols Mary as a model of self-knowledge and compares her to a lamp or vessel "in which the light of true knowledge thrives and burns."[288]

The capacity to enter into oneself for the sake of self-knowledge is what Catherine means by the "interior cell," which, as we saw in the previous chapter,[289] is a habit she learned when her family took away her room and solitude and "she made for herself a secret cell within her own heart, and made up her mind never to go forth from it no matter the business in which she was engaged."[290] Years later, in a letter to her close friend and follower Alessa dei Saracini, Catherine recommends the interior cell, a "dwelling place [that] is spiritual, and you carry it with you constantly."[291]

"Holy Prayer Made in the House of Self-Knowledge"

We have already noted the close connection between prayer and self-knowledge and the "ease in which Catherine can pass from self-knowledge to contemplation."[292] But when Catherine does speak explicitly about prayer, she does not use the word *preghiera* but rather *orazione:* "From its use, it seems that *pregare* expresses above all the act of asking (petitions, questions), while *orare* means rather a way of communicating with God by conversing with him."[293]

Catherine speaks of two types of prayer: mental and vocal.[294] By mental prayer she means contemplation, and by vocal prayer she means formal prayers, whether they are the church's official Liturgy of the Hours or devotions such as the recitation of the Our Father. Although she does not suggest the elimination of vocal prayer, Catherine prefers mental prayer as we can see in the following words of the eternal Father:

But do not think that such ardor and nourishment is to be had from vocal prayer alone, as many souls believe. Their prayer consists more in words than in affection, and they seem to be concerned only to complete their multitude of psalms and to say a great many Our Fathers. When they have finished the number they have set for themselves to say, they seem to think of nothing more. It seems they place the whole purpose of prayer in what is said vocally. But that is not how they should act, for if that is all they do they will draw little fruit from it and will please me little.

But if you ask me whether one should abandon vocal prayer, since it seems not everyone is drawn to mental prayer, the answer is no. A person has to walk step by step. I know well that, because the soul is imperfect before she is perfect, her prayer is imperfect as well. She should certainly, while she is still imperfect, stay with vocal prayer so as not to fall into laziness, but she should not omit mental prayer....

But if she looks only to the completion of her tally of prayers, or if she abandons mental prayer for vocal, she will never advance....[295]

The ultimate purpose of prayer is the same as that of self-knowledge and desire: loving union with God.[296] In prayer and self-knowledge we acquire the virtues that are lived out in our relationships with others.[297] Genuine prayer results in greater love of God and neighbor. If we refuse to help our neighbor during times of prayer out of fear of losing spiritual consolations, we are deceiving ourselves and actually have only selfish self-love in the guise of religion or virtue:[298] Catherine was squarely in the early Dominican tradition of not letting the regular life with its monastic observances stand in the way of "being useful to others."[299]

Catherine of Siena's Principal Teachings and Spiritual Development

"On Two Feet You Must Walk My Way": Love of God and Love of Neighbor

We first saw Catherine's strong emphasis on love of God *in* neighbor in the account of her own life, as recorded in the *Legenda major*, when the Lord commanded her to leave the cell:

> "Dearest daughter…it is right for you to fulfill *all* justice; for my grace in you must now begin to bear fruit not only in yourself but in other souls as well. I have no intention whatever of parting you from myself, but rather of making sure to bind you to me all the closer, by the bond of your love for your neighbour. Remember that I have laid down two commandments of love: love of me and love of your neighbor. 'On these two commandments,' as I myself bore witness, 'depend the Law and the Prophets.' It is the *justice* of these two commandments that I want you now to fulfill. On two feet you must walk my way; on two wings you must fly to heaven."[300]

"[M]y way" is the way of truth on which one goes as he or she progresses in the spiritual life. On this journey, as Catherine points out, the pilgrim traveler needs the two feet of love of God and love of neighbor. When she began dictating the *Dialogue* some nine years after the above experience, love of God expressed through love of neighbor emerges as an important theme:

> The service you cannot render me you must do for your neighbors. Thus it will be evident that you have me within your soul by grace, when with tender loving desire you are looking out for my honor and the salvation of your neighbors by bearing fruit for them in many holy prayers.[301]

For Catherine, spiritual development has an obligatory communal or horizontal dimension. No one can progress on the bridge in isolation from others:

> You must be thirsty, then, and you must gather together, as he said, either two or three more. Why did he say "two or three"? Because there are not two without three nor three without two. One alone is excluded from my companionship, since I cannot be "in the midst" of someone who has no companion. Those who are wrapped up in selfish love of themselves are alone, mere nothings, because they are cut off from my grace and from charity for their neighbors.[302]

Even after passing through the gate and into eternal life the communal dimension does not cease because the blessed in heaven share in each other's good and, owing to their ongoing desire to see God honored in his human creatures, pray for the salvation of those still on earth.[303]

In the cell of self-knowledge one comes to the knowledge of God and, seeing what he loves, loves what he loves:

> So she loves every person with the same love she sees herself loved with, and this is why the soul, as soon as she comes to know me, reaches out to love her neighbors. Because she sees that I love them even more than she does, she also loves them unspeakably much.
>
> Since she has learned that she can be of no profit to me, nor return to me the same pure love with which she feels herself loved by me, she sets herself to repaying my love through the means I established—her neighbors.[304]

The soul "shows her love by genuinely loving what I love and hating what I hate."[305] In the *Dialogue*, Catherine gives some "general" and "particular" examples of how we are to extend charity to our neighbor.[306] When we consider Catherine's involvement in secular affairs, it is evident that her love for others was very practical. We have only to think of her peacemaking among individuals, families, and city-states; her work with the poor and sick; her accompanying prisoners to the execution site; her tremendous letter writing to all types of people, including popes and bishops, kings and queens, a homosexual, a mercenary soldier, a Jewish man, a prostitute, and many others. Catherine's overarching concern, however, was always the salvation of souls—which was for her personally an intense desire that she referred to as "eating souls."[307] She encourages others to also "eat and savor souls."[308]

Love of neighbor, according to Catherine, is expressed concretely in the virtues. Evidence that we actually possess the virtues is seen in our loving relationships with others. In fact, the eternal Father insists that the virtues were never really present in the first place if they were not put into action in our relationships:

> If a woman has conceived a child but never brings it to birth for people to see, her husband will consider himself childless. Just so, I am the spouse of the soul, and unless she gives birth to the virtue she has conceived [by showing it] in her charity to her neighbors in their general and individual needs in the ways I have described them, then I insist that she has never in truth conceived virtue in her.[309]

This practical teaching reflects Catherine's consistent emphasis on "the other" and the fact that our relationship with God is mirrored in our relationships with others: "They love their neighbors with the same love with which they love me."[310] Faith must be seen in action: "[T]he faith of those souls is dead, you see, because it is not carried out in action."[311] Catherine even requires that mystical experiences, to be valid, must have some practical benefit for others:

> This, then, is how the soul can tell whether she is being visited by me or by the devil: In my visitation, she will find fear at the beginning; but in the middle and at the end, gladness and a hunger for virtue. When it is the devil, however, the

beginning is happy, but then the soul is left in spiritual confusion and darkness.[312]

For Catherine, virtues and the neighbor are inseparable and play a vital role in one's spiritual development.

Conclusion

We have completed an extensive examination of Catherine's principal teachings in relation to spiritual development that now enables us to present a synthesis of her teaching on the subject. Let us briefly summarize what we have said in this chapter by bringing together the various parts.

With the "light of faith" received in baptism we come to know the "truth of God the Father" as revealed in Jesus Christ and most especially in his blood. Catherine constantly urges us to "open the eye of the intellect," of which the "pupil is faith," to see the Crucified. The "truth" to be seen is that God loves us and has created us in his own image and likeness so that he can share his being and joy with us in an eternal love union; everything we have, including our very being, is his gift to us. Made in his image and likeness, there is deep within us the "desire" to love. This desire, however, can only be satisfied by something greater than ourselves (that is, by God himself).

Our first parents embraced falsehood and thereafter humanity's relationship with God was ruptured. The "road" to God was "broken" and truth, God's plan for us, could not be fulfilled. God, however, intervened out of love for us: In the incarnation, he became "little" so that we might begin to see the truth; in Christ's blood the truth was fully manifested. The Father made of his Son a "bridge" so that we could once again be in relationship with him. The "bridge of Christ crucified" is the "way of truth" because it is the only way in which the truth of God the Father is fulfilled. It is a bridge between our human nature and the divine nature.

We are drawn along the Christ-bridge toward our final end, union with God, by the attraction of Love.[313] This attraction is felt by the soul because it is made of love, for love, and always needs to love something. In the "cell of self-knowledge" the soul "gathers together" its three powers of memory, understanding, and will in Christ and comes to know the truth about God. To know God is to love him. "Love transforms one into what one loves"; the more we love God, the more we become like him. With our natural reason, assisted by faith and conscience, we see that sin (selfish "self-love," "self-will," "sensuality") stands between us and God and impedes our union of love with him. The "light" of faith received in baptism enables us to see the truth clearly and to move along the bridge; baptism also gives us a "knife" to uproot vice and plant the virtues.

To love God is to love what he loves; therefore, our love of God is reflected in our relationship with our neighbor. One cannot cross the bridge alone but always in relationship with others. Disordered desire and defective knowledge, caused by overattachment to self, persons, or things, "darkens" or "blinds" the "eye of the intellect" so that one cannot see the truth clearly and respond appropriately in love. Blinded to the truth, we choose to love finite things or sin (which is "no-thing") instead of infinite Love. The "worm of conscience," however, nibbles at us in an attempt to awaken us so that we might get out of the "river of sin."

The process of growing in the knowledge and love of God is gradual, involving the whole person. As we grow in knowledge and love of him, so too does the divine presence in us;[314] as our will conforms more and more with God's will, his image and likeness increase in us. This involves an ever-increasing contemplation of the truth about ourselves and God in the "cell of self-knowledge" where we "uproot" vice and "plant" virtue. The more we know God, the more we love. At the point of ultimate resemblance with him we pass through the "gate" and into God, the "peaceful sea."[315]

As we have seen, some of Catherine's themes, teachings, and images are not entirely original but were borrowed: the soul's three powers, the bridge, the staircase, desire, knowledge and love, the "fundamental maxim," and so on. She drew upon a diffuse, generalized Augustinianism, the spirituality of her day, which was "based on Scripture, and with influence from Thomas Aquinas and other medieval sources."[316] What is original, however, is the personal way in which she assimilates various truths, brings them together, and then applies them in a practical way. Hers was a "lived theology."[317] As Walsh says, she never regarded theological truths as abstract intellectual notions removed from real life but as expressions of God's love that she had personally experienced:

> She wrote of the mysteries of the Trinity, creation, the incarnation and the redemption. But these were not abstract terms for her. They were mysteries in the Pauline sense: they were mysteries, not because they could not be understood, but because their meaning was inexhaustible. They were a unified whole because they were expressions of God's love. They were part of God's plan to divinize man. These doctrines were an inadequate expression for a much deeper reality, a reality which had to be experienced by man in his whole being and not in his mind only. But St. Catherine was not anti-intellectual. For her "the intellect is the noblest part of the soul". But it was not only intellect but man's whole being, his person that gave him knowledge of God.[318]

We have said that pilgrim travelers pass on the Christ-bridge in different ways: imperfectly, more perfectly, and most perfectly. Next we will consider the three stages of spiritual development (*i tre stati dell'anima*).

3
"I Tre Stati dell'Anima":[1] Stages of Spiritual Development

Introduction

In the last chapter we looked at Catherine of Siena's principal teachings concerning God, the human person, and his or her return to God (that is, "spiritual development"). The gradual ascent on the bridge happens in stages *(stati)*, the subject of the present chapter. Before looking at Catherine's teaching, we will first briefly examine those parts of the *Dialogue* in which stages are mentioned. We will then try to untangle Catherine's rather difficult teaching on the two stairs, the *scaloni generali* and *scaloni particulari*, by which one ascends the Christ-bridge.

With this background in mind, we will then look at what Catherine has to say about the individual stages of spiritual development as symbolized by the three *scaloni* or stairs on the Christ-bridge. Before concluding the chapter, we will address the question of whether her own life, as described in chapter 1, bears any correspondence with her teaching on spiritual development.

Stages as a Principal Teaching in the Dialogue

The gradual ascent on the bridge is by way of stages as "the soul is imperfect before she is perfect."[2] As D'Urso says, "Catherine is not a fanatic about a system; she is just convinced that the life of grace cannot be disordered or on an even plane; that the line of spiritual development goes from the least to the most perfect."[3] However, as we said earlier,[4] the expression "stages of spiritual development" does not appear in the catherinian corpus; rather, she speaks of *scaloni*[5] and *stati* (or *gradi*)[6] *dell'anima*. While "state" suggests something stationary, "stairs" and "grades" connote ascent and movement; therefore, the expression "stages of spiritual development" seems justified in referring to Catherine's teaching on the "states," "grades," or "stairs" of the soul's perfection, what is today often called spiritual development.

The stages of spiritual development is one of her principal teachings in the *Dialogue* where it is found mainly in the sections "The Bridge" (*Dialogue* 26–87) and "Tears" (*Dialogue* 88–97), and to a lesser extent in the sections "Truth" (*Dialogue* 98–109) and "Divine Providence" (*Dialogue* 135–53).[7]

Before the pioneering work of Dupré Theseider in 1940,[8] it was generally thought that Catherine's teaching was the result of infused knowledge with little if any human input from others and thus had a charismatic or miraculous origin. However, he showed connections between many of her teachings and the Fathers of the church, theologians and contemporaneous spiritual writers. We now know that Catherine was "the daughter of a tradition"[9] insofar as she took (and adapted) what she regarded as useful from the spiritual patrimony available to her. One example of this is her teaching on the stages of spiritual development. The notion of "ages" or "ways" in the spiritual life goes back at least to Evagrius Ponticus (c. 364–99), who speaks of beginners, proficients, and the perfect, and Pseudo-Dionysius (c. 500), who speaks of purification, illumination, and perfection. Closer to Catherine's time, Aquinas develops the "three ages."[10] Bonaventure is the first to speak explicitly of the "three ways": purgative, illuminative, and unitive.[11] The threefold division of the soul's growth in charity was a common theme in medieval theology and spirituality.[12]

We recall from chapter 1 that, according to Caffarini, Catherine first encountered the notion of stages in her youth when Christ appeared once and showed her *tres status* at his feet, opened side,

"I Tre Stati dell'Anima": *Stages of Spiritual Development*

and mouth, by which she was to ascend in order to be acceptable to him.[13] And, as we saw in chapter 2, the first mention of stages of spiritual development is found in letters T74, in which she seems to refer to this above-named experience,[14] and in T75. These two letters were probably written between February and April 1376[15] before she began dictating the *Dialogue*, in which the stages emerge as a major theme.

Let us now look at those sections of the *Dialogue* in which Catherine's teaching on stages is found.

"The Bridge" (Dialogue 26–87)

In chapter 2 we looked at Catherine's image of the bridge of Christ crucified: its possible origin and development in her thought, its description, the tempestuous river underneath it, and the "stones of virtue" embedded in the bridge. Now we turn our attention to the three *scaloni* on the Christ-bridge that represent the three stages of spiritual development.

The doctrine of "The Bridge" *(La dottrina del ponte)* constitutes the central and more important part of the *Dialogue*[16] where the first explicit mention of stages is found. Moreover, this first explicit description also provides the most complete treatment of the subject:

> This bridge, my only-begotten Son, has three [*scaloni*] [=stairs]. Two of them he built on the wood of the most holy cross, and the third even as he tasted the great bitterness of the gall and vinegar they gave him to drink. You will recognize in these three [*scaloni*] three spiritual stages *(tre stati dell'anima)*.
>
> The first [*scalone*] is the feet, which symbolizes the affections *(l'affetto)*. For just as the feet carry the body, the affections carry the soul. My Son's nailed feet are a [*scalone*] by which you can climb to his side *(giognere al costato)*, where you will see revealed [the secret of the heart]. For when the soul has climbed up on the feet of affection and looked with her mind's eye into my Son's opened heart, she begins

Catherine of Siena

to feel the love of her own heart in his consummate and unspeakable love....Then the soul, seeing how tremendously she is loved, is herself filled to overflowing with love. So, having climbed the second [*scalone*], she reaches the third. This is his mouth, where she finds peace from the terrible war she has had to wage because of her sins.

At the first [*scalone*], lifting the feet of her affections from the earth, she stripped herself of [vice]. At the second she dressed herself in love for virtue. And at the third she tasted peace.[17]

Here is the "core image" of Catherine's teaching on stages: the three *scaloni* on the body of Christ. She uses this image as a figure for (1) the soul's three powers of memory, understanding, and will, and (2) the three stages (*stati* or *gradi*) of the soul. Into the latter, as we will see, she inserts other patterns of three, particularly (a) imperfect, perfect, and most perfect love, and (b) mercenary servant, faithful servant, child (or servant, friend, child). While she speaks of stages in other parts of the *Dialogue*, it is only in the "The Bridge" that she speaks of them as *scaloni*.

The image of stairs on a staircase (or steps on a ladder) to describe the soul's spiritual progress was not unknown in the history of Christian spirituality and was in fact common in the Middle Ages.[18] Catherine is original, however, in placing the staircase on the body of the crucified Christ, conceived as a bridge, and in saying that the three stairs are the soul's three powers: "That is why I have made of him a bridge with three [*scaloni*], the latter being an image of...three spiritual stages."[19]

Going to the feet, opened side (or heart), and mouth of Christ may well be an adaptation of Bernard of Clairvaux's well-known commentary on the Song of Songs 1:1,[20] in which he describes three kisses, one on the feet, one on the *hands*, and one on the mouth of Christ.[21] Catherine may have been indirectly influenced by Bernard's image through homilies, teachings, or the popular works of Cavalca. However, in Bernard's commentary, the second

"I Tre Stati dell'Anima": *Stages of Spiritual Development*

stage is at Christ's hands, which represent good works; Catherine's second stage is at the opened side where one enters and sees the secret of the heart.

Catherine does not use the traditional vocabulary (beginners, proficients, perfect; purgative, illuminative, unitive) for the three "ages" or the three "ways" but rather speaks of the three stages as "imperfect, perfect [or more perfect], and most perfect" to describe different ways of going *(andare)*:[22]

> Now I want to show you what I, Truth, promised you; that is, those who [go] *(vanno)* imperfectly, perfectly, and most perfectly *(con la grande perfezione)*, and how they behave....[23]

> The first of these stages is imperfect, the second more perfect *(più perfetto)*, and the third most perfect.[24]

> ...three spiritual stages: the imperfect, the perfect, and finally the most perfect stage *(perfettissimo)*.[25]

We may wonder where Catherine got the idea of identifying the three stages in this way and why.[26] D'Urso doubts that she would have derived it from Aquinas because his division was too "abstract and inanimate."[27] Grion has his own explanation:[28]

> [I]n the name of the Trinity the crucified Christ invites us, but even more it is the Trinity that invites us by "means" of Him. To pass from death to life and to the life of grace is to pass through Jesus Christ in virtue of his Blood; to pass from the misery of the present life to the beatitude of eternal life in the Trinity is to go up through the steps *(gradini)* of the crucifix in which the Christian "unites the soul in God following the footsteps of Christ crucified, and so through desire, affection and union of love [God] makes another himself" [*Dialogue 1*]. There is no other reason to limit to "three" the *scaloni* of mystical ascent when there are many more "wounds" on the crucifix.

The number hides a pre-determined intention in Catherine: to show that it is the Trinity that invites us to Itself, eternal beatitude, and the effective union of man graced according to the steps in which one finds himself in relation to Christ: the imperfect (or incipient) is at the "feet," the more perfect (or proficient) at the "side," and the most perfect (or perfect) at the "mouth." The three stairs of the crucified Word correspond to the "three grades and states of the soul."[29]

D'Urso, on the other hand, says, "The triple division reminded her of the blessed Trinity, so familiar to her spirit, and of the soul that is an image of the Trinity with its three powers; but this thought suggested the end and not the stages on the way to reaching it."[30] He believes that she may have derived it from reading Cavalca's *Lo specchio della croce* in 1374, the year she was called to the Dominican general chapter in Florence, after which time the triple division began to appear in her writings.[31] D'Urso's thesis seems more plausible.

In chapter six of *Lo specchio*, Cavalca speaks of four grades of love, the first one being the human person's natural love of happiness that disguises an instinctive love of God.[32] At the second grade of love one begins to see the way of God and to sense his mercy, goodness, and benefits. Of this grade, Cavalca says *"non è però perfetto"* ("it is not, however, perfect"). At the third grade one finds delight and consolation in God. This type of love he describes as *"buono"* although it cannot persevere during times of tribulation when consolations cease. Finally, there is the fourth grade of love which is *"perfetto"* in which one loves God purely, looking for his glory and honor and not for one's own benefit. In effect, Cavalca describes three grades of love in terms of "not perfect," "good," and "perfect."

Catherine may well have had contact with Cavalca's threefold division and terminology. Besides having favored it possibly because the number "three" relates to the Trinity and the soul's three powers (a strongly recurrent theme in the *Dialogue*), she may have chosen the threefold model simply because it was the most natural division

"I Tre Stati dell'Anima": *Stages of Spiritual Development*

to describe the beginning, middle, and end of a journey or project; or to represent infancy, adolescence, and adulthood.[33] In any case, the threefold division was a very well-known model and she may have just accepted it as something more or less standard on which she could develop her own teaching.

If "imperfect, perfect, and most perfect" refer to ways of going, then Catherine's other image of "mercenary servant, faithful servant, child" refers to types of relationships. It first appears in *Dialogue* 56, in which the *scaloni particulari* are introduced for those who are going the way of great perfection:

> Now I want to tell you about those who have begun to climb the [*scalone*] and want to follow the perfect road by actually living out the counsels as well as the commandments. I will show you these in three stages, explaining to you specifically now the three [grades] or stages of the soul and the three [*scalone*] that I have already set before you more generally in terms of the soul's three powers. The first of these stages is imperfect, the second more perfect, and the third most perfect. The first is a mercenary [servant], the second my faithful servant, and the third my child (*figliuolo*) who loves me with no regard for selfish interests.
>
> These are three states for which many have the capacity, and all three can be present in one and the same person. This is done when a person runs along the way perfectly careful to make good use of time, and from the mercenary stage reaches the [liberal] (*liberale*) and from the [liberal] the filial.[34]

Catherine may have been influenced by the grades of charity found in the widely read *Conferences* of Cassian, in which one passes from the fear of the servant to the hope of the mercenary to the affection of the child:[35]

> "If a person is tending to perfection, then, he will mount that first degree of fear—which we have properly designated as

servile and about which it is said: 'When you have done everything, say: We are useless slaves'—to the higher level of hope, progressing by a degree. Here the comparison is not with a slave but with a hireling, because now the person looks forward to the payment of a wage and is as it were untroubled by the absolution of his sins and the fear of punishment and is conscious of his own good works. Although he seems to strive for a reward for what is pleasing, still he is unable to attain to the disposition of a son who trusts in the generosity of his father's indulgence and who has no doubt that everything which belongs to his father is his.

"To this even the prodigal, who had abandoned even the name of son along with his father's property, did not dare to aspire when he said: 'I am no longer worthy to be called your son.'… But his father, hurrying to meet him, accepted these words of humble repentance with a love greater than that with which they had been spoken. Not content to grant him less, he passed over the other two degrees without delay and restored him to his former dignity of sonship.

"Hence we also, mounting by the indissoluble grace of love to the third degree of sons, who believe that everything which belongs to their father is theirs, must strive to be worthy of receiving the image and likeness of the heavenly Father and of being able to proclaim in imitation of the true Son: 'All that the Father has is mine.' [John 16:15]…

"We shall, then, be unable to mount to that true perfection unless, just as he first loved us for no other reason than our salvation, we also love him for no other reason than sheer love of him. Hence we must strive to mount, in perfect ardor of mind, from this fear to hope and from hope to the love of God and the love of virtue itself, so that we may attain to a disposition for the good itself and, to the extent possible to human nature, hold firmly to what is good."[36]

"I Tre Stati dell'Anima": *Stages of Spiritual Development*

Catherine, as we will see, adapts the sequence of mercenary servant, faithful servant, and child by inserting the image of friend before that of child.

In conclusion, Catherine brings together various patterns of three in her own teaching on spiritual stages. As Foster says:

> Within a general movement four patterns of three, at least are discernable. (a) A meditation on the three parts of Christ's body: the feet, the wounded side, the mouth. (b) To the soul's attention to these three parts of Christ's body correspond three stages in her progress towards union with him: purification, illumination, and union; corresponding in turn to the stages of being a servant, a friend, and a friend who is now also a child, a reborn son of God. Again (c) our three spiritual faculties, memory, understanding, and will, have each its particular correspondence with one of the above stages: memory to the stage of purification, understanding to illumination, and the will to union. Finally (d) the whole pattern reflects the three Persons of the Trinity, inasmuch as the soul's imaging of the Trinity is more and more perfectly restored as she enters into ever deeper union with the crucified God-Man. The Father's image is restored in the memory through a purifying fear and self-knowledge, which of course involve concomitantly a working of the other two faculties, understanding and will. The Son's image is restored particularly in the understanding at the stage of illumination, presupposing again the other two faculties, memory and will. Lastly the image of the Spirit is restored in the will at the stage of union, presupposing again the activities of understanding and memory. Such is the general pattern expressed in concrete terms as a climbing up the Christ-bridge as a ladder with three steps: the feet, the side and the mouth.[37]

Later in this chapter we will consider the three *scaloni* and stages in detail. Before doing so, let us briefly consider the other parts of the *Dialogue* in which Catherine speaks of, or alludes to, stages.

Catherine of Siena

"Tears" (*Dialogue 88–97*)

The second major teaching on spiritual stages in the *Dialogue* is found in "Tears" *(La dottrina delle lagrime)*. Here Catherine considers spiritual development not so much from the perspective of the growth of charity, as in "The Bridge," but rather from the aspect of "the heart," the affective or emotional side.[38] In this section knowledge is not emphasized as much as it is in "The Bridge." Tears, Catherine says, "come from the fountain of the heart"[39] when it is renewed by grace:

> Just as green wood, when it is put into the fire, weeps tears of water in the heat because it is still green (for if it were dry it would not weep), so does the heart weep when it is made green again by the renewal of grace, after the desiccating dryness of selfishness has been drawn out from the soul.[40]

Her teaching on tears represents the spiritual stages as experienced in the sufferings of the heart and expressed outwardly in weeping: "[A]ll tears come from the heart...for the more the heart loves, the more sorrow it has."[41] Catherine affirms the inevitability of suffering and the role it plays in bearing the soul to perfection just as Christ chose the cross as the indispensable means of redemption.[42] Catherine does not insist on the necessity of physical tears *(lagrima d'occhio)*; for those who are unable to shed them there is the weeping of fire *(pianto di fuoco)*, of true and holy desire.[43] The teaching on tears amplifies her previous teaching on the *scaloni*, providing a "psychological accentuation" of it.[44]

"Tears" is in answer to Catherine's request

> to know something about the spiritual stages God had described to her. She saw that the soul passes through these stages with tears, so she wanted Truth to show her the difference among the kinds of tears, what was their source, how they came to be, what fruit was to be had from such weeping, and what different reasons were for it.[45]

"I Tre Stati dell'Anima": *Stages of Spiritual Development*

Then gentle first truth replies:

> Open your mind's eye wide, and I will show you, through the spiritual stages I have described for you, those imperfect tears whose source is fear.
> First of all, there are the tears of damnation, the tears of this world's evil ones.
> Second are the tears of fear, of those who weep for fear because they have risen up from the sin out of fear of punishment.
> Third are those who have risen up from sin and are beginning to taste me. These weep tenderly and begin to serve me. But because their love is imperfect, so is their weeping.
> The fourth stage is that of souls who have attained perfection in loving their neighbors and love me without any self-interest. These weep and their weeping is perfect.
> The fifth stage (which is joined to the fourth) is that of sweet tears shed with great tenderness.[46]

This may refer to five kinds of emotion:

> (1) the servile fear of God suffered by those who refuse to follow Christ; (2) the servile fear of those who follow him but still only for selfish motives; (3) the consolations experienced by those who have begun to serve Christ out of pure love; (4) the compassion felt by those who love their neighbors for Christ's sake; (5) the perfect peace and joy of those finally united to God in love.[47]

The second to the fifth stages, the life-giving tears *(le lagrime che cominciano a dare vita)*, as we will see in the course of this chapter, correspond to the four stages in "The Bridge." However, as already noted, the emphasis here is more on the affective side. For example, the unitive stage is now described as the union of one's *heart* with God.[48]

Catherine of Siena

The fruits of the various life-giving tears are explained in *Dialogue* 95 with an unusual analogy to housekeeping and eating. In the first stage the soul is afraid of punishment and so begins to empty her house of filth; once it is clean she begins to experience consolations. In the second stage she furnishes the house with virtue; her fear is replaced by love and she receives consolation and joy. In the third stage "she prepares the table of the most holy cross in her heart and spirit and finds the food of the Word and feeds on God's honor and the salvation of souls."[49]

The image of tears also has a noble precedent in the history of Christian spirituality:

> A rich, unbroken tradition of the Christian East and West up to the recent past sees tears as a normal feature of spiritual life. The gift is seen as purifying and perfecting loving union with God and neighbor under the action of the Holy Spirit.... Absence of tears is seen as signifying resistance to grace, e.g. Peter's tears (Mark 14:72) and Judas's lack of tears (Matthew 27:5).[50]

Gregory of Nazianzen regarded tears as a type of baptism; John Climacus, in the seventh step of his *Scala paradisi*, spoke of different types of tears; Cassian had five categories of tears: tears of fear, of compunction, of sorrow for others' sins, tears of love and desire for God, and the cry of the poor and the oppressed; Gregory the Great described tears of fear and love. Cavalca and Jacopo de Voragine[51] also had teachings on tears.[52] D'Urso, however, is convinced that Catherine's treatment of the subject is something new:

> It can be said that there is no other example in Christian ascetical literature of the little treatise [on tears], either in the West or the East. The mysticism of weeping that was for long centuries a rich tributary in the Christian spiritual stream attains in these ten chapters a summit never before reached through its expository perfection, the breadth of its

concepts, the logic of its development, and its high psychological connections.[53]

He says that the soul's passage through the stages with tears is completely original to Catherine.

"Truth" (**Dialogue** *98–109*)[54] *and "Divine Providence"* (**Dialogue** *135–53*)

These parts of the *Dialogue* provide, to a lesser extent, some additional teachings on the spiritual stages.

In "Truth" spiritual growth is seen more from the perspective of the intellect.[55] Here God teaches Catherine that he is the true Light that leads people to the Truth. He then describes three types of people who live in the three lights that come forth from him: Those who live in the common light that they receive at baptism and who follow the way of common charity; it is "imperfect" but sufficient to bring one to God. Then there are those who live in the second light and are following the way of perfection; they are "guided by the light of discernment" and truly know themselves and God, and they are "wholly subject to the judgments of [God's] will rather than to those of other people"[56] and are "perfect." Finally, there are those who live in the "glorious" third light and who are, by implication, most perfect. They see God's will in everything that happens; they have "completely drowned [their will] in this light and knowledge."[57] She describes at some length the characteristics of those who are in this unitive state, which we will consider later.

"Divine Providence" is centered "on Christian hope, because it stresses God's loving care for the world which extends to every single person and every event in their lives, so that all things happen for the best for those who love God."[58] In this section Catherine again has many different teachings, some of which apply to the stages of spiritual development. In one place she refers explicitly to the three stages from the perspective of hope:

This true and perfect hope is more or less perfect in proportion to the soul's love for me, and thus she experiences my providence more or less perfectly. Those who serve me in the simple hope of pleasing me receive and enjoy it more perfectly than those who serve in hope of the reward or pleasure they might find in me.

The former are those in the final spiritual stage, whose perfection I have described for you. The others are those of the second and third stage, whose hope is set on pleasure and reward, the imperfect ones of whom I told you when I was speaking of the stages of the soul.[59]

Catherine breaks new ground in this section when for the first time she speaks of the perfect as being instruments of mediation (*mezzi*), "other Christs," who have taken his office (*l'officio*) upon themselves.[60] We will consider this in our examination of the third *scalone* later in this chapter.

Problems regarding Precision

Catherine's teaching on the stages is incredibly rich but also tangled, repetitive, and sometimes appears contradictory. This lack of precision is something that both D'Urso and Grion have also noted. Grion says:

We enter now into the more interesting and complex part of the catherinian works: the mystical ascent of the Christian through the cross and in Him, towards the beatitude of grace in the Trinity. The complexity is owing to different factors: inconsistency of terminology, overlapping of arguments, interruptions and repetitions, precise and categorical affirmations of principles which are not always applied with the same clarity; above all, without doubt, the lack of [our own] experience that would permit us to judge the case with some knowledge.[61]

"I Tre Stati dell'Anima": *Stages of Spiritual Development*

This problem, D'Urso says, makes it impossible to arrive at a precise catherinian teaching on spiritual development:

> He who attempts to reconstruct an itinerary of the spiritual life according to the concepts of Catherine of Siena finds before him a complex of ideas and images which would discourage anyone. It is not easy, in fact, to reduce so many diverse elements and figures into unity.
>
> There are allegories, such as that of the Bridge, which seem to give us a complete panorama and a well-articulated development of the spiritual journey. But quickly we notice that too many thoughts, including important ones, do not fit easily and that it is impossible to make them enter into the scheme of these allegories.[62]

The problem can be seen in the different way commentators have placed Catherine's "patterns of three" into the first, second, and third *scaloni*. For example, D'Urso puts the mercenary servant in the first stage, the faithful servant in the first and second stages, the friend in the second and third, and the child in the third. Grion and Riccardi, on the other hand, put the mercenary servant in the first stage, the faithful servant in the second, and the child in the third. Cavallini puts both types of servant in the first stage, friend in the second, and child in the third. Foster has yet another schema: servant in the first stage, friend in the second, and both friend and child in the third.[63]

We can speculate as to the reasons for Catherine's inconsistencies. First, we should remember that Catherine was a mystic who, while in a mystical state, dictated the *Dialogue* in installments over a period of approximately one year. D'Urso says that she might have given us a more logical and organized spiritual itinerary had she lived longer and in more peaceful times. In addition, Catherine may have not felt free to substantially rethink or change what she herself regarded as having been received under divine inspiration but rather could only add to it at different times.[64]

There may be another reason besides these, one that can be found in the *Dialogue* itself. In *Dialogue* 56, after introducing the three stages, the eternal Father says, "These are three stages for which many have the capacity, *and all three can be present in one and the same person*."[65] This may be an allusion to the fact that one's spiritual development can never be neatly contained in any of the spiritual stages. The notion of steps or stages on a journey is a "distinction…chiefly in the theoretical order; in the concrete reality it is difficult—as most spiritual writers acknowledge—to establish a well-defined break between the three steps."[66] The spiritual journey is something fluid, not mechanical, making distinctions difficult; elements of one stage can overlap into the next.[67] Catherine may have had this in mind when she says, "For we don't cease being God's servants and true friends once we have become his [child] (*figliuolo*)."[68]

While the three stages are successive

> [i]n another sense…[they] are commingled and each has its place in all the stages of the spiritual life. The sinner whose contrition is inspired by love is already united to God; such was the case of Augustine in the garden of Milan….At the other extreme, the mystic united to God finds himself in need of being purified.[69]

This "commingling" of stages is perhaps nowhere more evident than in Catherine's own various mystical experiences that occurred throughout her life. For example, during the extended period of penance in her cell she had mystical experiences (such as the mystical espousals) suggestive of the unitive stage; or, after her first vision (of the royal Christ) as a child, during which, according to Raymond, she was "transformed into him," she began scourging herself—an action characteristic of the first stage although she was apparently now in the last stage, the unitive.[70]

The problem of the placement of images into three stages, while it can be aggravating, is secondary to the core of her teaching.

"I Tre Stati dell'Anima": *Stages of Spiritual Development*

Scaloni Generali *and* Particulari

The Ways of Common Charity and Perfect Charity

Everyone is invited to ascend the Christ-bridge in order to reach their end *(termine)* and attain eternal life.[71] However, everyone is *not* required to ascend the bridge in the same way. The majority of good, ordinary Christians go the way of common charity. An example of such a person would be Catherine's beloved father Giacomo. Other Christians, on the other hand, strive to follow the way of perfect charity.[72] This group includes those who have publicly professed the evangelical counsels of poverty, chastity, and obedience but it is not limited to them. It also includes anyone, such as Catherine herself, who has great "thirst" and who is, therefore, striving after sanctity or *grande perfezione:*

> All of you are invited generally and particularly by my Truth when he cried out in the temple with restless desire saying: "Let he who is thirsty come to me and drink, for I am the fount of living water."...
> ...[T]hat is, to go by way of perfect charity *(carità perfetta)* or by common charity *(carità commune)*, as I told you earlier. Through whatever way that you pass and come to him, that is by following his doctrine, you will find what to drink, finding and tasting the fruit of the blood through the union of the divine nature united in the human nature.[73]

What matters most for Catherine is not whether one has professed vows but rather one's desire: "I am not a respecter of creatures or of states *(stati)* but of holy desires."[74]

As we saw in chapter 2, the Christ-bridge has three *scaloni* or stairs.[75] Catherine introduces two new images in "The Bridge" to illustrate the two different ways of ascending the bridge: three *scaloni generali* for those going the way of common charity and three *scaloni particulari* [sic] for those going the way of perfect charity.[76] She does not attempt to reconcile these new images with her original description of the bridge's three *scaloni*, and the reader is hard-pressed to imagine different sets of stairs on a bridge.[77]

Scaloni Generali: *An Interior Ascent*

The *scaloni generali*, as we have said, is the way of ascent on the Christ-bridge for ordinary Christians. However, the word *"generali"* means "for everyone"[78] and even those who are pursuing perfect charity and who therefore will ascend the bridge via the *scaloni particulari* must first begin on the *scaloni generali*:

> This is the way you must *all* keep to no matter what your situation, for there is no situation that rules out either your ability or your obligation to do so. You can and you must, and *every person* gifted with reason has this obligation to do so. No one can draw back saying, "My position or my children or other earthly obstacles keep me from following this way." Nor can the difficulties you encounter along this way excuse you. You are not to talk that way, because I have already told you that every state of life is pleasing and acceptable to me if it is held to with a good and holy will.[79]

In *Dialogue* 54 and 55 Catherine unfurls a new teaching in which the three *scaloni generali* are a figure of the soul's three powers. The ascent on the Christ-bridge via the *scaloni generali* requires gathering together the soul's three powers. Earlier, in chapter 2, we saw that it is by means of the soul's three powers that the human person is united to the Trinity.[80] This important teaching can also be found in the opening chapter of "The Bridge" where the eternal Father says, "If these three powers are in accord and gathered *(congregate)* together in my name, all the other actions that the human person does, actually or mentally, will be pleasing and *united in me* through the affection of love."[81] The "gathering together" of the soul's three powers "in my name" means, as we have said, that the soul remembers, understands, and loves that which is consonant with the truth of God the Father in a gradual progression leading

"I Tre Stati dell'Anima": *Stages of Spiritual Development*

to union with the Godhead.[82] The soul's powers also remember, understand, and *hate* that which is *not* consistent with the truth and thus detach from it: "memory to recall [vice], understanding to see the punishments they expect for their [fault] *(colpa)*, and finally the will to hate it."[83] In other words, the ascent on the Christ-bridge is a matter of increasing and successive identification with truth.

We have said that everyone is obliged to go on the *scaloni generali* even if they intend to follow the way of perfect charity. Having climbed them, those going the way of perfect charity then ascend the *scaloni particulari*:

> And I have showed you the perfection of the third stage of those who have attained peace at his mouth. These have run with [restless desire] *(ansietato desiderio)* across the bridge of Christ crucified. They have climbed the three [*scaloni generali*], have gathered their souls' powers and all their works in my name…and they have climbed the three [*scaloni particulari*] and passed from imperfection to perfection.[84]

> [A]s if drunk and ablaze with love, this soul has gathered herself together and climbed the three [*scaloni generali*] that I interpreted for you as the soul's three powers, and also the three [*scaloni attuali*] that I interpreted for you as the body of my only-begotten Son, Christ crucified.[85]

The gathering together of the soul's three powers on the *scaloni generali* is an "ascent of the soul, an interior 'rising above' at the end of which the soul reacquires its wonderful harmony, and from the same it receives the impulse to the exterior ascent through the way of the Christ-bridge."[86] The soul's gathering together of its three powers is "at the base of the entire ascent in love, where it finds its perfection."[87] G. Anadol also sees the *scaloni generali* and the gathering of the soul's powers as an "interior ascent" preliminary to the "exterior ascent" on the body of Christ crucified:

In the *Dialogue* the *"scaloni"* are also a figure of the soul's powers, with a new attribution given to the image of the *scaloni* that does not appear in the letters. The soul must first of all "gather together" its three powers—memory, understanding, will—which is already an ascent above oneself, following the superior attractions and crushing the inferior ones (and here the three powers can be figured as the three *scaloni*). When it has completed this interior ascent, the soul, having re-acquired that integrity which sin had disrupted, stays in *"carità commune"* and God rests in it through grace. Then the soul feels prompted to climb the three stairs on the body of Christ which he offers it.[88]

Stages of Ascent on the Scaloni Generali

Dialogue 56–86, a major part of the *Dialogue*, pertains generally to the stages of ascent on the Christ-bridge via the *scaloni particulari* for those following the way of perfect charity. This will be examined at length in this chapter. By comparison, it is only in *Dialogue* 54 where we find any mention of the "stages" of ascent for those going the way of common charity via the *scaloni generali*:

> When these three powers of the soul are gathered together, I am in their midst by grace. And as soon as you are filled with my love and love of your neighbor, you will find yourself in the company of the multitude of solid virtues. Then your soul's appetite is ready to be thirsty—thirsty for virtue and my honor and the salvation of souls. Every other thirst is now exhausted and dead, and you [go] securely, without any [servile] fear. You have climbed the first [*scalone*], that of [affection] (*affetto*). Once [affection] is stripped of selfish love, you rise above yourself and above passing things. What you decide to keep, you love and hold not apart from me but with me, that is, with true holy fear and love of virtue.

"I Tre Stati dell'Anima": *Stages of Spiritual Development*

> Then you find that you have climbed the second [*scalone*]. This is the enlightenment of the [intellect] *(intelletto)*, which sees itself reflected in the warmhearted *(cordiale)* love I have shown you in Christ crucified, as in a mirror. Then you find peace and quiet, for memory is filled with my love and no longer empty....
>
> After you have climbed you find that you are gathered together.[89]

We note several things in this text. While the first two *scaloni* are mentioned explicitly, there is at best only an allusion to the third: reference to finding "peace and quiet" that, as we will see later in this chapter when we consider the stages of spiritual development for those on the *scaloni particulari*, is a characteristic of those who are going on the *scaloni particulari* and who reach the third stage where they receive the kiss of Christ's mouth. We also note that in this text there is no mention of states, "imperfect, perfect, most perfect," "feet, opened side, mouth," or "servant, friend, child." Catherine uses these images only for the *scaloni particulari*.

Does this omission of any explicit reference to the third *scalone* suggest that the spiritual development of those on the *scaloni generali* bears resemblance to those who have reached only the first and second stages ("perfect") of spiritual development?[90] It would seem so. In her description of the three *scaloni generali*, Catherine may have stopped short of mentioning the third *scaloni* because of any possible correspondence it might have had with the third stage of the *scaloni particulari* where mystical phenomena such as levitation might occur and which would obviously *not* be a characteristic of the ordinary Christian who is following the way of common charity.

Why is Catherine's description of the "stages" for those on the *scaloni generali*, found only in *Dialogue* 54, so sparse and incomplete? The most likely answer is simply that her subsequent much-longer treatment on the spiritual stages of those on the *scaloni particulari* (*Dialogue* 56–86) also applies, to some extent, to everyone.[91]

Catherine of Siena

That Catherine's teaching on the *scaloni particulari* and thus the three stages pertains, more or less, to those who are also on the *scaloni generali* is, if true, of great importance because it clears away any doubt that Catherine intended a major portion of the *Dialogue* for everyone and not just for a minority of consecrated persons and some zealous "friends"[92] of God like herself. The following facts confirm this position:

- "The Bridge" is in answer to Catherine's third petition for God's providence over the *whole* world.[93] It is unlikely, then, that she intended the major part of thirty-one chapters (56–86), the very core of the *Dialogue*, for only a select few.

- We see in *Dialogue* 61, in the midst of Catherine's teaching on the *scaloni particulari*, a teaching that is applied explicitly to both those in common and perfect charity. Here the eternal Father speaks of three manifestations *(manifestazioni)* of himself to souls in which the first manifestation is of the Word's affection and charity "in two ways" according to whether one is following the way of common charity or, by implication, the way of perfect charity:

  > This charity manifests itself in two ways. One is general, for ordinary people *(gente commune)*, that is those who stay in common charity. It is manifested, I say, in them [as they] see and experience *(provando)* my charity in the many and different benefits they receive from me. The other way is particular to those who are made friends, [and is] added *(agionto)* to the manifestation of common charity, in which they taste, know, experience and feel him through feeling *(sentimento)* in their souls.[94]

  This text suggests that the difference between the experience of those in common charity and those in perfect charity is one of degree or something that is merely added and thus is not fundamentally different.

- In *Dialogue* 57, after Catherine has begun her teaching

"I Tre Stati dell'Anima": *Stages of Spiritual Development*

on the *scaloni particulari*, she says that the first and second stages apply to "many":

> Then that soul, restless with burning desire and gazing into God's gracious mirror, saw how people took different ways for different motives to get to their goal. She saw *many* who began to climb when they felt the grip of [servile] fear, that is, fear of personal suffering. And *many* by responding to that first call reached the second. But few seemed to reach the greatest perfection.[95]

Admittedly, it is ambiguous whether "many" refers only to those God has called to follow the perfect way or to everyone. It is more likely that "many" refers to all those going on the Christ-bridge, including those on the scaloni generali. This text also supports our position that those on the scaloni generali experience stages of spiritual development that are similar to the first and second stages of the scaloni particulari.

- We note that Catherine never says in any way that the two ways of common charity and perfect charity are absolutely separate, irreversible calls from the Lord. She does, however, imply that the way in which one goes is a response to God's general invitation according to one's desire, which, through the exercise of our free will, we can increase.[96]

- References to common charity and perfect charity are completely absent in "Tears," the second most important source on stages of spiritual development in the *Dialogue* after "The Bridge."[97] Surprisingly, those on the *scaloni generali* in "Tears" are even able to reach the unitive stage!

> What tongue could describe the marvel of this final unitive stage and the many fruits the soul receives when its powers are so filled? This is that sweet gathering together that I told you about when I spoke of

the three [*scaloni generali*], based on the word of my Truth.[98]

- In Catherine's teaching on *scaloni particulari* in *Dialogue* 59, the first *scalone* is described as the "first gathering together," which would imply successive gatherings on the other *scaloni*. This would seem to represent a combination of the teachings on the two types of *scaloni*, thus suggesting that the two are not entirely different. In any case, *all* spiritual development involves the soul and the "gathering together" of its three powers whether or not one is following the way of common charity or perfect charity.

In summary, this is Catherine's teaching on the two *scaloni*: Everyone, not just consecrated persons, is called by God to holiness. We generally respond to this call in two ways: the way of common charity and the way of "great perfection," the perfection of charity, represented by the *scaloni generali* and *scaloni particulari* on the bridge of Christ crucified. Those going the way of common charity are living out the graces received in baptism while those following the way of the perfection of charity do the same but have also freely taken on the evangelical counsels of poverty, chastity, and obedience "actually and mentally."[99] Both ways, however, have the same end and point the soul in the same direction of holiness.

Catherine's teaching that laypeople, with God's grace, can attain the same holiness as consecrated persons is a departure from the ordinary thinking of the church of her day and prefigures one of the most important teachings of the Second Vatican Council almost six hundred years later. In "The Universal Call to Holiness," chapter 5 of *Lumen Gentium*, "The Dogmatic Constitution on the Church" (1964), the council Fathers declared that "all the faithful of Christ of whatever state or walk in life are called to the fullness of the Christian life and the perfection of charity."[100] This new teaching is repeated in the later *Catechism of the Catholic Church* (1994):

"I Tre Stati dell'Anima": *Stages of Spiritual Development*

Spiritual progress tends toward ever more intimate union with Christ. This union is called "mystical" because it participates in the mystery of Christ through the sacraments—the "holy mysteries"—and, in him, in the mystery of the Holy Trinity. God calls us all to this intimate union with him, even if the special graces or extraordinary signs of the mystical life are granted only to some for the sake of manifesting the gratuitous gift to all.[101]

Everyone, therefore, may, by grace, attain holiness no matter whether they follow the way of common charity on the *scaloni generali* or the way of the perfection of charity on the *scaloni particulari*.[102] The characteristics of the journey to holiness via these two ways are similar, just as two pilgrims who take different routes to a mountain sanctuary may encounter the same climactic conditions, more or less, along the way. Catherine's teaching on the *scaloni generali* and *particulari*, which at first glance may appear as simply confused and incomplete, actually reflects an intuition of a truth that the church would proclaim centuries later.[103]

Now let us turn to what Catherine says about the actual stages of spiritual development on the *scaloni particulari*. Although the bulk of her teaching is contained in the section "The Bridge" in the *Dialogue*, we will, of course, also look at other sections of the work as well as her letters and prayers so as to arrive at a clearer understanding.

The First *Scalone*

Out of the River of Sin

In chapter 2 we described the tempestuous river of sin beneath the bridge and the people in it.[104] Because of their defective knowledge and selfishness, they have loved wrongly. However, it is possible to get out of the river. In *Dialogue* 49 the process is described:

> Now there are some, I tell you, who when they feel the pressure of trouble are prompted to remove the cloud [off themselves caused] by their very suffering and by what they see must be the consequence of their sin. In this [servile] fear they begin to make their way out of the river. They vomit out the venom with which the scorpion had stung them under the guise of gold. They had embraced him without any reservation, and so he had stung them. [They] begin to get up and turn toward the shore to gain access to the bridge.
>
> But to [go] merely in [servile] fear is not enough. It is not enough for eternal life to sweep the house clean of deadly sin. One must fill it with virtue that is grounded in love, and not merely in fear.[105]

This is a pre-stage, an "awakening," that Catherine calls "the first change" *(la prima mutazione)*.[106] Several movements can be discerned in the above passage. First, there is a crisis: the suffering caused by one's sins and the fear of future punishment. Second, this prompts one to "remove the cloud" that previously blocked one's understanding. Third, with servile fear one makes one's way out of the river and onto the shore. Fourth, there one vomits out the poison of sin, implying repentance and sacramental confession: "I send a prod of conscience *(uno stimolo di coscienzia)* to rouse these people to open their mouths and vomit out the filth of their sins in holy confession."[107] Fifth, then one gets up and goes toward the bridge. Fear has caused the soul "to sweep the house clean of deadly sin" but fear cannot fill it; only love and virtue can do that.

Servile fear is not enough to bring one to eternal life. One's tears at this stage are "heartfelt but sensual; that is, although they have not yet come to perfect hatred for sin as an offense against me, they do get up with heartfelt sorrow because of the punishment that must follow upon the sin they have committed."[108]

The gradual process of going from servile fear to love and virtue involves the replacement of defective knowledge with true knowledge of self and God, as we see in "Tears": "When the soul begins to practice virtue, she begins to lose this fear.... So she rises up in love to know herself and my goodness to her, and she begins to hope in mercy."[109] The more one sees the truth about oneself and God's love, servile fear gradually gives way to holy fear *(timore santo)*, which contains the first "glimmer" of love.[110]

Some people turn back before getting to the bridge. They are the lukewarm who have gone sluggishly, with *tiepidezza*, toward their goal. The winds of prosperity (disordered pleasures) or adversity blow them back into the river for various reasons: disordered love of things and people, fear, discouragement, complacency, impatience, the inability to persevere during times of suffering: "All this happens to them because the root of selfishness *(amore proprio)* has never been dug out of them."[111]

Arrival at the First Scalone

Now restored to grace, albeit imperfectly, the human person becomes a "pilgrim traveler" on the first *scalone* at the feet of the Crucified, the first stage of spiritual growth. Here begins the ascent on the Christ-bridge in which the divine likeness increases in us to the point of ultimate resemblance with God. Although this stage is "imperfect," it is a necessary one for everyone.

The Mercenary Servant

Having vomited out the scorpion's venom, the pilgrim traveler goes in the direction of the bridge. "Then one must put both feet on the first *[scalone]* of the bridge. And the two feet that carry the soul into the [affection] of my Truth, of whom I have made a bridge for you, are affection and desire."[112] At this point the pilgrim is a mercenary servant *(servo mercenario)*[113] who works for pay (good feeling, spiritual consolations, the hope of material benefits) more than love; his or her service is marked by the vestiges of servile fear (of punishment and loss). "Mercenary love is for the most part self-love, directed to oneself, in the search of what is useful to oneself;

in short, it is not genuine."[114] Our relationship with God is mirrored in our relationship with our neighbor; mercenary servants "love their neighbors with the same imperfect love."[115]

In *Dialogue* 59 two characteristics of mercenary love are given: lukewarmness and the inability to persevere during times of even the mildest suffering:

> But there are many who begin to climb so [slowly] *(lentamente)* and pay what they owe me in such bits and pieces, so indifferently and ignorantly, that they quickly fall by the way. The smallest wind makes them hoist their sails and turn back. They had climbed only imperfectly to the first [*scalone*] of Christ crucified, and so they never reach the second, which is that of the heart.[116]

The pilgrim, out of ignorance and blindness to the truth, relates to the Lord neither as friend nor father but as a somewhat frightening master. If there is to be any progress, one must continue to respond to the attraction of love and, as we will see, completely "lift" and "nail" both feet to the cross so as to become a faithful servant and continue on the pilgrimage upward.

"Two Feet of Affection and Desire"[117]

The first stage of spiritual development commences when the soul's "two feet of affection *(affetto)* and desire *(desiderio)*" are on the first *scalone*.[118] Affection and desire are practically the same thing for Catherine; both pertain to the will.

The word *affection* appears often in the church Fathers as well as in many medieval spiritual writings. Unlike the word's present-day meaning of "tender feeling," *affection* in medieval spirituality refers to our noncognitive interior reactions: intense feelings, spontaneous thoughts, desires, deep emotions, and any combination of these.[119] Affections are our initial subjective reactions to sense perceptions. At this stage on the Christ-bridge the affections are disordered and manifest themselves as inordinate attachments to

"I Tre Stati dell'Anima": *Stages of Spiritual Development*

"created goods": one's self, others, material things—in short, "the world."[120] The affections are not yet directed to God, as eventually they will be further along the Christ-bridge, but instead are directed to temporal things that only weaken the soul and make it lukewarm in the removal of vice and the acquisition of virtue. This initial point on the Christ-bridge pertains, therefore, primarily to our disordered desires, which are manifested in worldly attachments; it is not about our actions. It is the dimension of the heart, not the mind. As the pilgrim traveler goes higher on the Christ-bridge, his or her affections and desires, now no longer disordered, gradually attain union with the divine Essence.[121]

The feet as a symbol of the affections was not unknown in spiritual writings during Catherine's time. The image may have originated in Augustine's commentary on the Gospel of John where to wash the feet means to purify the affections.[122] It is possible that Catherine may have had indirect contact with Augustine's image through *Lo specchio della croce*, in which Cavalca says that "just as the feet carry the body, so the *will* carries the soul."[123] In her own original way, Catherine, in the *Dialogue* and letters, speaks of affection as if it were an extension or tentacle of desire that goes in search of something to love and then unite with.[124] For example, she speaks of the "feet of affection"[125] or affection as "love's hand,"[126] the two parts of the body that can go in search of something.

Two actions pertain to the feet on the first *scalone* and constitute the task of the pilgrim traveler at this initial point on the bridge: "*lifting* the feet of [the soul's] affections from the earth" and then *nailing* them to the cross. The pilgrim traveler's feet are lifted up on the cross, thereby *detaching* one's affections (disordered desires) from inordinate worldly attachments (created goods). Next, the affections are *attached* ("nailed") to Christ's feet on the cross:

> In the chapter [of God's book, his Son the Word] that is his feet, we see that they are nailed so that we may nail our affection to him by stripping it of all inordinate willfulness.

In this way, it will neither want nor seek anything but Christ crucified.[127]

The affections, now stripped of disordered love[128] and self-will,[129] are fixed entirely on Christ; our heart becomes more "Christ-like" and we now begin to "walk" like him.[130]

The nailing of our affections or disordered desires to Christ's feet is a prerequisite to removing vice and then acquiring virtue, which Catherine describes in terms of undressing and dressing: "At the first *scalone*, lifting the feet of affection from the earth, one stripped oneself *(si spogliò)* of vice, in the second clothed oneself *(si vesti)* with the love of virtue, and in the third tasted peace."[131] Putting the affections at the beginning of the Christ-bridge, on the first *scalone*, reflects Catherine's knowledge of basic moral principles: that until our disordered desires are brought under control, one will not have the energy to remove vice and progress in the virtues. To be free *for* God, one must be free *from* all disordered desires.

Because "the soul is always afraid until she has attained true love,"[132] the removal of "vice," "disordered love," "selfish-will," and every other disordered desire reduces the mercenary servant's servile fear and makes it possible to *see* the truth more clearly, thus fostering spiritual growth. Fear is only good for cleaning out the house of one's soul; it cannot furnish it nor does it suffice for positive growth in the spiritual life. This requires love!

The Faithful Servant

The gradual transformation of the mercenary servant into the faithful servant involves knowledge and desire: "Unless their desire for perfection makes them recognize their imperfection, it is impossible for them not to turn back."[133] The "desire for perfection" is the result of the attraction of love felt by the pilgrim traveler:

> So you see him up high in pain and disgrace, mocked, abused, tormented, insulted, sated with shame and so tortured with thirst that he dies of thirst for our salvation. This

"I Tre Stati dell'Anima": *Stages of Spiritual Development*

> is how the gentle Lamb, so in love, ate. And this is why he said, "If I am lifted up high I will draw everything to myself." For because of our rebirth in the blood of Christ crucified we are drawn to love him—if only we follow reason instead of abandoning it in love for our selfish sensuality. Once our heart has been drawn to love our benefactor, everything is drawn: heart, soul, and will, along with everything we do spiritually and physically.[134]

At this point there is an imperfect knowledge of God and self. Nevertheless, the pilgrim must act on it with free will or else fall back:

> There were others who had begun to climb. They were beginning to recognize their sinfulness; yet, they were abandoning sin only for fear of the punishment that follows upon sin, and fear of punishment is imperfect. She saw many of these running from imperfect to perfect fear, and they were going eagerly through the second stage and on to the last. But there were many who because of this [servile] fear were sitting down apathetically at the entrance to the bridge. They had begun to climb so [halfheartedly] *(tepidamente)*, without adding a spark to the fire of knowing themselves and God's goodness [in] them.[135]

The great enemy of progress, at every stage, is selfish self-love, which causes one to turn back especially in times of crisis.

As love gradually replaces servile fear, the faithful servant emerges:

> There are others who become faithful servants. They serve me with love rather than that [servile] fear which serves only for fear of punishment. But their love is imperfect, for they serve me for their own profit or for the delight and pleasure they find in me. Do you know how they show that their love is imperfect? By the way they act when they are

deprived of the comfort they find in me. And they love their neighbors with the same imperfect love. This is why their love is not strong enough to last.[136]

The faithful servant's love for God and neighbor is imperfect: He or she expects a reward, and when no reward is forthcoming the faithful servant falls back. The apostle Peter initially had this imperfect love: He loved the pleasure of Christ's companionship, but denied him out of a fear of suffering.[137]

Catherine's use of the two images in the *Dialogue* of "mercenary servant" and "faithful servant" brings out the internal movement within this first stage more so than if she had used the single image of "servant" (which in fact she does in letter T94)[138] or "mercenary servant." Also, the image of the faithful servant (as well as the subsequent "friend" and "child") is taken from the Gospel of Matthew.[139] The faithful servant is an image Catherine carries over into the second stage.

In conclusion, Catherine says that the first *scalone* is "a first general raising *(uno levare generale)* that the servants of the world commonly do."[140] The pilgrim traveler arrives as a mercenary servant with servile fear. Here purification takes place as seen in the lifting and nailing of the two feet of affection and desire and the stripping away of vice. Fear and the cloud caused by sin diminish to the point that the mercenary servant is able to see something of God's love and his or her own imperfection. Then a desire, although imperfect, for perfection results. Without this knowledge and desire, the mercenary servant cannot be transformed into the faithful servant and cannot proceed to the second *scalone*.

This knowledge of God and self is the result of reason and faith:

> And let us consider this to be the first ascent…which should be exercised with the light of the intellect inside of which is the pupil of holy faith, which looks not only at the punishment [for sin] but the fruit of the virtues and the love which I bear.…[141]

"I Tre Stati dell'Anima": *Stages of Spiritual Development*

The first *scalone* can be seen in terms of the theological virtue of faith.[142] Catherine, in her teaching on the *scaloni generali*, associates, by implication, the first *scalone* with the first of the soul's powers: memory.[143]

The pilgrim traveler is now ready to ascend to the second *scalone*.

The Second Scalone

Loving the Gift More Than the Giver

As the faithful servant increases in love, more joy and consolations are experienced:

> In the beginning [the soul] was imperfect, living in [servile] fear. By dint of practice and perseverance she came to the love of pleasure and self-advantage because in me she found both pleasure and profit.[144]

> After [the soul who wants to attain perfection] has risen from the guilt of deadly sin and recognized herself for what she is, she begins to weep for fear of punishment. But then she rouses herself to ponder my mercy, and in this finds delight and profit for herself. This is imperfect....[145]

The deceit comes from selfish self-love that attaches itself to these consolations because of the delight found in them to the point that one is more interested in the gift of God than God himself.[146]

> Thus I give spiritual consolation in prayer, now in one way, now in another. But it is not my intention that the soul should receive this consolation foolishly, paying more attention to the gift than to me. I want her to be more concerned about the loving charity with which I give it to her, and to her unworthiness to receive it, than to the pleasure of her own consolation.[147]

The faithful servant's love is imperfect because it is tinged by selfishness; without realizing it, God is used for the sake of spiritual, psychological, or material rewards. The goal is not yet an authentic encounter with God but consolations.[148] Such people relate to their neighbor in the same way, for self-advantage.

> These [souls] grow lax *(allentano)*, desisting from the service they were giving their neighbors and pulling back from their charity if it seems they have lost their own profit or some comfort they had formerly found in them. And this comes about because their love was not genuine. They love their neighbors with the same love which they love me—for their own profit.[149]

An indication that our love of neighbor is selfish is the distress we experience when someone we love does not return our love, loves someone more than us, or in general does not reciprocate our love.[150] We may, to some extent, possess the virtues but only imperfectly and because there is some personal advantage in doing so.[151]

This selfish attachment to spiritual pleasures leaves the faithful servant particularly vulnerable to the snares of the devil, who "gives whatever he sees the mind disposed to desire and receive"[152] sometimes by way of visions purportedly of angels, saints, or even Christ himself. As to the situation of the faithful servant in general, Garrigou-Lagrange notes that

> [t]he Christian who stops at that point does not take into account enough that God is infinitely better than his gifts and the created satisfaction one finds in him. If, because of the vestiges of egoism, one is content with this then it constitutes an obstacle that impedes loving God only for himself, subordinating to him the pleasure that is granted. It is just like a child who loves maternal caresses more than the mother.
>
> There is, in this imperfect love, a perpetual ebb and flow: the ebb of charity that draws the soul towards God; and the flow produced by the residue of egoism, that paralyzes

"I Tre Stati dell'Anima": *Stages of Spiritual Development*

the impulse of the Spirit towards total abandonment in God—the soul, in its seeking God, secretly, treacherously, seeks itself.[153]

Many remain at this stage or fall back.

Out of love and a desire to bring the pilgrim traveler to perfect love, God now intervenes.

The Crisis of Loss of Consolations

Catherine compares the period of spiritual consolations just described with the forty days after the resurrection when the risen Christ was with the disciples. The next experience of the faithful servant she compares with Christ's withdrawal at the ascension:

> [S]o to bring [the soul] to perfection, after the forty days (the first two stages) have passed, I withdraw from the soul now and again, but in feeling only, not in grace.
>
> My Truth showed you this when he said to the disciples, "I will go away and I will return to you."… So I tell you, it is to make the soul rise from imperfection that I withdraw from her feelings and deprive her of the comfort she had known.[154]

The experience of being deprived of consolations is described in "Divine Providence":

> Sometimes I vex her with evil thoughts *(molestie di molte e diverse cogitazioni)* and a sterile mind *(mente sterile)*. It will seem to her that I have left her completely, without any feeling whatever. She does not seem to be in the world, because she is in fact not there; nor does she seem to be in me, because she has no feeling at all other than that her will does not want to sin.[155]
>
> I do not let these [struggles] last forever. They come and go as I see necessary for her. Sometimes she will think she is

in hell, and then, through no effort of her own, she will be relieved and will have a taste of eternal life.[156]

An indication of God's abiding love and presence throughout this painful ordeal is the fact that he never withdraws his grace from the soul.

God allows all this to happen in order to raise the pilgrim traveler from imperfect to perfect love. This is brought about in two ways. First, God allows us to know the truth about ourselves so that we may become humble and learn to trust in him:

> And why do I keep this soul, surrounded by so many enemies, in such pain and distress? Not for her to be captured and lose the wealth of grace, but to show her my providence, so that she will trust not in herself but in me. Then she will rise up from her carelessness and her concern will make her run for protection to me her defender, her kind Father, the provider of her salvation. I want her to be humble, to see that of herself she is nothing and to recognize that her existence and every gift beyond that comes from me, that I am her life.[157]

The trials are permitted in order to bring the human person to knowledge of that same fundamental truth that the Lord revealed to Catherine in her early days: "Do you know, daughter, who you are and who I am?... You are she who is not, and I AM HE WHO IS."[158] In other words, the trials foster knowledge of one's own nothingness apart from God and make us realize that we have nothing of our own and that everything is a gift from God.

If the faithful servant is to persevere on the journey, then this truth must be contemplated in the cell of self-knowledge where one watches and waits for the Lord's promised return:

> Here is what she does. Though she feels that I have withdrawn into myself, she does not turn back. Rather, she perseveres in her exercise with humility and remains locked up

"I Tre Stati dell'Anima": *Stages of Spiritual Development*

in the house of self-knowledge. There, with lively faith, she waits for the coming of the Holy Spirit, for me, the flame of love. How does she wait? Not lazily, but in watching and constant humble prayer. And her watching is not only physical but spiritual as well. Her mind's eye *(l'occhio dell'intelletto)* never closes, but watches by the light of faith and with contempt tears out her heart's wandering thoughts. She watches in love of my charity, knowing that I want only her sanctification. My Son's blood stands witness to this.

By the very fact that her eye is watching in the knowledge of me and of herself, the soul is praying continuously. This is the prayer of a good and holy will, and this is continuous prayer. But she watches also in acts of prayer—prayer, I mean, that is made at the regular times ordained by holy Church....

I left her so that she might see and know her shortcomings. For when she felt bereft of comfort she would feel distressed and weak, incapable of constancy or perseverance. Here she would find the root of her spiritual selfishness and have reason to know it for what it is and to rise above herself and mount the judgment seat of her conscience. She would dig out the root of selfish love with the knife of contempt for such love and with love for virtue....[159]

Here we see the faithful servant's task at this crucial juncture. First, with the eye of the intellect and faith one "watches" or perseveres in the exercise of knowledge of self and God.[160] "[P]ain makes her enter into knowledge of herself."[161] One trusts God and perseveres because the blood of Christ has removed all doubts about his love and desire to bring us to perfect love. In the house of self-knowledge

> [w]e rise above ourselves, calling ourselves to account with a holy self-contempt, considering ourselves deserving of the suffering and struggles but undeserving of the fruit we see follows upon the suffering. In humility, we consider ourselves undeserving of spiritual peace and calm.[162]

There is the realization that one's service has not been that of a good child to a parent with no regard for one's own interest but rather with the expectation of reward.[163] We have loved consolations and not God; our love for consolations is nothing more than our selfish self-love and its rapacious appetite for good feeling cloaked in a religious mantle of false piety.[164] At this point prayer and self-knowledge must be continuous: "You must not break away from holy prayer for any reason except obedience or charity."[165]

Secondly, like the disciples in the Upper Room, the faithful servant "waits" for the Lord's promised return, the coming of the Holy Spirit, when one will no longer feel abandoned. Two scholars appropriately ascribe the theological virtue of hope to the second *scalone*.[166] "[O]ut of darkness is born the light."[167]

Finally, this new knowledge of self and God must issue in the renewed rooting out of selfish love and the planting of virtue if there is to be spiritual growth.[168] The entire process is described in similar terms in "Tears," where one's neighbor is explicitly mentioned as the object of unselfish love and of virtue:

> But as she grows and exercises herself in the light of self-knowledge, she conceives a kind of contempt for herself. From this she draws [some of] my goodness, aflame with love, and she begins to join and conform her will with mine. She begins to feel joy and compassion: joy for herself because of this impulse of love, and compassion for her neighbors....[169]

As this process continues a profound transformation occurs: The faithful servant of God gradually becomes a friend.[170]

> The faithful servant enjoys more and more the pleasure of serving God and, knowing his goodness better, and receives everything looking less at the gift and the hands that give them and more to the giver. If he persists in this way of living, he finishes by changing his service into love and becomes a friend.[171]

"I Tre Stati dell'Anima": *Stages of Spiritual Development*

This transition from faithful servant to friend is founded on John 15:15[172] and is described in *Dialogue* 60:

> If you love me the way a servant loves a master, I as your master will give you what you have earned, but I will not show myself to you, for secrets are shared only with a friend who has become one with oneself.
>
> Still, servants can grow because of their virtue and the love they bear their master, even to becoming his very dear friend.... They can sit in judgment on themselves so that motives of [servile] fear and mercenary love do not cross their hearts without being corrected in the light of most holy faith. If they act in this way, it will please me so much that for this they will come to the love of friendship.
>
> And then I will show myself to them, just as my Truth said: "Those who love me will be one with me and I with them, and I will show myself to them and we will make our dwelling place together."[173]

The pilgrim traveler now loves more perfectly. Up to this point growth has been primarily in knowledge of self. Now is the time to discover the "secrets" of God.

The Friend at the Opened Side

The love of friendship (*amore dell'amico*) is one of excellence.[174] At this point on the second *scalone* there is a correspondence between the illuminative stage where one grows in knowledge of God and "increasing consciousness of one's *being loved*":[175]

> Then you find that you have climbed the second *[scalone]*. This is the enlightenment of the mind (*lume de l'intelletto*), which sees itself reflected (*si specula*) in the warmhearted love I have shown you in Christ crucified, as in a mirror.[176]

Here the God-man reveals himself "especially in his saving *recreative* love of [the soul]."[177] The friend continues to serve God but now, says the eternal Father, "in the simple hope of pleasing me,"[178] with no selfish motives,[179] and with a sincere and generous love *(l'amore schietto e liberale)*.[180] He or she loves virtue only for the love of God[181] and one's neighbor without any self-interest.[182]

Friendship love is "a reciprocal fusion of souls, or reciprocal communion of thoughts and sentiments."[183]

> And then I will show myself to them, just as my Truth said: "Those who love me will be one with me and I with them, and I will show myself to them and we will make our dwelling place together." This is how it is with very dear friends. Their loving affection makes them two bodies with one soul, because love transforms one into what one loves. And if these two souls are made one soul [with me], nothing can be kept [secret]. This is why my Truth said, "I will come and we will make a dwelling place together." This is the truth.[184]

Friendship love has a unitive quality that comes into its own in the third stage.[185]

The friend is also the recipient of three extraordinary manifestations of the Lord. First, he manifests himself to the friend in such a way that one can taste, know, experience, and feel his love and affection in the soul by means of the Word. The second manifestation is the possible gift of prophecy, which allows one to see into the future. Thirdly, the appropriations of the Trinity are manifested: the Father's power, the Son's wisdom, and the clemency and charity of the Spirit that result in conceiving virtue for one's neighbors.[186]

The second *scalone* leads to Christ's opened side and heart and is mentioned for the first time in *Dialogue 26*:

> My Son's nailed feet are a *[scalone]* by which you can climb to his side *(giognere al costato)*, where you will see revealed [the secret of the heart]. For when the soul has climbed up

"I Tre Stati dell'Anima": *Stages of Spiritual Development*

on the feet of affection and looked with her mind's eye into my Son's opened heart, she begins to feel the love of her own heart in his consummate and unspeakable love.[187]

Catherine does not say whether the faithful servant's stripping off of selfish self-love, the emergence as friend, and the arrival at the opened side happen simultaneously. D'Urso, for one, thinks they do not, saying that the opened side/heart is the "finishing line" *(traguardo)* of friendship love or its goal where it fully arrives.[188] At the opened side it is possible for the friend to see what Catherine calls "the secret of the heart" because "secrets are shared only with a friend who has become one with oneself."[189]

The secret of the heart at the opened side is a theme found in medieval piety and spiritual writing. Catherine may have derived the expression indirectly from a sermon of Bernard of Clairvaux on the Song of Songs 2:14, in which he says "the secret of his heart is laid open through the clefts of his body."[190] The theme also appears in one of Augustine's sermons: "Christ is the door; the entrance was opened for you when his side was pierced with a lance."[191] William of St. Thierry (d. 1150) says that one should "enter completely inside the wound of the side…up to the heart of Jesus."[192] Catherine's German Dominican contemporary, Henry Suso (d. 1366), also speaks of entering into the opened side and the wounded heart where one finds a dwelling place and is purified and united with God.[193] Starting in the thirteenth century, the Dominican order celebrated a feast of the wounded side of Christ on the Friday after the octave of Corpus Christi.[194]

Catherine refers to the opened side/heart using several images, particularly those of a *channel,* an *open window,* and a *cavern.*[195]

> So, since we need to provision the ship of our soul, let's proceed to provision it there, at that sweetest of channels, the heart and soul, and body of Jesus Christ. We will find that this channel *(canale)* flows with so great a love that we will easily be able to fill our souls. So I say to you: don't be slow to put your eye to this [open window] *(finestra aperta).*[196]

> But among them all there is one channel flowing with blood and water mixed with fire, and to the eye that rests on this channel is revealed the secret of the heart.[197]

> Your place, where you will be, shall be Christ crucified, my only-begotten Son, living and hiding yourself *(nascondendovi)* in the cavern *(caverna)* of his side, where you will [have a] taste, through the affection of love, in that human nature and my divine nature. In that opened-heart you will find charity for me and for your neighbors....[198]

We will see how Catherine uses each image to convey a different aspect of the meaning of the opened side/heart. However, all three images convey to varying degrees the re-creative quality of God's love particularly as one becomes increasingly conscious of being loved.

The Opened Side/Heart as a Channel

In the first two passages above we see the opened side/heart described as a channel of God's love, blood, water, and fire. The church has traditionally seen in the blood and water pouring from Christ's wounded side a type of baptism and Eucharist.[199] Catherine incorporates this in her own teaching but goes further:

> Climbing up with the feet of the soul's affection, they reach as far as the side where they find the secret of his heart and know the baptism of water, that takes its efficacy from the blood *(à virtù nel sangue)*; here the soul finds the grace of holy baptism, disposing *(disposto)* itself as a vase to receive grace, united and kneaded *(impastata)* with the blood.
>
> Where may the soul know the highest dignity of seeing itself united and kneaded in the blood of the Lamb, receiving holy baptism in virtue of the blood? It finds it in the side of Christ crucified, where it can know the fire of divine charity.[200]

"I Tre Stati dell'Anima": *Stages of Spiritual Development*

At the opened side the soul sees that, by virtue of its baptism, it is united with the blood of the Lamb and occupies a place of the highest dignity. Here at the opened side "it can know the fire of divine charity." The opened side is where one receives grace: the grace of baptism as well as the "ongoing baptism of blood" *(il continuo battesimo del sangue)*, the sacrament of confession. In letter T97, the opened side is a channel of grace and the fire of charity: "Put your mouth to the open side of God's Son, put it there; for his side is a mouth that emits the fire of charity and pours out blood to wash away your sin."[201] Perhaps more significantly for the pilgrim traveler, who presumably is baptized, is the possibility of knowing "the fire of divine charity" at the opened side.[202] It is mentioned again in *Dialogue 76*:

> By what way did she come [to the mouth]? By way of the heart, that is, through the remembrance of the blood in which she was baptized once again *(si ribattezò)*, abandoning imperfect love for the knowledge of hearty love *(cordiale amore)* she drew from seeing and tasting and experiencing the fire of my charity.[203]

In seeing the secret of the heart one has the "remembrance of the blood," and sees, tastes, and experiences the fire of divine charity, thus enjoying a radical encounter with divine Love that re-creates ("re-baptizes") the pilgrim traveler.[204] The last remnants of imperfect love have now largely fallen away.

The Opened Side/Heart as an Open Window

Through the window of the opened side we see the secret of the heart, God's *amore cordiale* (warmhearted love):

> There [in the opening of my side] you find my heart's secret and it shows you, more than any finite suffering could, how I love you.[205]

For that splitting open of his body has made it clear to us that God loves us without measure and wants nothing other than our good.[206]

Through this window one sees the truth of God the Father.[207] Cavallini says:

> [O]nce it arrives at the second *scalone* the soul no longer knows effort or fatigue because in the opened-side of Christ crucified it reads "the secret of the heart," that truth which Catherine considers as belonging to God, "his truth:" the truth of the love that is at the origin of creation and redemption, truth manifested in the world more evidently in the "opening" of the side. The soul tastes this truth in the blood that flows from the wounded side where it is submerged and inebriated; its love is no longer mixed with fear but is nearly perfect.[208]

This newly acquired knowledge of the truth of God the Father is not experienced in some cold, purely rational way but is totally engaging: One sees it, tastes it, and experiences it in an unprecedented way. The fire of divine charity "ignites" the heart of the pilgrim traveler who, seeing it, is "swallowed up and clothed in the fiery gift of the blood of God's son."[209]

In the light of God's radical *amore cordiale* and the "fire of divine charity" the pilgrim traveler's own love is revealed.

> For when the soul has climbed up on the feet of affection and looked with her mind's eye into my Son's opened heart, she begins to feel the love of her own heart in his consummate and unspeakable love.[210]

> Then you find that you have climbed the second [*scalone*]. This is the enlightenment of the mind *(lume de l'intelletto)*, which sees itself reflected *(si specula)* in the warmhearted love *(amore cordiale)* I have shown you in Christ crucified....[211]

"I Tre Stati dell'Anima": *Stages of Spiritual Development*

In a sense, God now reflects back to us the "secrets" of *our* heart: "If [two friends] are made into one soul there can be no secret between them."[212] With this double knowledge of the truth of God's love and one's own, the pilgrim traveler's love is drawn toward ever greater perfection.

The Opened Side/Heart as a Cavern

Christ's opened side is a refuge from our enemies and a secure dwelling place:[213]

> For us you have made a cavern in your open side where we might have a refuge in the face of our enemies, and in this cavern we can come to know your charity because by this you have shown that you wanted to give us more than you could give by your finite actions. There we have found the bath in which we have washed our soul's face clean of the leprosy of sin.[214]

The cavern is like a hearth at which we are warmed by the fire of love: "The cavern of your body is open for the warmth of the fire of love for our well-being."[215] As a place where one sees and knows God and oneself, it is the cell of self-knowledge par excellence.[216] It is a portal into the Divine: "Hide yourself in the wounds of Christ crucified; flee from the world; leave your family home; take refuge in the cavern, the side of Christ crucified, and so come to the promised land."[217] Catherine may have derived the image of the cavern from the Song of Songs 2:14: *"columba mea in foraminibus petrae in* caverna *maceriae."*[218]

In her teaching on the love of God, Catherine relentlessly insists on the dimension of "the other," love of neighbor, indicated often by the word *virtù*, which, as we recall from chapter 2,[219] must always be put into practice in our relationship with our neighbor: "[T]he soul, as soon as she comes to know me, reaches out to love her neighbors."[220] Charity is the supreme virtue from which all others proceed. The more one's love of God is brought to perfection, so too is love of neighbor since one mirrors the other, and vice versa.[221]

Catherine often describes virtue and love of neighbor using the images of dressing oneself and childbearing:

> At the first *scalone*, lifting the feet of affection from the earth, one stripped oneself *(si spogliò)* of vice, in the second clothed oneself *(si vestì)* with the love of virtue....[222]

> On the first [*scalone*] they will undress *(spogliarono)* the feet of affection of the love of vice; on the second they will taste the secret and affection of the heart and then they will conceive love in virtue *(concepettero amore nella virtù)*....[223]

D'Urso says that the second *scalone*

> is the time to consider virtue and the virtuous life in their positive value; that is, no longer as an antidote to moral evil but as an enrichment of intrinsic goodness. Then the soul comprehends that "if they do not get up for love of virtue, their servile fear is not enough to win them eternal life."[224]

The virtues are acquired through one's knowledge of the goodness of God in oneself:

> [T]hrough that way we come to virtue, that is through knowledge of the goodness of God, and through the light of which we see his humility and charity. In him we will acquire them, looking for them inside our soul; elsewhere, in no other way, we will ever find them. This is the foundation and the beginning, means and end, of every virtue and our perfection.[225]

In seeking and finding the virtues in God's goodness (particularly in Christ) we discover the seeds of the same virtues within ourselves.

"I Tre Stati dell'Anima": *Stages of Spiritual Development*

Once acquired, the virtues are meant to grow in us by the "fire of holy desire," which increases the more we put "wood" on it:

> What wood? Recalling to mind the many and infinite benefits received from God, which are innumerable; the greatest being the benefit of the blood of the Word, his only begotten Son, which manifests the ineffable love that God has for us.[226]

In conclusion, we have seen that on the second *scalone* the pilgrim traveler enters as the faithful servant and how he or she is then gradually "raised to the status of a friend of God incarnate"[227] by persevering through the crisis of loss of consolations, entering Christ's opened side where one sees the secret of the heart and sees, tastes, and experiences the truth of God the Father in the totality of one's being, while acquiring virtue that is put into practice in one's relationship with others. This is the *liberale* stage of "perfect,"[228] which corresponds to the soul's power of understanding. Compared to the first *scalone*, this stage is more positive and centered on God and the attraction of his love.

Re-created by the fire of divine charity, the pilgrim traveler on the second *scalone* "knows and acquires so much fire of love that immediately [she] runs *(corre)* to the third."[229] After the secret of the heart, the soul, in the grip of God's love, is thereafter *running* in its ascent on the Christ-bridge, which is no surprise as "love does not stay idle."[230]

The Third Scalone

The third *scalone* consists of two *stati* or stages: the third stage of (most) perfect love and the fourth stage of perfect union:

> And this unites them with the fourth stage *(quarto stato)*, that is, from the third stage, which is the perfect stage, in which one tastes and gives birth to charity in one's neighbor,

one receives a final stage of perfect union in me. These two stages are united together, so that one is not without the other, for there cannot be love of me without love of neighbor nor love of neighbor without love of me: one cannot be separated from the other."[231]

Both stages are unitive:[232] In the third stage the unitive love of God in one's neighbor is emphasized; in the fourth the unitive love of God in his divinity is emphasized.[233] The two stages are inseparable; each "flavors" *(condisce)* the other.[234]

Although many people reach the first and second *scaloni*, "few seemed to reach the greatest perfection."[235]

The Third Stage
At the Mouth

At the third *scalone* the friend arrives at the mouth of Christ and receives the kiss of peace:

> Then the soul, seeing how tremendously she is loved, is herself filled to overflowing with love. So, having climbed the second *[scalone]*, she reaches the third. This is the mouth, where she finds peace from the terrible war she has had to wage because of her sins.[236]

As we noted earlier, arrival at the mouth is "by way of his heart, through the remembrance of his blood in which she was baptized once again."[237] Implied here is that arrival at this stage is a flowering of baptismal grace and therefore is "a sign that the journey of perfection is a normal development of the first grace and of the call to all the baptized to salvation."[238]

The kiss received at Christ's mouth is reminiscent of the liturgical kiss of peace. In *Dialogue* 76, Catherine elaborates:

> This is how the soul acts who has in truth reached the third *[scalone]*. This is the sign that she has reached it: Her selfish

"I Tre Stati dell'Anima": *Stages of Spiritual Development*

> will died when she tasted my loving charity, and this is why she found her spiritual peace and quiet in the mouth. You know that peace is given with the mouth. So in this third stage the soul finds such a peace that there is nothing that can disturb her. She has let go of and drowned her own will, and when that will is dead there is peace and quiet.[239]

The last vestiges of the selfish will are crushed, at least for now. The "war" between one's higher and lower self has been won by the former and peace ensues.

It is interesting to note that there is no reference to union or spousal imagery in the kiss of the mouth in the *Dialogue* even though Catherine makes such an allusion in two letters written perhaps only a few months before beginning the *Dialogue:*

> When you see the third [*scalone*], I mean when you reach the mouth of God's Son, you are nourished in peace.... The giver of peace unites himself with the one to whom he gives it. So once we are clothed in virtue we experience God in the movement of love, and we join the mouth of our holy desire with God's desire and so are united [with him] in peace and tranquility.[240]

> This is how you will pass over by way of me, the bridge, as I have said, and you will be spouses and children of my truth.[241]

The reason she avoids spousal imagery, according to D'Urso, is that since it represents "the maximum of carnal and sensual love, it could not effectively represent without confusion the most spiritual and perfect love one can conceive."[242] Also, we believe that Catherine's teaching on the stages was intended for everyone; spousal imagery, on the other hand, may have implied an exclusion of the laity, particularly men.[243]

Catherine of Siena

Friend and Child

At the third *scalone* the friend becomes the son or child: "One is my mercenary servant, one is my faithful servant, and the other my son *(figliuolo)*, that is one who loves me without respect [to himself]."[244] It is worthwhile to note that Catherine does not specify when the child actually emerges. The child, however, does not cease to be a friend:

> and being made friend [one] is made *figliuolo*....[245]

> This is the way, and through this passes he who desires to arrive at perfect love, that is to love of friend and [child] *(figliuolo)*.[246]

> For we don't cease being God's servants and true friends once we have become his [child] *(figliuolo)*.[247]

There is no absolute separation between the friend and child in the third stage. It is in Catherine's teaching on the third stage that friendship love is beautifully described in terms of gift and Giver:

> When a soul has reached the third stage, the love of friendship and filial love, her love is no longer mercenary. Rather she does as very close friends do when one receives a gift from another. The receiver does not look just at the gift, but at the heart and the love of the giver, and accepts and treasures the gift only because of the friend's affectionate love. So the soul, when she has reached the third stage of perfect love, when she receives my gifts and graces does not look only at the gift but with her mind's eye looks at the affectionate charity of me, the Giver.[248]

The friend, therefore, has completely surmounted all selfish attachment to the gift.

The most perfect form of love is filial love *(amore filiale)*, which Catherine describes generally under two aspects. Seen from the human side, it is the love that serves God devoid of any self-interest:

"I Tre Stati dell'Anima": *Stages of Spiritual Development*

> Souls who climb this first [*scalone*] with only [*servile*] fear and mercenary love fall into all sorts of troubles. What they need is to get up and be my children *(figliuoli)* and serve me without regard for their own interest.[249]

> Those who serve me in the simple hope of pleasing me receive and enjoy it more perfectly than those who serve in hope of the reward or pleasure they might find in me.
> The former are those in the final spiritual stage, whose perfection I have described for you.[250]

Seen from God's side, it is the love that makes one an heir to the Father's wealth:

> Filial love, I tell you, is perfect. For with filial love one receives the inheritance *(eredità)* from me the eternal Father. But no one attains filial love without the love of friendship, and this is why I told you that one progresses from being my friend to becoming my child.[251]

The child can be seen as a more important friend and as the fruit of friendship love: Filial love is perfect because "the state of the child is firm and stable, connected to a bond that goes beyond the fleeting tenderness of friendship and the fluctuations of sentiment."[252]

The child is Catherine's person image for union with God: The child is in a permanent bond with the Father, who desires to share his joy with his children. The soul's power of the will and the theological virtue of charity, both of which are necessary for union, can thus be ascribed to this stage. This image of the Father's child and heir is rooted in the New Testament:

> "Then the father said to him, 'Son, you are always with me, and all that is mine is yours.'"[253]

> For you did not receive a spirit of slavery to fall back into fear, but you have received a spirit of adoption. When we

> cry, "Abba! Father!" it is that very Spirit bearing witness with our spirit that we are children of God, and if children, then heirs, heirs of God and joint heirs with Christ....[254]
>
> So you are no longer a slave but a child, and if a child then also an heir, through God.[255]

For Catherine, therefore, the entire spiritual journey aims at the full realization of being a child of God. By placing the child instead of the spouse or friend at the pinnacle of the spiritual ascent we see her profound comprehension of the essence of Christianity. Blessed Columba Marmion, a Benedictine spiritual writer of the early twentieth century, says:

> [W]e shall understand nothing—I do not say merely of perfection, but even of simple Christianity—if we do not grasp that its most essential basis is constituted by the state of child of God, participation—through sanctifying grace—in the eternal filiation of the incarnate Word.... All Christian life, all holiness, is being by grace what Jesus is by nature: the Son of God.[256]

Characteristics of the Third Stage

As we have seen, Catherine provides a description of the practical and recognizable characteristics of the pilgrim traveler at each stage of the spiritual journey. The third stage has numerous characteristics, some of which are described in *Dialogue* 76:

> She runs briskly along the way of the teaching of Christ crucified. Nor does she slacken her pace for any assault that may befall her, or any persecution, or any pleasure the world may offer her. All these things she overcomes with true strength and patience, her will clothed with my loving charity and enjoying the food of the salvation of souls in true and perfect patience. Such patience is a sure sign that

the soul loves me perfectly and without self-interest, for if she loved me and her neighbors for her own profit she would be impatient and would slacken her pace.

But she loves me for myself, because I am supreme Goodness and deserve to be loved, and she loves herself and her neighbors because of me, to offer glory and praise to my name. And therefore she is patient and strong in suffering, and persevering.[257]

First, we see that self-will has died and "the soul's ordinary will is alive in me, clothed in my eternal will, but dead to the sensitive will."[258] Her strong emphasis toward the neighbor continues even in the highest reaches of the spiritual journey—in fact, it is found expressly here.

The pilgrim traveler now glories not in spiritual pleasures but in suffering. Catherine compares this stage with the disciples when they left the Upper Room:

They left the house and fearlessly preached my message by proclaiming the teaching of the Word, my only-begotten Son. They had no fear of suffering. No, they even gloried in sufferings. It did not worry them to go before the tyrants of the world to proclaim the truth to them for the glory and praise of my name.[259]

[Peter] loved Christ tenderly, but he wasn't strong, and so he faltered at the time of the crucifixion. But later, after the coming of the Holy Spirit, he distanced himself from this sweet love. He let go of fear and progressed to a love that was strong, tested in the fire of many tribulations. Once he had progressed to this filial love, he bore all these things with true patience. Indeed, he ran after them as joyfully as if he had been going not to torment but to a wedding.[260]

The child's attitude toward suffering is reflected in 1 Corinthians 4:12–13, "When reviled, we bless; when persecuted, we endure;

when slandered, we speak kindly."[261] Because the selfish will is dead, good works are no longer painful or tiring because "she has cut from herself that thing that gave pain, that is her own will which was grounded in self-love."[262] The child finds God's will in everything and reacts in the same way to adversity as to prosperity.[263]

We recall that on the second *scalone* the soul "conceives" the virtues. On the third *scalone* she "gives birth" to them in one's relationship with neighbor, whom she serves "courageously" with no self-concern.[264] All the virtues are branches of the tree of charity, with the "preeminent" virtue being patience: It is a "litmus test" of the authentic presence of all the virtues and Catherine repeatedly commends it.[265] The two other "glorious virtues" at this stage are fortitude and perseverance, although obedience and humility and "compassion for the soul of one's abuser" are also important.[266] The perfect are both sad and happy: sad "at the offense done to me and the harm done to their neighbors. They are happy…because the delight of charity that makes them happy can never be taken away from them, and in this they receive gladness and blessedness."[267]

Now the pilgrim traveler is supremely concerned with God's honor and the salvation of souls.[268] The connection between the two is explained in letter T55:

> In the blood of Christ we let go of this selfish love. And we gain an ineffable love when we see how he has given his life out of love to buy back this adopted child, the human race. When we see such love, love is drawn by love, and our desire is lifted up to love what God loves and to hate what God hates. And because we see that God loves human beings most of all, we conceive a seemingly insatiable love for the salvation of souls.[269]

Giving honor to God and working for the salvation of souls are in fact closely related: God is honored *in* the holiness of souls.[270] Catherine relates the image of the mouth and its function of eating with the salvation of souls: "She eats the food of souls for my honor at the table of the most holy cross."[271] One "eats" souls ("saves"

"I Tre Stati dell'Anima": *Stages of Spiritual Development*

them for eternal life) in proportion to one's own perfection: "So one's catch will be as perfect as one's cast. But those who are perfect catch plenty and with great perfection."[272]

In "Divine Providence" the apostolic vista of the perfect is dramatically broadened. The eternal Father now says that he wants the perfect to be the instruments of mediation *(mezzi)* between himself and those at war with him, to be "another Christ," and to take on his office:

> And the perfection of the perfect is augmented and made to grow, because they are prepared to grow, and I want to make of them good and perfect [instruments of mediation] *(mezzi)* for those who are at war with me. For I have already told you, if you recall, that it is by means of my servants and their great sufferings that I would be merciful to the world and reform my bride.
>
> Truly these last can be called another Christ crucified *(un altro Cristo crocifisso)*, my only-begotten Son, because they have taken [to do his office] *(preso a fare l'officio suo)*. He came as a mediator *(tramezzatore)* to put an end to the war and reconcile humanity to me in peace by suffering even to the shameful death of crucifixion. In the same way must these be crucified and become [an instrument of mediation] *(mezzo)* in prayer, in word, in good holy living, setting themselves up as an example to others.[273]

There is only one other instance in the catherinian corpus where Catherine refers to the nonordained as *"cristi,"* prayer 19 (XII): "But, as I see it, you are calling your servants *christs*, and by means of them you want to relieve the world of death and restore it to life."[274] This extension of the laity's apostolate to the office of Christ can be seen in light of the complete reintegration of human nature at this stage. Grion says:

> Such dignity of office for the children is founded on the full re-integration of their human nature. To the extent it had

been corrupted by sin it vanished. Overcoming sin and corruption, the most perfect have integrally reacquired in Christ crucified the gift of grace in the Trinity.[275]

Another daring extension of the work of the nonordained at this level is found in "The Mystic Body of Holy Church" where the eternal Father commands Catherine "and the others" to

> be humbly attentive *(attendete)* to my honor, the salvation of souls, *and the reform of holy Church (alla reformazione della santa Chiesa)*. This will be a sign to me that you and the others love me in truth. You know well, for I have shown you, that I want you and the others to be little sheep who graze continually in the garden of holy Church, putting up with weariness right up to the moment of death. If you do this, I will fulfill your [desires] *(desideri)*.[276]

As partakers in the office of Christ who said, "See, I am making all things new,"[277] and as other *cristi*, the most perfect pray and work as instruments of mediation for the reform of the church. In letter T282, Catherine relates a time when the Lord once spoke to her, saying:

> [U]nderstand that you cannot have desire for the salvation of souls apart from desire for the salvation of holy Church.... But now I want you and am telling you to increase your hunger and desire, and prepare yourself specifically to lay down your life if necessary in the mystic body of Church for my bride's reform. For if she is reformed, the good of the entire world will follow. [278]

The Fourth Stage of Perfect Union

The pilgrim traveler in the fourth stage has arrived at the gate at the end of the bridge where, as it were, one can glimpse the other side.[279] This stage is a "fruit that comes from this third stage."[280] It is the perfection of grace in this life, an experience of unitive love

"I Tre Stati dell'Anima": *Stages of Spiritual Development*

with God, and is termed the *stato unitivo*.[281] Here the soul experiences a pledge or foretaste of the final end of the Christ-bridge, a "sharing in my being and enjoying my supreme eternal tenderness and goodness," with the assurance of full payment when the soul separates from the body in death.

Foster says that Catherine's teaching at this point "leaves much to be understood," that "her eloquence falters, becomes less copious and more confused."[282] On the contrary, Catherine is most prolific at this stage, employing a variety of effective and arresting images to convey *something* of the essence of the experience in this stage. In the *Dialogue*, approximately eleven chapters are given over to the unitive stage—greater treatment than that afforded any of the other three stages.[283] Catherine is not confused but rather, like all other mystics, obliged to explain an experience that is in fact indescribable, as she herself declares:

> [T]he body loses its feeling. For the eye sees without seeing; the ear hears without hearing; the tongue speaks without speaking (except that sometimes, because of the heart's fullness, I will let the tongue speak for the unburdening of the heart and for the glory and praise of my name, so that it speaks without speaking); the hand touches without touching; the feet walk without walking. All the members are bound and busied with the bond and feeling of love. By this bond they are subjected to reason and joined with the soul's [affection] so that, as if against their own nature, they all cry out to me the eternal Father with one voice, asking to be separated from the soul, and the soul from the body.[284]

> But the inmost feeling, the ineffable sweetness and perfect union—you cannot describe it with your tongue, which is a finite thing![285]

Catherine most often communicates the experience of the unitive stage with images pertaining to *uniting, seeing, clothing*, and *filling*.

Catherine of Siena

Images of Union

Catherine has more to say about the fourth stage as union than any of the other images for this stage.[286] It is not unusual for her to mix images. Her more important images to describe union are those of the infant at the breast, the coal in the fire, and the peaceful sea.

In *Dialogue* 96 ("Tears"), the soul in the fourth stage is compared to an infant nursing quietly at the breast of its mother, Christ:

> Such a soul receives the fruit [of the quieting of the mind] *(quiete di mente)*, [a union made through sentiment in] my gentle divine nature in which she tastes milk, just as an infant when quieted rests on its mother's breast, takes her nipple, and drinks her milk through her flesh. This is how the soul who has reached this final stage rests on the breast of my divine charity and takes into the mouth of her holy desire the flesh of Christ crucified....So the soul rests on the breast of Christ crucified who *is* my love, and so drinks in the milk of virtue. In this virtue she gets the life of grace, and *tastes within herself my divine nature*, which gives the virtues their sweetness.[287]

The soul at the breast experiences union with the divine nature, through "feeling" *(sentimento)* and "tasting," and receives virtue and "the life of grace." Nothing now stands between the soul and God: "Not even the soul's own will stands between us, because she has become one thing with me."[288] In letter T164 Catherine further develops the teaching that when nothing stands between the soul and God, the result is divine union:

> You know...that to join two things together there must be nothing between them or there cannot be a perfect fusion. Now realize that this is how God wants our soul to be, with-

"I Tre Stati dell'Anima": *Stages of Spiritual Development*

out any selfish love of ourselves or of others in between, just as God loves us without anything in between.[289]

The union is effected by means of the soul's three powers that unite with God through love in such a way that the memory is *filled*, understanding *gazes*, and the will (affection) *unites* with him:

> So the memory, all imperfection past, is *filled (s'empie)* at this breast because it has remembered and held within itself my blessings.
>
> Understanding *(l'intelletto)* receives the light: *gazing (mirando)* into the memory it comes to know the truth, and shedding the blindness of selfish love it remains in the sunlight of Christ crucified [where] it knows both God and humanity. Beyond this knowledge, because of the union [with me] that she has realized, the soul rises to a light acquired not by nature nor by her own practice of virtue but by the grace of my gentle Truth who does not scorn any eager [desire] or labors offered me.
>
> Then [the affection], which follows understanding, *unites* itself [with me] in a most perfect and burning love. And if anyone should ask me what this soul is, I would say: She is another me *(è un altro me)*, made so by the union of love.[290]

This union at the breast is also characterized by peace, calmness, and rest—characteristics that began in the third stage at the kiss of the mouth. Now the soul constantly feels the abiding presence of Christ:

> To such as these it is granted never to feel my absence. I told you how I go away from others (in feeling only, not in grace) and then return. I do not act thus with these most perfect ones who have attained great perfection and are completely dead to every selfish impulse. No, I am always at rest in their souls by both grace and by feeling. In other words, they can join their spirits with me in loving affection

whenever they will. For through loving affection their desire has reached such union that nothing can separate it [from me]. Every time and place is for them a time and place of prayer.²⁹¹

When they reach perfection I relieve them of this lover's game of going and coming back.²⁹²

As wonderful as the experience of union is, it is merely a "pledge" or foretaste in this life of what is to come in the next:

I told you that these souls receive the pledge *(l'arra)* of eternal life. They receive the pledge, I tell you, but not the full payment *(pagamento)*. This they are waiting to receive in me, Life everlasting, where they will have life without death, satiety without boredom, and hunger without pain....²⁹³

The fourth stage is "perfect in grace" but imperfect compared to the soul's union with God in the next life.²⁹⁴ The apostle Paul's experience of being "caught up to the third heaven,"²⁹⁵ which Raymond compares to one of Catherine's own mystical experiences,²⁹⁶ was "the feeling of union" *(sentimento d'unione)* rather than actual union itself. Elsewhere, however, Catherine gives the impression that actual union *is* at least momentarily possible in this life. The eternal Father says:

I told you that all the body's feelings are drawn along by the force of the soul's affection when she is united with me more perfectly than soul is united with body, thus drawing that union into myself. For the body is not capable of bearing such a union constantly. That is why, though I remain in grace and in feeling, I withdraw so far as union is concerned.²⁹⁷

Levitation may occur in this stage when the soul is more united to God than to the body.²⁹⁸ However, for Catherine mystical gifts

"I Tre Stati dell'Anima": *Stages of Spiritual Development*

should never be sought but rather spurned.[299] In fact, the primary proof that one is experiencing the authentic pledge of eternal life in the unitive stage is not in extraordinary gifts but rather in the hunger for the salvation of souls:

> This is how they receive and enjoy the pledge in this life: The soul begins to hunger for the honoring of me, God eternal, and for that good which is the salvation of souls. And because she is hungry she feasts on that charity for her neighbors which she so hungers and longs for, for her neighbors are indeed a food that, when she feeds on it, never satisfies her. She remains insatiably and continually hungry.[300]

This hunger for God's honor and for the salvation of souls continues in heaven where the blessed experience "satiety without boredom, and hunger without pain."[301]

Another image Catherine employs to describe the union of the soul with God is the coal or ember in the fire. We remember that the pilgrim traveler forcefully encountered "the fire of divine charity" at the opened side/heart where God's love is seen, tasted, and experienced.[302] We also recall how Catherine uses the image of fire to show the infinite nature of God's love that cannot be contained in Christ's blood, which is finite.[303] "[I]t is a fire that comes forth from me and carries off their heart and spirit, accepting the sacrifice of their desires."[304] The coal image appears in *Dialogue* 78:

> They [those in the third and fourth stage] are like the burning coal *(tizzone)* that no one can put out once it is completely consumed in the furnace, because it has itself been turned into fire. So it is with these souls cast into the furnace of my charity, who keep nothing at all, not a bit of their own will, outside of me, but are completely set afire in me. There is no one who can seize them or drag them out of my grace. They have been made one with me and I with them.[305]

The soul is united with the fire of divine charity and transformed into it; it is made one with God and becomes fire itself.[306] The will is not eradicated but assumed into the divine will. In letter T137, the soul is now a log *(legno)* and God is the fire that heats it and turns it into himself, giving it his own characteristics:

> I long to see you so totally ablaze with loving fire that you become one with gentle First Truth. Truly the soul's being united with and transformed into him is like fire consuming the dampness in logs. Once the logs are heated through and through, the fire burns and changes them into itself, giving them its own color and warmth and power.[307]

The soul's powers are now "immersed and set afire in me."[308] It "is a fire that converts everything into itself."[309]

Catherine has several expressions for the soul becoming one with God. For example, "*[L]ove transforms one into what one loves.*"[310] All love, as a matter of fact, is *amore unitivo* in that it unites the lover and the beloved.[311] Another saying appears twice in the opening paragraph of the *Dialogue* where we are told that through the soul's union with God "*he makes of her another himself*" (ne fa un'altro sé) or "*another me*" (un altro me).[312] In *Dialogue* 96, in another reference to the soul's union, the eternal Father says: "And if anyone should ask me what this soul is, I would say: She is another me, made so by the union of love."[313] Another saying, found in several places, that pertains to the divinization of the soul is: "*God was made human and humanity was made God.*"[314]

Another image that Catherine uses for the soul's union with God is the peaceful sea *(mare pacifico)*, which itself is an image for the divine Essence,[315] the high eternal Godhead,[316] the Trinity.[317] The peaceful sea is an image that Catherine acquired, as we said in chapter 2,[318] when she saw the sea during her stay in Pisa in 1375. In our earlier consideration of self-knowledge[319] we recall that the soul sees itself reflected in the peaceful sea of which it is an essential part:

"I Tre Stati dell'Anima": *Stages of Spiritual Development*

> This water is a mirror in which you, eternal Trinity, grant me knowledge; for when I look into this mirror, holding it in the hand of love, it shows me myself, as your creation, in you, and you in me....[320]

In the peaceful sea the soul realizes its divine origin and that it is made in God's image and likeness. But the peaceful sea is also an image of the soul's destiny, that of ultimate union with God. Catherine repeatedly invites us to "enter into," "find ourselves," "fill our vessels," in the peaceful sea.[321] She also speaks of the soul's union with it:

> For once souls have risen up in eager [desire], they run in virtue along the bridge of the teaching of Christ crucified and arrive at the gate with their spirits lifted up to me. When they have crossed over and are inebriated with the blood and aflame with the fire of love, they taste in me the eternal Godhead, and I am to them a peaceful sea with which the soul becomes so united *(à fatta tanta unione)* that her [mind] *(mente)* knows no movement but in me. Though she is mortal she tastes the reward of the immortals....[322]

As D'Urso notes, "the soul is completely immersed in God ('and nothing remains outside of me') so much so that he is like its atmosphere, its entire world of thoughts and interests."[323] Catherine's use of the word "taste" *(gustare)* sometimes signifies a pledge or a glimpse in this life of what is to come when the soul separates from the body. The blessed, on the other hand, no longer simply "taste" eternal life but will be totally and definitively immersed in the sea: "They pass through the gate of truth and find themselves in me,"[324] all filled according to their individual capacity.[325]

Because the soul's union with God in this life is a matter of grace it is not a static union but can grow:

> I grant the soul this grace and give her this light to make her continue to grow. For the soul is never so perfect in this

life that it cannot become yet more perfect in love. My beloved Son, your head, was the only one who could not grow in any sort of perfection, because he was one with me and I with him. His soul was beatified in his union with my divine nature. But you, his pilgrim members, can always grow to greater perfection. Not that you would advance to another stage once you had reached that final [state of union with me]. But you can make that very union grow in whatever kind of perfection you choose with the help of my grace.[326]

But I always return with a greater increase of grace and with more perfect union. So it is always with a heightening of my truth that I return, revealing myself to the soul with greater knowledge.[327]

Growth in union, then, involves free will ("in whatever kind of perfection you choose"), the free gift of grace ("the help of my grace"), and a greater knowledge of the truth ("heightening of my truth… greater knowledge").

Growth in union and grace, even at the height of the spiritual life, requires a return to the cell of self-knowledge.

This is that final stage in which the soul is both happy and sorrowful. She is happy because of the union with me that she has felt in experiencing divine love. She is sorrowful because she sees my goodness and greatness offended. For she has seen and tasted that goodness and greatness in knowledge of herself, and it was this self-knowledge that brought her to this final stage….

It is therefore essential that the soul be constant in her charity for her neighbors and in true knowledge of herself. In this way she will feed the flame of my charity within her, because charity for others is drawn from my charity, that is, from the knowledge the soul gained by coming to know herself and my goodness to her, which made her see that I love her unspeakably much.[328]

"I Tre Stati dell'Anima": *Stages of Spiritual Development*

Nor should she rest in her union with me, but rather return to the valley of self-knowledge.³²⁹

As we said before, knowledge of oneself and of God's goodness in oneself, like grace, is also meant to grow.³³⁰

Images of Seeing, Clothing, Filling

It is perhaps not surprising, given her stress on "seeing" and "knowing," that Catherine would describe the fourth stage in identical terms. At the point of union with God, the soul's power of understanding *(intelletto)* "gazes *(specolandosi)* into [God's] Truth."³³¹ She also describes the intellect *(l'occhio de l'intelletto)* as "fixing" or "gazing" on the Truth:

> Having gone by this means, that is, by the teaching of my only-begotten Son, the eye of the intellect fixed *(fermato)* on me, sweet first Truth. Having seen the Truth, it knows it; and knowing it, loves it. Affection, drawn behind the intellect, tastes my eternal Deity in which it knows and sees the divine nature united with your humanity.³³²

> Then the eye of the intellect raises up and gazes *(specolandosi)* into my Deity, where affection, drawn behind the intellect, is nourished and united [with me]. This is a vision through infused grace *(grazia infusa)* that I give to the soul who in truth loves and serves me.³³³

Catherine does not say that there is a face-to-face vision of God in this life but rather a vision of the Truth, or seeing and knowing the Son's divine nature united to our human nature. The beatific vision is reserved for the blessed who have passed through the gate:

> Once, however, the soul is separated from the body, her [desire] is fulfilled and so she loves without suffering. She is sated, but her satiety is far removed from boredom. Though sated she is hungry, but her hunger is far removed

from pain. For once the soul is separated from the body, her vessel is filled up in me in truth, so steadied and strengthened that she can desire nothing but that she has it. Because she deserves to see me, she sees me face to face.[334]

The vision enjoyed by the most perfect in this life is "darksome when compared with the vision the soul has when separated from the body."[335]

The vision experienced in this life by the most perfect is the result of an unprecedented gift of supernatural light *(lume sopranaturale)* that allows one to see, taste, and love the Truth:

I have told you this, my dearest daughter, to let you know the perfection of this unitive state in which souls are carried off by the fire of divine charity. In that charity they receive supernatural light, and in that light they love me. For love follows upon understanding. The more they know, the more they love, and the more they love, the more they know. Thus each nourishes the other. By this light they reach that eternal vision of me in which they see and taste me in truth when the soul is separated from the body.[336]

This "supernatural light and knowledge infused by grace"[337] is given by God and is not acquired by any human effort. It is beyond the ordinary light of faith: "You are the light above all light who gives the [eye of the intellect] supernatural light in such fullness and perfection that you bring clarity even to the light of faith."[338] Those in the fourth stage remain in "this most perfect light."[339]

Although Catherine says more about the fourth stage as union,[340] nonetheless she gives more emphasis to vision in her great hymn of praise at the end of the *Dialogue*:

Now that the soul had seen the truth and the excellence of obedience with the eye of her understanding, and had known it by the light of most holy faith; she had heard it with feeling and tasted it with anguished [desire] in her will as she *gazed* into the divine majesty.[341]

For by the light of understanding within your light, I have tasted and *seen (veduto)* your depth, eternal Trinity, and the beauty of your creation.[342]

In the gradual realization of the final end of the Christ-bridge, the divinization of the human person, Catherine uses some images that pertain neither to union nor vision. Among these is the image of clothing oneself, which appears twice in the first chapter of the *Dialogue* and then appears in various places of the work right through to the final chapter. We have already seen how the process of stripping or undressing oneself of vice is a principal occupation on the first *scalone* and comes to completion in the third. As vice is shed, the pilgrim traveler puts on clothing variously described as virtue, truth, God's will, Christ's teaching, Christ himself, the eternal Father, and, especially, "the wedding garment of charity."

And loving, she seeks to pursue truth and clothe herself in it.[343]

But beyond the beauty I have given the soul by creating her in my image and likeness, look at those who are clothed *(vestiti)* in the wedding garment of charity *(vestimento nuziale della carità)*, adorned with many true virtues: They are united with me through love.[344]

The image of the wedding garment is taken from Matthew 22:1–14, the parable of the marriage feast, where it is a symbol of conversion for the Gospel writer as well as Catherine herself.[345] It is not a spousal image: In the parable, the garment is worn by the guests.

The wedding garment *"of charity"* represents the fact that the soul takes only charity with her into eternal life.[346] In letter T72 we see how clearly Catherine connects the wedding garment with charity:

> You have been called and invited by Christ to the wedding feast of eternal life. But no one should go to that feast not [properly] dressed. So you should be wearing the wedding garment; otherwise you will be expelled from the wedding feast as a wicked servant. It seems to me that gentle First Truth has sent messengers to announce the wedding to you and to bring you the garment. These messengers are the good holy inspirations and sweet desires given you by the Holy Spirit's [clemency]....Let your soul be clothed in love, and with that love you will enter eternal life.[347]

As charity includes every other virtue, Catherine describes the garment or clothing in a variety of ways. Clothing oneself in the wedding garment of charity is, of course, a gradual process and so it is mentioned at each stage of spiritual development.

Another image of the human person's gradual divinization is that of filling. As we have seen, Catherine compares the human person (or the heart or soul) traveling along the Christ-bridge to a vessel that is gradually emptied of transitory things and is then filled, variously, with love, Truth, grace, eternal life.[348] The image bears a parallel to the preceding one of undressing and dressing. In *Dialogue* 89 the vessel is filled with God himself:

> O most beloved daughter, how glorious is the soul who has truly learned to cross the stormy flood to come to me, the peaceful sea! The vessel of her heart is filled *(empito)* with the sea that is my very self, the most high eternal Godhead![349]

Although earlier the soul was united with the peaceful sea, now the vessel of the soul is filled with it.

Moreover, the same term *filled* is also used by Catherine to describe the soul's power of memory as it unites with the Deity: "[T]he memory finds itself filled *(piena)* with nothing but me."[350]

Let us now conclude our detailed consideration of the third *scalone*, the only one that has two stages. The existence of a fourth stage reflects Catherine's originality in that she departs from the traditional schema of the "three ways." Her third and fourth stages are both unitive, the former stressing the unitive love of God in the neighbor and the latter the unitive love of God by way of Jesus Christ's divinity "united with [our] humanity." The two stages are inseparably connected. Few people reach the third *scalone*, although no one is excluded from trying. After all, it is a flowering of the grace received in baptism.

In the third stage the predominant images are the mouth of Christ and the friend who becomes a child. At this stage the friend is more concerned with the Giver than the gift. When one receives the kiss of the mouth, the "war" waged with self-will is over, vice is vanquished, and lasting peace established. There is no longer any internal conflict. The friend spiritually matures into the child, and yet remains a friend.

The child is characterized by selfless service to the Father, by being an heir to the Father's wealth, by belonging to God's family, and by a firm and stable bond with him. At this stage the virtues conceived in the second stage are "born" in the lives of our neighbor, who is loved in the same selfless way. The soul now loves others even if not loved itself[351] and is consumed with God's honor and the salvation of souls. Suffering holds no fear. In fact, the soul actually glories in suffering. At this high stage one becomes "another Christ" and takes on his office as an instrument of mediation between humanity and God. Arising from concern for God's honor and the salvation of souls is another concern: the reform of the church.

A continuation and intensification of the third stage, the fourth stage is its "fruit." It is primarily a pledge or foretaste in this life of the beatitude of eternal life. As such, it is basically indescribable, although Catherine uses images to convey something of its essential reality. She frequently speaks of *uniting, seeing, clothing,* and *filling* to describe this. It is an experience in which the soul "tastes within herself the divine nature." With the assistance of the gift of supernatural light, one can clearly "see" the Truth. Further illustration of this unitive stage is derived from the images of the infant nursing at the breast and of the coal becoming one with the fire. In the fourth and unitive stage the soul never feels God's absence, continuously united with him through feeling and grace. The experience of union can grow and demands a return to the cell of self-knowledge. As the soul gradually becomes divinized, the Father's will is realized and the soul becomes "another [himself]."

Patience and the "hunger for souls" (craving for the salvation of others) indicate whether one has truly arrived at this stage. Mystical gifts like levitation and prophecy may be given, but they are not important and should never be sought. The soul longs for death in order to "pass through the gate" at the end of the bridge.

It is only charity that one takes into the next life. It is only charity that fosters progress: "You are rewarded not according to your work or your time but according to the measure of your love."[352] The blessed, who in their "humanity will be conformed *(si conformerà)* to the humanity of the Word and will delight *(diletterà)* in it,"[353] will see God's face and be united to him in proportion to their love. Then the final end of the Christ-bridge will be fully realized: *"You will all be like him in joy and gladness."*[354]

Catherine's Life in Relation to Her Teaching

In chapter 1 we traced the development of Catherine's spiritual life as reflected in her actions, mystical experiences, and her own words during various periods of her life: her childhood and the years in the "cell" (c. 1363–67); her work in and around Siena (c. 1367–75); and the last five years of her life spent beyond Siena (1375–80). Since Catherine's spiritual thought must have flowed, to a certain extent, from her own experience, and because she herself insisted that "[b]y these *[scaloni]* you must go if you would have me with you,"[355] we now ask whether her own life bears any correspondence

"I Tre Stati dell'Anima": *Stages of Spiritual Development*

to her teaching on stages of spiritual development that we have just considered.

It is not an easy question to answer for several reasons. First, there is obviously a difference between Catherine's actual life and the biographical record of it that in many cases is in the genre of medieval hagiography. In any biographical record there are events that go unrecorded. Moreover, it is impossible to provide a correct and absolute interpretation of the significance of the events that *are* recorded.[356] The most we can do is to recognize that our conclusions are based—however unsatisfactorily—on the biographical record.

Second, Catherine's life was utterly extraordinary. She had her first vision at the age of six and, soon thereafter, levitated in a cave on the outskirts of Siena. At first glance it seems that Catherine's life was so exceptional that it could bear no possible resemblance to her actual teaching on spiritual development. However, at this point of my research I will demonstrate my convinced opinion that there is in fact a *general* correspondence between the life and teaching of Catherine of Siena.

It must be admitted that Catherine's many and varied mystical experiences (especially her first vision, mystical espousals, drinking at the opened side, exchange of hearts, mystical death, and stigmata) pose a serious challenge to any hypothesis concerning *stages* in her life.[357] We agree, however, with D'Urso, who says that these events "demonstrate the generosity of the Lord, but do not always reveal that which the Spirit has done inside of her, nor the grade of perfection she attained."[358] This in fact will be our guiding principle regarding the relation between Catherine's mystical experiences and her actual stages of spiritual development.

Of course it is not possible to examine in detail the entire biographical record vis-à-vis every point of possible correspondence with her teaching on the stages of spiritual development.

Catherine of Siena

Childhood Experiences: The Invitation to Ascend the Christ-Bridge

Catherine's first vision at the age of six, the vision of the royal Christ, had such a tremendous impact on her that, as Caffarini says, it "transformed her entire life."[359] It was, in a sense, Christ's invitation to her to ascend the bridge of his crucified body. The vision was an attraction of love to which she responded in love. Years later, in her own teaching, Catherine would say that progress on the Christ-bridge is the result of love's attraction. To this end we recall her interpretation of John 12:32:

> In this way he drew everything to himself: for he proved his unspeakable love, and the human heart is always drawn by love....
>
> So my Truth indeed spoke truly when he said, "If I am lifted up high, I will draw everything to myself." For everything you do will be drawn to him when he draws your heart and its powers.[360]

This experience left her "thirsty" and desirous to be in an eternal communion of love with God. In her teaching she would later insist on the necessity of such thirst in order to persevere in the spiritual journey.[361]

There was a weakening in Catherine's resolve when, around the age of fifteen, she chose to listen to her beloved older sister Buonaventura and agreed to pay more attention to her appearance. Buonaventura's sudden death brought Catherine back to her original intention in a traumatic way. It was an experience that may be reflected in her teaching on "the four winds" that God sends for our spiritual well-being:

> While the wind of fear is battering them the wind of trouble and adversity (the very thing they feared) joins in and takes away their possessions, sometimes this thing or that, sometimes life itself, when the power of death deprives

them of everything. Sometimes, though, it takes only now one thing, now another: health, children, riches, position, honor—whatever I the gentle doctor see to be necessary for their salvation and so allow it to happen.[362]

The experience taught her to listen always to God and to seek to please him alone instead of any person. After this, Catherine took the radical step of cutting off her hair and boldly addressing her family, telling them of her vow of virginity and the irreversibility of her decision. With these two actions, Catherine firmly put her "two feet" on the Christ-bridge and never turned back.

The little "community" of girls that she gathered around her after her first vision, together with her attraction to the Order of Preachers with its emphasis on the salvation of souls, reveals the incipient and firm emphasis on others that would subsequently emerge more clearly in her later life and in her teaching.[363]

In the Cell (c. 1363–67): First and Second Scaloni

This period of Catherine's life and spiritual development corresponds generally to her teaching regarding the first and second *scaloni*.

In the cell Catherine clearly underwent a period of purification typical of the first *scalone*. Her purpose was to achieve complete dominion over her nature, both body and soul, so as to remove all selfish self-love. During this period she developed her profound teaching on the "cell of self-knowledge," one of the fundamental tenets of her entire doctrine. Perhaps her experience in the cell is reflected in her later statement, "It is impossible to keep one's mind pure while indulging in [much conversation] *(molta coversazione)*, bodily delicacy, and inordinate eating without watching and prayer."[364] It may have been during this time that the Lord revealed to Catherine her "hidden sickness" of judging others, particularly priests, "under the pretext of working for [God's] honor and their salvation."[365] Although there is absolutely no evidence of her ever having servile fear, her extreme reluctance to leave the cell for fear of losing consolations betrays an element of mercenary love that is typical of the pilgrim traveler on the first *scalone*.

The cell is also, it seems, where her experience reflected that of the pilgrim traveler on the second *scalone*. It was a time of enlightenment and divine visitation in which, among other things, various principles of the spiritual life were revealed to her, especially the fundamental maxim: "You are she who is not, and I AM HE WHO IS,"[366] which would become the cornerstone of her spiritual doctrine. On this second *scalone* her attention is drawn more to God than to herself. Her experience of the loss of divine consolations is subsequently reflected with clarity in the *Dialogue* where Catherine asserts the importance of perseverance during such deprivations and insists that love for God is never indicated by the enjoyment of spiritual pleasures. During this period in the cell she experienced the "mystical espousals" and, according to Raymond of Capua, was "called on by [the Lord] to bear children to him in the spirit."[367] In other words, it was at this time that she "conceived" the virtues for her neighbors, indicative of the second *scalone*. In Catherine's momentous decision to obey the Lord and leave her cell we see the triumph of her love of God over selfish self-love. The second *scalone* at which Catherine had so clearly arrived, albeit incompletely, was brought to completion in the next stage of her life.

Siena and Its Environs (c. 1367–75): Completion of the Second Scalone*; Third* Scalone

In 1370 Catherine, as far as the record indicates, had her first mystical experience of drinking at the opened side of Christ, an image that would become prominent in the *Dialogue* vis-à-vis the second *scalone*. In retrospect, the significance of the experience can be interpreted in Catherine's own teaching on the opened side/ heart, which she calls a "re-baptism" by which we are re-created by divine love.[368] In the biographical accounts Catherine primarily experiences the opened side as a channel of grace. Baptism (or "re-baptism") fashions a "new heart,"[369] and so a few weeks after

"I Tre Stati dell'Anima": *Stages of Spiritual Development*

drinking at the opened side the "mystical exchange of hearts" occurs, after which she tells her confessor, "[I] am no longer the same person, but have become totally transformed."[370] Her condition now is perhaps that described in *Dialogue* 60: "This is how it is with very dear friends. Their loving affection makes them two bodies with one soul."[371] It was also after drinking at the opened side that she was given the gift of prophecy, another characteristic of the second *scalone*,[372] and her future apostolate of more intensive labors for the salvation of souls is foretold.[373]

Characteristics of the third *scalone* (both its third and fourth stages) begin to appear at this point in her life. After emerging from her cell, she gives "birth" to the virtues in her neighbors by performing various corporal works of mercy for people in and around Siena that reach their climax in her "hiding herself in the wounds" and "drinking at the opened side" of the aged Mantellata Andrea. Caffarini records that during one of Catherine's experiences of drinking at Christ's opened side he "embraced her and kissed her, giving her peace. So she always had an inexpressible tranquility and peace."[374] As we know, the mouth of Christ is where the kiss of peace is received, a characteristic image of the third *scalone*.

There are other characteristics of the third *scalone* during this phase of Catherine's life. Caffarini says she levitated many times after receiving holy communion.[375] Raymond records an incident deserving of attention:

> Then, when she had received the sacrament, she felt her soul enter into God, and God into her soul, in the same way as a fish in the sea is in the water, and the water is in the fish. All drawn in and gripped by God, she could barely totter home to her tiny cell. Once there, she sank down and lay motionless on that bed of boards which I described earlier. Then, after a long time, her body found itself raised aloft into the air, and remained suspended, without any material support. This took place in the presence of three witnesses....[376]

Catherine of Siena

The incident recorded by Raymond of Capua is strikingly similar to Catherine's teaching in the *Dialogue:*

> She found herself eager for the next day's Mass—it would be Mary's day—because in communion the soul seems more sweetly bound to God and better knows his truth. For then the soul is in God and God in the soul, just as the fish is in the sea and the sea in the fish.[377]

In *Dialogue* 142, we read another description of one of her experiences of levitation that occurred when, after much longing, she was not able to receive the sacrament. In this passage the eternal Father tells Catherine that levitation is characteristic of the unitive stage (fourth stage).

> Then I who exalt the humble drew to myself this soul's love and [desire] and gave her knowledge in the abyss of the Trinity, myself, God eternal.... That soul was so perfectly united with me that her body was lifted up from the earth, because in the unitive stage I am telling you about, the union of the soul with me through the impulse of love is more perfect than her union with her body. And in this great abyss, to satisfy her [desire], she received holy communion from me.[378]

As we have seen in this chapter, Catherine uses the image of clothing, particularly "the wedding garment of charity," for the gradual divinization of the human person and as a pledge of future glory. It is not impossible that the image is linked to one of her own mystical experiences in which the Lord gave her a scarlet dress:

> With that he drew out from the scar of the wound on his side, a dress of blood-red colour, refulgent with rays of light and made to measure for Catherine herself. With his own hands he clothed her in it, saying: "This dress, with all it stands for, I give you as your own while you are still on earth. It is the

"I Tre Stati dell'Anima": *Stages of Spiritual Development*

sign and the pledge of the garment of glory with which, when the time comes, you will be clothed in heaven."[379]

Years later she would write, "It is the blood that gives us patience and clothes us in the wedding garment we need to enter eternal life."[380]

Caffarini says that frequently while praying Catherine would laugh and cry.[381] In the *Dialogue*, simultaneous feelings of happiness and sadness are characteristics of the unitive stage:

> This is that final state in which the soul is both happy and sorrowful. She is happy because of the union with me that she has felt in experiencing divine love. She is sorrowful because she sees my goodness and greatness offended.[382]

Also characteristic of souls in the unitive stage is the desire for death and union with God, concern for God's honor and the salvation of souls, and mystical experiences that are indescribable. Similarly Catherine longed to die and be completely united with the Lord.[383] In the mystical death she experienced in the summer of 1370, Catherine's focus on the honor of God and the salvation of souls is intensified when she is commanded by the Lord to return to life because the salvation of souls demanded it. God also told her that she must, for the salvation of souls, leave Siena and appear before popes and rulers.[384] In *Dialogue* 76 Catherine relates the mouth, the image of the third scalone on the body of Christ, with "eating souls."[385] Mystical experiences at this stage are largely indescribable; when Raymond of Capua asked her what she saw during her mystical death, Catherine said, "[M]y memory no longer can recall all that I saw, nor would words suffice to express it."[386]

Beyond Siena (1375–80): Growing in More Perfect Union[387]

This last period in Catherine's life exemplifies her teaching on the reality of growing in perfect union with the Lord. As the eternal Father once said to her:

I always return with a greater increase of grace and with more perfect union. So it is always with a heightening *(con più altezza)* of my truth that I return, revealing myself to the soul with greater knowledge.[388]

And the perfection of the perfect is augmented and made to grow, because they are prepared to grow....[389]

This period of her life witnesses an increased intensity of her experience of the unitive stage of the third *scalone*, especially its fourth unitive stage, an intensity best regarded as the further fruition of her "re-baptism" at the opened side. Her dedication to the honor of God and salvation of souls becomes more resolute and profound. Significantly, it is during this period that her love of God results in a more intense concern for the reform of the church. "Her love of Jesus expands, grows insatiable, infinite, is transformed into love of His Mystical Body."[390] This period of her life is almost perfectly reflected in *Dialogue* 133 when the eternal Father tells her: "[B]e humbly attentive to my honor, the salvation of souls, and the reform of holy Church. This will be a sign to me that you and the others love me in truth."[391] During this time Catherine wrote to her mother Lapa and urged her to seek God's honor and the salvation of souls, adding, "Understand, dearest mother, that I your poor daughter have been put on this earth for no other purpose; this is what my Creator has chosen me for."[392]

Her entry into this new phase "beyond Siena" begins with her journey to Pisa early in 1375.[393] Not too long after her arrival on April 1, she received the invisible stigmata. It was as if the Lord was showing her that a completely new chapter of her life was about to begin. She herself is now "crucified" and thus takes on the "office of Christ" as an "instrument of mediation," indicative of her further growth in perfect union with the Lord. The significance of the event is demonstrated in *Dialogue* 146:

And the perfection of the perfect is augmented and made to grow, because they are prepared to grow, and I want to

"I Tre Stati dell'Anima": *Stages of Spiritual Development*

make of them good and perfect [instruments of mediation] *(mezzi)* for those who are at war with me. For I have already told you, if you recall, that it is by means of my servants and their great sufferings that I would be merciful to the world and reform my bride.

Truly these last can be called *another Christ crucified*, my only begotten-Son, because they have taken [his office] *(l'officio)* upon themselves. He came as a mediator *(tramezzatore)* to put an end to the war and reconcile humanity to me in peace by suffering even to the shameful death of crucifixion. *In the same way must these be crucified and become [instruments of mediation]* in prayer, in word, in good holy living, setting themselves up as examples to others.[394]

Further light is shed on the meaning the stigmata had for her in *Dialogue* 78:

Such souls [in the fourth stage] glory in the shame of my only-begotten Son, as my trumpeter *(banditore)* the glorious Paul said: "I glory in the hardships and the shame of Christ crucified." And in another place he says, "I bear in my body the [stigmata] *(stimate)* of Christ crucified." So these also run to the table of the most holy cross, in love with my love and hungry for the food of souls. They want to be of service to their neighbor in pain and suffering, and to learn and preserve the virtues while bearing the [stigmata] *(stimate)* of Christ in their bodies. In other words, their [crucified love] *(crociato amore)* shines forth in their bodies, evidenced in their contempt for themselves and in their delight in shame as they endure difficulties and suffering however and from whatever source I grant them.[395]

Here the stigmata is associated with "crucified love": love of neighbor to the point of suffering, following the example of the apostle Paul. It is "the wounds received in the persecutions endured for the love of Christ and the good of souls."[396] Such willingness to glory in suffering for the sake of the gospel is a characteristic of those in the highest stage of spiritual perfection.

On the first anniversary of the stigmata, Catherine had the remarkable "investiture vision" in which she enters into the opened side of Christ with all people of the world, believers and unbelievers alike. The Lord puts a cross on her shoulder and an olive branch in her hand and tells her to carry them to Christians and unbelievers, saying, "I am bringing you news of great joy." The vision is described in letter T219 to Raymond of Capua. After describing it, Catherine tells Raymond that she is now ready to give herself completely "to seeking God's honor, the salvation of souls, *and the renewal and exaltation of holy Church*" for the rest of her life.[397] Of all the accounts of Catherine's visions, this is the only one that seems to complement her very first vision of the royal Christ. In that first vision, Christ *blessed* her as if to bestow a mission on her; twenty-three years later she is invested with a universal mission. The "investiture vision" is Catherine's only known mystical experience in which Christ explicitly gives her a share in his office. The vision is also a fulfillment of the experience of the stigmata insofar as those with "crucified love" are to share in Christ's office and be "other Christs." The stigmata and investiture vision reflect an intensification of Catherine's love of Christ and the church and of her concern for God and the salvation of souls, which in turn manifests the reality of further growth in her perfect union with God.

The office that Catherine was given was that of conversion (the cross) and peacemaking (the olive branch); it was not to be exercised just in Italy or Avignon but universally, among "believers and unbelievers," for the sake of God's honor, the salvation of souls, and the reform of the church. The universal dimension of genuine love of God is reflected in *Dialogue* 7: "[T]he soul in love with my truth never ceases doing service for all the world, universally and in particular."[398] Peacemaking can be associated with the "kiss of the mouth," the kiss of peace, which is experienced at the third *scalone*.

The climax of Catherine's entire life was her final mystical experience in which she offered her life for the reform of the

"I Tre Stati dell'Anima": *Stages of Spiritual Development*

church. It took place on January 29, 1380, exactly three months before her death, and is recounted in letter T371:

> "O eternal God, receive the sacrifice of my life into this mystical body of holy Church. I have nothing to give except what you have given me, so take my heart and squeeze it out over the face of the Bride." Then, turning [to me] the eye of his Loving-kindness, God eternal plucked out my heart and squeezed it out into holy Church.[399]

"Washing the face of the Church" is an image also found in the *Dialogue* where, instead of the heart's blood, "tears and sweat" are mentioned: "Bring, then, your tears and your sweat, you and my other servants. Draw them from the fountain of my divine love and use them to wash the face of my bride. I promise you that thus her beauty will be restored."[400]

In conclusion, we have seen how there is indeed a general correspondence between Catherine's own spiritual development as indicated in the biographical sources (including the autobiographical portions of her writings) and her teaching on spiritual growth and the various stages. We have seen how some of her experiences are most definitely elements of her teaching: the stripping of self-love, the cell of self-knowledge, the experience of consolations and the painful loss of same, the mercenary love of consolations, the opened side and breast, the kiss of the mouth, the clothing with a garment, and various unitive experiences.

Notably and generally absent in the *Dialogue* and Catherine's other writings are explicit references to many of her major mystical experiences such as the mystical espousals, exchange of hearts, mystical death, and stigmata.[401] Absent from the biographical sources is any mention of Catherine ever having servile fear or coming out of the "river of sin," two important elements of her later teaching. The absence of such is no doubt related to the purpose of hagiography: to edify.

Catherine's various mystical experiences, which started when she was a child, seem to contradict any theory of stages of spiritual

Catherine of Siena

development in her life. On the other hand, a definitive interpretation of these experiences vis-à-vis Catherine's interiority or the stage of her perfection is impossible.[402] However, we can say with certainty that her major mystical experiences preceded, provoked, or confirmed new passages in Catherine's life. D'Urso notes:

> [T]he principal turning points of her life were preceded or provoked by an ecstasy which came to indicate new passages, new horizons for her interior journey or her apostolic activity. The ecstasies were a determinative moment in her practical decisions and of her mystical ascension, more intuitive than active. This is a rule almost constant in her life.... These visions, which could be called "operative," signal the developments of her apostolically active conscience and demonstrate the journey of her spirit, its advancements, the tone of her decisions, which are therefore promoted and orientated under the sign of grace; they also confirm her more or less conscious desires and impulses.[403]

We note that the biographical accounts of her mystical experiences almost always describe these experiences with reference to serving "the other," particularly in relation to service involved in the salvation of souls. For example, during her mystical espousals she is prepared for her later work for the sake of others when the Lord tells her that henceforth she is to accept any task given to her. After the mystical exchange of hearts she has a boundless love for her neighbor for whom she is prepared to do anything. At her mystical death she is commanded to return to life and work for the salvation of souls and is told that it would take her out of Siena. The stigmata signaled her entrance into the passion and death of Christ for the salvation of sinners. Interestingly, Catherine hardly mentions her extraordinary mystical experiences in her teaching on spiritual development.

> All through her life she was the recipient of extraordinary manifestations of God's love: revelations, ecstasies, visions,

exchange of hearts, stigmata, mystical marriage. In her life, as written by her first biographers, we read many stories about these various mystical experiences. However, she never saw these extraordinary experiences as essential to a deep life of prayer. For her, the way to an authentic relationship with God was the "ordinary" way of faith, hope and love. Her relationship with God manifested a quality of great simplicity.[404]

Indeed, Catherine puts no emphasis on mystical experiences in her teaching on spiritual development.

It is possible that Catherine's mystical experiences, which generally are indicative of the unitive stage and yet occurred in all the stages of her own spiritual development, exemplify Catherine's own statement in the *Dialogue*, "These three stages that can be and are in many creatures and are in the same creature"[405] in the sense that all the stages "are commingled and each has its place in all the stages of the spiritual life."[406] That Catherine's mystical experiences occurred in the different stages of her own spiritual development may be an example of the "commingling" of stages might also be reflected in her statement that souls in the unitive stage need to return to the "valley of self-knowledge."[407] In other words, even in the unitive stage one must return to the first stage of purgation.

Conclusion

This, then, is Catherine of Siena's teaching on spiritual stages. However, as we said earlier, she is not a "fanatic" about a system.[408] Within these stages of spiritual development there is tremendous latitude owing to the individuality of each person, the uniqueness of each person's call, and God's infinite nature; no one goes along the Christ-bridge in quite the same way as others.[409] Catherine herself says this in the *Dialogue*:

> These [souls who have clothed themselves in God's will] enjoy everything, and have not made themselves judges of

my servants, or of any creature who has reason, but also enjoy every state and every way they see, saying: "Thanks be to you, eternal Father, that in your house there are many mansions." And they enjoy more the different ways they see, than if they had seen everyone go one way, because seeing it manifests more the greatness of my goodness. In everything they enjoy and find the fragrance of the rose.[410]

This passage has an autobiographical ring to it undoubtedly borne out of Catherine's own suffering caused by the false judgment of those who did not appreciate her unusual way of life. The singular quality of her own life may have caused her to reflect on the fact that her teaching on the spiritual stages could apply to everyone only in a broad way, that within each stage there is an infinite number of variations owing to the individuality of the human person and God's infinite nature and freedom.[411] If her teaching on the stages of spiritual development is only reflected in a general way in the biographical sources of her own life, it is, in part, because the same could be said of *everyone*.

> [T]here is no absolute pattern of coming to the fullness of life in Christ but...each individual experiences purgation, illumination, and union within the uniqueness of her or her own mysterious call to holiness. The freedom of the God who calls and the freedom of the person who responds constitute an essential horizon for any interpretation of the three ways.[412]

The uniqueness of each person's journey to God, spiritual development, is reflected in the eternal Father's advice to Catherine in *Dialogue* 104: "Reprove yourself if ever the devil or your own short-sightedness should do you the disservice of making you want to force all my servants to [go] by the same [way] *(via)* you yourself follow."[413]

Every human being is made in the image and likeness of God, but that image and likeness is found in the unique individual just

"I Tre Stati dell'Anima": *Stages of Spiritual Development*

as the biological children of a human father bear his likeness and yet are unique. When the pilgrim traveler becomes a "child" at the third *scalone*, it is as a *unique* child of God who is a "pilgrim member" *(peregrino membro)* of the body of Christ.[414] There is nothing uniform about the manner of our union with God; it is multiple and personalized.[415] Each person is "perfect" and will thus be perfectly united with God in a unique way. This could be what Catherine is saying in *Dialogue* 89: "Not that you would advance to another stage once you had reached that final [state of union with me]. *But you can make that very union grow in whatever perfection you choose with the help of my grace.*"[416]

With this in mind, let us consider some of the characteristics of Catherine's teaching on stages of spiritual development.

Catherine bases all spiritual development on the growth of one virtue, charity. Each stage represents a deepening of charity as the person moves toward greater interior unicity and union with God. Growth in charity entails greater knowledge of self and of the truth of God. The blood of Christ gives us the most knowledge of such truth. As long as faith and reason are not blinded by selfishness and we are "thirsty," have the desire, we will see the truth and then, with this knowledge, will love Truth more and more. Gradually, we are transformed into what we love and God makes of us "another himself."

Self-knowledge is at the beginning and end of each stage.[417] The "process" of self-knowledge mirrors the stages; it is a "miniature three stages." The exercise of self-knowledge, with its various moments as we identified them in chapter 2,[418] is a kind of passing through the three *scaloni*: knowledge of ourselves, knowledge of God, and union. We see this partially in letter T104 when Catherine speaks of "the night of self-knowledge, which is a sort of moonlight. And after this knowledge of ourselves comes the day, with the great light and warmth of the sun."[419] In fact, we would go so far as to say that Catherine's teaching on spiritual stages is, in one sense, an elaboration of her doctrine of self-knowledge.

Catherine reminds us that spiritual progress, at every stage, is by means of the neighbor. There is a consistent emphasis on "the other" in her teaching, especially in her repeated teaching on virtue (which is nonexistent until it is expressed in our relationships with others), as being the primary indicator of the authenticity of our love of God. Mystical experiences and emotions, on the other hand, are usually not reliable indicators—*unless* they result in an increase in virtue.[420] In Catherine's teaching, as well as her life, we see the same concern for the salvation of souls, reform of the church, and, toward the end of her life, her readiness to embark on a universal mission of faith and peace to "believers and unbelievers." G. Getto remarks:

> There is also in Catherine the absence of that solitary atmosphere, closed, individualistic, which is usually found with the concept of mystical marriage. In such currents of religious experience there is, in the end, never more than two protagonists: the soul on one side and God on the other. It is a drama in which voices other than these two are not raised, and in which everything is reduced to an incessant song between the two. On the other hand, in Catherine there is a view which is more ample, like a choir with different notes. There is not only God, not only the saint, but alongside there is also the neighbor, the Church, and the whole world.[421]

Catherine's teaching reflects a deep assimilation of divine truth and its application in a personal way to the daily life of ordinary people. As we have seen, she often borrows images and elements from others but, once having done so, "she continues to develop each idea in her own way and to integrate it uniquely into her own theological tapestry."[422] As the first censor noted in the *"positio"* in preparation for Catherine's proclamation as doctor of the church:

> When truths or doctrines have been personally assimilated, when traditional elements borrowed consciously or unconsciously, directly or indirectly, have passed through a temperament whose personal spontaneity illumined by grace

"I Tre Stati dell'Anima": *Stages of Spiritual Development*

imposes a new order on them, one can say that such teaching is truly personal.... If what she says comes from a common spring of Christian verities, the insistent accents she places on certain of these give her work an original tone that is very much her own.[423]

In Catherine's teaching we recognize many "old" truths of the catechism, but she proposes them as living truths for the present. She has a gift for cutting right to the heart of things: Sin is selfishness, serving God out of fear or for the sake of the pleasure is also selfishness, we love God in the same way we love our neighbor, and so forth. Catherine has an "intuitive grasp of what is essential in the Christian life, and flowing from that, her ability to offer new depths of insight into the central Christian message of God's love for humanity in Jesus Christ."[424]

We have also seen in this chapter how much of Catherine's teaching on the stages of spiritual development is actually inspired by scripture. For example, progress over the bridge, and the bridge itself, she explains in terms of John 12:32, "And I, when I am lifted up from the earth, will draw all people to myself." The images of the "servant," "friend," and "child" are all found, as we have seen, in the New Testament. The transition from servant to friend is inspired by John 15:15, and, as we have shown, her use of the image of "child" instead of spousal imagery is profoundly consistent with the New Testament message. The images of the opened side, the breast, the mouth, and the gate are also taken from scripture.[425] We need not mention the numerous allusions to scriptural passages.

Catherine's spiritual-theological outlook is very positive and optimistic. Her repeated emphasis on the human person as made in the image and likeness of God, a reality that even original sin did not substantially alter, is a fine example of this positive attitude as is the possibility of, indeed humanity's *vocation* to, divinization, to be "another God." We have a glimpse into this facet of her personality and teaching when, after describing the "investiture vision" to Raymond of Capua, she ends by saying: "Then I was marvelously happy. I was so confident about the future that it seemed I was already possessing and enjoying it."[426]

The very heart and purpose of the Christ-bridge and its *scaloni* are seen in the account by Raymond of Capua of what the Lord once said to Catherine in her cell:

> And since I in the beginning created man to my own image and likeness, and afterwards took your image on myself by assuming human nature, it is always my endeavour, in so far as you are fit for it, *to intensify that likeness between me and you*. What took place in my own body at the resurrection, I am ever working to bring about in your own souls, even here below.[427]

The necessity of ascending the bridge and its *scaloni* can be seen when, years later, the Lord again spoke to Catherine:

> It is as if this gentle loving Word, my Son, were saying to you: "Look, I have made the road and opened the gate for you with my blood. *Do not fail, then, to follow it.*"[428]

Conclusion

We have examined the principal tenets of Catherine's doctrine as they pertain to spiritual development as well as her teaching concerning the stages of the spiritual journey. We have seen how her own spiritual development, as described in the biographical sources, generally corresponds with her teaching. We now ask: What is the *fundamental* message of Catherine's teaching and life?

Catherine's Teaching

Mystics often illuminate particular aspects of revelation afresh and make certain accepted but neglected truths astonishingly clear.[1] Such is the case with Catherine of Siena. She has several illuminating key ideas that recur in the course of her writings. These are sayings or teachings that play an important role in her spiritual thought and, when considered together, constitute the fundamental message of her teaching:

- The human person is made in the image and likeness of God and, though wounded by the original fall, fundamentally reflects the divine beauty. Made out of love and for love, we cannot live without it and want always to love. Only something greater than ourselves can ultimately satisfy our craving to love. The only thing greater than ourselves is God himself.

- The blood of the God-man reveals to us in the most indubitable way the radical, self-sacrificing love of God for us. This knowledge of God's unfathomable love causes us to love him in return. The more we know him, the more we love him. To love God is to love what he loves and hate what he hates. In particular, God loves people; in loving him, we likewise love others. The extent to which we actually love God is mirrored in our relationship with our neighbor, and vice versa.

- "Love transforms one into what one loves."[2] As we grow, by stages, in our knowledge and love of God, Christ is "born" in us through grace, a participation in God's life.[3] Just as our knowledge and love of God increase, so does his presence in us. As the divine presence develops in us, our humanity is more and more conformed to Jesus' humanity and we share in his divinity.[4] We become *supernatural* images and likenesses of God who, at the point of ultimate resemblance with the Deity, are transformed into him and united with him.[5] The "gentle loving Word" then will say of us: "[T]hey are another me."[6] At death, we pass into the "peaceful sea" where we are completely immersed in God.

One important truth that can be deduced from the fundamental message of Catherine's teaching pertains to the study of theology. Although she was unlettered, Catherine had great regard for the intellect and knowledge. There was no such thing for her as theoretical or neutral knowledge of God. Knowledge of God, she would insist, is *always* transformative. Catherine asserts that genuine knowledge of God, if it is to be complete and life-giving, requires our being in a love relationship with him. This has important implications for theologians as Foster notes:

> It is at once paradoxical and strangely appropriate that the Order that is doctrinal par excellence, whose motto is Truth and special concern is theology, should have come to see in this young unlettered woman so authentic a representative of what it essentially stands for. Catherine is the supreme witness in our [Dominican] history, and perhaps in all Christian history, to the charismatic nature of Christian wisdom, *to the truth that intellectual growth in the faith comes, essentially, from a love-union with Christ,* and so from the Holy Spirit who "gives to

Conclusion

each one as he wills" for the common good of the Church. One can hardly think of her without recalling the great texts on this matter of her master St. Paul; especially, perhaps I Corinthians 1:18—2:16 and 12:4–11. No one better than St Catherine can teach us, by example even more than precept, that in theology the root of the matter is not a professional technique (however useful this may be) but docility to the Spirit: *non solum discens sed et patiens divina* [*ST* II–II, 45, 2].[7]

Catherine's great regard for knowledge did not prevent her from being critical of learned people who rejected the "supernatural light" of grace and "never understood learning [*scienzia*] because the horns of pride kept them from understanding its sweet marrow (*merollo*)."[8] Overattachment to self in the form of pride prevents us from seeing the truth about ourselves and God. The "knowledge" that is attainable in such circumstances is at best incomplete and defective; such people, Catherine says, know only the surface or "outer rind" instead of the "marrow." Fra' Bartolomeo Dominici, in his deposition for Catherine's canonization process, relates a particular incident he had personally witnessed, when she helped a well-known Franciscan theologian to go beyond superficial knowledge or the "outer rind" of scripture:

> Among the principal persecutors of the virgin [Catherine] there was a certain Fra' Lazzarino da Pisa of the Order of the Friar Minors, who at that time, in Siena, was a professor in philosophy in the convent of his order and who enjoyed great fame not only for his intelligence and speech but also for his sermons with which the people were very pleased. He, hearing how the fame and good odor of sanctity of the virgin were spreading through the city, prompted by envy, looked for a way to belittle her fame either secretly with his confreres or in public with outsiders. And he was so inflamed with zeal that he not only hated the virgin but also her friends. So also myself, who at that time taught in the convent the *Sentences* [of Peter Lombard], he tried in every

way to make me to be hated by the students, especially when, as we used to do, we would come together in a single room for disputations. But having tried denigrating her and having obtained nothing, and, on the contrary, the fame of her sanctity increased, he decided to denigrate her as much as he could in his public sermons before the people. And since not even in this way did he obtain good results, he had recourse to a cunning trick: to visit her, that is, apparently for devotion but in reality to take her by surprise through her words and actions so as to find something that he could use against her with the law.

Therefore on the vigil before the feast of the blessed virgin and martyr Catherine [of Alexandria], he came to my cell toward evening and begged me to conduct him to Catherine for a discussion. I, believing him to be really conscience stricken, and with the permission of her confessor Fra' Tommaso della Fonte, accompanied him. So we went into the cell of the virgin, and Fra' Lazzarino sat on top of a chest, she sat at his feet on the floor, and I stood opposite. For some time both were quiet. Finally he stood up and said, "Having heard so much about the fame of your sanctity and knowing you to be supplied by the Lord of the virtue to comprehend sacred scripture, I came gladly to hear some edifying words and, at the same time, consoling words for my soul." To this she replied, "At your arrival I instead rejoiced, believing that the Lord had sent you so that you, possessing the knowledge of sacred scripture with which souls are nourished every day, moved by charity, would console my poor little soul."

The time passed with such discourses and it was nearly approaching night, the friar, not having been able to trap her as he had thought to do, still thinking that she was a poor little woman and despising her, said, "I see that it's late and I believe that it would be better to go; I will come back again at a more suitable time." And he stood up to go away.

Conclusion

The virgin followed him and knelt down with her arms folded and asked him for the blessing, obtained it immediately, and begged him to keep her in his prayers. Then, more through shame than devotion, he asked her to pray for him, which the virgin promised to do gladly. So the friar went off with some regard for her, but thinking that she was not worthy of the fame that was heaped on her.

The following night, getting up early to prepare the lecture that he usually gave in the morning to his pupils, there immediately began to flow from his eyes copious tears such that, as much as he dried them, so much more they multiplied and came down abundantly. The friar was amazed and he examined himself for the cause of so much weeping but was not able to find any. And he was uncertain that what happened was from excessive drink the evening before or because he had slept with his head uncovered, but neither of the two seemed to him to be the true cause. Meanwhile, time flew and the usual hour of the class approached. The pupils were calling the master to come to the classroom. Bracing himself as much as he could, he quickly went to the classroom and, after having given the lecture with diligence and exactness, he left immediately because he wasn't able to hold back the tears. He entered his cell, let open the floodgate of tears, and was crying clamorously, angry at himself, when he began to harshly reproach himself, saying, "What ails me? What do I want? Has my mother suddenly died, or was my brother killed by the sword?" Passing that day in such talk, taking scarcely any food and drink, [the friars] were all very grateful when the silence of the night arrived. Overpowered by weariness and fatigue, he fell asleep but would soon awake and the tears would begin to flow again. He began now to reflect if it were the case that he had offended God with some grave sin, and if the weeping was therefore a means on the part of the Lord to remind him. While he examined himself, not materially but mentally, a voice resounded strongly in his ears and said, "Have you forgotten so quickly that the other day you despised with such pride my faithful servant Catherine, and that you falsely commended yourself to her prayers?"

Having heard this interior voice, he brightened up and tried to cry with joy but this was impossible for him because the river of tears had completely dried up so that not even a single tear flowed. Now his heart was inflamed and burned with desire to visit the holy virgin. And since daybreak had not come as quickly as he ardently desired so that he could go and visit the virgin, he became restless. Therefore, not waiting for sunrise, he left his convent and quickly ran, without any shame, to her house. Arriving at the door of the little cell, he knocked and the holy virgin, who was aware of that which her Spouse had done for the man, opened the door. He had scarcely seen her before entering the cell when he fell prostrate at her feet, but the virgin could not bear this and so she also fell to the ground and begged him to stand up. He refused to do this until finally both of them together stood up. They entered the cell and Fra' Lazzarino steadfastly refused to take a seat but instead sat on a mat on the ground and the virgin also sat on the ground, as she usually did.

After a long and holy discussion, now cheerful in mind and soul, the friar offered himself to the holy virgin, begging her with all his strength to adopt him as a son and to teach him and guide him in the way of the Lord. Refusing to accept her words that he knew the sacred scriptures and the way of the Lord better than herself, he objected saying that *he knew the outer rind [corteccia] while she had penetrated the sweet essence [sostanza].*[9]

Dominici finishes the account by describing the many virtuous ways in which Lazzarino changed after his encounter with Catherine. Commenting on these changes, Levasti observes that, among other things, the Franciscan's "preaching was now reformed, being no longer based on knowledge learnt in the Schools and in the books, *but on a living experience, born of contact with love.*"[10]

Catherine's Life

We now turn to the question of the fundamental message of Catherine's life for us today. This question should first be seen in the context of the part played generally by mystics in the church. R. Cantalamessa, the preacher to the papal household, points out that "mystics are not a category of Christians who are apart; they do not exist to amaze us, but to show all, in a magnified way, what the full development of the life of grace is."[11] In this regard, Pope John Paul II, on the occasion of the six-hundredth anniversary of Catherine's death, described her as a person of "complete dimensions":

> Today we look to St. Catherine in the first place to admire in her what immediately struck those who approached her: the extraordinary richness of humanity, not dimmed in any way, but on the contrary increased and perfected by grace, which made of her almost a living image of that true and wholesome Christian "humanism," the fundamental law of which is formulated by Catherine's confrere and teacher, St. Thomas Aquinas, in the well-known aphorism: "grace does not suppress, but presupposes and perfects nature" (*Summa Theol.* I, q. 1, a. 8 ad 2). The man of complete dimensions is the one who is fulfilled in Christ's grace.[12]

The life of Catherine of Siena is a superb example of how our journey on the Christ-bridge does not diminish our humanity but rather enhances, increases, and perfects it. Catherine exemplifies the person completely open to Christ to whom Pope Benedict XVI referred in his homily at Mass for the inauguration of the Petrine ministry on April 24, 2005, in St. Peter's Square. Quoting the words of his predecessor, John Paul II, "Do not be afraid! Open wide the doors of Christ," Pope Benedict closed his homily by addressing the world's youth:

> Are we not perhaps all afraid in some way? If we let Christ enter fully into our lives, if we open ourselves totally to him, are we not afraid that He might take something away from us? Are we not perhaps afraid to give up something significant, something unique, something that makes life so beautiful? Do we not then risk ending up diminished and deprived of our freedom? And once again [John Paul II] said: No! If we let Christ into our lives, we lose nothing, absolutely nothing of what makes life free, beautiful and great. No! Only in this friendship are the doors of life opened wide. Only in this friendship is the great potential of human existence truly revealed. Only in this friendship do we experience beauty and liberation. And so, today, with great strength and great conviction, on the basis of long personal experience of life, I say to you, dear young people: Do not be afraid of Christ! He takes nothing away, and he gives you everything. When we give ourselves to him, we receive a hundredfold in return. Yes, open wide the doors to Christ—and you will find true life.[13]

Catherine undoubtedly is one of the greatest examples in the history of the church of someone who "let Christ enter fully into [her] life" and who, far from being "diminished and deprived," became "free, beautiful and great." It is no surprise that biographies and other works continue to be written with enthusiasm and read with interest. The biographical sources portray Catherine as someone fully alive who, as a young, faithful, and intelligent (even if quasi-illiterate) fourteenth-century Tuscan woman "of the people," followed the attraction of Love to the end and was willing to do absolutely anything for God. The sources reveal a personality that was incredibly balanced and attractive to others as evidenced by the testimony of those who said that the mere sight of Catherine made

Conclusion

them happier.[14] She had a "special charm" that made people from different social ranks want to be with her.[15]

Catherine was a celibate whose personality was so well integrated that she was naturally warm and affectionate with others. She was not afraid to love others and show it.[16] We are afforded another glimpse into her humanity when she once awoke from a mystical experience and told those around her that she "enjoyed a sense of great peace and perfect purity and that she felt a great desire to be with children, to kiss and caress them."[17] She positively delighted in being with others, singing, and making crosses out of flowers.[18]

This spiritual sensitivity was balanced, however, by her great strength of character: We see her boldly confronting Gregory XI in Avignon, ready to undertake a universal mission to "unbelievers" in remote corners of the world, addressing a murderous mob in Florence that had come to lynch her, and following the young Niccolò di Toldo to the execution site only to be splattered by his blood moments later.[19] Catherine was, in short, fully human.

The rich and splendid life of Catherine of Siena validates the authenticity of our spiritual journey on the "bridge of Christ crucified," "the way of truth."

Appendix

Outline of the *Dialogue* of Catherine of Siena[1]
(numbers refer to chapters)

PROLOGUE: Catherine's Four Petitions (1)
                  Catherine's Self–Offering (2)

A. THE ETERNAL FATHER ANSWERS THE PETITIONS

    First Petition: For Herself: *The Way of Perfection* (3–12)
                          12—Summary
    Second Petition: For the Church (13–15)
    Third Petition: For the Whole World (16–18)
    Fourth Petition: For God's Providence over All, Especially for Her Spiritual Father, Raymond of Capua (19–20)

B. ELABORATION OF THE ANSWERS

    Teaching on the Bridge   (21–86)
        21–22   The Bridge—its Three *Scaloni* (Stairs)
        23–24   The Vine and Workers in the Vineyard
        25–30   Explanation of the Bridge
        31–35   Evil Tree and Four Vices
        36–50   Three Judgments, Temptations, Thorns
        50–55   Three *Scaloni* and Three Powers of the Soul
                        55—Summary
        56–76   Mounting the Three *Scaloni*, Three Stages *(Stati)* of the Soul
        77   Patience, Courage, and Perseverance
        78–85   Fourth Stage of the Soul
        86   Summary

    Tears   (87–97), Five Kinds of Tears, Four Winds

    Truth   (98–109), Three Lights

    The Mystic Body of Holy Church (110–34)
        110–18   Dignity of the Sacraments and Priests
                        118—Summary
        119   Virtues of Priests
        120   Summary
        121–33   Sins of Priests
        134   Prayer for the Reform of the Church

    Divine Providence   (135–53)

    Obedience   (154–65)

CONCLUSION: Summary of the Whole Book (166)
                     Prayer of Praise (167)

NOTES

Introduction

1. François-Marie Léthel, OCD, preface to "'Gesù dolce, Gesù amore'; Il Cristo di Caterina da Siena," by Emanuele Massimo Muso (STD diss., Pontificium Institutum Spiritualitatis Teresianum, 2005), vi. Italics mine.

2. All Catherine's "writings" were dictated to others. The catherinian corpus consists of 381 extant letters, the *Dialogue (Il dialogo della divina provvidenza)*, and twenty-six prayers.

3. "...andare per la via della verità" *(Il dialogo della divina provvidenza di S. Caterina da Siena,* ed. Giuliana Cavallini, 2nd ed. [Siena: Cantagalli, 1995], LXXVII, 200). Henceforth the Cavallini edition of the *Dialogue* will be abbreviated as *D* followed by Roman numerals indicating the chapter.

4. "I told you that no one can cross over the bridge and so escape the river without [rising] *(salisse)* on the three stairs" *(Catherine of Siena: The Dialogue,* trans. and intro. Suzanne Noffke, OP, The Classics of Western Spirituality [New York and Mahwah: Paulist Press, 1980], 59, 112). Henceforth abbreviated as *D* followed by Arabic numerals indicating the chapter. The English translation of the *Dialogue* by Algar Thorold is not recommended because it is incomplete. The original 1896 edition is missing the section Divine Providence, and the 1943 edition (reprinted by TAN Books and Publishers) is more drastically abridged.

5. *D* LVI, 147.

6. See Richard Byrne, "Journey (Growth and Development in Spiritual life)," in *The New Dictionary of Catholic Spirituality,* ed. Michael Downey. A Michael Glazier Book (Collegeville, MN: The Liturgical Press, 1993), 566.

7. See Kenelm Foster, introduction to *I, Catherine: Selected Writings of Catherine of Siena*, ed. and trans. Kenelm Foster, OP, and Mary John Ronayne, OP (London: Collins, 1980), 29.

8. See E. Ancilli and D. de Pablo Maroto, "Caterina da Siena (santa)," *Dizionario enciclopedico di spiritualità*, nuova edizione (Roma: Città Nuova Editrice, 1990), vol. 1, 485.

9. Paul VI, Apostolic Letter, *Mirabilis in Ecclesia Deus. Acta Apostolicae Sedis* 63:9 (30 September 1971), §3, 679. Henceforth *AAS*.

10. Raymond of Capua, *The Life of Catherine of Siena*, trans. and intro. Conleth Kearns, OP (Wilmington, DE: Michael Glazier, 1980), §31, 30. Henceforth abbreviated as *Legenda major*.

11. Giuliana Cavallini, "La verità nell'ascesi cateriniana," *Nuova rivista di ascetica e mistica* I:1 (1976): 29. The literary form of a dialogue is very ancient and was the preferred genre of Plato. Early Christian writers such as Justin, Origen, and Augustine wrote some of their works in dialogue form. The genre was popular up through the early Scholastic period in the beginning of the twelfth century.

12. Mary O'Driscoll, OP, "Women and the Dominican Tradition with Particular Reference to Catherine of Siena," *Angelicum* 81:2 (2004): 449.

13. For an excellent introduction to the *Dialogue*, see Suzanne Noffke, OP, introduction to *Catherine of Siena: The Dialogue*, trans. Noffke, 1–22. For a more comprehensive treatment, see Giuliana Cavallini, introduzione, *Il Dialogo*, ed. Cavallini, xi–xlvii. Also of interest is Benedict Ashley's "Guide to Saint Catherine's Dialogue," *Cross and Crown* 29 (September 1977): 237–49. Also see appendix for an outline of the *Dialogue*.

14. Jean Galot, SJ, "Recognize the Charism in its Specific Value," *L'Osservatore Romano:* Weekly Edition in English, June 29, 1981, 2.

15. See *D* 29, 69; 96, 181.

16. *D* 147, 311.

17. In *D* 55, 110, Catherine says that climbing the staircase *(scala)* and crossing over the Christ-bridge is necessary for everyone: "This is the way you must all keep to no matter what your situation, for there is no situation that rules out either your ability or your obligation to do so. You can and you must, and every person gifted with reason has this obligation."

Notes

Biographical Notes

1. This is largely a translation, with some modifications, of Giacinto D'Urso's "Nota Biografica," in Santa Caterina da Siena, *L'estasi e la parola: Dialogo della divina provvidenza, lettere, orazioni,* testi scelti a cura di Giacinto D'Urso (Fiesole: Nardini Editore, 1996), 43–45. I have also consulted: Kenelm Foster, "Key Events in Catherine's Life," in *I, Catherine: Selected writings of Catherine of Siena,* ed. and trans. Kenelm Foster, OP, and Mary John Ronayne, OP (London: Collins, 1980), 49–50; Suzanne Noffke, OP, "Chronology of Catherine's Life," in Catherine of Siena, *The Letters of Catherine of Siena,* trans. Suzanne Noffke, OP (Tempe, AZ: Arizona Center for Medieval and Renaissance Studies, 2000), vol. 1, liii–lvi.

Chapter One

1. *Legenda major,* §30, 29.
2. See ibid., §32, 31.
3. See ibid., §33, 32, and *D* 79, 148.
4. *Legenda major,* §35, 35.
5. For a complete list of the primary biographical sources see Johannes Jorgensen, *Saint Catherine of Siena* (London, New York, Toronto: Longman, Green and Co., 1938), 401–12; Alice Curtayne, *Saint Catherine of Siena* (London: Sheed and Ward, 1929), Appendix I, 215–16; Edmund G. Gardner, *Saint Catherine of Siena: A Study in the Religion, Literature, and History of the Fourteenth Century in Italy* (London: J. M. Dent & Co.; New York: E. P Dutton & Co., 1907), 423–24; Eugenio Dupré Theseider, "Caterina da Siena," *Dizionario biografico degli Italiani* (Roma: Istituto della Enciclopedia Italiana, 1979), XXII: 378–79. For her writings see *Epistolario di S. Caterina da Siena,* ed. Eugenio Dupré Theseider (Roma: Istituto Storico Italiano, 1940), vol. 1 only; *Le lettere di S. Caterina da Siena,* ed. Piero Misciattelli (Firenze: Marzocco, 1939), 6 vols.; *Il dialogo della divina provvidenza di S. Caterina da Siena,* ed. Giuliana Cavallini, 2nd ed.; *Le orazioni di S. Caterina da Siena,* ed. Giuliana Cavallini (Roma: Edizioni Cateriniane, 1978). English translations: *Catherine of Siena: The Dialogue,* trans. Suzanne Noffke;

Catherine of Siena

I, Catherine: Selected Writings of Catherine of Siena, ed. and trans. Kenelm Foster, OP, and Mary John Ronayne, OP (St. James Place, London: Collins, 1980); *The Letters of Catherine of Siena*, trans., intro., and notes Suzanne Noffke, OP, 4 vols. (Tempe, AZ: Arizona Center for Medieval and Renaissance Studies, 2000, 2001, 2007, 2008); *Saint Catherine of Siena as Seen in Her Letters*, trans., ed., and notes Vida D. Scudder (London: J. M. Dent & Sons Ltd; New York: E. Dutton & Co.,1927); *The Prayers of Catherine of Siena*. 2nd ed., ed., trans., notes Suzanne Noffke, OP (San Jose: Authors Choice Press, 2001).

6. For the Latin text of the *Legenda major* see Bollandist *Acta Sanctorum* (Paris: Palmé, 1866), vol. 3, 826–967. English translation: Raymond of Capua, *The Life of Catherine of Siena*, trans. Kearns.

7. See Jorgensen, *Saint Catherine of Siena*, 407–8. Raymond's actual name was Raimondo delle Vigne (c. 1330–99). He was master of the Order of Preachers from 1380 to 1399 and was beatified in 1899. In 1374 he was appointed by the master of the order, Elias of Toulouse, as Catherine's confessor. For a biographical outline of Raymond, see Conleth Kearns, OP, introduction to Raymond of Capua, *The Life of Catherine of Siena*, xiii–liii.

8. "The testimony of this earliest confessor [Tommaso della Fonte] of St. Catherine fills so large a place in Raymond's narrative that a summary account of the part he played seems desirable. He was called Father Thomas della Fonte. He was a younger brother of a son-in-law of Catherine's father, Giacomo Benincasa, in whose house he was 'brought up from childhood.' Older than Catherine, Thomas became a Dominican about the year 1356, while she was still a child of 9 or 10 years of age. Even before she took the habit of the Sisters of Penance he had become her first confessor, and thereafter remained her chief spiritual guide and counselor until, in 1374, he gave place to Raymond. To Raymond he handed over the copious notes which he had taken regarding Catherine's spiritual experiences and way of life over the 12 preceding years. He remained her faithful helper and disciple until her death in 1380, and an attached friend and frequent fellow-worker of Raymond until his own death in 1390. From his written records and from his *viva voce* testimony Raymond quotes repeatedly to describe and authenticate events of Catherine's life in the period previous to his own acquaintance with her. Unfortunately, as far as is known, the invaluable note-books of

Notes

Thomas della Fonte have not survived" (Kearns, Raymond of Capua, *The Life of Catherine of Siena*, 33).

9. Jorgensen, *Saint Catherine of Siena*, 407.

10. See Thomas Antonii de Senis "Caffarini," *Libellus de Supplemento*, ed. Giuliana Cavallini and Imelda Foralosso (Roma: Edizioni Cateriniane, 1974). For an Italian translation of Pars I and Pars II (tract. I–VI), cf. *Vita di Santa Caterina da Siena*, scritta da Fr. Tommaso Caffarini, a cura del Giuseppe Tinagli, OP (Siena: Ezio Cantagalli, 1938). Caffarini entered the Dominicans in 1364 and was assigned to San Domenico in Siena c. 1372. He became a lifelong friend of Raymond of Capua after the latter's arrival in Siena in 1374. A devoted disciple of Catherine, after her death in 1380 "he dedicated himself to spreading the knowledge of her life and writings and, as a means towards this, to working for her canonization. From 1394 till his death in 1424 he was stationed for the most part in the convent of SS. John and Paul in Venice. Through his activity there that city became the main centre of devotion to Catherine. There he promoted the *Process* of Castellano (1411– 1414), multiplied copies of Raymond's *Legenda Maior* in Latin and in Italian, wrote his own *Legenda Minor* (1412–1417), and compiled his great collection of such reminiscences of Catherine as Raymond had no space for. This is known as the *Libellus de Supplemento*, or simply as *Supplementum*. He was also compiler and copyist of one of the first three main collections of *Letters* of Catherine" (Kearns, introduction to Raymond of Capua, *The Life of Catherine of Siena*, lxii, note). Caffarini also wrote or translated the *vitae* of other Dominican women: Giovanna (Vanna) of Orvieto (1264–1306), Margherita of Città di Castello (1287–1320), and Maria Sturion of Venice (c. 1379–99). See "Appendix: Medieval Dominican Penitent *beatae* in Italy," in *Dominican Penitent Women*, ed., trans., intro. by Maiju Lehmijoki-Gardner with contributions by Daniel E. Bornstein and E. Ann Matter, preface by Gabriella Zarri, The Classics of Western Spirituality (New York: Paulist Press, 2005), 244–49.

11. See M. H. Laurent, *Il Processo Castellano con appendice di documenti*, Fontes vitae S. Catharinae senensis historici IX (Siena: Università di Siena, 1942). For an Italian translation of the depositions of Cortona, Maconi, and Dominici, cf. Innocenzo Taurisano,

OP, *Santa Caterina da Siena nei ricordi dei discepoli* (Roma: Libreria Ferrari, 1957).

12. See Fra' Tommaso da Siena ditto "Il Caffarini," *S. Caterina da Siena: Legenda minor*, trans. Bruno Ancilli (Siena: Edizioni Cantagalli, 1998). Henceforth abbreviated as *Legenda minor*.

13. "For a summary of the various methodological approaches used today in the study of hagiography, see Enrico Menesto, 'La "Legenda" di Margherita di Città di Castello' in Roberto Rusconi, *Il movimento religioso femminile in Umbria nei secoli XII–XIV* (Perugia and Florence, 1984), 217–237, esp. 219–223; Coakley, 'The Representation of Sanctity,' 1–19, and Gajano and Redon, *'La Legenda Major,'* 15–18. For the position that hagiography can only tell us what other people thought about the Saint, see Vauchez, *La sainteté en occident*, 2–3; Pierre Delooz, 'Towards a Sociological Study of Canonized Sainthood in the Catholic Church,' in Ed. Stephen Wilson, *Saints and their Cults: Studies in Religious Sociology, Folklore, and History* (Cambridge, 1983), 189–216" (Karen Scott, "Not Only with Words, but with Deeds: The Role of Speech in Catherine of Siena's Understanding of Her Mission" [PhD dissertation, University of California, Berkeley, 1989], 89).

14. Kearns, introduction to Raymond of Capua, *The Life of Catherine of Siena*, lii.

15. See ibid., liii.

16. Ibid., lvii.

17. Suzanne Noffke, OP, "Demythologizing Catherine: The Wealth of Internal Evidence," *Spirituality Today* 32 (March 1980): 4.

18. See Kearns, introduction to Raymond of Capua, *The Life of Catherine of Siena*, liii; §§5–10 and 12–15, 4–9 and 10–14. Kearns notes that twenty-two of the twenty-four witnesses in the *Processo Castellano* were members of religious orders, all of them former disciples of Catherine, and *all* "were adherents within their respective communities of the movements for reform of religious life." See ibid., lv; Laurent, *Il Processo Castellano*, XI–XIII.

19. *Legenda major*, §34, 33.

20. I. Taurisano, OP, "Le fonti agiografiche cateriniane e la critica di R. Fawtier," Letture Cateriniane nella R. Univeristà di Siena, 8 agusto 1928 (Siena: Libreria Editrice Senese, 1928); reprinted in Curtayne, *Saint Catherine of Siena*, 247, note.

21. *Legenda major*, §21, 20.
22. Ibid., §123, 118.
23. Kearns, introduction to Raymond of Capua, *The Life of Catherine of Siena*, lviii.
24. See Robert Fawtier, *Sainte Catherine de Sienne, essai de critique des sources*, vol. 1, *Sources hagiographique* (Paris: DeBoccard, 1921); vol. 2, *Les oeuvres de Sainte Catherine* (Paris: DeBoccard, 1930); Robert Fawtier and Louis Canet, *La double expérience de Catherine Benincasa (Sainte Catherine de Sienne)* (Paris: Gallimard,1948). For a summary of the Fawtier controversy, see Kearns, introduction to Raymond of Capua, *The Life of Catherine of Siena*, lx–lxx; Scott, "Not Only with Words, but with Deeds," 76–98; Maxime Gorce, "Catherine de Sienne," *Dictionnaire de spiritualité* (Paris: Beauchesne, 1953), vol. 2, cols. 331–36.
25. See Taurisano, "Le fonti agiografiche cateriniane e la critica di R. Fawtier"; E. Jordan, "La date de naissance de Sainte Catherine de Sienne," *Analecta Bollandiana* XL: III–IV (15 Novembre 1922): 365–411; Mandonnet, "Sainte Catherine de Sienne et la critique historique," extract from *L'Année Dominicaine*, Janvier-Fevrier 1923; G. Pardi, "Elenchi di mantellate Senesi," *Studi Cateriniani* II: 2 (1924–25): 43–58.
26. Curtayne, *Saint Catherine of Siena*, 219.
27. Arrigo Levasti, *S. Caterina da Siena* (Torino: Tip. Sociale Torinese, 1947), 525, translated and quoted by Kearns in introduction to Raymond of Capua, *The Life of Catherine of Siena*, lxviii.
28. Mandonnet, "Sainte Catherine de Sienne et la critique historique," 6–7.
29. *Legenda major*, §43, 42.
30. See ibid., §42, 41; §69, 63–64; §120, 115; §270, 251–52; D 108, 202; D 64, 121; D 106, 199.
31. *Legenda major*, §35, 34.
32. *Legenda minor*, I, ii, 22.
33. *Legenda major*, §29–31, 28–30. The anonymous Florentine author of the small work "The *Miracoli* of Catherine of Siena," written during her lifetime (1374), has a somewhat different version of the vision of the royal Christ: The vision appeared in an "unsettled area" and "only a little bit above the ground." Christ has a pastoral staff. After the vision, we are told that Catherine

was "left with a great fear" and felt "deeply tormented." "From this moment, she was always tormented from inside, fearful, conscientious, and afraid of falling into sin" ("The *Miracoli* of Catherine of Siena," chapters 2–3, in Lehmijoki-Gardner, *Dominican Penitent Women*, 90–91).

34. Giuliana Cavallini, "Caterina da Siena tra mistica e apostolato," *La patrona d'Italia: S. Caterina da Siena* XLIV:3 (maggio-giugno 1989): 7.

35. Caffarini, *Vita di Santa Caterina da Siena*, ed. Tinagli, II, iii, 8, 114. Henceforth abbreviated as *Supplementum* (Tin.).

36. Mario Ismaele Castellano, OP, "S. Caterina e la bellezza di Dio e dell'anima," *Quaderni Cateriniani* (Siena: Edizioni Cantagalli, 1997), 3–13.

37. D 141, 290.

38. D 153, 325.

39. D 167, 366.

40. Cf. *Letter* T122, *The Letters of Catherine of Siena*, trans. Noffke, vol. 2, 393. Henceforth abbreviated as *L* followed by T indicating the numbering system of the letters of N. Tommasèo.

41. Cf. D 130, 261.

42. Cavallini, "Caterina da Siena tra mistica e apostolato," 7.

43. Giacinto D'Urso, OP, "L'itinerario ascetico di S. Caterina da Siena," *Rivista di ascetica e mistica* VI (Nuova Serie; luglio-ottobre 1961): 453–54.

44. D 54, 107.

45. *Legenda major*, §31, 30–31.

46. Ibid., §35, 34.

47. Ibid., §34, 32.

48. Cf. ibid., §35, 34–35.

49. Ibid., §35, 34.

50. Ibid., §35, 35.

51. Ibid., §38, 38. As Kearns points out in a note, Catherine may have known the story through the vernacular translation of *Vite dei Santi Padri* of Domenico Cavalca (c.1270–1342). Earlier in the *Legenda* (§27, 27), Raymond recounts how neighbors had given the nickname "Euphrosyne" to Catherine. In *D* 165 the eternal Father refers to Catherine having read the *Vitae Patrum*. See D CLXV, 574.

Notes

52. *Legenda major*, §45, 43.
53. Ibid., §45, 44.
54. Ibid., §46, 45.
55. Ibid., §48, 46.
56. Ibid., §49, 46–47.
57. D'Urso, "L'itinerario ascetico di S. Caterina da Siena," 456.
58. *Legenda major*, §51, 48.

59. A Dominican lay sisterhood, also known as the Sisters of Penance of St. Dominic, the forerunner of the Dominican third order. The word *Mantellate* comes from the mantle or outer cloak worn by the women. Raymond of Capua gives a history of the group in *Legenda major*, §§77–79, 70–73. For an excellent description of Dominican women penitents see Maiju Lehmijoki-Gardner's introduction to *Dominican Penitent Women*, 1–36.

60. *Legenda major*, §53, 50.
61. Ibid., §69, 63.

62. A Dominican friar, Dominici (1343–1415), was introduced to Catherine by his fellow Dominican novice Tommaso della Fonte. He became a lifelong friend and disciple of Catherine's and accompanied her to Pisa, Lucca, and Avignon. After her death he became active in the reform of the order as provincial of the Roman province and procurator of the order. According to A. T. Drane, he became "titular Bishop of Corona in the Morea" (Augusta Theodosia Drane, *The History of St. Catherine of Siena and Her Companions*, 4th ed., 2 vols. [London: Longman, Green and Co., 1915], vol. 2, 318). See also Noffke, *The Letters of Catherine of Siena*, vol. 2, 705.

63. Taurisano, *Santa Caterina da Siena nei ricordi dei discepoli*, 95. Henceforth abbreviated as *Processo* (Taur.)
64. *Supplementum* (Tin.), I, i, 4, 73.
65. *Legenda major*, §54, 51.
66. Ibid, §55, 51.
67. D'Urso, "L'itinerario ascetico di S. Caterina da Siena," 456.
68. *Legenda major*, §57, 54.

69. The church of San Antonio Abate was closer to her house than the church of San Domenico. Cf. Giacinto D'Urso, "L'ascesa alla santità di S. Caterina (I)" *S. Caterina da Siena*, ottobre 1961: 10.

Noffke says that it was demolished in 1937. See Noffke, *Catherine of Siena: Vision Through a Distant Eye*, 159. The memory of the church is preserved today in the official title of San Domenico: "S. Antonio Abate in San Domenico." Anthony is mentioned only once in the catherinian corpus: *L* T344.

70. The baths were like summer resorts or spas. See Arrigo Levasti, *My Servant, Catherine*, trans. Dorothy M. White (London: Blackfriars, 1954), 23.

71. *Legenda minor*, I, vii, 35.

72. Most commentators say it happened c. 1363 when Catherine was about sixteen. See Edmund G. Gardner, *Saint Catherine of Siena*, 12; Jorgensen, *Saint Catherine of Siena*, 37; D'Urso, "L'itinerario ascetico di S. Caterina da Siena," 457; Cavallini, "Caterina da Siena tra mistico e apostolato," 9. However, Dupré Theseider gives a somewhat later date of c. 1364–65. See Dupré Theseider, "Caterina da Siena," 364. The author of the *Miracoli* of Catherine of Siena makes the exceptional assertion that Catherine received the habit at twenty-three. See chapter 8 of "The *Miracoli* of Catherine of Siena" in Lehmijoki-Gardner, *Dominican Penitent Women*, 93.

73. Kenelm Foster, OP, "The Spirit of St. Catherine of Siena," *Life of the Spirit* 15 (April 1961): 437.

74. D'Urso, "L'ascesa alla santità di S. Caterina," 23.

75. See *Supplementum* (Tin.), I, i, 5, 74–75. Raymond does not mention it.

76. Jorgensen, *Saint Catherine of Siena*, 34.

77. *D* 44, 90.

78. D'Urso, "L'itinerario ascetico di S. Caterina da Siena," 458.

79. *Legenda major*, §82, 76.

80. Ibid., §63, 58. In *D* 3–12, Catherine emphasizes that penance without love or desire is of no value.

81. *Processo* (Taur.), 58.

82. *Legenda major*, §84, 77.

83. Ibid., §86, 78. Raymond goes on to say that "the solace of his visible presence was nearly always with her."

84. See *Processo* (Taur.), 54.

85. In *Supplementum* (Tin.), II, vi, 38, 164, we read: "When the preaching that is done every morning finished…"; "After the homily,

that is done every morning in the convent of Siena...." Ibid., II, vi, 45, 173. Yet this seems to be contradicted by: "There is a custom in our convent in Siena to preach in the morning *of every feast day*...." Ibid., II, vi, 53, 183. Italics mine.

86. All biblical quotations are taken from the New Revised Standard Version unless otherwise noted.

87. *Processo* (Taur.), 89.

88. Jorgensen, *Saint Catherine of Siena*, 43. Antoine Gardeil, OP, in *The Gifts of the Holy Ghost in the Dominican Saints* (Milwaukee: Bruce, 1937), 88–89, says that Catherine manifested most clearly the gift of understanding that is "present as a simple intuition, as a spiritual insight which goes beyond appearances, which penetrates, beneath the mere letter or the symbols into the hidden meaning and causes the hidden thought to gush forth."

89. *Legenda major*, §92, 85. Raymond comments, "Take note, Reader, that this is the solid foundation which our Lord laid down in the beginning for Catherine's life of union with him. This is his betrothal pledge to her. Assuredly it is a foundation fit to carry a building of the loftiest spiritual perfection, holding it erect and unshaken, come what may of wind or tempest" (Ibid., §96, 89).

90. See ibid., §85, 77–78.

91. Ibid., §92, 89. Later Raymond says that knowledge of this truth resulted in Catherine's absolute trust in God's providence. See ibid., §98, 90.

92. See ibid., §100, 92–93.

93. See ibid., §101, 93–94.

94. See ibid., §§105–11, 97–103.

95. Ibid., §105, 98.

96. Ibid., §109, 101.

97. Ibid., §110, 102.

98. Ibid., §111, 103.

99. *Legenda minor*, I, ix, 42.

100. *Legenda major*, §112, 103–4.

101. Ibid. §113, 105.

102. *Supplementum* (Tin.), II, iii, 18, 125.

103. See "Chronology of Catherine's Life," in *The Letters of Catherine of Siena*, trans. Noffke, vol. 1, liv. Benedict Ashley, in *Spiritual Direction in the Dominican Tradition* (New York: Paulist

Press, 1995), 142, notes that "[t]he symbolism of the spiritual union of the human person with God as a 'marriage' is perfectly biblical. The prophets portray the covenant between Yahweh and Israel as a marriage in which there is fidelity or infidelity on the part of Israel but not on the part of Yahweh who is always faithful. Traditionally, even among the rabbis, the Song of Songs was (and still is by some exegetes) read as an allegory of this mutual love of God and Israel, or perhaps of the Messiah and Israel. In the New Testament, Jesus refers to himself as the Bridegroom (Matt 9:15, 25:1, 6; Mark 20:19; Luke 5:34; John 3:29) and the kingdom of Heaven as a wedding banquet; 2 Corinthians 11:2; Ephesians 5:23 speak of Christ as the bride of his church, and the same metaphor is used in Revelation 19:7, 9; 21:2, 9:22:17. No wonder then that Christian mystics have adopted this same symbolism."

104. *Legenda major*, §114, 106. In Caffarini's version of the mystical espousals, Catherine asks the Lord to marry her. See also *Supplementum* (Tin.), I, i, 10, 79. The expression, "And I will espouse thee to me in faith" is taken from Hos 2:20 (Douay-Rheims). Poulain names only one person as having experienced mystical marriage before Catherine: Bl. Angela of Foligno (d. 1309), a Franciscan tertiary. See Augustin Poulain, "Marriage, Mystical," *The Catholic Encyclopedia* (London: The Encyclopedia Press, 1910), vol. 9, 703.

105. *Legenda major*, §115, 107. It is sometimes said that the ring given by Christ to Catherine was that of his foreskin (for example, Barbara W. Tuchman, *A Distant Mirror: The Calamitous 14th Century*, 1978). However, none of the biographical sources say this. In *L* T221 to a cloistered nun in Pisa, Catherine says: "You see very well that you are a bride and that he has espoused you—you and everyone else—and not with a ring of silver but with a ring of his own flesh. Look at that tender little child who on the eighth day, when he was circumcised, gave up just so much flesh as to make a tiny circlet of a ring!" (*L* T221, *The Letters of Catherine of Siena*, trans. Noffke, vol. 2, 184). Raymond says that the ring could only be seen by Catherine. See *Legenda major*, §115, 107. Caffarini says that she always saw the ring "except when it would happen that she would commit some negligence" (*Supplementum* [Tin.], I, 1, 10, 79). Gardner points out that St. Teresa of Avila and St. John of the

Cross drew a distinction between "spiritual espousal" and "spiritual marriage" and that the former was a kind of preparation or engagement. He says that for Catherine, mystical marriage as they understood it would probably not be attainable in this life—which may be attested to in the Lord's words to her, "That faith will be ever kept untarnished until the day when you will celebrate with me the everlasting wedding-feast in heaven." See Gardner, *Saint Catherine of Siena*. 24–25. For the notion of mystical marriage in spiritual theology, see Antonio Royo, OP, and Jordan Aumann, OP, *The Theology of Christian Perfection* (Dubuque, IA: The Priory Press, 1962), 556–60.

106. See *Legenda major*, §177, 108.

107. D'Urso, "L'itinerario ascetico di S. Caterina da Siena," 465.

108. *Legenda minor*, I, xii, 56. St. Catherine of Alexandria, whose cult was popular in the Middle Ages, is said to have undergone mystical marriage with Christ. She lived in the fourth century.

109. *Supplementum* (Tin.), II, ii, 8, 81. It is not clear whether the Lord's kiss happened after the mystical espousals; Caffarini describes it after his account of the espousals. The expression, "Let him kiss me with the kisses of his mouth" is taken from Song of Songs 1:1.

110. *Legenda major*, §118, 113.

111. Ibid., §131, 126.

112. Ibid., §120, 115.

113. Ibid. "As he was getting into the boat, the man who had been possessed by demons begged him that he might be with him. But Jesus refused, and said to him, "Go home to your friends, and tell them how much the Lord has done for you, and what mercy he has shown you" (Mark 5:18–19).

114. Ibid., §121, 116–17. Italics mine.

115. Cavallini, "Caterina da Siena tra mistica e apostolato," 9.

116. *Legenda major*, §119, 115.

117. See John 20:19. See also *D* 63, 119.

118. D'Urso, "L'itinerario ascetico di S. Caterina da Siena," 466.

119. D'Urso, "Caterina creatura dello Spirito," *Rivista di ascetica e mistica* V (1980): 20.

120. *Legenda major*, §131, 126.

121. See ibid., §§142–46, 138–41.
122. See ibid., §§147–49a, 141–45.
123. Ibid., §147, 142.
124. Ibid., §149, 144–45.
125. Ibid., §150, 145.
126. Ibid., §151, 146.
127. See ibid., §311, 288; §167, 160–61. Her fasting may have actually resulted in an eating disorder. Raymond says she could no longer digest food and any attempt to eat resulted in vomiting. See ibid., §174 in which Catherine expressed her desire to eat again but could not; §176 in which she rejoined her followers every day at the table to eat a little but found it impossible to do so. Dominici also describes her condition in such a way that some today would call it an eating disorder. See *Processo* (Taur.), 125.
128. *Legenda major*, §314, 291.
129. See *Supplementum* (Tin.), II, vi, 26, 155.
130. See *Processo* (Taur.), 129.
131. See *Supplementum* (Tin.), II, vi, 52, 180.
132. Ibid., II, vi, 32, 159. Caffarini says that there was a custom in those days that after receiving the host at Mass the faithful would be given the chalice with unconsecrated wine so as to cleanse the mouth. See *Supplementum* (Tin.), II, vi, 57, 187.
133. Ibid., II, vi, 38, 165.
134. *Legenda major*, §189, 181.
135. Ibid., §407, 371.
136. Ibid.
137. "Penitent women's mystical experiences became public spectacles that contributed to the later medieval sense of God's presence in all human affairs" (Maiju Lehmijoki-Gardner in the introduction to *Dominican Penitent Women*, 16).
138. *Legenda major*, §125, 120. Raymond says that he witnessed her in ecstasy "a thousand times" (Ibid., §126, 126).
139. *Processo* (Taur.), 26.
140. See *Supplementum* (Tin.), I, ii, 13, 83–84; II, iii, 1–2, 108–9; II, vi, 11, 148.
141. *Legenda major*, §154, 148.
142. Ibid., §155, 149.
143. Ibid., §158, 151.

144. *Processo* (Taur.), 62.

145. *Legenda major*, §162, 155. Medieval saints were sometimes drawn to extreme expressions of their faith and desire for self-conquest. Molly Morrison, in "Strange Miracles: A Study of the Peculiar Healings of St. Maria Maddelena de' Pazzi," *Logos* 8:1 (Winter 2005): 129–44, cites several examples: St. Francis of Assisi (1182–1226) strove to overcome his disgust for lepers by eating out of the same bowl with a leper who had putrefying hands; the Carmelite St. Maria Maddelena de' Pazzi (1566–1607) licked a woman's leprous wounds and ate the worms of another sick person; the Franciscan Blessed Angela of Foligno (c. 1248–1309) drank the bloody wash water and ate the scab of a leper whom she was caring for; St. Catherine of Genoa (1447–1510), a laywoman, ate the pus and lice of the impoverished sick; the Spanish Jesuit St. Francis Xavier (1506–52) and the Italian Franciscan St. Joseph of Copertino (1603–63) ate the pus from the wounds of the sick; the Spanish Jesuit St. Peter Claver (1585–1650) would suck out the pus from the sores of black slaves; the Peruvian Dominican St. Rose of Lima (1586–1617) drank the corrupted blood of a sick woman; the French Visitandine St. Margaret Mary Alacoque (1647–90) ate the vomit and excrement of sick people. Morrison says, on 134, that these "nauseating acts are frequently associated with an effort to gain control over personal repugnance, the achievement of heroic feats of self-conquest, or the performance of a penance."

146. *Legenda major*, §163, 156. The opened side will be Catherine's image for the second stage of spiritual development.

147. Ibid., §178, 173.

148. Giacinto D'Urso, OP, "Il mandato ecumenico a S. Caterina," *Nuovi Studi Cateriniani* 3 (Siena: Biblioteca Cateriniana, Cantagalli, 1988), 32.

149. *Legenda major*, §191, 183. The breast of Christ is an image found in the *Dialogue*. See *D* 96, 179. Raymond also records a mystical experience in which Catherine nurses at the breast of the Virgin Mary. See also *Legenda major*, §199, 189.

150. Ibid.

151. Ibid., §178, 173–74.

152. *Supplementum* (Tin.), I, ii, 17, 85–86.

153. See Caffarini, *Libellus de Supplemento*, II, ii, 7, 35–36. Tinagli's Italian translation of this part is not complete. See *Supplementum* (Tin.), II, ii, 7, 98–99. In this vision, which possibly occurred when Catherine was still quite young, we see the nucleus of her later teaching on the three stages of spiritual development. Years later she would refer to this particular experience in *L* T74, where the stages are mentioned for the first time in her writings: "This was the rule he taught on one occasion to a servant of his. He said, 'Get up, daughter, rise above yourself and climb up onto me. And to enable you to climb up I have made the stairway for you by being nailed to the cross. See that you first use your affection and desire to climb up to [my] feet....'" Noffke dates the letter to "February to April 1376, but more probably nearer 17 February." See *The Letters of Catherine of Siena*, trans. Noffke, vol. 1, 313–14.

154. *Supplementum* (Tin.), II, vi, 41, 168.

155. See *Legenda major*, §137, 132. Catherine is portrayed in the red dress in a painting in the chapel of the Holy Rosary in the Basilica of Santa Maria sopra Minerva, Rome.

156. *Supplementum* (Tin.), II, vi, 53, 184.

157. Ibid., II, vi, 51, 179.

158. *Legenda major*, §165, 158.

159. Ibid., §165, 158–59.

160. Ibid., §226, 214.

161. *Processo* (Taur.), 109–10.

162. See *Legenda major*, §278, 259.

163. Ibid., §365, 339; cf. ibid., §370, 343.

164. *Supplementum* (Tin.), II, iv, 22, 133.

165. Ibid., II, iv, 24, 133.

166. Ibid., II, vi, 26, 155.

167. *Processo* (Taur.), 58.

168. Ibid., 94.

169. *Legenda major*, §§250–56, 236–41.

170. Ibid., §§269–73, 250–55. Catherine was not keen about performing the exorcism as she hid in her house when the family of the girl came to ask her help. Dominici says that she believed herself to be incapable of doing it. See *Processo* (Taur.), 116–17.

171. *Legenda major*, §277, 258.

172. *Processo* (Taur.), 90–91.

173. Psalm 51:10.

174. *Legenda major*, §180, 175. "Christ fulfilled for [Catherine] the biblical promise to give his people 'a new heart' [cf. Ezek 36:26; 2 Cor 3:3]" (Ashley, "Guide to Saint Catherine's Dialogue," 242).

175. *Legenda major*, §180, 175. According to Gorce, the thirteenth-century German mystic St. Gertrude is also said to have experienced the mystical exchange of hearts. See Gorce, "Catherine de Sienne," col. 345. A. Poulain says that Ven. Ursula Benincasa (1547–1618, foundress of the Theatine nuns) and Dominican St. Catherine di Ricci (1522–89) also experienced the mystical exchange of hearts (Augustin Poulain, SJ, *Revelations and Visions*, trans. Leonora L. Yorke Smith [New York: Alba House, 1998], 23). Aumann adds the name of the Spanish Trinitarian St. Michael de los Santos (1591–1624). See Jordan Aumann, *Spiritual Theology* (London: Sheed and Ward, 1980), 434.

176. Jorgensen, *Saint Catherine of Siena*, 93–94.

177. *Legenda major*, §182, 176.

178. "You know I have no will but yours; you know I have no heart but yours." Ibid., §182, 177.

179. Levasti, *My Servant, Catherine*, 77.

180. *Legenda major*, §181, 175. In some of Catherine's prayers and mystical experiences she sees Christ as a youth (*fanciullo* or *giovane*). For example, see ibid., §206, 196; *Supplementum* (Tin.), II, iii, 17, 122; III, vi, 6, 145. Musso notes that youthfulness was regarded as a characteristic of the risen Christ. See Emanuele Musso, "Il Cristo risorto è 'giovane:' una puntualizzazione di Caterina da Siena," *La patrona d'Italia e d'Europa: S. Caterina da Siena*, LX:1 (gennaio–marzo 2005): 27–28. See also St. Thomas Aquinas, *Summa Theologica*, 3 vols., trans. Dominican Fathers of the English Dominican Province (New York: Benziger, 1947), III, 46, 9, 4. Henceforth abbreviated as *ST*.

181. *Legenda major*, §184, 178.

182. Ibid., §206, 196.

183. *Supplementum* (Tin.), II, ii, 1, 79.

184. Ibid., II, vi, 32, 160.

185. *Legenda major*, §192, 183–84. Caffarini says that Catherine levitated many times after receiving communion. See *Supplementum* (Tin.), II, iii, 3, 109; II, vi, 56, 186. This incident reflects some

of the major facets of Catherine's life: prayer, teaching, and intercession.

186. *Legenda major*, §193, 184–85. The stigma in the palm of her right hand is a preparation for the eventual stigmata five years later and is a continuation of those mystical experiences that, as we have said, prefigure it: the appearance of the crucified Christ to Catherine after her crisis in the cell, the Lord's offering of the two crowns, his appearance with the five wounds when he showed his opened side. See ibid., §109, 101; §158, 151; §163, 155–56.

187. *D* 108, 202.

188. *The Prayers of Catherine of Siena*, 2nd ed., ed., trans., and notes by Suzanne Noffke, OP (San Jose: Authors Choice Press, 2001), 12 (XXII), 117. Henceforth abbreviated as *P* indicating the Noffke translation of the prayers, followed by Arabic numerals indicating the number of the prayer and page number in Noffke and Roman numerals indicating the number of the prayer in *Le orazioni di S. Caterina da Siena*, ed. Giuliana Cavallini (Roma: Edizione Cateriniane, 1978).

189. *D* 50, 102.

190. *L* T119, *The Letters of Catherine of Siena*, trans. Noffke, vol. 2, 701.

191. *D* 64, 121.

192. *Legenda major*, §200, 190; see *Processo* (Taur.), 94. Dominici says the hermit in question was the English Augustinian William Flete, a well-known friend of Catherine's who lived in the nearby forest at Lecceto.

193. Ibid., §§202–3, 192–93. This incident is similar to her fundamental religious experience at the age of six: Both incidents involve Catherine momentarily removing her glance from a vision to look at one of her brothers. Dominici, in his deposition, has an indelicate variation: "She, in order to spit, had turned at that moment and saw him [her brother] and recognized him, but immediately she turned back towards me and began to cry bitterly." See *Processo* (Taur.), 96.

194. Even in her cell she received visitors such as Dominican friars Tommaso della Fonte, Dominici, and others.

195. *Legenda major*, §31, 30–31.

196. Dupré Theseider, "Caterina da Siena," 362.

Notes

197. *Legenda major*, §301, 279. F. Thomas Luongo, in *The Saintly Politics of Catherine of Siena* (Ithaca: Cornell University Press, 2006), 156, has convincingly shown how politically connected many of Catherine's disciples were: "[H]er network of followers gave her influence and a status within the political world that she, as a woman—even a saintly woman—would not otherwise have been able to claim."

198. See *Legenda major*, §301, 279. While in Rome the group numbered more men than women.

199. Ibid., §264, 246.

200. Ibid., §§415–16, 377–78.

201. Ibid., §§212–13, 201.

202. Ibid., §213, 202.

203. Ibid., §215, 203–4. Citing *Summa Theologiae (ST)* I, 56, 3, and *De Potentia* 7:5, Boulding says that "my soul saw the divine Essence" is "a phrase remarkably reminiscent of Aquinas." See M. Cecily Boulding, OP, "St. Catherine of Siena's 'Mystical Apprehension' of God," *New Blackfriars* 85: 996 (March 2004): 168.

204. *Legenda major*, §216, 204–5. This message should be seen in light of the one a few weeks before when Catherine had drunk at the opened side. See ibid. §165, 158–59. We recall that in this message the Lord said he would flood her soul with graces, that she would begin to take on an abnormal way of life and be filled with a burning zeal for the salvation of souls, that she was to plunge boldly into public activity, that he would use her to snatch souls from the jaws of hell, and that many would be scandalized by her, and so on. Catherine refers in passing to her mystical death in *L* T373 to Raymond, written some nine years later. See *I, Catherine*, ed. Foster and Ronayne, 267.

205. See Gardner, *Saint Catherine of Siena*, 107; *The Letters of Catherine of Siena*, trans. Noffke, vol. 1, xv. Foster also says "around 1370." See Foster, introduction to *I, Catherine*, trans. Foster and Ronayne, 40. The majority of the extant letters were written between 1374 and Catherine's death in 1380.

206. D'Urso, *Il genio di Santa Caterina*, 62.

207. *Legenda major*, §194, 185.

208. Dupré Theseider, on the other hand, says that the trip to Florence "signaled a notable turning point in the life of the young

Mantellata; her entrance into public life, or into the apostolate among those who live in the midst of the passions that shake the world. It was the desire of her heavenly Spouse, who said to her: 'From now on you will go anywhere I send you.' From the cell of her house she was hurled into the larger world stirred by human contrasts and also into that of the Church, which was in need not least of a purifying fire" (Dupré Theseider, "Caterina da Siena," 10).

209. Jorgensen, in *Saint Catherine of Siena*, (185), dates these "wanderings" to the late summer of 1374.

210. *L* T127. *The Letters of Catherine of Siena*, trans. Noffke, vol. 1, 40. Noffke dates this letter close to March 26, 1374.

211. *Legenda major*, §257, 241–42.

212. Ibid., §365, 339. Munio of Zamora, master general of the Dominicans from 1285 to 1291, wrote some *Ordinationes* for Dominican penitent women living in Orvieto. The exceptional quality of Catherine's traveling can be better appreciated after reading chapter 11 of the work: "There should be no unnecessary and curious wandering about the town. The sisters, especially the young ones, do not move around alone. The sisters do not attend wedding banquets, dances, or any mundane or indecent feast. They never attend any world spectacles. They absolutely do not leave the town without a license from the prior or his vicar, or, at least, their prioress, even in the case of emergency" ("Munio of Zamora: The *Ordinationes*," in Lehmijoki-Gardner, *Dominican Penitent Women*, 43).

213. On the relation of Mary Magdalene to the Dominican order, see Guy Bedouelle, OP, "Mary Magdalene: The Apostle of the Apostles and the Order of Preachers," *Dominican Ashram*, 18:4 (1999): 157–71.

214. See Jacobus de Voragine, *The Golden Legend*, trans. W. G. Ryan. vol. 2 (Princeton, NJ: Princeton University Press, 1993), 334–41.

215. *Legenda major*, §45, 44.

216. Ibid.

217. Ibid. §183, 177. See Kearn's comments in note 23 on the place of Mary Magdalene in the *Legenda* and Raymond's references to medieval legends about her.

218. *L* T61, *The Letters of Catherine of Siena*, trans. Noffke, vol. 1, 3–4. Italics mine. Catherine praises the Magdalene for her "blaz-

ing love," her self-knowledge, humility, perseverance, and love for others, adding that she "had no heart, since it was buried with [her] dearest Master." This latter statement is reminiscent of Catherine's own experience of the mystical exchange of hearts.

219. Voragine, *The Golden Legend*, vol. 1, 374–83.

220. *L* T165, *The Letters of Catherine of Siena*, trans. Noffke, vol. 2, 42. See Matthew 28:1–10; Mark 16:1–14; Luke 24:1–11; John 20:1–18.

221. McGinn says that the Magdalene provided "a female model and evangelical prototype for Catherine and the other women who took up apostolic roles in the Middle Ages." See Bernard McGinn, "Catherine of Siena: Apostle of the Blood of Christ," *Theology Digest* 48:4 (2001): 332. On page 331, he cites two medieval hagiographical works concerning the Magdalene: *Vita apostolica Mariae Magdalenae* and the *Life of Saint Mary Magdalene and of her Sister Saint Martha*, in which the Magdalene is described as the "apostle to the apostles." The cult of Mary Magdalene was popular in the Middle Ages. Scott, in a thought-provoking article, agrees that Mary Magdalene was a role model for Catherine but thinks that Catherine identified more with the male apostles of Christ. See Karen Scott, "St. Catherine of Siena, 'Apostola,'" *Church History* 61 (1992): 34–46. The evidence, however, is not very strong. On the other hand, it is worth noting how often Raymond of Capua in the *Legenda major* implicitly compares Catherine not to an apostle or saint but to Christ himself. A few examples: Catherine has a group of "disciples" (§360), she knows people's sins (§280), she makes bread with a small amount of flour (§299), she takes on the sins of the Romans when they wanted to kill the pope (§346), she has a "Judas" who afterward commits suicide (§408), in Florence she retires to a garden before her "arrest" (§426), the stigmata (§194), the numerous posthumous miracles she performs (§393), after her death she appears to a "disciple" and prepares food for her (§375). It could be argued that Raymond was to Catherine what Simon Peter was to Jesus. Raymond records a time in which Catherine's face changed into that of God the Father (§90). (Caffarini records the same event in the *Legenda minor*, I, ix.)

222. *Processo* (Taur.), 102.

Catherine of Siena

223. Cf. "Chronology of Catherine's Life," in *The Letters of Catherine of Siena*, trans. Noffke, vol. 1, liv.

224. *Legenda major*, §§194–95, 185–86. The invisible stigmata of Catherine would be fiercely defended by the Dominicans in the centuries that followed. The legitimacy of her stigmata was affirmed by popes Urban VIII (1625–44) and Benedict XIII (1724–30), who approved feasts in the Divine Office commemorating it and mentioning its invisibility. See Joseph C. Henchey, CSS, "St. Catherine of Siena: An Historic and Prophetic Synthesis of the Consecrated Life," *Congresso internazionale di studi cateriniani: Atti* (Roma: Curia Generalizia OP, 1981), 639. St. Francis of Assisi is said to have been the first person to have received the (visible) stigmata in 1224. Other saints prior to Catherine who were said to have received the stigmata include St. Lutgarde (d. 1246), St. Margaret of Cortona (d. 1297), St. Gertrude (d. 1302), St. Clare of Montefalco (d. 1308), and Bl. Angela of Foligno (d. 1309). Cf. Augustin Poulain, "Stigmata, Mystical," *The Catholic Encyclopedia*, XIV: 295.

225. *Legenda major*, §109, 101.

226. Ibid., §158, 151.

227. Ibid., §193, 184–85.

228. Ibid., §207, 197.

229. *Processo* (Taur.), 103–5. Dominici first says that Catherine felt the pain of three nails "nel capo, nel petto e nei fianchi" (104) but then changes it to "nei piedi, nelle mani e nel fianco" (105).

230. See Giacinto D'Urso, introduction to *L'estasi e la parola: Dialogo della divina provvidenza, lettere, orazioni*, testi scelti a cura di Giacinto D'Urso (Fiesole: Nardini Editore, 1996), 11.

231. See Jorgensen, *Saint Catherine of Siena*, 194.

232. *Processo* (Taur.), 106.

233. Reginaldo Garrigou-Lagrange, OP, "La stimmatizzazione di Santa Caterina da Siena," *Vita Cristiana* IX (1937): 51. Italics mine.

234. Cavallini, "Caterina da Siena tra mistica e apostolato," 9.

235. L T219. *The Letters of Catherine of Siena*, trans. Noffke, vol. 2, 91–93. Italics mine. "[F]or Catherine the side, the pierced and opened heart of the Crucified, is the bodily *locus theologicus*, the focal point of Jesus' body, where the beams of light of God's revelation as Love (1 John 4:8 and 16) are gathered, concentrated,

and projected" (Musso, "'Gesù dolce, Gesù amore': Il Cristo di Caterina da Siena," 99).

236. Jorgensen, *Saint Catherine of Siena*, 220.

237. D'Urso, "Il mandato ecumenico a S. Caterina," 31

238. Ibid., 32.

239. About a year after writing *L* T219, Catherine writes to a goldsmith in Siena: "Whether the devils want it or not, I will do my best to use my life for God's honor and the salvation of souls *throughout the whole world*, and especially for my city." *L* T122, *The Letters of Catherine of Siena*, trans. Noffke, vol. 2, 396. Italics mine.

240. D'Urso, "Il mandato ecumenico a S. Caterina," 33. Catherine's generally liberal attitude toward Muslims can be seen in *L* T218 to Gregory XI, written perhaps just a few months after the "investiture vision," in which she says that once converted, the Muslims would play an important role in the reform of the church. See *The Letters of Catherine of Siena*, trans. Noffke, vol. 2, 199–200.

241. D'Urso, "Il mandato ecumenico a S. Caterina," 27–28. By this time Catherine's letter "writing" was well under way. She may have written as many as eighty letters in 1376 alone. Dominici, who was a witness to her tremendous output, says, "I often saw her dictating to two and sometimes three writers simultaneously on different subjects, and she did not hesitate one moment to think what she had to dictate." *Processo* (Taur.), 90. Scudder, in her introduction to *Saint Catherine of Siena as Seen in Her Letters* (1), says, "Her letters were talked rather than written."

242. See "Chronology of Catherine's Life," *Letters of Catherine of Siena*, trans. Noffke, vol. 1, liv.

243. See *Letters of Catherine of Siena*, trans. Noffke, vol. 2, 192.

244. *Legenda major*, §289, 267–68. Catherine promoted the Crusade as a means of uniting warring Christian factions under the leadership of the pope and to convert "unbelievers." For the attitudes of medieval Europeans on the Crusade, see Benjamin Z. Kedar, *Crusade and Mission: European Approaches to the Muslims* (Princeton: Princeton University Press, 1984).

245. The letters to Gregory XI written prior to her arrival in Avignon: *L* T185, T196, T206, and T229; the letters written to him while she was in Avignon: *L* T255, T218, T233, T231, T238, and

T239 (in the order of Noffke's dating of the letters). See *Letters of Catherine of Siena*, trans. Noffke, vol. 2, 713.

246. See D'Urso, "Il mandato ecumenico a S. Caterina," 35. Catherine refers to the arrival of St. Birgitta's confessor in *L* T127 (*The Letters of Catherine of Siena*, trans. Noffke, vol. 1, 40).

247. *Processo* (Taur.), 110.

248. Ibid., 37. Noffke, in *The Letters of Catherine of Siena* (vol. 2, 723), says that Stefano di Corrado Maconi (1347–1424), a member of a noble Sienese family, became one of Catherine's most trusted disciples in 1376. He accompanied Catherine to Florence and Avignon and "was one of the three principal scribes for her *Dialogue*." After her death he became a Carthusian and later gave testimony for the *Processo Castellano*.

249. *Legenda major*, §152, 147.

250. See ibid., §247, 234; §277, 258; §335, 312; §224, 255; §367, 340; §264, 246; §344, 320.

251. Jorgensen, *Saint Catherine of Siena*, 214.

252. Foster, "The Spirit of St. Catherine of Siena," 437.

253. Ibid, 438.

254. *Legenda major*, §336, 313.

255. *L* T272. *The Letters of Catherine of Siena*, trans. Noffke, vol. 2, 494–506.

256. Noffke, introduction to *Catherine of Siena: The Dialogue*, 12–13.

257. *Legenda major*, §349, 324–25.

258. See Noffke, "Chronology of Catherine's Life," in *The Letters of Catherine of Siena*, trans. Noffke, vol. 1, lv. "Catherine's appearance in Florence as a public ally of the Parte Guelfa placed her at risk when opposition to the Parte erupted in a series of uprisings known collectively as the Revolt of the Ciompi. While this civic unrest was fostered and to some extent directed, in its early stages, by elements of the Florentine middle classes who opposed the Parte Guelfa, the revolt was driven by the poor and unenfranchised workers of the wool industry against their masters of the wool guild and other *popolo grasso* elites" (Luongo, *The Saintly Politics of Catherine of Siena*, 199).

259. *Legenda major*, §427, 386.

260. Ibid.

Notes

261. Catherine wrote *L* T326 to William Flete, the Augustinian hermit, urging him to leave his solitude at Lecceto for Rome. She also wrote *L* T327 and T328 to other hermits urging them to come to Rome. See Scudder, *Saint Catherine of Siena as Seen in Her Letters*, 306–16. Flete never went.

262. Caffarini records a vision of her death that Catherine had in St. Peter's Basilica in which she saw the *navicella* (little boat or bark) of the church descending on her shoulders and crushing her to death. See *Legenda minor*, III, ii, 187; Drane, *The History of St. Catherine of Siena and Her Companions*, vol. 2, 240–41.

263. *L* T373, in *I, Catherine*, trans. Foster and Ronayne, 266.

264. Ibid., 267.

265. Ibid., 269.

266. Ibid., 274.

267. Ibid., 275.

268. *L* T371, in *I, Catherine*, trans. Foster and Ronayne, 275–76. To properly understand Catherine's words, "I have nothing to give except what you have given me, so take my heart and squeeze it out over the face of the Bride," we should remember her words to the Lord after the miraculous exchange of hearts: "You know I have no will but yours; you know I have no heart but yours" (*Legenda major*, §183, 177). See Drane, *The History of St. Catherine of Siena and Her Companions*, vol. 2, 250.

269. *Legenda major*, §118, 113.

270. Ibid., §182, 176.

271. Jorgensen, *Saint Catherine of Siena*, 199.

Chapter Two

1. *Legenda major*, §257, 241. Italics mine.

2. "[I]magery is the very language of her theology!" (Suzanne Noffke, "Catherine of Siena: Justly Doctor of the Church?" *Theology Today* 60 [2003]: 59).

3. In the *"positio"* for the conferral of the title doctor of the church, the first censor acknowledged the "problem of certain formulations" in Catherine's images: "Does it mean that these formulations are completely perfect? There are some formulations or

expressions which will always be debatable especially when they are isolated from their context. For example, the formulations where it is said that God strongly loves the beauty of his creature, or where the pope is identified with Christ, or where there is some restriction about the concept of the Mystical Body....The theologians usually prefer to change those kinds of formulations. Some have the awkwardness of inadequate images. It should nevertheless be mentioned that there are other formulas which rebalance these expressions....If these expressions are not correct, they are not very frequent. Their inadequacy does not really disturb the religious truth which they claim to communicate" *(Urbis et Orbis, concessionis tituli doctoris et extensionis eiusdem tituli ad universam Ecclesiam necnon Officii et Missae de communi doctorum virginum in honorem S. Catharinae Senensis virginis Tertii Ordinis S. Dominici. Vota censorum theologorum,* [Città Vaticano], typis poliglottis vaticani, 1969, 4°, 45 [9]).

4. See Introduction, 3.

5. William A. Hinnebusch, OP, *The History of the Dominican Order*, vol. 2 (New York: Alba House, 1973), 361.

6. See D'Urso, *Il genio di Santa Caterina*, 79.

7. Although the theme of truth is important in the works of Augustine, Catherine's repeated emphasis on it is the clearest evidence of the influence of her Dominican confrere Thomas Aquinas. "Veritas," the motto of the Dominican order, is the first word in both the *ST* and *Summa Contra Gentiles* (henceforth, *SCG*). Beatitude, Aquinas says in *ST* I–II, 66, 3, 1, begins with a knowledge of the truth. In *ST* I, 16, 5, he says that God, whose essence is his intellect, is the cause and measure of all understanding. Truth is not only found in God but he is the source and highest form of truth, the immutable first truth and foundation of all other truths. Every other truth participates in this first truth.

8. "Catherine moves on the plane of the 'truth' to be known and verified: not discursive, theoretical, or abstract truth, such as the demonstration of the existence of God...but 'his truth *towards* us,' that which constitutes the true reason for which we exist, by the work of the Creator, and through which every man will continue to exist with this being that one has; it is, in short, the reason for God's conduct toward all of us, from our creation..." (Giacinto D'Urso,

Notes

OP, "Il mistero di Cristo nella verità del Padre," *Angelicum* LXIV [1987]: 195–96). Noffke says that Catherine "inherits a scholastic tradition that defines truth as what *is*" (Noffke, "Catherine of Siena: Justly Doctor of the Church?" 59).

9. *D* 21, 58. See also *Le lettere di S. Caterina da Siena*, ed. Misciattelli: *L* T195, vol. 3, 158; *L* T227, vol. 3, 302; *L* T317, vol. 5, 42; *L* T259, *The Letters of Catherine of Siena*, trans. Noffke, vol. 2, 610.

10. "I have said these things to you so that my joy may be in you, and that your joy may be complete" (John 15:11). Foster, introduction to *I, Catherine*, trans. Foster and Ronayne (31), says that the "truth of the eternal Father" means "the whole divine plan and process with regard to man." See also Sr. Dominic, OP [Ann Walsh, OP], "St. Catherine of Siena: Doctor of the Church," *Supplement to Doctrine and Life* 8 (1970): 139.

11. *D* 13, 49.

12. "Why then, eternal Father, did you create this creature of yours? I am truly amazed at this, and indeed I see, as you show me, that you made us for one reason only: in your light you saw yourself completely compelled by the fire of your charity to give us being…" (*P* 13 [IV], 129).

13. *L* T227, *Le lettere di S. Caterina da Siena*, ed. Misciattelli, vol. 3, 303.

14. *D* 14, 51. The image of the earthen or clay vessel is taken from 2 Corinthians 4:7.

15. *D* 21, 58.

16. See *D* 14, 52.

17. *D* 21, 58. McGinn says that "[t]he notion of humanity as made in the image and likeness of God (Gen 1:26) was the central theme of the theological anthropology of the patristic period and for much of the Middle Ages as well." The restoration of God's image in the human person is the essential task of Augustinian spirituality. Cf. Bernard McGinn, *The Foundations of Mysticism*, vol. 1, *The Presence of God: A History of Western Christian Mysticism* (New York: Crossroad, 1991), 243.

18. Kenelm Foster, OP, "St. Catherine's Teaching on Christ." *Life of the Spirit* 16 (1962): 310–23. 316–17

19. See *D* 14, 51.

20. *D* 153, 325. The motif of God as a lover who goes in search of his beloved is taken from the Song of Songs.

21. See *D* 12, 46; *D* 13, 50.

22. See *D* 12, 46.

23. See *D* 72, 2.

24. See *P* 17 (X), 175–76.

25. *D* 62, 117. Italics mine.

26. *D* 12, 46. Italics mine.

27. *D* 26, 65. Italics mine.

28. *P* 13 (IV), 124–25. Italics mine. *Rinchiudendo* can also mean to shut oneself up (for example, in a room or house).

29. John 14:6 and 18:37. Italics mine.

30. *L* T177, *The Letters of Catherine of Siena*, trans. Noffke, vol. 2, 97.

31. *D* 13, 50.

32. *D* 12, 46. See also *P* 17 (X), 175–76. Catherine says that fallen humanity is brought back to life and able to bear fruit again by the engrafting of divinity onto it.

33. Aquinas says that grace deifies. See *ST* I-II, 112, 1.

34. *L* T177, *The Letters of Catherine of Siena*, trans. Noffke, vol. 2, 99. In the next section we will consider Catherine's teaching on the redemption.

35. Foster, "St. Catherine's Teaching on Christ," 318–19.

36. "The circumcision is the beginning of the pouring out of Christ's blood in order to cleanse his bride. The blood that Jesus lost at the circumcision was but a pledge of the full payment he would make for the sins of the human race when every drop would be drained from his body" (Sr. Mary Jeremiah, "Catherinian Imagery of Consecration," *Communio* 17 [1990]: 365). Noffke points out that, as can be seen in *L* T50, T143, T221, T262, T330, "Jesus espouses the human race on the day of his circumcision with the ring of his flesh. But note that Catherine consistently calls her disciples to respond by espousing Truth with the ring of faith [cf. *L* T262, T330, T341]" (Suzanne Noffke, OP, "The Physical in the Writings of Catherine of Siena," *Annali d'Italianistica* 13 [1995]: 118–19). The word *sangue* appears more than 1,800 times in Catherine's writings.

37. Giacinto D'Urso, OP, "Santa Caterina da Siena." *Temi di predicazione* XVI: 84 (1970): 13–125. 48.

Notes

38. God's love and mercy are closely related. "[F]or her God is not so much one who loves, as one who has mercy. Mercy is love that bends, reaches down to nothingness and brings it into being, reaches down even lower into sin and redeems it. Catherine sees the mercy, touches it, tastes it, smells it, wraps herself round with it and revels in it. So her wild preoccupation with blood—the Blood of Christ shed in a frenzy of unthinkable love for her who is nothing" (A. Stanley Parmisano, OP, "Mystic of the Absurd: Saint Catherine of Siena," *Religious Life Review* 21 [1982]: 214).

39. Foster says there are three principal themes found in Catherine's works: (1) the crucified Christ and the blood as the supreme sign and pledge of divine love and the chief motive of our love, (2) self-knowledge, (3) the doctrine of the soul as created in the image of the divine Trinity, Father, Son, and Holy Spirit. See Foster, introduction to *I, Catherine*, 29. In the *"positio"* the first censor listed the following as principal elements of her doctrine: (1) knowledge of oneself and knowledge of God, (2) the human person created in the image and likeness of God, (3) intelligence and will, (4) disordered and sensual self-love, (5) human freedom, (6) the spiritual battle, (7) vices and virtues, (8) redemption in the blood of the immaculate Lamb, (9) love of neighbor as proof of one's love of God, (10) love of the church and suffering for the church, (11) the communion of saints. See *Urbis et Orbis, concessionis tituli doctoris...*, 4°, 7–22.

40. Foster, "The Spirit of St. Catherine of Siena," 445.

41. *L* T304, *Le lettere di S. Caterina da Siena*, ed. Misciattelli, vol. 4, 275.

42. *L* T181, ibid., vol. 2, 41. In various places Catherine uses the images of blood and fire (or God's desire) to express the fact that God's infinite love cannot be entirely contained in something finite such as the blood or the passion of Christ: "He gave you not only his blood but fire as well, for it was through the fire of love that he gave you his blood" (*D* 127, 247). See also *L* T8, T11, T12, T16, T34, and T185.

43. *L* T227, *Le lettere di S. Caterina da Siena*, ed. Misciattelli, vol. 3, 302.

44. *L* T102, *Le lettere di S. Caterina da Siena*, ed. Misciattelli, vol. 2, 127.

45. *D* 14, 51–52. The above text reflects the traditional theory of the redemption as Christ's vicarious atonement that the Fathers propounded in various ways. In the text Catherine portrays the work of redemption as satisfaction (that is, restoring God's honor and removing humanity's guilt caused by original sin so that we could be in a right relationship with God again). Lampe says that patristic thought was dominated by two central ideas: deification and "the interpretation of the saving work of Christ as an 'exchange of places' by which the Logos/Son took upon himself, or entered into, the human state in order to enable sinful, alienated, and perishing human beings to enter through incorporation into himself, the state of sonship towards God" (G. W. H. Lampe, "Christian Theology in the Patristic Period," in *A History of Christian Doctrine*, ed. Hubert Cunliffe-Jones [Edinburgh: T. & T. Clark Ltd., 1978], 149).

46. Catherine was perhaps influenced by her fellow Dominican Thomas Aquinas, who downplays Anselm's satisfaction theory, although he does not reject it, in favor of the Father's gift of beatitude as the reason for the incarnation. See Jean-Pierre Torrell, OP, *Saint Thomas Aquinas*, vol. 2, *Spiritual Master*, trans. Robert Royal (Washington, DC: The Catholic University of America Press, 2003), 110.

47. *D* 14, 52. In *L* T260 Christ is compared to a doctor who gives his blood as medicine. See *The Letters of Catherine of Siena*, trans. Noffke, vol. 2, 317. "In the *De Gestis* [V, xiii, 216b] and *Evangelii* [of Simone Fidati da Cascia, II, xv, 199] there is a wealth of Augustinian imagery, some of which we have already noted as typical of Catherine's writing. For example, Simone, following Augustine, depicts Christ as the heavenly doctor who drank first himself the bitter medicine of suffering lest his weak patients might fear to take it" (Benedict Hackett, OSA, "Simone Fidati da Cascia and the Doctrine of St. Catherine of Siena," *Augustiniana* XVI [1966]: 397). Domenico Cavalca, OP, also describes Christ as both doctor and medicine. See Domenico Cavalca, *Lo specchio della croce*, testo originale e versione in italiano corrente, a cura di Tito Sante Centi, OP (Bologna: Edizioni Studio Domenicano, 1992), capitolo 37: 288–97.

48. "You hold us to your breast like a wet-nurse, and have given us the milk of divine grace. You took the bitterness, and in

this way we receive health" (*L* T260, *The Letters of Catherine of Siena*, trans. Noffke, vol. 2, 318).

49. Aquinas also says that the redemption is a greater work of God's than creation: "The justification of the wicked, which has as its end the eternal good of our divine participation, is a greater work than the creation of heaven and earth, for the latter only results in a perishable natural good" (*ST* I–II, 113, 9).

50. Foster, introduction to *I, Catherine*, 35.

51. *D* LXXV, 139.

52. *D* 4, 29. "So if you would receive the fruit of this blood, you must first rouse yourself to heartfelt contrition, contempt for sin…" (*D* 23, 60).

53. See F. Valli, "Il sangue di Cristo nell'opera di S. Caterina da Siena," *Studi cateriniani* IX: 1 (1932): 18; *L* T333, *Le lettere di S. Caterina da Siena*, ed. Misciattelli, vol. 5, 98.

54. See D'Urso, "Santa Caterina da Siena," 50.

55. Foster, "St. Catherine's Teaching on Christ," 318–19.

56. *D* 100, 188.

57. *L* T235, *The Letters of Catherine of Siena*, trans. Noffke, vol. 2, 219, and *L* T316, *I, Catherine*, trans. Foster and Ronayne, 202.

58. *D* 154, 329.

59. *D* 14, 152.

60. See Foster, introduction to *I, Catherine*, 36.

61. *L* T272, *The Letters of Catherine of Siena*, trans. Noffke, vol. 2, 494. This is the only place in the letters where the image of the bridge appears; it is altogether absent in the prayers.

62. *L* T272, *Le lettere di S. Caterina da Siena*, ed. Misciattelli, vol. 4, 162.

63. *D* XX, 59.

64. *D* 21, 58.

65. Giuliana Cavallini, "La dottrina dell'amore in S. Caterina da Siena: concordanze col pensiero di S. Tommaso d'Aquino," *Divus Thomas* LXXV: 4 (ottobre-dicembre 1972): 373.

66. John 14:6. Italics mine. See *D* 27, 66. "Her Christology can be understood as a commentary of the account [Jesus] gave of himself, which she quotes more than once: 'He said: I am the way and truth and the life'" (Giuliana Cavallini, OP, *Catherine of Siena*,

Outstanding Christian Thinkers Series [London and New York: Geoffrey Chapman, 1998], 68).

67. *D* 55, 110.

68. See D'Urso, *Il genio di Santa Caterina*, 145–54.

69. See chapter 1, 27 and also *Supplementum* (Tin.), I, i, 5, 74–75.

70. See *D* 44, 90. In five of Catherine's extant letters (*L* T34, T101, T108, T120, T139) she identifies the tree with the cross.

71. Foster, *I, Catherine*, 144, dates *L* T34 to before the schism (September 20, 1378). Noffke dates *L* T74, T75, and T120 between February 1376 and late September 1377. See Noffke, *The Letters of Catherine of Siena*, vol. 1, 312, and vol. 2, 75 and 120.

72. Cf. Caterina da Siena, *Epistolario di Santa Caterina da Siena*, ed. Dupré Theseider, 258. Noffke, however, dates it to "in or near October 1377." See *The Letters of Catherine of Siena*, trans. Noffke, vol. 2, 514.

73. *L* T75, *The Letters of Catherine of Siena*, trans. Noffke, vol. 2, 517–18. In *L* T74, written around the same time, Catherine refers to the early vision in her cell of the "three ways" on the body of Christ. Although Caffarini's account of the vision does not include any mention of *scaloni* but rather three places on Christ's body, *L* T74 does. See chapter 1, 43–44. See also Caffarini, *Libellus de Supplemento*, ed. Cavallini and Foralosso, II, ii, 7, 35–36. In *L* T34, which Foster dates to sometime before the schism of September 30, 1378, Catherine puts the staircase of Christ's body on the *tree* of the cross. See *L* T34, *I, Catherine*, trans. Foster and Ronayne, 145–46. Throughout this work, we have retained Catherine's distinctive Tuscan word *"scalone"* in preference to the English words "stair" or "step."

74. See Noffke, introduction to *Catherine of Siena: The Dialogue*, 12–13.

75. *D* 26, 64.

76. See *L* T272, *The Letters of Catherine of Siena*, trans. Noffke, vol. 2, 500.

77. See D'Urso, *Il genio di Santa Caterina*, 152.

78. See *D* 26, 64, note. E. di Rovasenda says its is more likely that Catherine conceived the image of the bridge in Avignon where she undoubtedly saw the famous Saint Bénezet bridge over the Rhône, which was built and rebuilt in the twelfth and fourteenth

centuries by a confraternity of friars. A chapel stands midway on the bridge. See Enrico di Rovasenda, OP, *Introduzione al Dialogo di S. Caterina da Siena* (Genova: Biblioteca Franzoniana, 1984), 48. Another possible source for the image of the bridge is Jacopo de Voragine (c.1226–98), Dominican archbishop of Genova, who wrote hundreds of sermons that were used by preachers in the Middle Ages. In a second sermon for Passion Sunday based on John 8:59 he says: "The present world was like a stormy sea, and [also] to be compared with a swift and deep river that endangered everyone; therefore God made a bridge to be built over it which everyone could securely pass towards the heavenly fatherland. But when a bridge is to be built it is customary to first set the foundation stones and then to build pillars on them and then on these pillars the bridge is constructed. Today's Gospel speaks about the founding of pillars when it says: 'The Jews took up stones.' Indeed the epistle speaks about the building of the bridge, when it says: 'Christ assisting as 'pontifex'—that is 'builder of bridges'.... Concerning the second take note that Christ is called builder of bridges...." D'Urso asserts that "Blessed Iacopo da Varazze [Voragine] is surely counted among the indirect teachers of St. Catherine." See Giacinto D'Urso, *Giacomo da Varazze, maestro di S. Caterina da Siena*, Quaderni Caterinati 47–48 (Siena: Associazione Ecumenica Caterinati and Edizioni Cantagalli, 1986), 7–8, 17. It is also possible that beginning with Catherine's childhood vision of Christ as a *pontefice* (pontiff) she may have associated him with a *ponte* (bridge) owing to the similarity in sound of the two words. She may also have been aware of the fact that the word *pontifex* means "bridge builder." *Pontifex* appears numerous times in Hebrews (Vulgate) in reference to Christ the "high priest" and Catherine, of course, may have heard it at Mass.

79. Jorgensen, *Saint Catherine of Siena*, 313. See ibid., 428, note 5: "(MS C. VI, 8 Bibl. Comm. Siena. Stated to me by Signorina Lina Tamburini on St. Galgano. Cf. Olmi: *I Senesi d'una volta* 298–305; Rondoni: *Legende di Siena*)."

80. See D'Urso, *Il genio di Santa Caterina*, 147–48. D'Urso credits Puccetti with the conjecture but gives no citation. He says that the story can be found in the 1538 edition of Cavalca's *Vite dei Santi Padri* published by "Dom. Zio e fratelli," an edition he

describes as "rare, if also imperfect." I have not seen it; subsequent editions do not have it. For more on Cavalca, see Benedict M. Ashley, OP, "Dominic Cavalca and a Spirituality of the Word," Internet: www.oorg/domcentral.study/ashley.cavalca.htm. Accessed on February 20, 2005. See also Gregory the Great, *The Dialogues of St. Gregory the Great*, ed. by Henry James Coleridge (London: Burns and Oates, 1874), Chapter XXXVI, 267, and *Patrologiae cursus completus. Series Latina.* (Paris, 1844–), 77, 384–88, henceforth abbreviated as *PL*.

81. D'Urso, in *Il genio di Santa Caterina* (112–14), cites teachings in every chapter of Cavalca's *Lo specchio* that he says are echoed in Catherine's writings. Also, in *D* 165 there is a reference to Catherine once reading the *"Vita patrum."*

82. See Musso, "Possibili fonti del simbolo cateriniano del 'ponte,'" appendix in "'Gesù dolce, Gesù amore': Il Cristo di Caterina da Siena," 165–77.

83. See *D* 26, 64.

84. The spiritual stages are the subject of chapter 3.

85. See *D* 27, 66.

86. See ibid.

87. Cf. Girolamo Gigli, *Vocabulario cateriniano*, parte prima (Firenze: Tito Giuliani, 1866), 58–59.

88. Cavallini, *Catherine of Siena*, 92. *Bottiga* also appears in *D* 66, 77, 126; *L* T37, T75, T87, T163, T273.

89. See *D* 45, 93.

90. "I am the gate. Whoever enters by me will be saved, and will come in and go out and find pasture" (John 10:9). *Porta* can also mean door. "After this I looked, and there in heaven a door stood open!" (Rev 4:1).

91. *D* 27, 66.

92. *D* 42, 87.

93. *D* XXIX, 77

94. Ibid., 79.

95. See *D* 68, 129; *D* 75, 137; *D* 79, 147. Italics mine.

96. *D* 29, 70. Aquinas says that all of Christ's actions and words, including his teaching, are redemptive. See *ST* III, 48, 6.

97. See *D* 27, 66.

98. *D* 1, 25. Italics mine.

Notes

99. Servais Pinckaers, OP, *Morality: The Catholic View*, with a preface by Alistair MacIntyre, trans. Michael Sherwin, OP (South Bend, IN: St. Augustine's Press, 2001), 19. Aquinas say that "beatitude is the reward of virtue. Therefore, they who tend to beatitude must be virtuously disposed" (*SCG* IV, 54 [7], 231).

100. *D* 66, 122–23. Later in this chapter we will consider Catherine's teaching on self-knowledge.

101. Charity is the mother and root of all virtue. See *ST* I, 62, 4. "'God is Love' and love is his first gift, containing all others" (*Catechism of the Catholic Church*, 2nd ed., 1997, §733. Henceforth abbreviated as *CCC*). See also 1 John 4:8, 16.

102. *D* 63, 118. See D'Urso, "Santa Caterina da Siena," 33–34. Charity is something we owe God as a debt; however, his charity toward us is absolutely gratuitous.

103. See *D* 77, 142. The opposite of charity is selfish self-love, the "mother" of all sins in Catherine's teaching.

104. *D* 95, 178. "In a way [patience] is her moral touchstone or test-virtue, as the typical virtue of the Christian in this world, the *viator*, of the soul on its pilgrimage, beset by temptation. As she saw it, I think, patience is simply the strength of the soul cleaving to God despite everything to the contrary. Patience, in this sense, is active rather than passive; temptations and difficulties are things to be used rather than avoided" (Foster, "The Spirit of St. Catherine of Siena," 445).

105. In *D* 160 charity is a queen who alone enters eternal life while faith and hope do not. See also *D* 160, 346–47.

106. L T69, *The Letters of Catherine of Siena*, trans. Noffke, vol. 1, 65. Noffke dates the letter to "[e]arly 1375, perhaps about 15 March." Grion relates the three theological virtues to the three divine Persons: hope to the Father, faith to the Son, and charity to the Holy Spirit, but without giving citations to Catherine's writings. See Alvaro Grion, OP, "S. Caterina: Maestra di contestazione," *Stella di S. Domenico*, numero speciale: "Santa Caterina da Siena, dottore della Chiesa." LVI: 10 (ottobre 1970): 249. However, this could be a deduction based on Catherine's relating of the three virtues to the three stages of spiritual development that she implicitly relates to the three Persons. See Foster, "St. Catherine's Teaching on Christ," 321–22. Hackett says that Catherine's teaching on the

virtues was influenced by Augustine. See Hackett, "The Augustinian Tradition in the Mysticism of St. Catherine of Siena," 500–1.

107. "But through her love of [the soul's primary virtue] she attracts all the other virtues to herself, since they are all bound together in loving charity" (*D* 7, 37–38).

108. In translating *discrezione*, I prefer "discretion" instead of "discernment." Discretion is a virtue and occupies a venerable place in early monastic spirituality. See *D* 9, 40, and *D* 11, 44, where Catherine speaks of discretion. It is important to note that discretion, in this context, does not mean the ability to keep a secret or a sense of reserve in words and actions. The word appears more than sixty times in Catherine's writings.

109. John Cassian, c. 360–c. 435. See *John Cassian: The Conferences*, translated and annotated by Boniface Ramsey, OP, Ancient Christian Writers: The Works of the Fathers in Translation 57 (New York, NY, and Mahwah, NJ: Newman Press, 1997), Second Conference on Discretion, 77–112.

110. Regis Appel, OCSO, "Cassian's *Discretio*—a Timeless Virtue," *American Benedictine Review* 17 (1966): 24.

111. See *L* T213 in *Saint Catherine of Siena as Seen in Her Letters*, trans. Scudder, 144–53.

112. "Human virtues acquired by education, by deliberate acts and by a perseverance ever-renewed in repeated efforts are purified and elevated by divine grace" (*CCC*, §1810).

113. *D* 27, 66. Catherine is expressing traditional Catholic teaching: that after Christ's passion, the virtues were infused with sanctifying grace, a share in God's own life. See *CCC*, §1810–11.

114. *L* T181, *I, Catherine*, trans. Foster and Ronayne, 96.

115. *D* 96, 179–80.

116. *D* 29, 71.

117. *L* T272, *The Letters of Catherine of Siena*, trans. Noffke, vol. 2, 497–98.

118. *D* 21, 58.

119. *D* 42, 87.

120. See *D* 31, 73. The worm of conscience is an image found in scripture: The agonies of hell are represented by the "worm [that] shall not die" (Isa 66:24; Mark 9:44, 46, 48). Aquinas rea-

soned that the worm of conscience is the worm of regret and conscience. See *ST*, Suppl., Appendix 1, 1.

121. *D* 42, 87.

122. "Objective redemption is the gift of communion offered to us, and subjective redemption is our personal acceptance of this communion through faith and the sacraments" (Roch A. Kereszty, OCist, *Jesus Christ: Fundamentals of Christology*, rev. ed. [Staten Island, NY: St. Paul's, 2002]), 221. John Paul II in *Redemptor hominis* speaks of the importance of personal acceptance of the redemption, which he sees in terms of drawing near to Christ and assimilating the reality, and then knowing oneself and God. See John Paul II, Encyclical Letter *Redemptor hominis*, *AAS* LXXI (1979): 274–75.

123. Aquinas says that the "general remedy" of Christ's suffering must be applied to the individual through faith and the sacraments, "which derive their power from Christ's sufferings" (*ST* III, 49, 1).

124. John 12:32.

125. See *D* 26, 65. "We read in the *Dialogo:* 'the heart of man is drawn by love,' which is simply another way of rephrasing Augustine: 'The mind is ever drawn by love'" (*Tractatus in Evangelium Ioannis* XXVI, 4: *Corpus Christianorum. Series Latinae*, [Turnhout, 1953–], XXXVI, 261–62. Henceforth *CCSL*). Michael B[enedict] Hackett, OSA, "The Augustinian Tradition in the Mysticism of St. Catherine of Siena," in *Collectanea Augustiniana: Augustine, Mystic and Mystagogue*, ed. Frederick Van Fleteren, Joseph C. Schnaubelt, OSA, and Joseph Reino (New York: Peter Lang, 1994), 501.

126. *D* 119, 226; see *D* 155, 330. "God made you without your knowing it; he justifies you with your willing consent to it" (*Sermo* 169, 13). See Benedict Hackett, OSA, *William Flete, OSA, and Catherine of Siena: Masters of Fourteenth Century Spirituality*, ed. John E. Rotelle, OSA, foreword by Francis X. Martin, OSA, The Augustinian Series, vol. 15 (Villanova, PA: Augustinian Press, 1992), 112.

127. *D* 54, 107.

128. *D* XXXVII, 73.

129. See *D* 29, 71.

130. "[T]he soul is a vessel ready to receive grace and to make it grow" (*D* 14, 52).
131. John 4:10.
132. *D* 54, 109.
133. Cf. D'Urso, "Santa Caterina da Siena," 46.
134. *D* 36, 78.
135. Aquinas says that Christians "can attain to [God] by their own operations of knowing and loving" (*ST* I, 65, 2).
136. L T113, *The Letters of Catherine of Siena*, trans. Noffke, vol. 2, 675. Maximus the Confessor (d. 662) had said as much centuries before: intelligent beings move toward God by knowledge and love. See Etienne Gilson, *The Mystical Theology of St. Bernard*, trans. A. H. C. Downes (New York: Sheed and Ward, 1940), 25.
137. *D* 1, 25. "One who knows more, loves more" (*D* 66, 126). Kearns says that love following knowledge is "one of the most characteristic in the theology of Saint Thomas Aquinas.... Love, he repeatedly says, follows knowledge" (Conleth Kearns, "The Wisdom of Saint Catherine," *Angelicum* 57:3 [1980]: 335). See *ST* I–II, 27, 2, 2, in which Aquinas says: "[I]t suffices, for the perfection of love, that a thing be loved according as it is known in itself." McGinn says that knowledge and love are intertwined in Augustine's mysticism. See McGinn, *The Foundations of Mysticism*, vol. 1, *The Presence of God: A History of Western Christian Mysticism*, 235. "Catherine worked out in a practical way the Thomistic principle inherited from St. Augustine: 'Nothing is loved except it be first known' [*De Trinitate* X, 1] (*ST* I-II, 3, 4, 4)" (Marie Walter Flood, "St. Thomas's Thought in the *Dialogue* of St. Catherine," *Spirituality Today* 32 (1980): 30).
138. See 1 John 4:16.
139. Gilson, *The Mystical Theology of St. Bernard*, 22.
140. *D* 60, 115. Aquinas says that "love transforms the lover into the beloved" (*Scriptum super Sententiis*, III, 27, 1, 1, 4. Henceforth abbreviated as *Sent*).
141. See *D* 58, 111–12.
142. *D* 1, 26.
143. Mario Ismaele Castellano, OP, "Antropologia cateriniana," *Quaderni Cateriniani* 90 (Siena: Edizioni Cantagalli, 1996): 6.

144. *D* 2, 27. See also *D* 112, 211 (in which the expression is a commentary on John 6:56: "Those who eat my flesh and drink my blood abide in me, and I in them") and *P* 20 (XII), 226. God's presence in the human person, and the person's presence in God, is contained in the dogma of God's omnipresence. God fills the whole created space and every one of its parts: "Where can I go from your spirit? Or where can I flee from your presence? If I ascend to heaven, you are there; if I make my bed in Sheol, you are there. If I take the wings of the morning and settle at the farthest limits of the sea, even there your hand shall lead me, and your right hand shall hold me fast" (Ps 139:7–10); "[I]n him we live and move and have our being" (Acts 17:28). See also *ST* I, 8, 1. As L. Ott makes clear, besides the "natural presence of God, there is also a special natural presence or indwelling of God, by the supernatural efficacy of His grace in the soul of the just man (John 14:23; 1 Cor 3:16 and 6:19), in the house of God (Ps 132:13 et seq.) and in Heaven (Matt 6:9)" (Ludwig Ott, *Fundamentals of Catholic Dogma*, trans. Patrick Lynch, ed. James Bastible [Cork: The Mercier Press, 1955], 38). Aquinas says that the divine indwelling can be understood in terms of love: "God manifestly loves in the greatest degree those whom He has made lovers of Himself through the Holy Spirit, for He would not confer so great a good save by loving us.... Of course, every beloved is in the lover. Therefore, by the Holy Spirit not only is God in us, but we also are in God. Hence, we read in I John (4:16,13): 'He that abideth in charity abideth in God, and God in him'; and: 'In this we know that we abide in Him and He in us: because He hath given us His spirit'" (*SCG* IV, 21, [4], 122–23). See also Royo and Aumann, *The Theology of Christian Perfection*, 566–67.

145. "Cognoscimento di me in te" (*D* LXXXVI, 226).

146. *L* T70, *The Letters of Catherine of Siena*, trans. Noffke, vol. 1, 42.

147. *P* 14 (VII), 142.

148. *D* 1, 26. The "'bright garment of charity' is the supreme virtue, a foretaste, *arra*, of eternal life." Foster, introduction to *I, Catherine*, 37.

149. "[T]hrough this union of the divine nature with the human, God was made human and humanity was made God *(l'uomo è fatto*

Dio e Dio è fatto uomo)" (*D* 15, 53); see also *D* 110, 205. We will consider Catherine's teaching on union with God in chapter 3.

150. Sr. Dominic [Walsh], "St. Catherine of Siena: Doctor of the Church," 139.

151. Not all medieval writers had such a positive anthropology. Pourrat quotes an anonymous writer of the period: "What then is man that he should commune with God his creator? Alas! what am I Lord, who speak to thee? I am a decaying body, the food of worms, a fetid vessel, fuel for the fire. What again am I, Lord, who speak to thee? I am an unfortunate, *born of a woman, living for a short time, filled with many miseries* (Job xiv, I).... What again, O Lord? I am a dark abyss, miserable earth, a child of wrath...born in corruption, living in tribulation, and destined to die in pain.... I shall tell thee my misery, O my God, I do not hesitate to confess to thee my baseness. Help me, Lord, thou who art my strength by which I shall rise" (P[ierre] Pourrat, *Christian Spirituality in the Middle Ages*, trans. S. Jacques, vol. 2 [New York: J. Kenedy and Sons, 1924], 296).

152. In the two English translations of the *Dialogue*, that of Thorold (1896) and of Noffke (1980), feminine pronouns are used throughout to refer to the soul. This is legitimate because *l'anima* is feminine. Also, the particular soul being spoken of in the work is often Catherine's. See Catherine of Siena, *The Dialogue of the Seraphic Virgin Catherine of Siena*, trans. Thorold.

153. See chapter 1, 37–38.

154. *D* 51, 103.

155. According to Aquinas, human beings, because they are made in God's image and likeness, have a natural inclination to know and love God; through grace we know and love God imperfectly but in the light of glory we shall know him perfectly. See *ST* I, 93, 4. Catherine's teaching on the *imago Dei* and our vocation to divinization is echoed in the famous saying of Meister Eckhart in his treatise *On the Nobleman*: "God's seed is within us. If it had a good, skillful and industrious gardener to tend it, it would thrive all the better and grow up to God, whose seed it is, and the fruit would be like God's nature. The seed of a pear-tree grows into a pear-tree, that of a nut-tree into a nut-tree, God's seed into God" (*Meister Eckhart: Sermons and Treatises*, trans. M. O'C. Walshe [London:

Watkins, 1985], vol. 3, 107). "Those who have been born of God do not sin, because God's seed abides in them" (1 John 3:9).

156. *D* XXXIII, 89. Caffarini records that once when Catherine was upset about not being able to receive communion, the Lord said to her: "My daughter, where do you want to go? Your soul is my habitation and wherever you go, you will always be with me and I with you" (*Supplementum* [Tin.], II, vi, 49, 177).

157. *D* 151, 320. This doctrine of the mystical birth of Christ in the soul is based on Galatians 4:19: "My little children, for whom I am again in the pain of childbirth until Christ is formed in you." The mystical birth of Christ in the Christian is a theme found in Irenaeus of Lyon and Origen. See Walter H. Principe, CSB, *Introduction to Patristic and Medieval Theology*, 2nd ed. (Toronto: Pontifical Institute of Medieval Studies, 1982), 60. F. Vandenbroucke, in a flawed presentation of Catherine, is obviously wrong when he says that the birth of the Word in the soul "is altogether foreign to her thought" (Jean Leclercq, François Vandenbroucke, Louis Bouyer, *A History of Christian Spirituality*, vol. 2, *The Spirituality of the Middle Ages* [Wellwood, Kent: Burns and Oates, 1968], 415). For a critique of Vandenbroucke, see Francesco Scalvini [Innocenzo Colosio], "La vera Caterina da Siena e la Caterina del benedettino fr. Vandenbroucke," *Rivista di ascetica e mistica* VI (1961): 503–36.

158. See *D* 159, 342, etc.

159. See *D* 23, 60, etc.

160. See *D* 144, 299.

161. See *D* 144, 299 and *L* T114, *The Letters of Catherine of Siena*, trans. Noffke, vol. 2, 340. Catherine also speaks of the "little boat of the soul" *(navicella dell'anima)* in *D* 95, *L* T126, T127, T132, T139, T195, T246, T331, etc. Hackett says that she may have conceived the image from the Italian version of St. Bernard's *De Gestis*. See Hackett, "Simone Fidati da Cascia and the Doctrine of St. Catherine of Siena," 406.

162. See *D* 11, 45

163. *D* 13, 49. Italics mine. "Catherine explains the likeness of the memory with the power of God, not because man has the power to create but because he has the power to *preserve* in his memory all that the intellect knows. God in fact creates, but

also *preserves in himself* all created things, and maintains them in life" (Castellano, "Antropologia cateriniana," 12). "The last term, *clemenza* [sic], is curious and raises historical questions.... *Clementia* in Thomistic theology denotes a virtue in man rather than an attribute of God" (Foster, "St. Catherine's Teaching on Christ," 316). In a sermon on the dignity of the mother of God for Saturday of the third week of Lent, Jacopo de Voragine (Iacopo da Varazze) says: "And so the Father made her powerful so as to help us, the Son made her wise so as to be our advocate, the Holy Spirit made her *clement* in the exercise of mercy." Voragine was author of the immensely popular medieval hagiographical work the *Legenda aurea*. D'Urso says Catherine very likely had contact with its legends. See Giacinto D'Urso, "Iacopo da Varazze ispiratore di S. Caterina," *La patrona d'Italia, Santa Caterina* XXX:3 (1975): 14.

164. Her contact with Augustinianism may have been principally through the English Augustinian hermit William Flete in nearby Lecceto. Catherine may have met Flete (c. 1325–c.1390) as early as 1368. The two had many conversations. A room is preserved today at the Augustinian monastery in Lecceto where Catherine is said to have slept whenever she visited Flete. The extent to which Flete influenced Catherine, and vice versa, is disputed. See Hackett, *William Flete, OSA, and Catherine of Siena*, 79–106. Seven of Catherine's extant letters were addressed to him: *L* T55, 64, 66, 77, 227, 292, 326. Hackett, in "The Augustinian Tradition in the Mysticism of St. Catherine of Siena," 503, says: "The comparison of the soul and its three faculties, which Catherine obviously considered as distinct, to the Trinity ultimately derives from Augustine, who also suggests, but cautiously, that the memory or *reminiscentia* may be likened to the Father, the intellect to the Son, and the will to the Holy Spirit. But he refrains from appropriating, as Catherine seems to do, power to the Father, wisdom to the Son, and love (the equivalent of Catherine's mercy) to the Holy Spirit. For once it would appear that she is more Thomistic than Augustinian, though her proximate source is more likely to have been Simone da Cascia, the Augustinian spiritual writer and mystic who died in 1348...." Augustine speaks of *memoria, intelligentia,* and *voluntas* as the three faculties of the soul. See *De Trinitate* XV, xx, 39–xxiii, 43: *CCSL* (A), 516–21, and *Sermo* LII VI, 17–X, 23: *PL* 38, 360–64.

165. See Benedict Ashley, "St. Catherine of Siena's Principles of Spiritual Direction," *Spirituality Today* 33: 1 (March 1981): 52, n. 12.

166. *P* XXIII, 264; Sr. M. Jeremiah, "The Theological Anthropology of Catherine of Siena," *Communio* 20 (1993): 459.

167. *D* 54, 107–9.

168. Matthew 18:20.

169. *D* 126, 246.

170. *D* 51, 104.

171. *D* 59, 113.

172. *L* Gardner II, *The Letters of Catherine of Siena*, trans. Noffke, vol. 2, 618. Riccardi says that true love for Catherine is "the love that derives from 'true knowledge' of oneself and of God in the soul. While this love is unifying, disordered and egotistical love is disintegrative and dispersive: it breaks the unity and harmony of the human being and leaves him weak and alone." See "C.R." [Carlo Riccardi, C.M.], "La carità, fonte di unità interiore e di armonia sociale, nell'insegnamento di Caterina da Siena," *Rassegna di ascetica e mistica*, "S. Caterina da Siena," XXII: 2 (aprile-giungno 1971): 138.

173. See *D* 147, 310. Likewise, the soul's three powers can produce an evil sound. See *D* 126, 246.

174. See *D* 96, 179.

175. Cf. *D* 54, 108.

176. *D* 26, 65. Catherine sometimes interchanges the words *heart* and *soul*.

177. "The ultimate purpose of man's creation is that he may share in God's eternal joy. But this will only be the climax of a communication *already* established (but at the risk of being lost by sin) in the original 'forming' of the soul to the image of the created Trinity. Catherine's treatment of this theme is a variant of the Augustinian tradition" (Foster, introduction to *I, Catherine*, 34).

178. J. R. Quinn, "Divine Nature," *New Catholic Encyclopedia* (New York: McGraw-Hill Book Company, 1967), 916. Italics mine.

179. "l'unione fra l'anima e il corpo" (*D* XIX, 57).

180. *D* 1, 25.

181. See *D* 98, 185. "So I find it to be a law that when I want to do what is good, evil lies close at hand. For I delight in the law of God in my inmost self, but I see in my members another law at war

with the law of my mind, making me captive to the law of sin that dwells in my members" (Rom 7:21–23).

182. Self-will, Catherine says, is the source of our suffering. See D 48, 98. She uses the words *sensuality, selfish self-love,* and *self-will* somewhat interchangeably.

183. D 46, 94. "One of the effects of self-love [according to Catherine] is that the mind is darkened. It needs to be purified. Catherine's teaching on this aspect of the spiritual life is a further and highly significant indication of the Augustinian trend of her thought. According to Augustine, the eye of the soul—the intellect—is liable to be darkened by error, self-love and its offshoots, namely cupidity, hatred and worldliness. It has turned away its gaze from the light of God and is therefore no longer healthy; indeed the light is hateful to the eye. Hence there can be no advance towards the truth unless the eye of the soul is first healed and cleansed, and be able to see and receive the light which illumines the way and in which the soul contemplates Truth itself" (Hackett, "The Augustinian Tradition in the Mysticism of St. Catherine of Siena," 497). As stated in 1 John 1:6, to be in a state of sin is to be in darkness: "If we say that we have fellowship with him while we are walking in darkness, we lie and do not what is true."

184. The sin which is "most hateful and so darkens the human mind" is lust (D 32, 74).

185. Foster, "The Spirit of St. Catherine of Siena," 442. Augustine also speaks of self-love *(amor sui)* as the root sin that is directly opposed to God. See Oliver O'Donovan, *The Problem of Self-Love in St. Augustine* (New Haven and London: Yale University Press, 1980), 93 and 137. Augustine teaches that all evil is rooted in the will: "I inquired then what villainy might be, but I found no substance, only the perversity of a will twisted away from you, God, the supreme substance, towards the depths—a will that throws away its life within you and swells with vanity abroad" (Augustine of Hippo, *The Confessions*, intro., trans., notes Maria Boulding, OSB, The Works of St. Augustine: A Translation for the 21st Century, ed. John E. Rotelle, OSA [Hyde Park, NY: New City Press, 1997], 176). See *Confessiones* VII, xvi, 22: *CCSL* XXVII, 106.

186. Sr. Dominic [Walsh], "St. Catherine of Siena: Doctor of the Church," 140. Catherine never relents in her tremendous assaults

on selfish self-love and is very realistic about human weakness and the tendency to turn away from God. Yet, as we have said before, her overall teaching on the human person is very positive, as Walsh attests: "Generally speaking…St. Catherine's vision of man is a very positive one. If she stressed his sinfulness, she stressed even more the possibilities that are in man and the glorious destiny that can be his. This was her approach especially in her letters. Instead of condemnation, she assured the recipients of pardon and put before them the beauty and holiness of a loving response to God. The remedy for those who had sinned was easy and was given to all. 'Bathe thee in the blood of Christ crucified'" (ibid).

187. See *D* 33, 75.

188. *D* 35, 77. See also *D* 15, 53.

189. *L* T164, *The Letters of Catherine of Siena*, trans. Noffke, vol. 2, 31.

190. See *D* 6, 34–35.

191. *L* T29, *The Letters of Catherine of Siena*, trans. Noffke, vol. 1, 207.

192. *D* 18, 56. Aquinas says that "evil, as evil, is nothing, because it is a deprivation, as blindness" (I *Sent.* 36, 2, 3, 1).

193. *D* 21, 58.

194. McCabe, *God Matters*, 35.

195. *D* 6, 33. See *D* 6, 34 and *P* 15 (VIII), 150.

196. See *D* XXXV, 91. *Cavelle* is Tuscan for "something" or "nothing." See Caterina da Siena, *Il messaggio di Santa Caterina da Siena*, ed. Carlo Riccardi, CM, 2nd ed. (Roma: CLV Edizioni, 1988), L.

197. *D* 93, 173–74.

198. *D* 143, 297.

199. See *L* T260, *The Letters of Catherine of Siena*, trans. Noffke, vol. 2, 317. Also see Michele Fortuna, OP, "Struttura dell'anima nel linguaggio metaforico di S. Caterina da Siena," *Rassegna di ascetica e mistica*, "S. Caterina da Siena," XIII:3 (luglio–settembre 1972): 258.

200. *D* 73, 135. Catherine describes conscience using various images: a watchdog (*D* 129, *L* T2, T22, T114, T313), a guard at the door of the will (*L* T313, T321), a worm that nibbles (*D* 31, 156; *L* T80), a light (*L* T90), a judgment seat (*L* T154, T315, T331,

T358), an advocate or attorney (*L* T3), and a prod *(stimolo)* that helps to vomit out sins (*D* 94). Its purpose is self-correction: "And if difficulties make her selfish sensuality want to rise up against reason, her conscience must use [holy] hatred to pronounce judgment and not let any impulse pass uncorrected. Indeed, the soul who lives in [holy hatred] finds self-correction and self-reproach in everything..." (*D* 73, 135).

201. *L* T205, *Le lettere di S. Caterina da Siena*, ed. Misciattelli, vol. 3, 201.

202. *L* T265, ibid., vol. 4, 133.

203. *D* XXIX, 79.

204. *D* 29, 70.

205. *D* 14, 52.

206. *D* 23, 60. "Hatred and love unite, rather as allies, because one cannot think that Catherine's ascetical norms would be only negative, and thus inhuman; on the contrary, because one sees that the double-edged weapon is not so much for destruction as for building up that edifice of virtue which, through the work of knowledge, must begin from the valley of humility" (D'Urso, "Santa Caterina da Siena," 36).

207. *L* T69, *I, Catherine*, trans. Foster and Ronayne, 65–66.

208. Foster, introduction to *I, Catherine*, 32. See also *P* 15 (VIII) and *L* T28. "Who will separate us from the love of Christ? Will hardship, or distress, or persecution, or famine, or nakedness, or peril, or sword?"(Rom 8:35).

209. *D* 43, 88.

210. "Levandosi una anima ansietata di grandissimo desiderio..." (*D* 1, 25).

211. For more on the theme of desire in Catherine of Siena, see Foster, "St. Catherine's Teaching on Christ," 315; Mary O'Driscoll, "St. Catherine of Siena: Life and Spirituality," *Angelicum* 57 (1980): 317.

212. Bernard of Clairvaux embraced the theme of desire and saw it as an essential part of the spiritual life. See Michael Casey, *A Thirst for God: Spiritual Desire in Bernard of Clairvaux's Sermon on the* Song of Songs, Cistercian Studies Series, 77 (Kalamazoo: Cistercian Publications, 1988), 59; McGinn, *The Foundations of Mysticism*, 259. Leclercq calls Gregory "the doctor of desire." See

Jean Leclercq, OSB, *The Love of Learning and the Desire for God: A Study of Monastic Culture*, trans. Catharine Misrahi (New York: Fordham University Press, 1960), 39–40. Desire for God is mentioned in *CCC*, §27–30.

213. "My soul thirsts for God, for the living God. When shall I come and behold the face of God?" (Ps 42:2). For more scriptural references and information on "desire of God" in the history of spirituality, see Henri Martin, "Désirs," *Dictionnaire de spiritualité* (Paris: Beauchesne, 1957), vol. 3, cols. 606–23.

214. Torrell, *Saint Thomas Aquinas*, vol. 2, *Spiritual Master*, 343. See also 327.

215. *L* T29, *The Letters of Catherine of Siena*, trans. Noffke, vol. 1, 208.

216. "There is, therefore, a certain suffering involved in the creature's desire for God. In one of her letters [*L* T211] Catherine speaks of the 'torment of desire—those who have experienced it know that it is the heaviest of crosses'" (O'Driscoll, "St. Catherine of Siena: Life and Spirituality," 317).

217. See ibid., 318. The right relationship between human beings and created things will be given greater attention when we consider Catherine's teaching on the neighbor later in this chapter.

218. Foster, introduction to *I, Catherine*, 33.

219. See Foster, "St. Catherine's Teaching on Christ," 315; introduction to *I, Catherine*, 32. Affection *(affetto)* is an extension or manifestation of the soul's desire. See chapter 3, 164–66.

220. *L* T8, *The Letters of Catherine of Siena*, trans. Noffke, vol. 2, 356. See John 19:28, *L* T12 and T136. Christ's suffering on the cross was finite, but his desire for our salvation is infinite. See *D* 75, 139 and *P* 18 (XI), 193–94.

221. *D* 4, 31.

222. *D* 51, 101.

223. "To his servants which, in fact, he calls his christs, who may or may not be his [ordained] ministers, the Lord has assigned the task of prolonging through the ages his desire; to the Church he has left his Blood, expression of his love and of the Savior's desire" (D'Urso, "Santa Caterina da Siena, " 57–58).

224. *D* 3, 28; cf. 1 Chr 18:38.

225. Innocenzo Colosio, OP, "La infinità del desiderio secondo S. Caterina da Siena," in *S. Caterina tra i dottori della Chiesa*, ed. Tito S. Centi, OP (Firenze: Casa Editrice A. Salani, 1970), 74.

226. "Knowledge of the faith does not pacify desire; rather it stirs it up" (*SCG* III, 40).

227. *D* 92, 170.

228. *D* 66, 126; see 1 Thess 5:17. Giardini notes that Catherine follows Augustine in saying that desire is St. Paul's "prayer without ceasing." Cf. Fabio Giardini, *Pray Without Ceasing: Toward a Systematic Psychotherapy of Christian Prayerlife* (Herefordshire and Rome: Gracewing and Millennium Romae Editrice, 1998), 346–49. Augustine distinguishes between the desire to desire something, and the desire for the thing itself. See *Expositions of the Psalms (Enarrationes in Psalmos)* 99–120. III/19, trans. and notes Maria Boulding, OSB, ed. Boniface Ramsey, OP, The Works of St. Augustine: A Translation for the 21st Century (Hyde Park, NY: New City Press, 2003), 376. Aquinas, like Augustine, says that desire is "prayer without ceasing"; he also says it is the cause of prayer and should always be present in us. See *ST* II–II, 83, 14.

229. *L* T26, in *Catherine of Siena: Passion for the Truth, Compassion for Humanity: Selected Spiritual Writings*, ed. and intro. Mary O'Driscoll, OP (Hyde Park, NY: New City Press, 1993), 22.

230. *D* 92, 170–71. According to Giardini, Catherine's teaching on the continuation of desire in heaven is a departure from Augustine. See Giardini, *Pray Without Ceasing*, 349.

231. Colosio, "La infinità del desiderio secondo S. Caterina da Siena," 78. On the other hand, Aquinas says that beatitude is "capable of entirely pacifying desire" (*ST* I-II, 2, 7).

232. "Cell" (*cella*) connotes a monastic cell. Catherine uses a variety of other words to describe self-knowledge: a house, tomb, valley, stable, night, moonlight, grace, abyss, tug, wood, enclosed garden, dew, fire, light, vessel, cave, well. Catherine's teaching on self-knowledge does not pertain to psychological self-knowledge in the modern sense.

233. See *D* 1, 25.

234. In the opening chapter of the *Dialogue*, Catherine speaks of "continual humble prayer, grounded *[fondata]* in the knowledge of [oneself] and of God" (*D* 1, 25).

235. "And find your pleasure in prayer, where you will come to a better knowledge of both yourself and God" (*L* T264, *The Letters of Catherine of Siena*, trans. Noffke, vol. 2, 483).

236. See Pourrat, *Christian Spirituality in the Middle Ages*, vol. 2, 291; Louis de Bazelaire, "Connaissance de soi," *Dictionnaire de spiritualité* (Paris: Beauchesne, 1953), vol. 2, cols. 1511–43. The theme is clearly seen in the famous fifteenth-century work *The Imitation of Christ:* "The humble man's knowledge of himself is a surer way to God than any deep researches into the truth" (Thomas à Kempis, *The Imitation of Christ*, trans. Ronald Knox and Michael Oakley [New York: Sheed and Ward, 1959], 21).

237. Hackett, "The Augustinian Tradition in the Mysticism of St. Catherine of Siena," 494. "In books VIII–X [of *De Trinitate*] Augustine seeks to discover the true nature of man: the first step in search of God is to seek to discover one's self. Without true self-knowledge man has only a distorted idea of the image of God in himself, and so the way to God is flawed from the start" (Andrew Louth, *The Origins of the Christian Mystical Tradition from Plato to Denys* [Oxford: Clarendon Press, 1981], 148).

238. Pourrat, *Christian Spirituality in the Middle Ages*, vol. 2, 291.

239. "The Greeks say: Know thyself that thou may'st know that thou are not a god, but only a mortal. The Christians say: Know thyself that thou may'st know thyself a mortal, but the image of God" (Gilson, *The Mystical Theology of St. Bernard*, 232).

240. Domenico Abbrescia, OP, "La conoscenza di sè," in *Lineamenti di spiritualità cateriniana* (Roma: Coletti Editore, 1964), 8.

241. *Legenda major*, §92, 85. Italics mine.

242. Ibid., chapter X, 85.

243. Ibid., §96, 89.

244. Exodus 3:13–14.

245. D'Urso, "Santa Caterina da Siena," 29. See Sr. Mary Jeremiah, OP, "'To Be or Not to Be': Catherine of Siena on Sin and Salvation," *The Canadian Catholic Review*, September 1990: 298.

246. Ignazio Paci, OP, "Intelletto, memoria, e voluntà," in *L'anima dominicana di S. Caterina da Siena*, Quaderni Caterinati 39 (Siena: Associazione Ecumenica Caterinati, 1985), 17.

247. *D* 18, 56. "I am who I am" *(Io sono colui che so')* can also be rendered "I am He (or the One) who is."

248. *D* 134, 273. "But these presumptuous wretches do not reflect that I am who I am and they are the ones who are not." *D* 119, 226.

249. *D* 144, 301.

250. Sr. Dominic [Walsh], "St. Catherine of Siena: Doctor of the Church," 138.

251. *L* T94, *Le lettere di S. Caterina da Siena*, ed. Misciattelli, vol. 2, 96.

252. *D* LXXXVI, 226.

253. *L* T49, *Le lettere di S. Caterina da Siena*, ed. Misciattelli, vol. 1, 191. Walsh notes that knowledge of God for Catherine was "seen in terms of the biblical meaning of the word knowledge. This is essentially the knowledge one person has of another" (Sr. Dominic [Walsh], "St. Catherine of Siena: Doctor of the Church," 136).

254. *L* T41, *The Letters of Catherine of Siena*, trans. Noffke, vol. 1, 7–8. Noffke dates the letter to "possibly 1368, but certainly before May 1374." Dupré Theseider dates it to "before May 1374" (Caterina da Siena, *Epistolario di Santa Caterina da Siena*, trans. Dupré Theseider, 18).

255. *L* T94, *Le lettere di S. Caterina da Siena*, ed. Misciattelli, vol. 2, 96.

256. *L* T49, ibid., vol. 1, 191.

257. *L* T49, *The Letters of Catherine of Siena*, trans. Noffke, vol. 2, 601–2. Noffke dates the letter to "late October or November 1377." See also *L* T94, ibid., 672, which Noffke dates to "November or December 1377" and *L* T104, ibid., 652, which she also dates to the same period.

258. *L* T41, ibid., vol. 1, 8.

259. "Through that way we come to virtue, that is through knowledge of the goodness of God, and through the light of which we see his humility and charity. In him we will acquire them, looking for them inside our soul; elsewhere, in no other way, will we ever find them" (*L* T345, *Le lettere di S. Caterina da Siena*, ed. Misciattelli, vol. 5, 160.

260. *D* 112, 211.

261. *L* T49, *The Letters of Catherine of Siena*, trans. Noffke, vol. 2, 602. "The soul cannot have two foundations; either one or the other will be thrown to the ground" (*L* T213, *Le lettere di S. Caterina da Siena*, ed. Misciattelli, vol. 3, 233).

262. *D* 10, 141.
263. *D* I, 1.
264. *D* 66, 124.
265. *L* T226, I, *Catherine*, trans. Foster and Ronayne, 171–72. Foster and Ronayne date the letter to April 14, 1378. Noffke, however, dates the letter to "about 17 February 1376" (*The Letters of Catherine of Siena*, trans. Noffke, vol. 2, 2).
266. See *D* 45, 92.
267. *D* 126, 246.
268. *D* 98, 184. See *D* 100, 187; *D* 111, 209; *L* T184, *The Letters of Catherine of Siena*, trans. Noffke, vol. 2, 310.
269 "Oh God eternal! Oh God eternal! You tell me to gaze into you" (*P* 12 [XXII], 111).
270. See *L* T146, *The Letters of Catherine of Siena*, trans. Noffke, vol. 1, 96.
271. *D* 167, 365–66. C. S. Lewis, in *Mere Christianity* (New York: Macmillan, 1952), 174–75, uses the image of a mirror to show how, in the kingdom, we shall be mirrors of God that perfectly reflect back to him his joy and love: "[God] said (in the Bible [Ps 82:6]) that we were 'gods' and He is going to make good His words. If we let Him—for we can prevent Him, if we choose—He will make the feeblest and filthiest of us into a god or goddess, dazzling, radiant, immortal creature, pulsating all through with such energy and joy and wisdom and love as we cannot now imagine, a bright stainless mirror which reflects back to God perfectly (though, of course, on a smaller scale) His boundless power and delight and goodness. The process will be long and in parts very painful; but that is what we are in for."
272. *D* 13, 48.
273. "[L]ove transforms one into what one loves" (*D* 60, 115–16).
274. *D* 1, 25.
275. *D* 21, 18.
276. *L* T226, I, *Catherine*, trans. Foster and Ronayne, 171.
277. *D* 13, 48.
278. Hackett suggests that Catherine's teaching on self-knowledge is virtually the same as found in Augustine's *True Religion*, *Expositions of the Psalms*, and *Confessions*. He summarizes the process

as (1) the creature knows its own nothingness, (2) then it begins to sense at its deepest point an overwhelming goodness, and (3) it craves union with God. But this misrepresents Catherine's teaching on self-knowledge, at least in its final form. Catherine first stresses our realization of God's beauty *and* his beauty in us and then moves on to the human person's nothingness and sinfulness. Her anthropology, therefore, starts on a positive note. See Hackett, *William Flete, OSA, and Catherine of Siena*, 110–11.

279. Herbert McCabe, OP, *God Matters*, Contemporary Christian Insights Series (London and New York: Mowbray, 1987), 20.

280. *L* T362, *I, Catherine*, trans. Foster and Ronayne, 255.

281. Foster, introduction to *I, Catherine*, 30.

282. *L* T101, *The Letters of Catherine of Siena*, trans. Noffke, vol. 2, 71. This is another example of Catherine's positive anthropology: We do not "hate" ourselves as God's creatures but only as rebels.

283. *D* 73, 135.

284. *L* T30, *The Letters of Catherine of Siena*, trans. Noffke, vol. 1, 49. In *D* 10, Catherine describes a circle written on the ground with a tree in the center. The tree represents the soul and the circle represents knowledge of oneself and of God within oneself. The circle is broken when these two dimensions of self-knowledge are separated from one another; the circle expands, however, in proportion to the growth of self-knowledge. Nurtured by self-knowledge and the soil of humility, the tree "bears many-fragranced blossoms of virtue" and its fruit is grace for oneself and blessings for one's neighbors. See *D* 10, 41–42.

285. *L* T30, *Le lettere di S. Caterina da Siena*, ed. Misciattelli, vol. 1, 111.

286. See *D* 151, 320.

287. See Sr. Jean Marie, OP, "Aquinas's Theology of Trinitarian Mission and the *Dialogue* of Catherine of Siena," *Dominican Monastic Search* 95 (1995): 64.

288. *P* 18 (XI), 186.

289. See chapter 1, 24.

290. *Legenda major*, §49, 46. See also D'Urso, "Santa Caterina da Siena," 40.

Notes

291. *L* T49, *The Letters of Catherine of Siena*, trans. Noffke, vol. 2, 601. For more on Catherine's teaching on self-knowledge, see Mary O'Driscoll, "Catherine the Theologian," *Spirituality Today* 40 (Spring 1988): 4–17, especially 12–13, and Mary Ann Fatula, OP, *Catherine of Siena's Way*. The Way of the Christian Mystics Series (Wilmington, DE: Michael Glazier, 1987), 76–91. Aquinas says that God's self-knowledge is the Word and his self-love is the Spirit: "God exists as the known in the knower and the beloved in the lover" (*ST* Ia, 43, 3).

292. Foster, introduction to *I, Catherine*, 31.

293. Giacinto D'Urso, OP, "Nozione teologale dell'orazione secondo S. Caterina," *Caterina da Siena* XVI (gennaio–febbraio 1965): 31. A computer word search of Catherine's writings reveals that *orazione(i)* appears 510 times while *preghiera(e)* appears only once (*L* T338).

294. See *D* 66, 126.

295. Ibid., 124–25. In the same chapter she speaks of "prayers of obligation," the Liturgy of the Hours that clerics and religious are obliged to recite.

296. "For by such prayer the soul is united with God..." (*D* 1, 25).

297. See *D* 66, 122.

298. *D* 68, 130–31.

299. See *Early Dominicans: Selected Writings*, ed. and intro. by Simon Tugwell, OP, preface by Vincent de Couesnongle, OP, The Classics of Western Spirituality (Mahwah, NJ: Paulist Press, 1982), 22. Augustine also gives priority to both charity and prayer: "No man has a right to lead such a life of contemplation as to forget in his own ease the service due to his neighbor; nor has any man a right to be so immersed in active life as to neglect the contemplation of God" (Augustine of Hippo, *City of God* 19.19. *PL* 41, col. 647). For an English translation, see St. Augustine of Hippo, *Basic Writings of St. Augustine*, vol. 2, ed. Whitney J. Oates (New York: Random House, 1948), 495.

300. *Legenda major*, §121, 116.

301. *D* 7, 36. See also *D* 64, 121.

302. *D* 54, 107. McGinn says that for Augustine progress toward God is also communal and not individual. See McGinn, *The*

Catherine of Siena

Foundations of Mysticism, 262. Aquinas, in *ST* I, 65, 1, 3 says: "In themselves, creatures do not turn us from God but lead us to him."

303. See *D* 41, 83–84.

304. *D* 89, 164–65.

305. *D* 96, 180.

306. *D* 6, 33. In general, we extend charity to our neighbors by loving them as ourselves, assisting them spiritually with prayer, counsel, and, when necessary, material things. In particular, we do it by helping others in "word and *teaching* and good example, indeed in every need of which you are aware, giving counsel as sincerely as you would to yourself, without selfishness" (*D* 6, 33). Italics mine. It is noteworthy that Catherine includes teaching among the particular ways in which we practice charity.

307. The expression is probably related to Christ's words, "My food is to do the will of him who sent me and to complete his work" (John 4:34) and "I am thirsty" (John 19:28), which Catherine, in keeping with a certain tradition, interprets as "I thirst for souls." "Though he was very thirsty, his thirst of holy longing for the salvation of souls was greater" (*L* T16, *The Letters of Catherine of Siena*, trans. Noffke, vol. 2, 114).

308. *L* T134, ibid., vol. 1, 297.

309. *D* 11, 45.

310. *D* 60, 114. "[F]or Catherine, the way one tries to practice the selfless love of neighbor provides not only the necessary expression, but also a basic testing and self-revelation of the level of one's love for God" (Karen Scott, "'This is why I have put you among your neighbors': St. Bernard's and St. Catherine's Understanding of the Love of God and Neighbor," *Atti del simposio internazionale cateriniano-bernardiniano: Siena, 17–20 aprile 1980* [Siena: Accademia Senese degli Intronati, 1982], 290). According to Gilson, Bernard of Clairvaux teaches that the two signs of God's charity in us are the love we bear our neighbor and the expulsion of all fear. See Gilson, *The Mystical Theology of St. Bernard*, 23–24. McGinn says that Augustine also stresses the love of neighbor as a reflection of one's love of God and as such is necessary for the restoration of the trinitarian image in the soul. See McGinn, *The Foundations of Mysticism*, 246.

311. *D* 46, 95.

312. *D* 71, 134. The "hunger for virtue" can only be enacted in our relationships with others.

313. The attraction to Christ felt by the pilgrim traveler is that of an "image and likeness" to its model and is reflected in Christ's words, "Be perfect, therefore, as your heavenly Father is perfect" (Matt 5:48) and in Paul's words, "[B]e imitators of God, as beloved children." (Eph 5:1). See Torrell, *Saint Thomas Aquinas*, vol. 2, *Spiritual Master*, 126–27.

314. Catherine speaks variously of God's presence in us: He inhabits the soul (*D* 33, 75), he is present through grace when the soul's three powers are "gathered together," (*D* 54, 108), and Christ is "born" in the soul through self-knowledge (*D* 151, 320).

315. To pass into the peaceful sea is to enter the kingdom, of which H. McCabe says: "In the Kingdom, God will no longer be standing over against us either to judge us or to reward us. He will not be the Other, over there or out there or up there. He will be all in all." Herbert McCabe, *God, Christ, and Us* (London and New York: Continuum, 2003), 86. See 1 Corinthians 15:28.

316. O'Driscoll, "St. Catherine of Siena: Life and Spirituality," 311–12. "It is also evident that the theological milieu in which [Catherine] moved and which exercised in human terms the most potent influence on the development of her mystical teaching was not the scholastic world, still less the setting Thomistic. Her spiritual thought was very much the product of the writings of near-contemporary Italian authors, though ultimately, as far as non-scriptural sources go, Augustine was her master" (Hackett, "Simone Fidati da Cascia and the Doctrine of St. Catherine of Siena," 414). Catherine mentions Augustine by name only twice in the *Dialogue* (*D* 85 and 119) and quotes him explicitly in only four letters: *L* T96, T97, T110, T260.

317. John Paul II, Apostolic Letter *Novo millennio ineunte*, January 6, 2001, *AAS* XCIII:5 (3 maii 2001), para. 27, 283–84.

318. Sr. Dominic [Walsh], "St. Catherine: Doctor of the Church," 137. Catherine's understanding of the doctrines of the faith is consistent with McCabe's description of mystery: "[M]ystery always refers to the not-so-obvious, deeper meaning that is perhaps hidden at first. So mystery concerns what shows itself but does not show itself easily. Mysteries are not for concealment but for revelation; it

is because the revelation is so important and so profound that we have to work to understand it" (McCabe, *God Matters*, 76).

Chapter Three

1. "I tre stati dell'anima" ("three states of the soul") is an expression found in five chapters of the *Dialogue: D* 26, 51, 63, 86, and 166.

2. *D* 66, 124.

3. D'Urso, "Santa Caterina da Siena," 78.

4. See Introduction, 2.

5. As indicated in chapter 2, Catherine's distinctive word *scalone* has been retained instead of *stair* or *step*.

6. *D* LVI, 147.

7. The division of the *Dialogue* into various sections with titles is the work of later copyists and translators. Noffke largely follows the division of Cavallini, giving the name "Truth" to the section *La dottrina della luce*, as Cavallini has it in her first edition.

8. See Dupré Theseider's notes in Caterina da Siena, *Epistolario di Santa Caterina da Siena*, ed. Dupré Theseider, the first critical edition of eighty-eight of the letters. He was the first to bring to light the many similarities between Catherine's teaching and that of Cavalca, as found especially in his *Lo specchio della croce* (or *Specchio di croce*).

9. Giacinto D'Urso, "Il 'trattato delle lacrime' di S. Caterina da Siena," *La nuova rivista di ascetica e mistica* I:2 (1976): 199.

10. Incipients, proficients, and perfect. *ST* II–II, 24, 9.

11. See Aimé Solignac, "Voies," *Dictionnaire de spiritualité* (Paris: Beauchesne, 1994), vol. 16, cols. 1200–15; Thomas D. McGonigle, OP, "Three Ways," *The New Dictionary of Catholic Spirituality*, 963–65.

12. See Gabriella Anadol, "Le immagini del linguaggio cateriniano e le loro fonti: La scala," *Rassegna di ascetica e mistica* XXIII (1972): 337.

13. See chapter 1, 43–44; See Caffarini, *Libellus de Supplemento*, ed. Cavallini and Foralosso, II, ii, 7, 35–36. "Tres status" appears in the Latin text.

Notes

14. "This was the rule he taught on one occasion to a servant of his. He said, 'Get up, daughter, rise above yourself and climb up onto me.'" *L* T74, *The Letters of Catherine of Siena*, trans. Noffke, vol. 1, 313.

15. See chapter 2, p. 92.

16. See Cavallini, introduzione, S. Caterina da Siena, *Il dialogo* (1995), xx.

17. *D* 26, 64–65.

18. The image was often inspired by Jacob's ladder to heaven (Gen 28:12). The most well-known work in which the image is employed is the *Scala paradisi* of John Climacus (c. 525–c. 606), who envisioned a ladder with thirty steps to heaven.

19. *D* 51, 105. The *"scaloni generali"* and *"scaloni particulari"* will be considered later in this chapter.

20. "Let him kiss me with the kisses of his mouth!"

21. See Bernard of Clairvaux, *The Works of Bernard of Clairvaux*, vol. 2, *On the Song of Songs I*, trans. by Kilian Walsh and intro. by M. Corneille Haflants (Spencer, MA: Cistercian Publications, 1993), 19; M. Basil Pennington, OCSO, "Three Stages of Spiritual Growth According to St. Bernard," *Studia Monastica* 11 (1969): 315–26.

22. In reference to the soul's spiritual progress, Noffke frequently translates *vanno* as "walking" instead of "going" but this seems too casual in the catherinian context: The soul runs *(corre)* to the third stair, Christ is running *(correndo)* to his death on the cross. See *D* 76, 140 and *D* 140, 289. She tells Bartolomeo Dominici, "Run! Run! Run!" in *L* T149 (*The Letters of Catherine of Siena*, trans. Noffke, vol. 1, 97). *Camminare* and its variants appear only five times in the catherinian corpus, whereas *correre* and its variants appear seventy-one times.

23. *D* 29, 71.

24. *D* 56, 111,

25. *D* 166, 362.

26. In *D* 78, 144, Catherine speaks for the first time of a fourth stage that is inseparable from the third; she also speaks of five stages of tears in *D* 88, 161, that represent the three spiritual stages (with the fourth) plus a first "stage" of tears for those condemned to

damnation. However, she consistently speaks of only *tre scaloni* and *tre stati dell'anima*.

27. See D'Urso, *Il genio di Santa Caterina*, 83.

28. His emphasis on the Trinity as Catherine's fundamental truth is reflected in the titles of several of the chapters: "The Trinity at the Origin of the 'Most Precious Blood,'" "The Crucified Bridge-Staircase Towards the Beatitude of the Trinity," "The Fruits of the Blood in the Glory of the Eternal Trinity."

29. Grion, *La dottrina di Santa Caterina da Siena*, 137–38. J. Arintero also concludes that Catherine's three *scaloni* are the three grades and states of the soul. See Juan G. Arintero, OP, *Las escalas de amore y la verdadera perfección cristiana* (Salamanca, Convento de San Esteban: Editorial FIDES, 1926), 109–23.

30. D'Urso, *Il genio di Santa Caterina*, 83.

31. D'Urso, as mentioned before, shows that in almost every chapter of *Lo specchio della croce* (the original name of the work) similarities with Catherine's teachings can be found. He cites many. See D'Urso, *Il genio di Santa Caterina*, 112–14. In Ashley's summary of Cavalca's main themes in *Specchio* we indeed detect an echo in Catherine's teachings: "In the whole work three points are stressed which are of special significance for the Dominican tradition of spirituality. The first is that one of the chief consequences of sin is the darkening of the intellect so that we need to be illumined through the Cross as to what we should love and what we should hate. The second is that the sanctification that comes through the Cross consists principally in the growth of charity confirmed by the gifts of the Holy Spirit and the beatitudes which they produce. The third is that this charity must bear fruit in practical ministry to our neighbor, both in material and spiritual matters, but especially in spiritual works of which the preaching of the faith is the greatest" (Benedict M. Ashley, OP, "Dominic Cavalca and a Spirituality of the Word," Internet: www.op.org/domcentral.study/ashley.cavalca.htm. Accessed on February 20, 2005 [no page numbers given]).

32. See Cavalca, *Lo specchio della croce*, a cura di Centi, Capitolo 6, 61–65.

33. See Reginald Garrigou-Lagrange, OP, "La prima conversione secondo Santa Caterina da Siena," *Vita Cristiana* V:3 (maggio–giungo 1933): 258.

34. *D* 56, 110–11. Catherine equates "faithful servant" with *stato liberale* (openhanded, generous). For Aquinas on liberality, see *ST* II–II, 117, 2.

35. See Anadol, "Le imaggini del linguaggio cateriniano e le loro fonti: *La scala*," 337. St. Dominic is known to have carried with him Cassian's *Conferences* along with the Gospel of Matthew and the letters of Paul.

36. *John Cassian: The Conferences*, trans. Ramsey, Conference XI on perfection: VII: 1–2, 412–13. Aumann says that Maximus the Confessor (c. 580–662) also "classifies Christians into three groups: the beginners who are led by fear; the advanced souls, who have the well-founded hope of a reward and are therefore somewhat mercenary; and the perfect, who are true children of God and motivated by filial love" (Jordan Aumann, *Christian Spirituality in the Catholic Tradition* [London: Sheed and Ward, 1985], 56).

37. Foster, "St. Catherine's Teaching on Christ," 320–21. The word *unitive* is found in several places in the *Dialogue* in reference to the third *scalone*. The words *purgative* and *illuminative* do not appear.

38. Benedict Ashley, OP, "Guide to Saint Catherine's Dialogue," 243. "It is noteworthy that chapter 166, the summary of the whole book, mentions the doctrine of tears only briefly and omits any reference to the doctrine of truth. This treatment of these two doctrines shows that they do not play an essential role in the central argument of the book, but are like appendices" (Ibid., 249).

39. *D* CLXVI, 581.

40. *D* 92, 170.

41. *D* 93, 171.

42. See D'Urso, "Il 'trattato delle lacrime' di S. Caterina da Siena," 128.

43. *D* XCI, 243.

44. See D'Urso, "Il 'trattato delle lacrime' di S. Caterina da Siena," 126.

45. *D* 87, 160.

46. *D* 88, 161.

47. Ashley, "Guide to Saint Catherine's Dialogue," 243.

48. See *D* 89, 163.

49. *D* 95, 177.

50. M. Clare Adams, OSC, "Tears, gift of," *The New Dictionary of Catholic Spirituality*, 957. Poulain notes: "It is said that a person has the gift of tears when certain pious thoughts cause him to weep often and abundantly, and when this facility can only be attributed to the divine action. This has been the case with many saints....Tears may...come from other causes than the divine action. The Devil can produce them, either to enfeeble the health or to give rise to pride" (Poulain, *Revelations and Visions*, 99). An example of tears caused by divine action is the story of Lazzarino da Pisa, recounted in the conclusion, 227–30.

51. See chapter 2, 266–67, n. 78.

52. See Maria Agnes Karasig, OP, "Affective Self-Transcendence in Catherine of Siena's Beatitude of Tears," *Review for Religious* 49 (1990): 419. For more on the subject of tears in the history of Christian spirituality, see Adnes, "Larmes," *Dictionnaire de spiritualité* (Paris: Beauchesne, 1976), vol.9, cols. 287–303.

53. D'Urso, "Il 'trattato delle lacrime' di S. Caterina da Siena," 118.

54. In Cavallini's edition: *La dottrina della luce*, D XCVIII–CVIII.

55. See Ashley, "Guide to Saint Catherine's Dialogue," 244. The teaching on the lights (or "Truth") can also be found in *L* T64 to William Flete. See *Saint Catherine of Siena as Seen in Her Letters*, trans. Scudder, 60–65.

56. *D* 99, 186.

57. *D* 100, 188.

58. Ashley, "Guide to Saint Catherine's Dialogue," 246. A computer word search reveals that more than half the occurrences of the word *speranza* in the *Dialogue* are in "Divine Providence."

59. *D* 136, 281.

60. See *D* 146, 307.

61. Grion, *La dottrina di Santa Caterina da Siena*, 128.

62. D'Urso, *Il genio di Santa Caterina*, 79.

63. See D'Urso, "Santa Catherina da Siena," 74–110; Grion, *La dottrina di Santa Caterina da Siena*,141–80; Carlo Riccardi, CM, *Il pensiero filosofico e mistico di S. Caterina da Siena* (Siena: Edizioni Cantagalli, 1994), 113–35; Cavallini, *Catherine of Siena*, 131–50; Foster, "St. Catherine's Teaching on Christ," 320.

64. See D'Urso, *Il genio di Santa Caterina*, 89.

65. *D* 56, 111. "Questi sono tre stati che possono essere e sono in molte creature, e sono in una creatura medisma" (*D* LVI, 147).

66. Solignac, "Voies," col. 1201. Also see Karl Rahner, "Reflections on the Problem of the Gradual Ascent to Christian Perfection," *Theological Investigations*, vol. 3, trans. by Karl-H. and Boniface Kruger (Baltimore: Helicon Press; London: Darton, Longman, & Todd, 1967), 3–23.

67. See D'Urso, "Santa Caterina da Siena," 96.

68. *L* T94, *The Letters of Catherine of Siena*, trans. Noffke, vol. 2, 673.

69. Solignac, "Voies," col. 1213.

70. See *Legenda major*, §§ 30–31, 29–30.

71. See *D* 52, 105.

72. In *D* XLVII, 125, Catherine says that those who go the way of common charity observe the commandments in action and the evangelical counsels mentally while those following the way of perfect charity observe the commandments and counsels in both action and thought. See also *D* 47, 96–97.

73. *D* LIII, 139. Catherine is referring to *D* 47.

74. *D* XLVII, 125. *Stati* in this context connotes states of life: lay, religious, clerical. Catherine belonged to the lay state.

75. See chapter 2, 93.

76. Catherine's teaching on the *scaloni generali* is primarily found in *D* 51–56; the first appearance of the words are in *D* 55. Her teaching on the *scaloni particulari* is found in various places in *D* 57–86, although the expression itself appears only in *D* 86, the summary of "The Bridge" (*D* LXXXVI, 227). She also refers to the *scaloni particulari* as *scaloni attuali* in *D* 75 (*D* LXXV, 191).

77. Catherine's teaching on the *scaloni generali* and *particulari*, because of its lack of clarity, is her most difficult teaching to understand.

78. For example, *battesimo generale* in *D* 75; *lume generale* in *D* 98; *chiave generale* in *D* 166; *generale obedienzia* in *D* 157.

79. *D* 55, 110. Italics mine.

80. See chapter 2, 107. "Thus by memory we resemble and are united to the Father, to whom Power is attributed; by the intellect we resemble and are united to the Son, to whom Wisdom

is attributed; and by the will we resemble and are united to the Holy Spirit to whom Clemency is attributed..." (*P* XXXIII).

81. *D* XXVI, 72. Italics mine.

82. See chapter 2, 107–109.

83. *D* 59, 113.

84. *D* 86, 158–59.

85. *D* 75, 137. As previously mentioned, this is the only place where Catherine refers to the *scaloni particulari* as *scaloni attuali*.

86. Cavallini, "La dottrina dell'amore in S. Caterina da Siena: concordanze...," 380–81.

87. Ibid., 385.

88. Anadol, "Le imaggini del linguaggio cateriniano e le loro fonti: *La scala*," 335. D'Urso likewise sees the *scaloni particulari* as an exterior ascent on the body of Christ: "In both a generic sense and in terms of perspective, the three *scaloni* are the three spiritual powers—memory, understanding, and will—that come together in unity in God. This is for those who respond only to the 'universal call' that is for the good and simple Christians who do not aspire to sanctity but live according to common charity. In a more proper sense, or '*in particulare*,' as Catherine says, the three *scaloni* carved on the Bridge in correspondence to the three characteristic signs on the body of Christ crucified are for those who are called to the '*grande perfezione:*' the first is at the wound of the feet, the second at the wound of the side, the third at the mouth" (D'Urso, "Gli scaloni cateriniani del ponte e le notti di S. Giovanni della Croce," 12).

89. *D* 54, 108.

90. De Blasio, for one, is of the opinion that those going the way of common charity go no further than even the *first* stage of spiritual development: "At this point one needs to note that St. Catherine makes a clear distinction between simple Christians and religious in the progress of the spiritual life. She corresponds the grade of common charity to the state of Christians who live in the world observing the commandments but not the counsels. Then it could be asked: Must the Christians who do not have vocations always remain as beginners? For St. Catherine all souls are called to perfection, but not all to the '*grande perfezione*' of the second and third stage. The call to this particular perfection corresponds ordinarily with the call to religious life: 'He who does not feel that he can reach this perfection

because of what his fragility may not bear can stay in the common state, everyone according to his state' (*D* XLVII)" (De Blasio, OP, "Gli stati di perfezione nel Dialogo di S. Caterina," 10). This, however, would not seem to be the case because in *D* 54, the treatise on the *scaloni generali*, the second *scalone* is clearly mentioned.

91. This is the opinion of D'Urso, who says: "The particulars of the soul's advance [on the *scaloni generali*] are most visible in the study of the Bridge and its *scaloni particulari* regarding those that have chosen through grace the state of perfect charity" (D'Urso, "Santa Catherina da Siena," 80).

92. The "friends" of God are those who know his love in a special way. See *D* 61, 116.

93. See *D* 16, 55.

94. *D* LXI, 156.

95. *D* 57, 111. Italics mine.

96. Desire can increase; see chapter 2, 116. An example of Catherine urging someone to change, in effect, from following the way of common charity and aspire to the way of perfect charity may be her own mother, Lapa. Sometime after the death of her husband, Lapa became, like Catherine herself, a Mantellata. In *L* T117 Catherine enjoins her to be "set ablaze in the fire of divine charity, seeking always God's honor and the salvation of souls" (*The Letters of Catherine of Siena*, trans. Noffke, vol. 2, 442). Concern for God's honor and the salvation of souls is characteristic of those in the third stage who are on the *scaloni particulari*.

97. However, brief references to common charity and perfect charity appear in "Truth." See *D* 98–99 and 102.

98. *D* 96, 181. As we will see, the third *scalone*, comprising the third and fourth stages, is the unitive stage.

99. "[A]ttualmente e mentalmente." See *D* XLVII, 123.

100. Second Vatican Council, Dogmatic Constitution on the Church *Lumen Gentium*, §40. English translation: *Vatican Council II: The Basic Sixteen Documents*, ed. Austin Flannery, OP (Northport, NY: Costello Publishing Company; Dublin, Ireland: Dominican Publications, 1996), 59–60. The universal call to holiness should be seen in relation to the work prior to the council of (Venerable) Juan González Arintero, OP (1860–1928), and Reginald Garrigou-Lagrange, OP (1877–1964), on the general

call to the mystical life. It is summarized in the second chapter of Richard Peddicord's *The Sacred Monster of Thomism: An Introduction to the Life and Legacy of Reginald Garrigou-Lagrange, OP* (South Bend, IN: St. Augustine's Press, 2005), 178–210.

101. *CCC*, §2014.

102. Ibid., §915, says that "all the faithful are called" to the "perfection of charity."

103. In *D* 76, 40, the soul experiences rebaptism on seeing the secret of Christ's heart at the second *scalone*. The pilgrim traveler's arrival at the third *scalone*, says D'Urso, is a flowering of baptismal grace that all the baptized may attain. See D'Urso, "Santa Caterina da Siena," 97.

104. See chapter 2, 99–101.

105. *D* 49, 100.

106. Ibid., 102.

107. *D* 94, 175.

108. *D* 89, 162. This is traditionally known as imperfect contrition. See *CCC*, §1453.

109. Ibid.

110. See D'Urso, "Santa Caterina da Siena," 76.

111. *D* 49, 102.

112. Ibid., 100.

113. See *D* 56, 111.

114. D'Urso, "Santa Caterina da Siena," 82. *Mercennaio* occurs twenty-nine times in the catherinian corpus.

115. *D* 60, 113.

116. *D* 59, 60.

117. *D* 49, 100.

118. In *D* 26, 54, Catherine mentions only affection: "The first [*scalone*] is the feet, which symbolize the [affection]. For just as the feet carry the body, the [affection] carries the soul." In "The Mystic Body of Holy Church" (*D* 110–34), Catherine speaks of "the feet of the will" (*D* 126, 246). She obviously uses the words *affection*, *desire*, and *will* somewhat interchangeably. *Affetto* occurs 873 times in the catherinian corpus, 260 times in the *Dialogue* alone.

119. Affection is "[t]he intense feeling of the soul moved towards an object that favors the good or its obstacle" ("Affettività," in *Dizionario enciclopedico di spiritualità*, ed. Ancilli. vol. 1, 36). Aquinas

says that "[t]he passions of the soul are the same as the affections" (*ST* I–II, 22, 2). Further information on the passions or affections is found in *CCC*, §§1771–75: "The term 'passions' refers to the affections or feelings. By his emotions man intuits the good and suspects evil. The principal passions are love and hatred, desire and fear, joy, sadness, and anger. In the passions, as movements of the sensitive appetite, there is neither moral good nor evil. But insofar as they engage reason and will, there is moral good or evil in them. Emotions and feelings can be taken up in the virtues or perverted by the vices. The perfection of the moral good consists in man's being moved to the good not only by his will but also by his 'heart.'"

120. "Just as there are two kinds of bodily stain, one consisting in the privation of something required for beauty, e.g. the right color or the due proportion of members, and another by the introduction of some hindrance to beauty, e.g. mud or dust; so too, a stain is put on the soul, in one way, by the privation of the beauty of grace through mortal sin, *in another, by the inordinate inclination of the affections to some temporal thing, and this is the result of venial sin*" (*ST* III, 87, 2). Italics mine.

121. See *D* 78, 145.

122. See Anadol, "Le immagini del linguaggio cateriniano e le loro fonti: *La scala*," 340. Augustine, in Tractate 48 on John 10:22–42, says, "The soul is not moved by the feet but by the affections" (Augustine of Hippo, *Homilies on the Gospel According to St. John by S. Augustine, Bishop of Hippo*, trans. with notes and indices in two volumes [Oxford: John Henry Parker; London: F. and J. Rivington, 1898], vol. 2, 638).

123. See Cavalca, *Lo specchio della croce*, a cura di Centi, capitolo 45: 362. Italics mine. The will and affection are closely related. For example, in "The Mystic Body of Holy Church" (*D* 110–34), Catherine speaks of "the feet of the will" (*D* 126, 246).

124. *Desiderio*, as we said in the last chapter, is the human person's holy longing for fulfillment, union with the divine Essence. See chapter 2, 114–17.

125. See *D* 35, *L* T26, T74, T96, T150, and T301.

126. *D* 53, 103.

127. *L* T309, *The Letters of Catherine of Siena*, trans. Noffke, vol. 2, 539. Aquinas says that our passions (affections) must be moderated by reason. See *ST* I–II, 24, 3.

128. See *L* T120, *The Letters of Catherine of Siena*, trans. Noffke, vol. 2, 438.

129. See *L* T75, ibid., vol. 2, 517.

130. "Ordinarily, the reason many people do not have diligence and eagerness for the acquisition of virtue is that their appetites and affections are not fixed purely on God" (John of the Cross, *The Ascent of Mount Carmel*, Book One, 11:4, in *The Collected Works of St. John of the Cross*, trans. Kieran Kavanaugh, OCD, and Otilio Rodriguez, OCD [Washington, DC: I.C.S. Publications, 1991], 141). "[W]hoever says, 'I abide in him,' ought to walk just as he walked" (1 John 2:6).

131. *D* XXVI, 70. The action of stripping and clothing is a motif that begins in the first stage and continues into the third.

132. *D* 63, 119.

133. *D* 60, 114.

134. *L* T259, *The Letters of Catherine of Siena*, trans. Noffke, vol. 2, 611.

135. *L* T272, ibid., vol. 2, 500.

136. *D* 60, 113.

137. See *D* 60, 115.

138. "It is true that God loves some people as his [children] *(figli)*, some as friends, some as servants" (*L* T94, *The Letters of Catherine of Siena*, trans. Noffke, vol. 2, 668).

139. "His master said to him, 'Well done, good and faithful servant'" (Matt 25:21 [Revised Standard Version]). The mercenary servant is also found in John 10:12–13 as the "hired hand" (NRSV).

140. *D* XLIX, 130.

141. *D* LIX, 151.

142. See Grion, *La dottrina di Santa Caterina*, 151; Foster, "St. Catherine's Teaching on Christ," 321.

143. "And I showed you the three [*scaloni generali*] that are set up in the soul's three powers" (*D* 86, 158). In *L* T259, where the gathering of the soul's three powers is considered, the removal of vice is associated with memory. See *The Letters of Catherine of Siena*, trans. Noffke, vol. 2, 614. Foster says that the soul's power

of memory is appropriate to this stage. See Foster, "St. Catherine's Teaching on Christ," 320–21.

144. *D* 63, 118.
145. Ibid., 119.
146. See D'Urso, "Santa Caterina da Siena," 87–88.
147. *D* 68, 129.
148. "[H]er goal *(fine)* is not consolation but only virtue built on me" (*D* 68, 130).
149. *D* 60, 114.
150. See *D* 64, 121.
151. See ibid.
152. *D* 70, 132.
153. Reginald Garrigou-Lagrange, *L'unione mistica in S. Caterina da Siena*, edizioni di *Vita Cristiana* (Firenze: Libreria Editrice Fiorentina, 1938), 46.
154. *D* 63, 119 (John 14:28).
155. *D* 144, 299.
156. Ibid., 301.
157. *D* 144, 301.
158. *Legenda major*, §92, 85.
159. *D* 63, 120. See also *D* 73, 136; *L* T94, *The Letters of Catherine of Siena*, trans. Noffke, vol. 2, 671.
160. See *D* 86, 158, where Catherine says that knowledge of self and knowledge of God in us must always be kept together.
161. *D* 144, 302.
162. *L* T335, *The Letters of Catherine of Siena*, trans. Noffke, vol. 2, 586.
163. See *D* 60, 115.
164. "[Y]ou will see that this is your own sensitive will, cloaked *(ammantellata)* with the spiritual mantle" (*L* T71, *Le lettere de S. Caterina da Siena*, ed. Misciattelli, vol. 1, 269).
165. *D* 65, 122.
166. Grion also ascribes the virtue of hope to the second *scalone* but without giving a reason. See Grion, *La dottrina di Santa Caterina*, 151. Foster, in "St. Catherine's Teaching on Christ" (322), does the same but is not totally convincing: "St. Catherine relates this stage of illumination to hope. The explanation, I think, is to be sought in her own experience. To the preliminary stage of purification

corresponded, in her mind, those early years she spent as a recluse in her father's house, self-enclosed from the world. Then she received her mission to go out into the world and declare the love of Christ, to declare, that is, her enlightenment by the blood. And for this new phase of apostolic activity the virtue of hope, with its concomitants of courage and endurance, was particularly appropriate and necessary." It is not clear that Catherine herself ever intended the three *scaloni* to correspond with the three theological virtues. As was said in chapter 2, she seldom refers to them as a group. See chapter 2, 97–98.

167. *L* T211, *The Letters of Catherine of Siena*, trans. Noffke, vol. 2, 168.

168. See *D* 23, 60.

169. *D* 89, 163.

170. In *ST* I–II, 65, 5, Aquinas says, "Charity signifies not only the love of God, but also a certain friendship with Him."

171. D'Urso, "Santa Caterina da Siena," 86.

172. "I do not call you servants any longer, because the servant does not know what the master is doing; but I have called you friends, because I have made known to you everything that I have heard from my Father."

173. *D* 60, 115. "'They who have my commandments and keep them are those who love me; and those who love me will be loved by my Father, and I will love them and reveal myself to them.' Judas (not Iscariot) said to him, 'Lord how is it that you will reveal yourself to us, and not to the world?' Jesus answered him, 'Those who love me will keep my word, and my Father will love them, and we will come to them and make our home with them'" (John 14:21–23).

174. See *D* LXIII, 159.

175. Foster, "St. Catherine's Teaching on Christ," 321.

176. *D* 54, 108. The passage is rather unclear. *Specularsi* can mean to reflect or mirror oneself but also to observe oneself. Raschini, in her version of the *Dialogue* in modern Italian, translates it as follows: "Here then [the soul] has already climbed up to the second *scalone*, that is the light of the intellect, which contemplates my love in Christ crucified by the means of which I have shown you" (S. Caterina da Siena, *Dialogo della divina provvidenza*, ed.

Maria Adelaide Raschini, versione in italiano corrente [Bologna: Edizioni Studio Domenicano, 1989], 141).

177. Foster, "St. Catherine's Teaching on Christ," 321.
178. *D* 136, 281.
179. See *D* 56, 111.
180. See *D* LXV, 166.
181. See *D* 60, 114.
182. See *D* 64, 120.
183. D'Urso, "Santa Caterina da Siena," 92.
184. *D* 60, 115–16.
185. Aquinas, quoting Aristotle, says that "a friend is called a man's *other self* (Ethic. ix. 4)" (*ST* I–II, 28, 1).
186. See *D* 61, 116.
187. *D* 26, 64.
188. See D'Urso, "Santa Caterina da Siena," 93.
189. *D* 60, 115. "The goal to be reached by means of the pierced and open side is not just the heart, but its secret, its mystery. This is the 'mystery kept secret for endless ages' until revealed in the person of Jesus Christ. It is the mystery of God's love for humanity" (Sr. M. Jeremiah, *The Secret of the Heart: A Theological Study of Catherine of Siena's Teaching on the Heart of Jesus* [Front Royal, VA: Christendom Press, 1995], 100).
190. See D'Urso, "Santa Caterina da Siena," 93; Bernard of Clairvaux, *Sermo* 61 in *Canticum* 61, 3–4; *PL* 183, 1071–72.
191. Augustine of Hippo, *Sermones*, CCCXI, chapter III; *PL* 38, 1415, quoted in *The Letters of Catherine of Siena*, trans. Noffke, vol. 1, 8, n. 16.
192. See William of St. Thierry, *De Contempl. Deo*, I, 3; *PL* 184, 368, quoted in Valli, "Il Sangue di Cristo nell'opera di S. Caterina da Siena," 32.
193. See Henry Suso, *Livre de la Sapience*, IV, in *Oeuvres mystiques du B. Henry Suso*, trad. Thireot (Paris, 1899), vol. 2, 292, quoted in Valli, "Il Sangue di Cristo nell'opera di S. Caterina da Siena," 36.
194. See M. I. Bernadot, "Le développement historique de la devotion au Sacré Coeur," in *La vie spirituelle* II (1920): 193, quoted in Valli, "Il Sangue di Cristo nell'opera di S. Caterina da Siena," 33.

195. Other images for the opened side include a habitation or cell of self-knowledge (*L* T36, T158, T251), a bath of blood (*L* T262, T300), and an open storeroom *(bottiga aperta)* (*L* T75, T87, T273). These images, however, seem to be variations of the images of a window, cavern, and channel.

196. *L* T127, *The Letters of Catherine of Siena*, trans. Noffke, vol. 1, 39–40. Also see *L* T41.

197. *L* T208, ibid., vol. 2, 87; also see *D* 54 and *L* T318.

198. *D* CXXIV, 363; also see *L* T47, T306, T308, T329, *P* 19 (XII).

199. See John 19:34, 1 John 5:6–8, and *CCC*, §1225.

200. *D* LXXV, 191.

201. *L* T97, *The Letters of Catherine of Siena*, trans. Noffke, vol. 2, 105. Gregory the Great, in his commentary on Song of Songs 2:4, speaks of finding nourishment in Christ's wounds: "While imitating the patience of Christ in the remembrance of the Cross, while remembering his wounds, the simple soul, like a dove in the clefts, finds its nourishment to recover in the wounds" (S. Greg., *In Cantic.* II, 15; *PL* 79, 499l, quoted in Valli, "Il Sangue di Cristo nell'opera di S. Caterina da Siena," 31).

202. The pilgrim traveler's baptism is presumed since the Christ-bridge is the way in which one grows in grace. Also, on the shore of the tempestuous river pilgrim travelers vomit out their sins, an allusion to sacramental confession. See *D* 49, 100.

203. *D* 76, 140.

204. The friend is re-created into the child at the third *scalone*.

205. *D* 75, 139.

206. *L* T253, *The Letters of Catherine of Siena*, trans. Noffke, vol. 2, 423.

207. See chapter 2, 80–82.

208. Giuliana Cavallini, "La verità nell'ascesi cateriniana," 38.

209. *L* T146, *The Letters of Catherine of Siena*, trans. Noffke, vol. 1, 97.

210. *D* 26, 64.

211. *D* 54, 108.

212. *D* LX, 155–56. See D'Urso, "Santa Caterina da Siena," 94.

213. See *L* T158, *The Letters of Catherine of Siena*, trans. Noffke, vol. 2, 307.

214. *P* 19 (XII), 211.

215. *L* T253, *Le lettere di S. Caterina da Siena*, ed. Misciattelli, vol. 4, 73.

216. "[God's servants] must hide in the cavern of self-knowledge and knowledge of God" (*L* T214, *The Letters of Catherine of Siena*, trans. Noffke, vol. 2, 660). "This is why I refer to Christ's side as the cell where you will find knowledge of yourself and of his goodness" (*L* T36, ibid., vol. 2, 131).

217. *L* T329, *I, Catherine*, trans. Foster and Ronayne, 223. Catherine sees the soul of Niccolò di Toldo "plunged into his open side" where he was "received by God." (*L* T273, *I, Catherine*, 74).

218. See Valli, "Il Sangue di Cristo nell'opera di S. Caterina da Siena," 31. Vulgate, emphasis mine. "O my dove, in the clefts of the rock, in the covert of the cliff."

219. See chapter 2, 133.

220. *D* 89, 165.

221. "They love their neighbors with the same love with which they love me" (*D* 60, 114).

222. *D* XXVI, 70.

223. *D* LXXVIII, 206. After conceiving the virtues she gives birth to them in her relationship with her neighbors. See *D* 11, 45.

224. D'Urso, "Santa Caterina da Siena," 86; *D* 58, 111–12.

225. *L* T345, *Le lettere di S. Caterina da Siena*, ed. Misciattelli, vol. 5, 160.

226. *L* T290, ibid., vol. 4: 220.

227. Foster, "St. Catherine's Teaching on Christ," 321. Foster says that it is in Catherine's teaching on the opened side that she "develops her great theme of the blood. It is here perhaps, in her meditations on the open side and the wounded heart of Christ, that she most magnificently and individually expresses herself. It is here that she seems most 'inspired'...."

228. In one place, *D* LVI, 147, Catherine calls this stage "more perfect" (*più perfetto*). For *liberale* see also *D* 74, 137, and *L* T361, *Le lettere di S. Caterina da Siena*, ed. Misciattelli, vol. 5, 236.

229. *D* LXXVI, 195.

230. *L* T82, *Le lettere di S. Caterina da Siena*, ed. Misciattelli, vol. 2, 45.

231. *D* LXXIV, 190. This is an example of Catherine's incon-

sistency in terminology; she more often describes the third *scalone* as *perfettisimo*. See *D* LVI, 147; *D* CLXVI, 580.

232. In "Tears" the fourth stage is referred to as "the second unitive [stage]" (*D* LXXXIX, 236; *D* 89, 164).

233. "Thus she finds herself in the third stage of charity for her neighbors" (*D* 96, 180). In the fourth stage (= fifth stage of tears) affection "tastes my eternal Godhead and knows and sees therein the divine nature [united] with your humanity. She takes her rest then in me, the peaceful sea. Her heart is united with me [through the affection of love], as I told you at the fourth and unitive stage" (*D* 89, 163).

234. *D* 96, 179. Riccardi says that the reason Catherine always insists on the connection between the third and fourth stage is to show that "the life of mystical union must never be sought after for itself with all the mystical phenomena that may be connected to it. But the fourth stage must be and always remain well-anchored in the third which is the stage of essential holiness" (Riccardi, *Il pensiero filosofico e mistico di S. Caterina da Siena*, 107). This would seem to be supported by the fact that in both the summary chapter of "The Bridge," *D* 86, and in the summary of the entire work, *D* 166, there is no mention of the fourth or unitive stage.

235 *D* 57, 111.

236. *D* 26, 64. The image of the kiss is taken from Song of Songs 1:2, "Let him kiss me with the kisses of his mouth!"

237. *D* 76, 140. In comparing Catherine and Teresa of Avila, Léthel says that the teaching of both illustrate Jesus' words, "Remain in me and I in you" from different aspects: Catherine stresses "us in him" with an emphasis on the corporal aspect of Jesus, as we see here and in her repeated invitation to "enter the opened side," while Teresa stresses "he in us" with an emphasis on his spiritual presence in us. See François-Marie Léthel, "L'interiorité chrétienne," *La vie spirituelle*, mars 1996: 47–84; Léthel, *Theologie de l'amore de Jesus. Escrits sur la theologie des saints* (Venasque: Editions du Carmel, 1996), 73–91.

238. D'Urso, "Santa Caterina da Siena," 97.

239. *D* 76, 141. "For he is our peace; in his flesh he has made both groups into one and has broken down the dividing wall, that is, the hostility between us" (Eph 2:14).

240. *L* T120, *The Letters of Catherine of Siena*, trans. Noffke, vol. 2, 439. Noffke dates the letter to "late September 1377." The expression "mouth of holy desire" appears nineteen times in the catherinian corpus.

241. *L* T272, ibid., vol. 2, 501. As noted earlier, Noffke dates this to "10 October 1377 or shortly thereafter."

242. D'Urso, "Santa Caterina da Siena," 101.

243. In letters to nuns, Catherine sometimes stresses their spousal relationship to Christ. See *L* T50 and T221.

244. *D* LVI, 147. Catherine uses the word *figliuolo*, which means "son" but which can also mean "child." Noffke translates it as "child" and Thorold as "son." On one level, "son" is perhaps more correct since it corresponds with the biblical son who is the heir as well as with the Son of God. However, because Catherine's teaching applies to everyone it also would seem that the use of "child" can be justified. Foster, who was Reader in Italian at Cambridge University, translates it as "child." See Foster, "St. Catherine's Teaching on Christ," 320. However, it is important to note that *figliuolo* does not mean a little child or young person (*fanciullo*, which occurs in *D* 14, 96, and 159). For Catherine, the friend who becomes a child is a mature son or daughter of God. Aquinas also teaches that charity makes a servant become a friend and then a son: "[I]t is charity that causes man's greatness....Charity makes a friend out of a servant. Thus not only are we free, but we have become sons, bearing the name and being so in truth. 'The Holy Spirit himself gives to our spirit the witness that we are children of God. And if we are children, we are also heirs, heirs of God and co-heirs with Christ' (Rom 8:17)" (*De decem preceptis* II–IV, quoted in Torrell, *Saint Thomas Aquinas*, vol. 2, *Spiritual Master*, 364).

245. *D* LXIII, 159.

246. Ibid.

247. *L* T94, *The Letters of Catherine of Siena*, trans. Noffke, vol. 2, 673.

248. *D* 72, 134–35.

249. *D* 60, 115.

250. *D* 136, 281.

251. *D* 63, 118.

252. D'Urso, "Santa Caterina da Siena," 100.

253. Luke 15:31.
254. Romans 8:15–16.
255. Galatians 4:7.
256. Dom Columba Marmion, *Christ in His Mysteries* (St. Louis: B. Herder, 1924), 54–55.
257. *D* 136, 281.
258. *D* LXXVI, 198.
259. *D* 74, 136.
260. *L* T94, *The Letters of Catherine of Siena*, trans. Noffke, vol. 2, 671.
261. See Grion, *La dottrina di Santa Caterina*, 168.
262. *L* T108, *Le lettere di S. Caterina da Siena*, ed. Misciattelli, vol. 2, 147.
263. See *D* 77, 142; *D* 78, 145.
264. See *D* 77, 142.
265. See ibid., 143–44. Catherine's own patience is lauded by Raymond in *Legenda major*, §§ 395–430, 361–88.
266. *D* 77, 141–44; *D* 145, 303; *D* 155, 330–31.
267. *D* 78, 147.
268. No doubt Catherine's attraction to the Dominican order was owing to the fact that it "is known to have been established, from the beginning, for preaching and the salvation of souls, especially" (Prologue to the Primitive Constitutions, quoted in "The Fundamental Constitution," *The Book of Constitutions and Ordinations of the Brothers of the Order of Preachers* [Dublin: Dominican Publications, 2001], 25). "And look at the ship of your Father Dominic, my beloved son. He governed it with a perfect rule, asking [his followers] to be attentive only to my honor and the salvation of souls with the light of learning" (*D* 158, 237). Vernet says that Richard of St. Victor also "characterizes the highest mystical state…by apostolic zeal and the imitation of Christ" (Felix Vernet, *Medieval Spirituality* [London: Sands and Co.; St. Louis: B. Herder, 1930], 229). Vernet gives no citation.
269. *L* T55, *The Letters of Catherine of Siena*, trans. Noffke, vol. 2, 470.
270. "What these blessed ones want is to see me honored in you who are still on the way, pilgrims running ever nearer your end in death. Because they seek my honor they desire your salvation,

and so they are constantly praying to me for you" (*D* 41, 84). "The glory of God is man fully alive" (Irenaeus, *Adv. haeres.* 4, 20, 7: *PG* 7/1, 1037).

271. *D* 76, 140. "Eating souls" at "the table of the most holy cross" is an image possibly unique to Catherine that occurs several times in her writings, as can be seen in *D* 100, 124; *L* T37, T64, T210, T227, T242, and T322. On "eating souls," see chapter 2, 133.

272. *D* 147, 310.

273. *D* 146, 307. Noffke translates both *mezzo* and *tramezzatore* in *D* 146 as "mediator." Raschini's *strumenti di mediazione* (instruments of mediation) for the original *mezzi* seems more correct. See S. Caterina da Siena, *Dialogo della divina provvidenza*, versione in italiano corrente ed. Raschini, 397. Earlier in "Truth," the eternal Father tells Catherine to "[m]ake yourself a channel *(mezzo)* for giving each of them [that is, her spiritual Fathers] what he needs, according to their disposition and what I, your Creator, give to you" (*D* 109, 204).

274. *P* 19 (XII), 214. See *D* CXLVI, 484, n. 88.

275. Grion, *La dottrina di Santa Caterina*, 174.

276. *D* 133, 272–73. Italics mine. On her deathbed Catherine enjoined her followers "to yearn with burning desire for the reform and good estate of the holy Church of God and the welfare of the Vicar of Christ" (*Legenda major*, §362, 336–37).

277. Revelation 21:5.

278. *L* T282, *The Letters of Catherine of Siena*, trans. Noffke, vol. 2, 684. Noffke dates the letter to "November or December 1377."

279. See *D* 79, 147. Only when the soul is separated from the body in death does it pass through the gate and into eternal life. See *D* 82, 152.

280. *D* 78, 144; see *L* T154, *Le lettere de S. Caterina da Siena*, ed. Misciattelli, vol. 3, 10.

281. *Stato unitivo* appears first in *D* 85; altogether it appears eleven times in the *Dialogue*.

282. Foster, "St. Catherine's Teaching on Christ," 322.

283. See *D* 78–85, 89, 96, and 100.

284. *D* 79, 148.

285. *D* 96, 181.

286. To whatever extent she was influenced by Augustinian spirituality, Catherine does, of course, occasionally depart from it. According to McGinn, Augustine deliberately excluded the language of union: "Unlike some Greek fathers, he is not much concerned with individual 'union' with God.... When he does speak of union here below, it is the union of Christ and the church he had in mind" (McGinn, *The Foundations of Mysticism*, vol. 1, *The Presence of God: A History of Western Christian Mysticism*, 230 and 242). Bonner says that "Augustine makes it clear that deification will be attained only in the life to come" (Bonner, "Augustine's Conception of Deification," *Journal of Theological Studies* 37 (1986): 381).

287. *D* 96, 179. Italics mine. The image of resting on the breast of Christ may have been taken from John 13:23, "One of his disciples, whom Jesus loved, was lying close to the breast of Christ" (Revised Standard Version). In *D* 96, 181, the eternal Father says of the apostle John: "[W]hat light he imbibed at the priceless breast of Christ my Truth!" The image is also found in Isaiah 66:12 in which God's children nurse at Jerusalem's breast. "Augustine asks how fallen humanity can absorb the solid food of the Word, the second person of the Trinity. Following Paul (1 Cor 3:2) he says this is only possible because the Word has become milk in taking on flesh. He concludes that we must suck what he became for us in order to grow into what he is *(Suge quod pro te factus est, et crescis ad id quod est)*. (*Hom. on Ps.* 119.2 [*PL* 37:1599])" (McGinn, *The Foundations of Mysticism*, vol. 1, *The Presence of God: A History of Western Christian Mysticism*, 250). Catherine also speaks of nursing at the breasts of the eternal Father and the Holy Spirit. See *D* 151, 325; *D* 141, 292. McGinn says that "[m]edieval medical theory identified...breast milk with the mother's congealed blood" (McGinn, "Catherine of Siena: Apostle of the Blood of Christ," 337).

288. *D* 96, 181.

289. *L* T164, *The Letters of Catherine of Siena*, trans. Noffke, vol. 2, 31.

290. *D* 96, 180–81. Italics mine. Aquinas says that it is through intellect and will, the chief faculties of God and humanity, that God and humanity will unite. See *ST* I–II, 62 and 65, I, 12. Also see A. N. Williams, *The Ground of Union: Deification in Aquinas and Palamas* (New York and Oxford: Oxford University Press, 1999), 157.

291. *D* 78, 145.

292. Ibid., 147.

293. *D* 101, 192. "The thought satiety without boredom, and hunger without pain" is originally from Pseudo-Augustine (*Meditatio XXVII, PL* XL, 921). Catherine, however, probably encountered the passage in one of Cavalca's works, for example, *Descrizione de' dieci comandamenti*, 306: "We shall desire though we are sated, and we shall be sated even in our desiring. Yet satiety will not be a source of boredom, nor desire be accompanied by pain, as happens in this world" (Noffke in *The Letters of Catherine of Siena*, trans. Noffke, vol. 2, 49, n. 9). Cavalca also has another variation of the statement: "But, as St. Augustine says, 'sated you will still be hungry, and being hungry you will be sated'" (Cavalca, *Lo specchio della croce*, a cura di Centi, Capitolo 44, 352).

294. *D* 96, 181–82.

295. 2 Corinthians 12:2–4.

296. See chapter 1, 53.

297. *D* 84, 154. Here Catherine distinguishes between the continuous feeling of God's presence and the intermittent feeling of union with him, both of which occur in the fourth stage. John of the Cross, in *Spiritual Canticle*, sts. 20–21, no. 14, calls this continuous feeling "habitual embrace." In *The Living Flame of Love*, st. 1, no. 2, he compares the continuous feeling of God in the soul to a burning log in which the fire completely consumes and transforms it. From time to time the flame flares up and "bathes the soul in glory and refreshes it with the quality of divine life" (John of the Cross, *The Collected Works of St. John of the Cross*, 557 and 641–42). See also *D* 78, 145.

298. See *D* 79, 148.

299. See *D* 89, 166.

300. *D* 101, 192.

301. Ibid.

302. See *D* 75, 138; *D* 76, 140.

303. See chapter 2, 263, n. 42.

304. *D* 84, 154. See 1 Chronicles 18:38.

305. *D* 78, 147.

306. "In your nature, eternal Godhead, I shall come to know my nature. And what is my nature, boundless Love? It is fire, because

you are nothing but a fire of love. And you have given humankind a share in this nature for by the fire of love you created us" (*P* 12 [XXII], 117–18).

307. *L* T137, *The Letters of Catherine of Siena*, trans. Noffke, vol. 1, 181–82.

308. *D* 79, 148.

309. *L* T263, *Le lettere di S. Caterina da Siena*, ed. Misciattelli, vol. 4, 122.

310. *D* 60, 115; "l'amore si transforma nella cosa amata," *D* LX, 155. "Each person is what he loves" *(talis est quisque, qualis ejus dilectio est)* (Augustine, *Hom. on 1 John* 2:14).

311. *Amore unitivo* appears twice in the *Dialogue*: *D* 4, 29; *D* 7, 37. See also *ST* I–II, 28, 1.

312. *D* 1, 25–26 and *L* T215.

313. *D* 96, 181.

314. *D* 15, 53. See also *D* 110, 205; *P* 11 (XXI), 102. "For this is why the Word became man, and the Son of God became the Son of man: so that man, by entering into communion with the Word and thus receiving divine sonship, might become a son of God" (Irenaeus, *Adv. haeres.* 3, 19, 1: *Patrologiae cursus completes. Series Graeca.* [Paris, 1844–], 7/1, 939. Henceforth abbreviated as *PG*). "For the Son of God became man so that we might become God" (Athanasius, *De inc.*, 54, 3; *PG* 25, 192B). "The only-begotten Son of God, wanting to make us sharers in his divinity, assumed our nature, so that he, made man, might make men Gods" (Aquinas, *Opusc.* 57:1–4).

315. *L* T129, *The Letters of Catherine of Siena*, trans. Noffke, vol. 1, 235.

316. See *D* 89, 164.

317. See *D* 167, 364. Mary is also referred to as a peaceful sea in *P* 18 (XI), 186.

318. See chapter 2, 125 and *L* T146, *The Letters of Catherine of Siena*, trans. Noffke, vol. 1, 95–97.

319. See chapter 2, 117–29.

320. *D* 167, 365–66.

321. See *D* 100, 188; *D* 82, 152; *D* 165, 357.

322. *D* 79, 147. In the patristic period, 1 Corinthians 6:17 ("But anyone united to the Lord becomes one spirit with him") was often cited as referring to the soul's union with God.

Notes

323. D'Urso, "Santa Caterina da Siena," 103. "Nothing remains outside of me" (*D* LXXIII, 208). The thought is similar to another expression: "Just as the fish is in the sea and the sea in the fish, so am I in the soul and the soul in me, the sea of peace" (*D* 112, 211). For variations on this expression, see *D* 2, 27 and *P* 20 (XIII), 226.

324. *D* 27, 67.

325. See *D* 165, 360. Catherine's teaching on beatitude agrees with that of Aquinas: It is enjoyment of God in a perfect communion of knowledge and love. See Torrell, *Saint Thomas Aquinas*, vol. 2, *Spiritual Master*, 180.

326. *D* 89, 166. For Aquinas, the gift of grace deifies or unites the soul with God. See *ST* I–II, 112, 1. "For him grace is a deiform structure, which is why God alone can give it to us. Thomas uses the terms 'deify' and 'deiform' so often as to leave no doubt on the subject.... Thomas speaks of saints as 'deified' by the grace of adoption, or through glorious knowledge of God in heaven. In this last context, he also talks about the saints who have become 'deiform' through the face-to-face vision of God. But he also uses the term for the saints still on the way, on earth. Grace and charity, as well as the gift of wisdom, make us deiform; but in fact, Christians are deiform from the moment of their baptism, for the Holy Spirit is the main agent" (Torrell, OP, *Saint Thomas Aquinas*, vol. 2, *Spiritual Master*, 126–27).

327. *D* 84, 154.

328. *D* 89, 164.

329. Ibid., 166.

330. See chapter 2, 128–29.

331. *D* 79, 148. "[W]hen he is revealed, we will be like him, for we will *see* him as he is" (1 John 3:2). Italics mine.

332. *D* LXXXIX, 235.

333. *D* LXXXIV, 222. The damned, on the other hand, must look at the devil face-to-face and "in seeing him they know themselves better: that is, they recognize that their sinfulness has made them worthy of him.... For my divine justice makes him look more horrible still to those who have lost me, and this in proportion to the depth of their sinfulness" (*D* 38, 80–81). There are three other torments the damned experience: loss of the beatific vision, the reproof of their own consciences, and continuous hellfire.

334. *D* 79, 149. D'Urso strongly disagrees with Grion's assertion that the beatific vision is communicated to the most perfect in this life: "In catherinian thought those on earth, even in the highest state of the Spirit, are not given the beatific vision but only a foretaste of it." See D'Urso, *Il genio di Santa Caterina*, 94. Cf. Grion, *S. Caterina da Siena, dottrina e fonti*, 134.

335. *D* 79, 149. This is in reference to Paul's vision (2 Cor 12:2–4).

336. *D* 85, 157. For other references to *lume sopranaturale*, see *D* 119, 124, 127, 131, 141, 151, 158, 167.

337. *D* 158, 339. This expression alludes to the gifts of the Holy Spirit, particularly the gifts of understanding (insightful faith) and knowledge (mature faith). Although the expression "gifts and graces of the Holy Spirit" occurs in several places in her writings, Catherine's only reference to "the seven gifts of the Holy Spirit" is in *D* 140, 289. Congar says that this omission is not unusual among the saints and mystics who "themselves make no distinction in their own experience between the grace of the virtues and that of the gifts of the Spirit. It is their spiritual directors, biographers or interpreters who speak here of the action of the 'gifts' and who even state precisely which gift is active." See Yves Congar, *I Believe in the Holy Spirit*, trans. David Smith (New York: Crossroad Herder, 2000), 2:134. What is significant is that Catherine distinguishes between the "light" of faith received in baptism and the "supernatural light" received further along on one's spiritual journey.

338. *D* 167, 365.

339. *D* 99, 187. Catherine says that the holy doctors and saints, such as Aquinas, had this light and were thus able to explain scripture and be lights for others. This light, by which we are enlightened to understand the truths of the faith, is given to anyone who grows in charity, even to the unlettered such as Catherine herself. See *D* 96, 181. The light is incompatible with "pride, indecency, and sinful living." Learned people without the light know only the outer rind but not the marrow. See *D* 127, 249–50; *D* 85, 157. Catherine often distinguishes between the outer surface and the marrow (*mirollo, merollo*) of things (for example, bad priests "never understood learning because the horns of pride kept them from tasting its sweet marrow" [*D* 132, 267]).

340. She herself had experienced great mystical union in the mystical espousals.

341. *D* 167, 363–64. Italics mine.

342. Ibid., 365. Italics mine.

343. *D* 1, 25.

344. Ibid., 26. "Man through sin lost the clothing of innocence and of charity, that is the wedding garment *(vestimento nuziale)*, and was naked.... Christ came to re-clothe us in virtue, to make of himself our virtue and innocence.... [Man] is reclothed with the wedding garments of charity, without which no one can enter the heavenly banquet" (Cavalca, *Lo specchio della croce*, a cura di Centi, Capitolo 38, 300).

345. See Benedict T. Viviano, OP, "The Gospel According to Matthew," in *The New Jerome Biblical Commentary*, ed. Raymond E. Brown, SS, Joseph A. Fitzmyer, SJ, Roland E. Murphy, OCarm (London: Geoffrey Chapman, 1990), 665.

346. See *L* T345, *Le lettere di S. Caterina da Siena*, ed. Misciattelli, vol. 5, 158. See *ST* II–II, 26, 13.

347. *L* T72, *The Letters of Catherine of Siena*, trans. Noffke, vol. 2, 331. Patience reveals whether one's clothing is really the wedding garment of charity or not; impatience is a sign that virtue is "torn" or altogether missing. See *D* 95, 178, and *D* 163, 355.

348. "This is why I gave the Word, my only-begotten Son. The clay of humankind was spoiled by the sin of the first man, Adam, and so all of you, vessels made from that clay, were spoiled and unfit to hold eternal life.... Then [after baptism] the soul is as a vessel ready to receive grace and to make it grow within her as much as she chooses to fit herself, through affection and desire, to love and serve me" (*D* 14, 51–52).

349. *D* 89, 163.

350. *D* 79, 148. Memory is also portrayed as being filled with the memory of God's blessings. See *D* 96, 180.

351. See *D* 89, 165.

352. *D* 165, 357.

353. *D* LXII, 158. Jean Corbon, OP, in *The Wellspring of Worship* (San Francisco: Ignatius Press, 1988 and 2005), 217–18, says almost the same thing: "The beloved Son has united us to himself in his body, and the more he makes our humanity like his own,

the more he causes us to share in his divinity.... We become God by being more and more united to the humanity of Jesus."

354. *D* 42, 85.

355. *D* 54, 107.

356. A case in point, as we noted in chapter 1, 64–65, was Catherine's important investiture vision described in *L* T219 to Raymond and the fact that it is unrecorded in his *Legenda major*.

357. For example, Raymond suggests that Catherine's childhood vision of the royal Christ was an experience of the unitive stage: "So powerful was the grace this blessing brought her that she was transported out of herself, and *transformed into him* upon whom her loving gaze was fixed" (*Legenda major*, §30, 29). Italics mine.

358. D'Urso, "Caterina creatura dello Spirito," 7.

359. *Legenda minor*, I, ii, 22.

360. *D* 26, 65.

361. See *D* 54, 107.

362. *D* 94, 175.

363. See chapter 1, 21.

364. *D* 159, 342.

365. *D* 108, 202.

366. *Legenda major*, §92, 85.

367. Ibid., §118, 113.

368. See *D* 76, 140.

369. "A new heart I will give you, and a new spirit I will put within you" (Ezek 36:26).

370. *Legenda major*, §182, 176. The confessor at the time was Tommaso della Fonte.

371. *D* 60, 115. Catherine is explaining how faithful servants can become dear friends of their master. No particular stage or *scalone* is explicitly mentioned.

372. See *Legenda major*, §192, 56 and *D* 61, 116. Prophecy is also characteristic of the third *scalone*. See *D* 89, 166.

373. See *Legenda major*, §165, 159.

374. *Supplementum*, II, ii, 7, 98–99.

375. See ibid. II, iii, 3, 109; II, vi, 56, 186.

376. *Legenda major*, §192, 183–84.

377. *D* 2, 27.

378. *D* 142, 295.

Notes

379. *Legenda major*, §137, 132. "Silk then comes out of the worm's interior. As Christ says in the Psalms, 'I am only a worm, not a man.' In fact, he was so consumed with love that he will open his side, which means from every side of his body, to make for us our clothing of silk. And since men delight to be dressed in colored silk clothes, he sheds his blood to make the scarlet dye bright red" (Cavalca, *Lo specchio della croce*, a cura di Centi, Capitolo 38, 302).

380. *L* T264, *The Letters of Catherine of Siena*, trans. Noffke, vol. 2, 481.

381. See *Supplementum* (Tin.), I, ii, 13, 83; II, iii, 1, 108; II, iii, 4, 110–11.

382. *D* 89, 164. See also *D* 78, 147.

383. See *Legenda major*, §206, 196–97; *D* 84, 154.

384. See *Legenda major*, §216, 204–5.

385. See *D* 76, 140.

386. *Legenda major*, §215, 203–4.

387. "[Y]ou can make that union grow in whatever kind of perfection you choose with the help of my grace"(*D* 89, 166). See also *D* 167, 366. Aquinas says that there is no limit to the growth of charity here below. See *ST* II–II, 24, 7.

388. *D* 84, 154. "For the soul is never so perfect in this life that it cannot become yet more perfect in love" (*D* 89, 166).

389. *D* 146, 307.

390. Jorgensen, *Saint Catherine of Siena*, 199.

391. *D* 133, 272.

392. *L* T117, *The Letters of Catherine of Siena*, trans. Noffke, vol. 2, 441. Noffke dates it to late September 1377.

393. See Levasti, *My Servant Catherine*, 155.

394. *D* 146, 307. Italics mine.

395. *D* 78, 144. See 2 Corinthians 12:9–10 and Galatians 6:17. She also speaks of the stigmata shining in God's servants in *L* T333. See *Le lettere di S. Caterina da Siena*, ed. Misciattelli, vol. 5, 96.

396. D'Urso, "Santa Caterina da Siena," 106.

397. *L* T219, *The Letters of Catherine of Siena*, trans. Noffke, vol. 2, 92–93. Italics mine.

398. *D* 7, 37.

399. *L* T371, *I, Catherine*, trans. Foster and Ronayne, 276.

400. *D* 15, 54. See also *D* 86, 159–60. The soul is also described as having a face that is dirtied by sin in *D* 96, 180.

401. For example, as previously noted, in *D* 142 reference is made to her having levitated. Also, in *D* 44 her early vision of the tree is mentioned; in *D* 98 there is perhaps an indirect reference to the mystical espousals when the eternal Father calls her "my bride" (*sposa mia*).

402. We cannot be certain, for example, that Catherine's "vision of the royal Christ" during which, according to Raymond of Capua, she was "transformed into [God]" was actually indicative of her being in the unitive stage. See chapter 1, 18–20.

403. D'Urso, introduction to *L'estasi e la parola*, 21–22.

404. O'Driscoll, "Women and the Dominican Tradition with Particular Reference to Catherine of Siena," 449–50.

405. *D* LVI, 147. See also *D* 56, 111.

406. See chapter 3, 152.

407. *D* 89, 166. Instead of conceiving of the spiritual life as proceeding along a straight line consisting of three consecutive stages, it may be more helpful, and indeed closer to what Catherine herself actually had in mind, to think of the three stages as three points on a circle, any one of which can be a beginning point at various moments in one's life. Alternatively, we can imagine the spiritual life as an upward spiral in which one passes through the three stages at a progressively higher point each time while allowing for the possibility of backsliding.

408. See chapter 3, 137.

409. See *ST* I, 103, 4.

410. *D C*, 279.

411. Raymond refers to how much Catherine suffered under inept spiritual directors who "were obstinately set on making her keep to the beaten path that suits the common run of men. They did not bow to the Majesty of God, present with her and leading her by ways beyond the ordinary" (*Legenda major*, §80, 74).

412. McGonigle, "Three Ways," 964.

413. *D* 104, 196.

414. See *D* 89, 166.

415. See Solignac, "Voies," col. 1215.

416. *D* 89, 166. Italics mine.

Notes

417. See Ancilli and Maroto, "Caterina da Siena (santa)," 487.
418. See chapter 2, 117–29.
419. *L* T104, *The Letters of Catherine of Siena*, trans. Noffke, vol. 2, 654.
420. Regarding mystical experiences see *D* 71, 134; for emotions see *D* 106, 199; *D* 145, 305.
421. Giovanni Getto, *Saggio letterario su S. Caterina da Siena* (Firenze, 1939), a revised edition of which was later published as *L'intuizione mistica e l'espressione letteraria di S. Caterina da Siena* (Firenze, 1967). No page number is given. Quoted in Carlo Riccardi, CM, *Il messaggio di Santa Caterina da Siena dottore della Chiesa*, 2nd ed. (Roma: CLV Edizioni, 1988), 786–87.
422. Noffke, "Catherine of Siena, Justly Doctor of the Church?" 57–58.
423. *Urbis et Orbis, concessionis tituli doctoris et extensionis eiusdem tituli ad universam Ecclesiam necnon Officii et Missae de communi doctorum virginum in honorem S. Catharinae Senensis virginis Tertii Ordinis S. Dominici. Vota censorum theologorum,* [Città Vaticano], typis poliglottis vaticani, 1969, 4°, 5, quoted in Noffke, "Catherine of Siena, Justly Doctor of the Church?" 52.
424. O'Driscoll, "Women and the Dominican Tradition with Particular Reference to Catherine of Siena," 5.
425. For example, for "opened side" see John 19:34; for "breast" see John 13:23; for "mouth" see Song of Songs 1:2; and "gate," see John 10:1.
426. *L* T219, *The Letters of Catherine of Siena*, trans. Noffke, vol. 2, 93.
427. *Legenda major,* §111, 103. Italics mine.
428. *D* 100, 188. Italics mine.

Conclusion

1. On the subject of private revelations, *CCC*, §66–67 states: "Yet even if Revelation is already complete, it has not been made completely explicit; it remains for Christian faith gradually to grasp its full significance over the course of centuries.... It is not [the role of private revelations] to improve or complete Christ's definitive

Revelation, but to help live more fully by it in a certain period in history."

2. *D* 60, 115. This statement, more than any other, expresses the whole of Catherine of Siena's spiritual thought.

3. "You see this gentle loving Word born in a stable while Mary was on a journey, to show you pilgrims how you should be constantly born anew in the stable of self-knowledge, where by grace you will find me born within your soul" (*D* 151, 320).

4. See *D* LXII, 158. Our destiny is to "become participants of the divine nature" (2 Pet 1:4).

5. According to Aquinas, "[k]nowledge is perfected by the thing known being united, through its likeness, to the knower. But the effect of love is that the thing itself which is loved is, in a way, united to the lover. Consequently, the union caused by love is closer than that which is caused by knowledge" (*ST* I–II, 28, 1).

6. *D* 1, 26. In relation to this, we are reminded of what Christ once said to Catherine, according to Raymond of Capua: "[S]ince I in the beginning created man to my own image and likeness, and afterwards took your image on myself by assuming human nature, it is always my endeavor, in so far as you are fit for it, *to intensify that likeness between me and you*" (*Legenda major*, §111, 103). Italics mine.

7. "Editorial" [Kenelm Foster, OP], *Life of the Spirit* 15 (April 1961): 432. Italics mine. "[T]his knowledge [of the divine Persons] from which love springs is found abundantly among those who are fervent in their love of God" and "cannot be perfect in persons who are not inflamed by this love" (*I Sent*. d. 15. q. 4 aa. 2 arg. 4 and ad 4, quoted in Torrell, *Saint Thomas Aquinas*, vol. 2, *Spiritual Master*, 98).

8. *D* CXXXII, 411. "I tell you, therefore, that it is far better to go for spiritual counsel to a humble and unlettered person *[uno idioto umile]* who has a holy and correct conscience than to a proud scholar schooled in much knowledge, for one cannot share what one does not have in oneself" (*D* LXXXV, 225).

9. *Processo* (Taur.), 132–36. Knowledge and/or love of the "outer rind" instead of the "marrow" of something (e.g., God, the church, scripture) is a subtheme in Catherine's writings. See *D* 85,

157; 124, 239; 127, 249; 132, 266–67; *L* T371, *I, Catherine*, trans. Foster and Ronayne, 273.

10. Levasti, *My Servant, Catherine*, 81. Italics mine.

11. Raniero Cantalamessa, OFMCap, "Advent 2003 in the Papal Household. Third Homily," [article on-line] available from http://www.cantalamessa.org/en/2003Avvento3.htm; Internet; accessed on May 28, 2006.

12. John Paul II, Homily at Mass for the Celebration of the Sixth Centenary of the Death of St. Catherine of Siena at St. Peters Basilica on April 29, 1980; English translation from *L'Osservatore Romano*, Weekly Edition in English, June 23, 1980, 7.

13. *L'Osservatore Romano*, 25 aprile 2005, 5.

14. See *Supplementum* (Tin.), II, iv, 22, 133.

15. See ibid.

16. In *L* T344 to Raymond of Capua, she seems to speak easily of having a "special love" for him. See *I, Catherine*, ed. Foster and Ronayne, 248.

17. *Supplementum* (Tin.), I, ii, 12, 83.

18. See *Processo* (Taur.), 94.

19. Regarding Niccolò di Toldo, see *L* T273, *The Letters of Catherine of Siena*, trans. Noffke, vol. 1, 82–90.

Appendix

1. An adaptation of Benedict Ashley's chart in his "Guide to Saint Catherine's Dialogue," *Cross and Crown* 29 (1977): 241.

WORKS CITED

Complete Works

Caterina da Siena. *Santa Caterina da Siena: Opera omnia. Testi e concordanze.* Recensione critica di testi: *Letture* a cura di Antonio Volpato; *Dialogo e Orazioni* a cura di Giuliana Cavallini. Fausto Sbafoni, OP, coordinatore. [CD-ROM]. Pistoia: Provincia Romana dei Frati Predicatori Centro Riviste, 2002.

Editions and Translations of the *Dialogue*

Caterina da Siena. *Il dialogo della divina provvidenza di S. Caterina da Siena.* Edited by Giuliana Cavallini. 2nd edition. Siena: Cantagalli, 1995.

———. *Dialogo della divina provvidenza.* Edited by Maria Adelaide Raschini. Versione in italiano corrente. Bologna: Edizioni Studio Domenicano, 2001.

———. *Dialogo della divina provvidenza.* Edited by Innocenzo Taurisano, OP. Roma: Libreria Editrice Ferrari, 1947.

Catherine of Siena. *Catherine of Siena: The Dialogue.* Translated and introduction by Suzanne Noffke, OP. Preface by Giuliana Cavallini. The Classics of Western Spirituality. New York/Mahwah, NJ: Paulist Press, 1980.

———. *The Dialogue of the Seraphic Virgin Catherine of Siena.* Translated by Algar Thorold. London: Kegan Paul, Trench, Trübner & Co., Ltd., 1896.

Editions and Translations of the *Letters*

Caterina da Siena. *Epistolario di S. Caterina da Siena.* Edited by Eugenio Dupré Theseider. Vol. I. Roma: Istituto Storico Italiano, 1940.

———. *Le lettere di S. Caterina da Siena*, con note di Niccolò Tommasèo. Edited by Piero Misciattelli. 6 vols. Firenze: Marzocco, 1939.

Catherine of Siena. *I, Catherine: Selected Writings of Catherine of Siena.* Edited by and translated by Kenelm Foster, OP, and Mary John Ronayne, OP. St. James Place, London: Collins, 1980.

———. *The Letters of Catherine of Siena.* Translated, introduction, notes by Suzanne Noffke, OP. 2 vols. Tempe, AZ: Arizona Center for Medieval and Renaissance Studies, 2000–2001.

———. *Saint Catherine of Siena as Seen in Her Letters.* Translated, edited, and notes by Vida D. Scudder. London: J. M. Dent & Sons Ltd; New York: E. P. Dutton & Co., 1927.

Edition and Translation of the *Prayers*

Caterina da Siena. *Le orazioni di S. Caterina da Siena.* Edited by Giuliana Cavallini. Roma: Edizioni Cateriniane, 1978.

Catherine of Siena. *The Prayers of Catherine of Siena.* Edited, translated, and notes by Suzanne Noffke, OP. 2nd edition. San Jose: Authors Choice Press, 2001.

Primary Biographical Sources and Translations

Raimondo da Capua. *Legenda major.* Bollandist *Acta Sanctorum.* Paris: Palmé, 1866. Aprilis tomus 3: 826–967.

Raymond of Capua. *The Life of Catherine of Siena.* Translated, introduced, and annotated by Conleth Kearns, OP. Wilmington, DE: Michael Glazier, 1980. English translation of Raymond's *Legenda major.*

Thomas Antonii de Senis "Caffarini." *Libellus de supplemento*. Edited by Giuliana Cavallini and Imelda Foralosso. Roma: Edizioni Cateriniane, 1974.

———. *Il Processo Castellano*. Edited by M. H. Laurent. Fontes vitae S. Catharinae senensis historici IX. Siena: Università di Siena, 1942.

———. *S. Caterina da Siena: Legenda minor*. Translated by Bruno Ancilli. Siena: Cantagalli, 1998.

———. *Santa Caterina da Siena nei ricordi dei discepoli*. Edited by Innocenzo Taurisano, OP. Roma: Libreria Ferrari, 1957. Italian translation of the depositions of Cortona, Maconi, and Dominici in Caffarini's *Processo Castellano*.

———. *Vita di Santa Caterina da Siena*. Edited by P. Giuseppe Tinagli, OP. Siena: Cantagalli, 1938. Italian translation of Pars I and II (tract. I–VI) of Caffarini's *Libellus de supplemento*.

Patristic and Medieval Works Cited as Possible Catherinian Sources

Augustine of Hippo. *Basic Writings of St. Augustine*. Edited by Whitney J. Oates. 2 vols. New York: Random House, 1948.

———. *The Confessions*. Translation and introduction by Maria Boulding, OSB. The Works of St. Augustine: A Translation for the 21st Century. Hyde Park, NY: New City Press, 1997.

———. *Expositions of the Psalms*. Translated by Maria Boulding, OSB. The Works of St. Augustine: A Translation for the 21st Century. Hyde Park, NY: New City Press, 2003.

———. *Homilies on the Gospel According to St. John by S. Augustine, Bishop of Hippo*. Oxford: John Henry Parker; London: F. and J. Rivington, 1898.

Bernard of Clairvaux. *The Works of Bernard of Clairvaux*. Vol. 2, *On the Song of Songs I*. Translated by Kilian Walsh. Introduction by M. Corneille Haflants. Spencer, MA: Cistercian Publications, 1993.

Cavalca, Domenico. *Lo specchio della croce*. Edited by Tito Sante Centi, OP. Bologna: Edizioni Studio Domenicano, 1992.

Gregory the Great. *The Dialogues of St. Gregory the Great.* Edited by Henry James Coleridge. London: Burns and Oates, 1874.
Jacobus de Voragine. *The Golden Legend.* Translated by W. G. Ryan. 2 vols. Princeton, NJ: Princeton University Press, 1993.
John Cassian. *The Conferences.* Translated by Boniface Ramsey, OP. Ancient Christian Writers: The Works of the Fathers in Translation 57. New York/Mahwah, NJ: Newman Press, 1997.
Thomas Aquinas. *Scriptum super Sententiis.* 4 vols. Paris, 1947.
———. *Summa Contra Gentiles.* 5 vols. Translated by Vernon J. Bourke. Notre Dame and London: University of Notre Dame Press, 1975.
———. *Summa Theologica,* Translated by the Fathers of the English Dominican Province. 3 vols. New York: Benziger Brothers, 1947.

Magisterial Texts

Second Vatican Council, *Lumen Gentium* (Dogmatic Constitution on the Church). English translation: *Vatican Council II: The Basic Sixteen Documents.* Edited by Austin Flannery, OP. Northport, NY: Costello Publishing Company; Dublin, Ireland: Dominican Publications, 1996, 1–95.
Paul VI. Apostolic Letter *Mirabilis in Ecclesia Deus.* (The Title of Doctor of the Universal Church is Conferred on Saint Catherine of Siena, October 4, 1970.) *AAS* 63:9 (September 30, 1971): 674–82.
John Paul II. Encyclical Letter *Redemptor hominis. AAS* LXXI (1979): 257–324.
———. Apostolic Letter *Amantissima Providentia, AAS* 72 (April 1980): 569–81; English translation: *L'Osservatore Romano,* Weekly Edition in English, June 23, 1980: 7–8.
———. Apostolic Letter *Novo millennio ineunte. AAS* XCIII (3 mai 2001): 266–309.
Catechism of the Catholic Church, 2nd edition. Città del Vaticano: Libreria Editrice Vaticana, 1997.

Benedict XVI. Homily at Mass at inauguration of Petrine ministry in St. Peter's square on April 24, 2005. *L'Osservatore Romano*, 25 aprile 2005: 5.

Annotated Bibliographies

Bibliografia analitica di S. Caterina da Siena 1901–1950. Edited by Lina Zanni. Roma: Centro Nazionale di Studi Cateriniani, 1971.
Bibliografia analitica di S. Caterina da Siena 1951–1975. Edited by Lina Zanni. Roma: Centro Nazionale di Studi Cateriniani, 1985.
Bibliografia analitica di S. Caterina da Siena 1976–1985. Edited by Maria Carlotta Paterna. Roma: Centro Nazionale di Studi Cateriniani, 1989.
Bibliografia analitica di S. Caterina da Siena 1986–1990. Edited by Maria Carlotta Paterna. Roma: Centro Nazionale di Studi Cateriniani, 2000.
Bibliografia analitica di S. Caterina da Siena 1991–2000. Edited by Maria Carlotta Paterna. Roma: Centro Nazionale di Studi Cateriniani, 2003.

Studies and Biographies on Catherine of Siena

AA.VV., *Urbis et Orbis, concessionis tituli doctoris et extensionis eiusdem tituli ad universam Ecclesiam necnon Officii et Missae de communi doctorum virginum in honorem S. Catharinae Senensis virginis Tertii Ordinis S. Dominici. Vota censorum theologorum.* [Città Vaticano:] typis poliglottis vaticani, 1969.
Abbrescia, Domenico, OP. "La conoscenza di sè." In *Lineamenti di spiritualità cateriniana*, 7–21. Roma: Coletti Editore, 1964.
Anadol, Gabriella. "Le immagini del linguaggio cateriniano e le loro fonti: *La scala*." *Rassegna di ascetica e mistica* XXIII (1972): 332–43.
Ancilli, E., and D. de Pablo Maroto. "Caterina da Siena (santa)." *Dizionario enciclopedico di sprituality*. Edited by Ermanno Ancilli

and the Pontificio Istituto di Spiritualità del Teresianum. Nuova edizione, completamente aggiornata e ampliata. Roma: Città Nuova Editrice, 1990.

Ashley, Benedict M., OP. "Guide to Saint Catherine's Dialogue." *Cross and Crown* 29 (September 1977): 237–49.

———. "St. Catherine of Siena's Principles of Spiritual Direction." *Spirituality Today* 33:1 (March 1981): 43–52.

Blasio, Bernardino de, OP. "Gli stati di perfezione nel Dialogo di S. Caterina." *S. Caterina da Siena: Bimestrale di vita e cultura cateriniana*. XVI: 4–5 (luglio–ottobre 1965): 6–16.

Boulding, M. Cecily. "St. Catherine of Siena's 'Mystical Apprehension' of God." *New Blackfriars* 85 (March 2004): 163–69.

C. R. [Carlo Riccardi, CM]. "La carità, fonte di unità interiore e di armonia sociale, nell'insegnamento di Caterina da Siena." *Rassegna di ascetica e mistica.* "S. Caterina da Siena." XXII: 2 (aprile–giugno 1971): 135–38.

Castellano, Mario Ismaele. "Antropologia cateriniana." *Quaderni Cateriniani* 90. Siena: Cantagalli, 1996.

———. "S. Caterina e la bellezza di Dio e dell'anima." *Quaderni Cateriniani*. Siena: Cantagalli, 1997: 3–13.

Cavallini, Giuliana. "Caterina da Siena tra mistica e apostolato." *La patrona d'Italia: S. Caterina da Siena* XLIV: 3 (maggio–giugno 1989): 7–9.

———. *Catherine of Siena*. Outstanding Christian Thinkers Series. London and New York: Geoffrey Chapman, 1998.

———. "La dottrina dell'amore in S. Caterina da Siena: concordanze col pensiero di S. Tommaso d'Aquino." *Divus Thomas* LXXV: 4 (ottobre–dicembre 1972): 369–88.

———. "La verità nell'ascesi cateriniana." *Nuova rivista di ascetica e mistica*. I: 1 (1976): 27–43.

Colosio, Innocenzo, OP. "La infinità del desiderio secondo S. Caterina da Siena." In *S. Caterina tra i dottori della Chiesa*, edited by Tito S. Centi, OP, 69–72. Firenze: Casa Editrice "A. Salani," 1970.

Curtayne, Alice. *Saint Catherine of Siena*. London: Sheed and Ward, 1929.

Works Cited

Dominic, Sr. [Ann Walsh, OP]. "St. Catherine of Siena: Doctor of the Church." *Supplement to Doctrine and Life* 8 (1970): 134–44.

Drane, Augusta Theodosia. *The History of St. Catherine of Siena and Her Companions*. 4th edition. 2 vols. London: Longman, Green and Co., 1915.

Dupré Theseider, E[ugenio]. "Caterina da Siena." *Dizionario biografico degli Italiani*. Roma: Istituto della Enciclopedia Italiana, 1979.

D'Urso, Giacinto, OP. "L'ascesa alla santità di S. Caterina (I)." *S. Caterina da Siena*. [No vol. number] ottobre 1961: 9–12.

———. "Caterina creatura dello Spirito." *Rivista di ascetica e mistica*. V (XLIX di *Vita Cristiana*; 1980): 5–23.

———. Introduzione. *L'estasi e la parola: Dialogo della divina provvidenza, lettere, orazioni*. Edited by Giacinto D'Urso. Fiesole: Nardini Editore, 1996: 7–45.

———. *Il genio di Santa Caterina: studi sulla dottrina e personalità*. Quaderni Cateriniani 8. Roma: Edizioni Cateriniane, 1971.

———. *Giacomo da Varazze, maestro di S. Caterina da Siena*. Quaderni Caterinati 47–48. Siena: Associazione Ecumenica Caterinati and Edizioni Cantagalli, 1986.

———. "Iacopo da Varazze, ispiratore di S. Caterina." *La patrona d'Italia. Santa Caterina* XXX: 3 (1975): 12–13.

———. "L'itinerario ascetico di S. Caterina da Siena." *Rivista di ascetica e mistica* VI (Nuova serie; anno XXX di *Vita Cristiana*; luglio–ottobre 1961): 452–66.

———. "Il mandato ecumenico a S. Caterina." *Nuovi studi Cateriniani* 3. Siena: Biblioteca Cateriniana, Edizioni Cantagalli, 1988: 27–38.

———. "Il mistero di Cristo nella verità del Padre." *Angelicum* LXIV (1987): 193–217.

———. "Nozione teologale dell'orazione secondo S. Caterina." *Caterina da Siena* XVI (gennaio-febbraio 1965): 31–36.

———. "Santa Caterina da Siena." *Temi di predicazione* XVI: 84 (1970): 13–125.

———. "Gli scaloni cateriniani del ponte e le notti di S. Giovanni della Croce." *I symposium catharinianum nel V centenario della canonizzazione di S. Caterina da Siena. Siena: 24–28 aprile, 1962*. Siena: Accademia degli Intronati, MCMLXII: 3–17.

———. "Il 'trattato delle lacrime' di S. Caterina da Siena." *La nuova rivista di ascetica e mistica* I: 2 (1976): 117–31.

Fatula, Mary Ann, OP. *Catherine of Siena's Way*. The Way of the Christian Mystics Series. Wilmington, DE: Michael Glazier, 1987.

Fawtier, Robert. *Sainte Catherine de Sienne, essai de critique des sources*. Vol. 1, *Sources hagiographique*. Paris: DeBoccard, 1921.

———. *Sainte Catherine de Sienne, essai de critique des sources*. Vol. 2, *Les oeuvres de Sainte Catherine*. Paris: DeBoccard, 1930.

——— and Louis Canet. *La double experience de Catherine Benincasa (Sainte Catherine de Sienne)*. Paris: Gallimard, 1948.

Flood, Marie Walter. "St. Thomas's Thought in the *Dialogue* of St. Catherine." *Spirituality Today* 32 (1980): 25–35.

Fortuna, Michele P., OP. "Struttura dell'anima nel linguaggio metaforico di S. Caterina da Siena." *Rassegna di ascetica e mistica*. "S. Caterina da Siena." XIII: 3 (luglio–settembre 1972): 251–62.

Foster, Kenelm, OP. "Editorial" [unsigned]. *Life of the Spirit* 15 (April 1961): 432–33.

———. Introduction to *I, Catherine: Selected Writings of Catherine of Siena*. Edited and translated by Kenelm Foster, OP, and Mary John Ronayne, OP. St. James Place, London: Collins, 1980: 11–44.

———. "St. Catherine's Teaching on Christ." *Life of the Spirit* 16 (1962): 310–23.

———. "The Spirit of St. Catherine of Siena." *Life of the Spirit* 15 (1961): 433–46.

Gardner, Edmund G. *Saint Catherine of Siena: A Study in the Religion, Literature, and History of the Fourteenth Century in Italy*. London: J. M. Dent & Co.; New York: E. P. Dutton & Co., 1907.

Garrigou-Lagrange, Reginald, OP. "La prima conversione secondo Santa Caterina da Siena." *Vita Cristiana* V: 3 (maggio–giugno 1933): 257–71.

———. "La stimmatizzazione di Santa Caterina da Siena." *Vita Cristiana* IX (1937): 36–54.

———. *L'unione mistica in S. Caterina da Siena*. Edizioni di *Vita Cristiana*. Firenze: Libreria Editrice Fiorentina, 1938.

Works Cited

Getto, Giovanni. "L'intuizione mistica e l'espressione letteraria di S. Caterina da Siena." In *Studi di letteratura religiosa*, 107–267. Firenze, 1967.

Gigli, Girolamo. *Vocabulario cateriniano*. Firenze: Tito Giuliani, 1866.

Gorce, Maxime. "Catherine de Sienne." *Dictionnaire de spiritualité*. Paris: Beauchesne, 1953. Vol. 2, cols. 331–36.

Grion, Alvaro, OP. *La dottrina di Santa Caterina*. Brescia: Morcelliana, 1962.

———. "S. Caterina: Maestra di contestazione." *Stella di S. Domenico*. Numero speciale: "Santa Caterina da Siena, dottore della Chiesa." LVI: 10 (ottobre 1970): 247–56.

———. *S. Caterina da Siena: dottrina e fonti*. Brescia: Morcelliana, 1953.

Hackett, Benedict, OSA. "The Augustinian Tradition in the Mysticism of St. Catherine of Siena." In *Collectanea Augustiniana: Augustine, Mystic and Mystagogue*, edited by Frederick Van Fleteren, Joseph C. Schnaubelt, OSA, and Joseph Reino, 493–512. New York: Peter Lang, 1994.

———. "Simone Fidati da Cascia and the Doctrine of St. Catherine of Siena." *Augustiniana* XVI (1966): 386–414.

———. *William Flete, OSA, and Catherine of Siena: Masters of Fourteenth Century Spirituality*. Edited by John E. Rotelle, OSA. Foreword by Francis X. Martin, OSA. The Augustinian Series, vol. 15. Villanova, PA: Augustinian Press, 1992.

Henchey, Joseph C., CSS. "St. Catherine of Siena: An Historic and Prophetic Synthesis of the Consecrated Life." *Congresso internazionale di studi cateriniani. Atti*. Roma: Curia Generalizia OP, 1981: 632–52.

Jean Marie, Sr. "Aquinas's Theology of Trinitarian Mission and the *Dialogue* of Catherine of Siena." *Dominican Monastic Search* 95 (1995): 60–66.

Jeremiah, Sr. Mary. "Catherinian Imagery of Consecration." *Communio* 17 (1990): 362–74.

———. *The Secret of the Heart: A Theological Study of Catherine of Siena's Teaching on the Heart of Jesus*. Front Royal, VA: Christendom Press, 1995.

———. "The Theological Anthropology of Catherine of Siena." *Communio* 20 (1993): 457–62.

———. "'To Be or Not to Be': Catherine of Siena on Sin and Salvation." *The Canadian Historical Review*. September 1990: 298–302.

Jordan, E. "La date de naissance de Sainte Catherine de Sienne." *Analecta Bollandiana* XL: III–IV (November 15, 1922): 365–411.

Jorgensen, Johannes. *Saint Catherine of Siena*. London, New York, Toronto: Longman, Green and Co., 1938.

Karasig, Maria Agnes, OP. "Affective Self-Transcendence in Catherine of Siena's Beatitude of Tears." *Review for Religious* 49 (1990): 418–29.

Kearns, Conleth, OP. "The Wisdom of Saint Catherine." *Angelicum* 57: 3 (1980): 324–43.

Léthel, François-Marie, OCD. Preface to "'Gesù dolce, Gesù amore': Il Cristo di Caterina da Siena." STD dissertation. Roma: Pontificium Institutum Spiritualitatis Teresianum, 2005: v–vi.

Levasti, Arrigo. *S. Caterina da Siena*. Torino: Tip. Sociale Torinese, 1947.

———. *My Servant, Catherine*. Translated by Dorothy M. White. London: Blackfriars, 1954.

Luongo, F. Thomas. *The Saintly Politics of Catherine of Siena*. Ithaca: Cornell University Press, 2006.

Mandonnet, P. "Sainte Catherine de Sienne et la critique historique." *L'Année Dominicaine*. Janvier–Fevrier 1923. 24-page extract.

McGinn, Bernard. "Catherine of Siena: Apostle of the Blood of Christ." *Theology Digest* 48:4 (2001): 329–42.

Musso, Emanuele Massimo. "Il Cristo risorto è 'giovane': una puntualizzazione di Caterina da Siena." *La patrona d'Italia e d'Europa: S. Caterina da Siena*. LX:1 (gennaio–marzo 2005): 27–28.

———. "'Gesù dolce, Gesù amore': Il Cristo di Caterina da Siena." STD dissertation. Roma: Pontificium Institutum Spiritualitatis Teresianum, 2005.

Noffke, Suzanne, OP. "Catherine of Siena, Justly Doctor of the Church?" *Theology Today* 60 (2003): 49–62.

Works Cited

———. *Catherine of Siena: Vision Through a Distant Eye*. A Michael Glazier Book. Collegeville, MN: The Liturgical Press, 1996.

———. "Demythologizing Catherine: The Wealth of Internal Evidence." *Spirituality Today* 32 (March 1980): 4–12.

———. "The Physical in the Writings of Catherine of Siena." *Annali d'Italianistica* 13 (1995): 109–29.

O'Driscoll, Mary, OP, ed. *Catherine of Siena: Passion for the Truth, Compassion for Humanity. Selected Spiritual Writings*. Hyde Park, NY: New City Press, 1993.

———. "Catherine the Theologian." *Spirituality Today* 40 (Spring 1988): 4–17.

———. "St. Catherine of Siena: Life and Spirituality." *Angelicum* 57 (1980): 305–23.

———. "Women and the Dominican Tradition with Particular Reference to Catherine of Siena." *Angelicum* 81:2 (2004): 445–57.

Paci, Ignazio, OP. "Intelletto, memoria, e voluntà." In *L'anima dominicana di S. Caterina da Siena*. Quaderni Caterinati 39. Siena: Associazione Ecumenica Caterinati, 1985: 16–29.

Pardi, G. "Elenchi di mantellate Senesi." *Studi Cateriniani* II: 2 (1924–25): 43–58.

Parmisano, A. Stanley, OP. "Mystic of the Absurd: Saint Catherine of Siena." *Religious Life Review* 21 (1982): 201–14.

Riccardi, Carlo, CM, ed. *Il messaggio di Santa Caterina da Siena*. Tutto il pensiero della vergine senese esposto con le sue parole in forma moderna. 2nd edition. Roma: C.L.V. Edizioni, 1988.

———. *Il pensiero filosofico e mistico di S. Caterina da Siena*. Siena: Cantagalli, 1994.

Rovasenda, Enrico di, OP. *Introduzione al Dialogo di S. Caterina da Siena*. Genova: Biblioteca Franzoniana, 1984.

Scalvini, Francesco [Innocenzo Colosio, OP]. "La vera Caterina da Siena e la Caterina del benedettino fr. Vandenbroucke." *Rivista di ascetica e mistica* VI (1961): 503–36.

Scott, Karen. "Not Only with Words, but with Deeds: The Role of Speech in Catherine of Siena's Understanding of Her Mission." PhD dissertation. Berkeley: University of California, 1989.

———. "St. Catherine of Siena: '*Apostola*.'" *Church History* 61 (1992): 34–36.

———. "'This is why I have put you among your neighbors': St. Bernard's and St. Catherine's Understanding of the Love of God and Neighbor." In *Atti del simposio internazionale cateriniano-bernardiniano: Siena, 17–20 aprile 1980,* 279–94. Siena: Accademia Senese degli Intronati, 1982.

Taurisano, I., OP. "Le fonti agiografiche cateriniane e la critica di R. Fawtier." *Letture Cateriniane nella R. Università di Siena, 8 agosto 1928.* Siena: Libreria Editrice Senese, 1928. Reprinted in Alice Curtayne, *Saint Catherine of Siena,* 225–47. London: Sheed and Ward, 1929.

Valli, F. "Il sangue di Cristo nell'opera di S. Caterina da Siena." *Studi cateriniani* IX: 1 (1932): 17–38.

Other Works Consulted

Adams, M. Clare, OSC. "Tears, gift of." *The New Dictionary of Catholic Spirituality,* Edited by Michael Downey. A Michael Glazier Book. Collegeville, MN: The Liturgical Press, 1993.

Adnes, P. "Larmes." *Dictionnaire de spiritualité.* Paris: Beauchesne, 1976. Vol. 9, cols. 287–303.

"Affetività." *Dizionario enciclopedico di spritualità.* A cura di Ermanno Ancilli e del Pontificio Istituto di Spiritualità del Teresianum. Nuova edizione, completamente aggiornata e ampliata. Roma: Città Nuova Editrice, 1990.

Appel, Regis, OCSO. "Cassian's *Discretio*—a Timeless Virtue." *American Benedictine Review* 17 (1966): 20–29.

Arintero, Juan G., OP. *Las escalas de amore y la verdadera perfección cristiana.* Salamanca, Convento de San Esteban: Editorial FIDES, 1926.

Ashley, Benedict, OP. "Dominic Cavalca and a Spirituality of the Word." Internet: www.op.org/domcentral.study/ashley.cavalca.htm. Accessed on February 20, 2005.

———. *Spiritual Direction in the Dominican Tradition.* New York: Paulist Press, 1995.

Aumann, Jordan, OP. *Christian Spirituality in the Catholic Tradition.* London: Sheed and Ward, 1985.

———. *Spiritual Theology.* London: Sheed and Ward, 1980.

Works Cited

Bazelaire, Louis de. "Connaissance de soi." *Dictionnaire de spiritualité*. Paris: Beauchesne, 1953. Vol. 2, cols. 1511–43.

Bedouelle, Guy, OP. "Mary Magdalene: The Apostle of the Apostles and the Order of Preachers." *Dominican Ashram* 18:4 (1999): 157–71.

Bonner, Gerald. "Augustine's Conception of Deification." *Journal of Theological Studies* 37 (1986): 369–86.

Book of Constitutions and Ordinations of the Brothers of the Order of Preachers. Dublin: Dominican Publications, 2001.

Byrne, Richard, OCSO. "Journey (Growth and Development in Spiritual Life)." *The New Dictionary of Catholic Spirituality*, edited by Michael Downey. A Michael Glazier Book. Collegeville, MN: The Liturgical Press, 1993.

Cantalamessa, Raniero, OFMCap. "Advent 2003 in the Papal Household. Third Homily." Internet: http://www.cantalamessa.org/en/2003Avvento3.htm. Accessed on May 28, 2006.

Casey, Michael. *A Thirst for God: Spiritual Desire in Bernard of Clairvaux's Sermon on the* Song of Songs. Cistercian Studies Series, 77. Kalamazoo, MI: Cistercian Publications, 1988.

Congar, Yves, OP. *I Believe in the Holy Spirit*. The Complete Three-Volume Work in One Volume. Translated by David Smith. New York: Crossroad Herder, 2000.

Corbon, Jean, OP. *The Wellspring of Worship*. Translated by Matthew J. O'Connell. San Francisco: Ignatius Press, 2005.

Eckhart, Meister. *Meister Eckhart: Sermons and Treatises*. Translated by M. O'C. Walshe. London: Watkins, 1985. Vol. 3: 107.

Galot, Jean, SJ. "Recognize the Charism in its Specific Value." *L'Osservatore Romano*. Weekly Edition in English. June 29, 1981: 2.

Gardeil, Antoine, OP. *The Gifts of the Holy Ghost in the Dominican Saints*. Translated by Anselm M. Townsend, OP. Milwaukee: Bruce Publishing Company, 1937.

Giardini, Fabio, OP. *Pray Without Ceasing: Toward a Systematic Psychotherapy of Christian Prayerlife*. Herefordshire and Rome: Gracewing and Millennium Romae Editrice, 1998.

Gilson, Etienne. *The Mystical Theology of St. Bernard*. Translated by A. H. C. Downes. New York: Sheed and Ward, 1940.

Hinnebusch, William A., OP. *The History of the Dominican Order*. 2 vols. New York: Alba House, 1973.
John Climacus. *The Ladder of Divine Ascent*. Translated by Colm Luibheid and Norman Russell. The Classics of Western Spirituality. New York: Paulist Press, 1982.
John of the Cross. *The Collected Works of St. John of the Cross*. Translated by Kieran Kavanaugh, OCD, and Otilio Rodriguez, OCD. Washington, DC: I.C.S. Publications, 1991.
Kedar, Benjamin Z. *Crusade and Mission: European Approaches to the Muslims*. Princeton: Princeton University Press, 1984.
Kereszty, Roch A., OCist. *Jesus Christ: Fundamentals of Christology*. Revised and updated edition. Staten Island, NY: St. Paul's, 2002.
Lampe, G. W. H. "Christian Theology in the Patristic Period." In *A History of Christian Doctrine*, edited by Hubert Cunliffe-Jones, 149–55. Edinburgh: T. & T. Clark Ltd., 1978.
Leclercq, Jean, OSB. *The Love of Learning and the Desire for God: A Study of Monastic Culture*. Translated by Catharine Misrahi. New York: Fordham University Press, 1960.
Leclercq, Jean, and François Vandenbroucke, Louis Bouyer. *A History of Christian Spirituality*. Vol. 2, *The Spirituality of the Middle Ages*. Wellwood, Kent: Burns and Oates, 1968.
Lehmijoki-Gardner, Maiju, ed. *Dominican Penitent Women*. The Classics of Western Spirituality. New York: Paulist Press, 2005.
Léthel, François-Marie. "L'interiorité chrétienne." *La vie spirituelle*. [No. vol. number] Mars 1996: 47–84.
———. *Theologie de l'amore de Jesus. Escrits sur la theologia des saints*. Venasque: Editions du Carmel, 1996.
Lewis, C. S. *Mere Christianity*. New York: Macmillan, 1952.
Louth, Andrew. *The Origins of the Christian Mystical Tradition from Plato to Denys*. Oxford: Clarendon Press, 1981.
Marmion, Dom Columba. *Christ in His Mysteries*. St. Louis: B. Herder, 1924.
Martin, Henri. "Désirs." *Dictionnaire de spiritualité*. Paris: Beauchesne, 1957. Vol. 3: cols. 606–23.
McCabe, Herbert. *God, Christ, and Us*. London and New York: Continuum, 2003.

Works Cited

———. *God Matters*. Contemporary Christian Insight Series. London and New York: Mowbray, 1987.

McGinn, Bernard. *The Foundations of Western Mysticism*. Vol. 1, *The Presence of God: A History of Western Christian Mysticism*. New York: Crossroad, 1991.

McGonigle, Thomas D., OP. "Three Ways." *The New Dictionary of Catholic Spirituality*. Edited by Michael Downey. A Michael Glazier Book. Collegeville, MN: The Liturgical Press, 1993.

Meister Eckhart. *Meister Eckhart: Sermons and Treatises*. Vol. 3. Translated by M. O'C. Walshe. London: Watkins, 1985.

Morrison, Molly. "Strange Miracles: A Study of the Peculiar Healings of St. Maria Maddelena de' Pazzi." *Logos* 8:1 (Winter 2005): 129–44.

O'Donovan, Oliver. *The Problem of Self-Love in St. Augustine*. New Haven and London: Yale University Press, 1980.

Ott, Ludwig. *Fundamentals of Catholic Dogma*. Translated by Patrick Lynch. Edited by James Bastible. Cork: The Mercier Press, 1955.

Peddicord, Richard, OP. *The Sacred Monster of Thomism: An Introduction to the Life and Legacy of Reginald Garrigou-Lagrange, OP*. South Bend, IN: St. Augustine's Press, 2005.

Pennington, M. Basil, OCSO. "Three States of Spiritual Growth According to St. Bernard." *Studia Monastica* 11 (1969): 315–26.

Pinckaers, Servais, OP. *Morality: The Catholic View*. Translated by Michael Sherwin, OP. Preface by Alistair MacIntyre. South Bend, IN: St. Augustine's Press, 2001.

Poulain, Augustin. "Mystical Marriage." *The Catholic Encyclopedia*. London: The Encyclopedia Press, 1910.

———. *Revelations and Visions*. [A reprint of Part IV of *The Graces of Interior Prayer*, 1910.] Translated by Leonora L. Yorke Smith. New York: Alba House, 1998.

———. "Stigmata, Mystical." *The Catholic Encyclopedia*. London: The Encyclopedia Press, 1910.

Pourrat, P[ierre]. *Christian Spirituality in the Middle Ages*. Translated by S. P. Jacques. Vol. 2. New York: P.J. Kenedy and Sons, 1924.

Principe, Walter H., CSB. *Introduction to Patristic and Medieval Theology*. 2nd edition. Toronto: Pontifical Institute of Medieval Studies, 1982.

Quinn, J. R. "Divine Nature." *The New Catholic Encyclopedia*. New York: McGraw-Hill Book Company, 1967.
Rahner, Karl, SJ. "Reflections on the Problem of the Gradual Ascent to Christian Perfection." *Theological Studies*. Vol. 3. Translated by Karl-H. and Boniface Kruger. Baltimore: Helicon Press; London: Darton, Longman, & Todd, 1967: 3–23.
Royo, Antonio, OP, and Jordan Aumann, OP. *The Theology of Christian Perfection*. Dubuque, IA: The Priory Press, 1962.
Sheed, F. J. *Theology and Sanity*. London: Sheed and Ward, 1978.
Solignac, Aimé. "Voies." *Dictionnaire de spiritualité*. Paris: Beauchesne, 1994. Vol. XVI: cols. 1200–15.
Thomas à Kempis. *The Imitation of Christ*. Translated by Ronald Knox and Michael Oakley. New York: Sheed and Ward, 1959.
Torrell, Jean-Pierre, OP. *Saint Thomas Aquinas*. Vol. 2, *Spiritual Master*. Translated by Robert Royal. Washington, DC: The Catholic University of America Press, 2003.
Tuchman, Barbara W. *A Distant Mirror: The Calamitous 14th Century*. New York: Ballantine Books, 1978.
Tugwell, Simon, OP. *Early Dominicans: Selected Writings*. Edited by Simon Tugwell, OP. Preface by Vincent de Couesnongle, OP. The Classics of Western Spirituality. Mahwah, NJ: Paulist Press, 1982.
Vernet, Felix. *Medieval Spirituality*. London: Sands and Co.; St. Louis: B. Herder, 1930.
Viviano, Benedict T., OP. "The Gospel According to Matthew." In *The New Jerome Biblical Commentary*, edited by Raymond E. Brown, SS, Joseph A. Fitzmyer, SJ, Roland E. Murphy, OCarm. London: Geoffrey Chapman, 1990.
Williams, A. N. *The Ground of Union: Deification in Aquinas and Palmas*. New York and Oxford: Oxford University Press, 1999.

INDEX

Affection, 164–66; *see also* Love
Alfonso da Vadaterra, Bishop, 67
Anadol, Gabriella, 155–56
Ancilli, E., 2
Anthony, St., 30
Aquinas, Thomas, St. *See* Thomas Aquinas, St.
Augustine, St., 101; desire, 114; feet as symbol of affections, 165; heart at the opened side, 177; self-knowledge, 118; triad of memory, understanding, and will, 106–7

Baptism: "light of faith," 113, 134, 135; tears as type of, 148
Benedict XVI, Pope, 231–32
Benedict, *Rule* of, 114
Benincasa, Buonaventura, 7, 17, 23, 208
Benincasa, Jacopo di (Giacomo), 7, 153
Benincasa, Lapa, 7, 13, 17, 26, 214
Bernard of Clairvaux, St., 140–41, 177

Blood of Christ, 28, 78, 81, 84–89, 221, 225–26
Bonaventure, St., 138
Bridge of Christ. *See* Christ-bridge
Byrne, Richard, 2

Caffarini, Tommaso, 25, 26, 47, 58, 213; Catherine's visions, 27, 31, 43, 92; levitation, 211; mystical espousals, 33–34; spiritual stages, 138–39; *Supplementum*, 12
Canet, L., 15
Cantalamessa, Raniero, 231
Cassian, 98, 114, 143; desire for God, 114; discretion, 98; grades of charity, 143–44; tears, 148
Catechism of the Catholic Church, 160–61
Catherine of Alexandria, 33, 59–60
Catherine of Siena, St.: in Avignon, 67–69; biographical notes, 7–10; biographical sources, 12–17; canonization, 15,

54; church reform, 9, 65–66, 75, 216–27; community, 53–55; crisis, 30–32, 74; death, 10, 63, 73, 75, 76; doctor of church, 1, 4–5, 10, 222–23; and Dominicans, 7, 13, 25, 26; ecstasies, 38–39, 42, 50, 51, 218; and Eucharist, 38, 50; exchange of hearts, 8, 49–50, 75, 76; exorcism by, 47; fasting, 7, 8, 38, 46; first vision (of the royal Christ), 7, 11, 18–21, 74, 208; in Florence, 70; gift of prophecy, 47–48; healing, 8, 47; "interior cell," 23–24, 26–34; "investiture vision," 64–67, 75–76, 216, 223–24; levitation, 11, 22, 51, 207, 211–12; and Mantellata Andrea, 39–41, 75, 211; and Mantellata Palmerina, 36–37; mystical death, 8, 50, 55–58, 63; mystical espousals, 7, 32–34, 63, 74, 76, 210; near martyrdom, 9, 69–70; peacemaking, 8–9, 46–47, 133, 216; penitential practices, 7, 8, 20–21, 22, 26, 28, 38, 46, 74; in Pisa, 58–64, 125, 214–15; promotion of Crusade, 8, 67; refusal to marry, 7, 23; in Rome, 71–73; salvation of souls, 22, 25, 37, 45–48, 50, 65–66, 75, 133, 216, 218; sins, 17, 23, 52–53; stigmata, 8, 61–64, 75–76, 214–16, 218; teachings, 3–5, 78–136, 225–31; virginity, 11, 17, 22, 23, 25, 28, 74, 233; *see also* specific topics, e.g.: Neighbor, love of; Self-knowledge

Cavalca, Domenico, 94, 140, 165; grades of love, 142; tears, 148

Cavallini, Giuliana, 3–4; Christ-bridge, 95; love, 91; spiritual stages, 151; truth of God the father, 180

Charity, 97, 153–54, 158–61, 181–82, 206, 221; "wedding garment" of, 203–4; *see also* Love; Neighbor, love of

Christ, blood of. *See* Blood of Christ

Christ-bridge, 2, 79, 139–45, 204; affection and desire, 164–66, 168; description of, 95–96; development of image of, 91–95; exterior ascent, 155; final end of, 203; interior ascent, 154–56; invitation to ascent, 208–9; and love, 134–35; *scaloni generali*, 153, 154–56, 159–60, 161; *scaloni particulari*, 143, 153, 154, 157–59, 160, 161; *scaloni* (stairs), 2, 34, 92–94, 95, 140, 161, 224; and self-knowledge, 105; and

self-love, 112; as spiritual development, 101–3; stages of ascent, 156–61; "stones of virtue" on, 96–99; stormy river, 99–101; as "way of truth," 89–103; *see also* Spiritual development
Clement VII, Antipope, 9
Colosio, Innocenzo, 116
Conferences (Cassian), 98, 114, 143
Crusade, 67
Curtayne, Alice, 15

Desire, 114–17, 164; *see also* Affection
Dialogue, The (Catherine of Siena), 3–4, 9, 12, 69–70, 131, 151; *see also* specific topics, e.g.: Christ-bridge; Truth
Discretion, 98
Dominic, St., 24, 53
Dominicans, 25, 27; reform movement, 13
Dominici, Bartolomeo, 8, 28, 29, 40, 46, 47, 48, 53, 58, 61, 63, 67; Catherine compared to Abraham, 61; Catherine's mystical death, 63; conversion of sinners, 46; deposition for Catherine's canonization, 227–30; healed by Catherine, 47
Double experience de Catherine Benincasa, La (Sainte Catherine de Sienne) (Fawtier and Canet), 15
Drane, Augusta Theodosia, 65
D'Urso, Giacinto, 27, 182, 185, 199, 207, 218; friendship love, 177; "investiture vision," 65–67; mystical espousals, 33; precision, 150, 151; spiritual stages, 137–38, 141, 142, 151; tears, 148–49

Eucharist, 38, 50
Euphrosyne of Alexandria, St., 22
Evagrius Ponticus, 138

Faith, 36, 168–69; "light of faith," 113, 134, 135
Fawtier, Robert, 15–16
Filial love, 186–87
Foster, Kenelm, 68–69, 193, 226–27; blood of Christ, 85, 89; Dominicans, 26–27, 226; patterns of three, 145, 151; self-knowledge, 127; self-love, 110–11; spiritual stages, 151
Free will, 113–14
Friendship love, 175–78, 186, 188; filial love and, 187, 188

Galot, J., 4
Gardner, Edmund G., 57
Garrigou-Lagrange, Reginald: "faithful servant," 170–71; stigmata, 63–64
Getto, Giovanni, 222

Gigli, Girolamo, 95
Gregory XI, Pope, 8–9, 67, 68, 233
Gregory of Nazianzen, St., 148
Gregory the Great, St., 94, 114, 148
Grion, Alvaro, 141–42, 150, 151, 191–92

Hackett, Benedict, 118
Hagiography, 12–14, 16–17, 30; role of, 16–17, 30
Healing. *See* Spiritual healing
Hinnebusch, William A., 79–80
Hope, 36, 149–50
Human person, 78, 81, 225; as clay vessel, 81; desire for God, 114–16; free will, 113–14; sensuality and reason, 110–13; truth of, 104–17; *see also* Charity; Soul
Humility, 36, 97, 118, 173

Incarnation, 82–84, 134
"Investiture vision," 64–67, 75–76

Jacopo de Voragine, 60, 148
John Climacus, St., 148
John Paul II, Pope, 10, 231–32
Jordan, E., 15
Jorgensen, Johannes, 27–28; Christ-bridge, 94; "investiture vision," 65

Kearns, Conleth, 12–13

Laity, 160, 191–92
Laurent, M. H., 16
Lazzarino da Pisa, 227–31
Legenda (genre), 12–13
Legenda aurea (Jacopo de Voragine), 60
Legenda major (Raymond of Capua), 12–16; attacks on, 15–16; *see also* Raymond of Capua
Legenda minor (Caffarini), 12
Levasti, Arrigo, 15–16, 230–31
Levitation, 11, 22, 51, 196, 207, 211–12
Libello de Supplemento. *See Supplementum* (Caffarini)
Love, 193, 226; filial love, 186–87; friendship love, 175–76; of God, 134–36; grades of, 142; mercenary love, 163–64; perfect love, 183–84; self-love, 81, 103, 110–11, 112, 127–28, 135, 169–71, 174, 177; *see also* Charity; Neighbor, love of
Lumen gentium, 160

Maconi, Stefano, 38–39, 67
Mandonnet, Pierre, 15, 16
Marmion, Columba, 188
Mary Magdalene, 60–61
Matteo di Centi, 8

Neighbor, love of, 35–37, 50, 53–54, 74, 75, 78, 131–34, 181, 189, 221–22; as selfish, 170

Index

Niccolò di Toldo, 8, 233
Noffke, Suzanne, 13, 57, 94

O'Driscoll, Mary, 4
Order of Preachers.
    See Dominicans
Order of St. Dominic.
    See Dominicans
Original sin, 81–82, 113

Pardi, G., 15
Patience, 36, 97
Paul, St., 69, 110, 215, 227; "caught up in the third heaven," 53, 196
Paul VI, Pope, 3, 10, 79
Pius IX, Pope, 10
Pius XII, Pope, 10
Prayer, 129–30
Processo Castellano, Il, 12, 38–39
Pseudo-Dionysius, 138

Raymond of Capua, 3, 9, 41, 68, 78, 90, 119–20; Catherine in Avignon, 67–68; Catherine leaving Siena, 35, 57–59; Catherine's crisis, 30, 31–32; Catherine's sins, 17, 52–53; Catherine's visions, 18–21, 29, 42–43, 44–45, 49, 50–52, 64–66, 70, 74; diplomatic mission to France, 9, 69; Dominicans, 13, 25; healed by Catherine, 8, 47; "interior cell," 24; *Legenda major*, 12–16; letters from Catherine, 64–66, 69–70, 71–73, 89, 124, 216, 223–24; levitation, 22, 51; Mary Magdalene, 60; mystical death, 55, 213; mystical espousals, 33, 34, 36, 210; penitentiary practices, 28; reform of Dominican order, 13; salvation of souls, 37, 76; spiritual stages, 152, 196, 211–12, 224; stigmata, 61–62
Reason, 112–13, 135, 168
Redemption. See Blood of Christ
Riccardi, Carlo, 151

Sainte Catherine de Sienne (Fawtier), 15
Saracini, Alessa dei, 24
Selfishness. See Self-love
Self-knowledge, 29, 78, 111, 117–30, 135; image of "peaceful sea," 124–20; prayer and, 78, 118, 129–30
Self-love, 81, 103, 110–11, 112, 127–28, 135, 169–71, 174, 177
Sensuality, 110, 112, 135; see also Self-love
Sin, 110–12; original sin, 81–82, 113; personal sin, 110
Soul, 105–9, 110; Catherine's ability to see beauty of, 7, 37, 38; powers of, 106–9, 118, 142, 143, 154–56, 195

Specchio della croce, Lo (Cavalca), 94, 142, 165
Spiritual development, 1–2, 5, 11; faithful servant, 166–75, 177, 183; friend and child, 186–88; friend at opened side, 175–78; image of clothing, 203–4, 205, 212–13; image of filling, 204, 205; image of seeing, 201–3, 205; images of union, 194–201; loss of consolations, 171–75; mercenary servant, 163–64, 168; opened side/heart as cavern, 181–83; opened side/heart as channel, 178–79; opened side/heart as open window, 179–80; perfect union, 192–206, 213–19; precision and, 150–52; stages of, 2, 137–52; unitive stage, 183–84, 152, 192–206, 214, 219; *see also* specific topics, e.g.: Christ-bridge; Tears
Spiritual healing, 8, 47
Stigmata, 8, 61–64, 75–76, 215–16
Supplementum (Caffarini), 12
Suso, Henry, 177

Taurisano, I, 15, 16
Tears, 2, 146–49, 162–63

Theseider, Dupré, 16, 54, 92–93, 138
Thomas Aquinas, St., 136, 138, 231
Tommaso d'Alviano, 9
Tommaso della Fonte, 12, 14, 29, 53, 121–22, 228
Tommaso di Antonio di Siena. *See* Caffarini, Tommaso
Trinity, 43, 106–7, 141–42, 145, 154
Truth, 78, 149; and Christ's blood, 84–89; "of God the Father," 80–82, 113, 134, 135; of human person, 104–17; and incarnation, 82–84; "light of faith," 113, 134, 135; and original sin, 81–82; and spiritual stages, 149; and theology, 226–27; *see also* Christ-bridge

Urban VI, Pope, 9, 68, 69, 71

Valli, F., 16
Vatican Council II, 160
Virtues, 36, 182–83; "stones of virtues," 96–99; *see also* specific virtues, e.g.: Charity
Vite dei santi padri (Cavalca), 94

Walsh, D., 136

William of St. Thierry, 177

Printed in the USA
CPSIA information can be obtained
at www.ICGtesting.com
LVHW020455260424
778447LV00004B/988